À

_____

de

Pour Amelia, Harriet,
Lucie et Jay
A. A.

Textes écrits et compilés par Lois Rock
Copyright des illustrations © 2003 Alex Ayliffe

L'auteure et de l'illustrateur conservent leurs droits moraux.

Tous droits réservés
© 2003 Lion Hudson
Édition originale publiée par Lion Children's Book

Pour le Canada
© Les éditions Héritage inc. 2010
Adaptation française de Florence Miglionico

Nous reconnaissons l'aide financière du gouvernement du Canada,
par l'entremise du Programme d'aide au développement de l'industrie
de l'édition (PADIÉ), pour nos activités d'édition.

ISBN : 978-2-7625-8985-6

Remerciements

Toutes les prières non attribuées sont de Lois Rock, copyright © Lion Hudson
à l'exception du Notre Père, en page 116. Les prières de Christina Goodings.
Mark Robinson et Sophie Piper : © copyright Lion Hudson.

Imprimé en Chine

Mes toutes premières
prières

Textes de
Lois Rock

Illustrations de
Alex Ayliffe

EH **Héritage jeunesse**

Table des matières

Le matin

Mon Dieu,
en cette nouvelle journée,
écoute ma prière.

Mon Dieu,
en cette nouvelle journée,
aide-moi dans les choses
    que je vais faire.

Faire mon lit,
plier et ranger mon pyjama.
Ouvrir les rideaux,
Laisser entrer le soleil.
Que cette nouvelle journée
soit remplie de joie et d'amour.

Qui a créé le soleil?
Qui a créé la journée?
Qui a créé les heures
pour travailler et s'amuser?

Dieu les a créés,
Dieu les a parfaits,
Dieu nous aide à vivre
comme on le devrait.

Je me réveille
Je me lève
Je m'habille
Je dis :

« Merci mon Dieu pour
cette nouvelle journée. »

Je lève les mains vers le soleil doré,
Une journée radieuse vient de commencer.
Je salue les cieux,
Que l'amour de Dieu me protège.

Ô mon Dieu,
Fais qu'aujourd'hui soit une bonne journée.

Que je pense à une bonne chose.
Que je dise une bonne chose.
Que j'apprenne une bonne chose.
Que je fasse une bonne chose.

Fais qu'aujourd'hui soit une bonne journée,
Ô mon Dieu !

C'est un jour pour agir comme un grand
Un jour pour être un enfant
Un jour bruyant et animé
Un jour pour les jeux calmes et la tranquillité
Un jour pour crier et chanter
Un jour bien rempli.

Mon Dieu,
Ton ciel est si grand
et je suis si petit.
Ne m'oublie jamais,
je t'en supplie.

Mon Dieu,

S'il te plaît sois mon ami de cœur :

plus proche qu'un câlin,

plus doux qu'un doudou,

plus courageux qu'un ours en peluche.

Merci, ô Dieu du ciel,
Pour cette nouvelle journée.
Merci pour la brise,
Merci pour le soleil.
Pour ce moment de joie,
Pour nos travaux et nos jeux,
Merci, ô Dieu du ciel,
Pour cette nouvelle journée.

Prière traditionnelle

Moi

Mon Dieu, du ciel, regarde en bas :
Ici, sur la terre, tu verras
Quelqu'un qui regarde vers toi.
Cette personne, c'est moi.

Bénis mes cheveux et bénis mes orteils,
Bénis mon nez et bénis mes oreilles,
Bénis mes yeux et bénis chacune de mes mains,
Bénis les pieds sur lesquels je me tiens,
Bénis mes coudes, bénis chacun de mes genoux.
Mon Dieu, bénis chaque partie de moi, bénis tout.

Je regarde dans le miroir et qu'est-ce que je vois?
Quelqu'un qui ressemble exactement à moi!
Je vais explorer dehors, mais je n'ai toujours pas rencontré
Quelqu'un qui, même un peu, me ressemblerait.

Mon Dieu,
On dit que chacun est spécial,
Aussi spécial qu'il est possible de l'être,
Mais à l'intérieur, je me sens bien normal.
Suis-je le seul à ne pas être spécial?

Mon Dieu,
Il n'y a qu'un seul moi.
J'aime ce que j'aime.
Je n'aime pas ce que je n'aime pas.
Je pense ce que je pense.
Je fais ce que je fais.
Tu n'as personne d'autre comme moi.
S'il te plaît prends soin de moi.

Content, boudeur, triste, souriant
Souvent gentil et parfois méchant
Mon Dieu, aide-moi à bien grandir
À travers les larmes et les rires.

Mon Dieu,
S'il te plaît aime-moi quand je suis gentil.
S'il te plaît aime-moi quand je suis méchant.
S'il te plaît aime-moi comme
  je me comporte habituellement.

Mon Dieu,
S'il te plaît, aide-moi à être moi-même
quand je suis avec ma famille.

Aide-moi à être moi-même
quand je suis avec mes amis.

Aide-moi à être moi-même
quand je suis tout seul.

Mon Dieu,

Certaines personnes me confondent
avec quelqu'un d'autre.

D'autres se trompent sur mon nom.

S'il te plaît souviens-toi de mon nom

Et souviens-toi de moi.

Dieu, qui a créé la terre,
L'air, le ciel, la mer,
Qui a donné naissance à la lumière,
Prends soin de moi!

Dieu, qui a créé l'herbe,
La fleur, l'arbre, le fruit,
Ainsi que le jour et la nuit,
Prends soin de moi!

Sarah Betts Rhodes

Les personnes que j'aime

Mon Dieu, bénis tous ceux que j'aime ;
Mon Dieu, bénis tous ceux qui m'aiment ;
Mon Dieu, bénis tous ceux qui aiment
   ceux que j'aime,
Et tous ceux qui aiment ceux qui m'aiment.

Prière de Nouvelle-Angleterre

Mon Dieu,
Lorsque maman est joyeuse,
Donne-nous l'occasion de rire et de jouer ensemble.

Lorsque maman est occupée,
Donne-nous l'occasion de travailler ensemble.

Lorsque maman est inquiète,
Donne-nous l'occasion de trouver une solution ensemble.

Lorsque maman est fatiguée,
Donne-nous l'occasion de nous asseoir et de nous
  reposer ensemble.

Mon Dieu,
Fais que papa devienne plus fort et plus sage,
Plus drôle et plus intelligent.

Mon Dieu,
Fais que maman devienne plus forte et plus sage,
Plus drôle et plus intelligente.

Mon Dieu,
Lorsque je suis avec papa et maman,
aide-moi à prendre soin d'eux.

Lorsque je ne suis pas avec papa et maman,
S'il te plaît prends soin d'eux pour moi
et fais que nous soyons vite réunis à nouveau.

Les grands-mamans sont gentilles
et les grands-mamans sont amusantes.
Merci de m'avoir donné une grand-maman
que j'aime tant.

Mon Dieu, bénis grand-papa
pendant le jour radieux.
Mon Dieu, bénis grand-papa
pendant la nuit sombre et grise.
Mon Dieu, bénis grand-papa
Lorsqu'il me serre dans ses bras.
Mon Dieu, bénis grand-papa
Même quand on ne se voit pas.

Je prie pour bébé.
« Que Dieu te garde et te bénisse,
Avec douceur et amour
Que Dieu te guide et t'assiste. »

Mon Dieu,
S'il te plaît aime-moi,
Aime ma sœur,
Aime mon frère.

Mon Dieu,
S'il te plaît prends soin de moi,
Prends soin de ma sœur,
Prends soin de mon frère.

Mon Dieu,
S'il te plaît bénis-moi,
Bénis ma sœur,
Bénis mon frère.

Merci, mon Dieu,
pour toutes les bonnes personnes
qui nous aident à avancer,
qui sourient lorsque nous sommes contents,
qui nous consolent lorsque nous sommes tristes,
qui nous protègent tout au long de la journée.

Mon Dieu,
Aide-moi à être doux et gentil,
   aimable et respectueux
      envers tous ceux que je rencontre.

À la maison

Garde la fenêtre et la porte.

Garde le plancher et le plafond.

Que cet endroit qui est notre maison
soit sous ta garde.

Bénis-nous, que l'on y entre ou
que l'on en sorte.

Lorsqu'il fait froid
Que notre maison soit pleine de chaleur.

Lorsqu'il pleut
Que notre maison soit toujours un bon abri.

Lorsque le soleil brille fort
Que notre maison soit un refuge de fraîcheur.

Quand il fait noir dehors
Que notre maison soit bien éclairée.

Prenons un moment pour remercier
Dieu pour la nourriture qu'il nous a donnée,
Pour les amis autour de la table
Et pour tout ce qui est agréable.

Cuillère, assiette,
Fourchette, couteau,
Que le repas
arrive bientôt.

Couteau, fourchette,
Cuillère, assiette,
Merci, mon Dieu,
Pour ce cadeau des cieux.

Le Seigneur est bon pour moi,
Et je le remercie alors
Pour toutes les choses qu'il me donne,
Le soleil, la pluie, le pépin de pomme.
Le Seigneur est bon pour moi.

Prière attribuée à John Chapman,
planteur de vergers

Pour la santé, la force
et les repas quotidiens,
nous louons ton nom,
Ô Seigneur.

Prière traditionnelle

Des sous-vêtements partout
Des chaussures en paires
Tant de vêtements
Que je m'y perds.

Je sais que je suis béni
D'avoir autant d'habits
Mais s'habiller
Est une véritable difficulté.

La chambre est presque rangée
Les jouets sont mis de côté
Je choisis un moment tranquille
Pour remercier Dieu de cette journée.

Merci, mon Dieu, pour toutes les peluches
Qui forment un berceau tendre et doux
Où je peux m'allonger
et comme dans un nid me reposer.

Les choses
que je fais

Mon Dieu, peux-tu entendre
ma prière ?
S'il te plaît, prends soin
de moi sur cette terre.

Mon Dieu,
Aide-moi à être patient
Pour apprendre de nouvelles
choses petit à petit.

Mon Dieu,
J'ai appris à marcher,
S'il te plaît apprends-moi à courir.
Et peux-tu m'aider à faire des galipettes
Pour que je puisse m'amuser et rire ?

Que mes mains puissent aider,
Si besoin est,
À transporter, à soulever et à tenir
Et à transformer toutes les tâches difficiles
en éclats de rire.

Que mes mains soient intelligentes
Pour tout ce que je fabrique et ce que je fais
Avec du sable, de la pâte et de l'argile
Avec de la colle, de la peinture et du papier.

Que mes mains soient gentilles et douces
Et que je n'ose jamais
Pousser, taper ou blesser,
Mais que je sache toucher avec tendresse
et amitié.

Les mots peuvent nous rendre heureux
Les mots peuvent nous attrister.
LES MOTS PEUVENT NOUS RENDRE FURIEUX !
Les mots peuvent nous calmer.
C'est pourquoi il faut faire attention
Aux choses que l'on dit.
Mon Dieu, aide-nous à choisir les mots
Que l'on emploie aujourd'hui.

Aide-nous à bâtir avec soin nos amitiés ;
Et si on devait se disputer et se brouiller
Aide-nous à reconstruire nos amitiés.

Mon Dieu,
S'il te plaît, apprends-moi à dire « je suis désolé ».
S'il te plaît, apprends-moi à dire « je pardonne ».

Lorsque je suis en colère,
Lorsque je suis très furieux,
Je peux être très méchant
Je peux être très dangereux.

Je suis aussi sauvage qu'un tigre
Je suis aussi sauvage qu'un ours
Je suis plus sauvage qu'un gnou
Et ça m'est bien égal.

Mon Dieu, qui a créé le tigre,
Mon Dieu, qui a créé l'ours,
S'il te plaît, dis-moi
    que tu m'aimes encore
Et que tu m'aimeras toujours.

Mark Robinson

Nous te remercions
pour toutes les choses que nous possédons.

Nous te remercions
pour toutes les choses que nous partageons.

Nous te remercions
pour toutes les choses que les autres partagent
avec nous.

Nous te remercions
pour toutes les choses que nous apprécions ensemble.

Mon Dieu, prends soin de nous tous
Jusqu'à ce que nous nous revoyions
Qu'il fasse soleil ou qu'il gèle,
Qu'il vente, qu'il grêle ou qu'il pleuve,
Protège-nous jusqu'à la prochaine fois.

Quand je me promène
Et que je me sens petit,
Mon Dieu, s'il te plaît,
Rattrape-moi si je fléchis.

Quand je me promène
Comme un grand
J'ai confiance en Dieu
Et je ne suis plus peureux.

Que Dieu veille sur nous
lorsque l'on se montre courageux.
Que Dieu veille sur nous
pour que l'on revienne heureux.

Les animaux

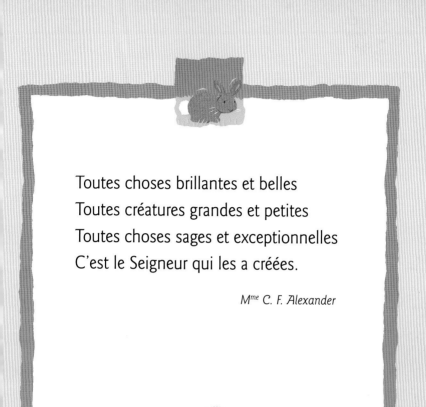

Toutes choses brillantes et belles
Toutes créatures grandes et petites
Toutes choses sages et exceptionnelles
C'est le Seigneur qui les a créées.

Mme C. F. Alexander

Les insectes qui courent partout,
Les petites bêtes qui rampent
Au milieu des pelouses et des herbes
Et là où la forêt est dense :
Tous ont été créés par Dieu
Et font partie de son dessein.
Rappelle-toi que notre monde
   est aussi le leur,
Pas seulement le tien et le mien.

Mon Dieu,

S'il te plaît donne beaucoup d'amour
et de tendresse

aux vers de terre, aux escargots,

aux serpents, aux grenouilles

et à toutes les bestioles étranges
et visqueuses.

Aide-nous à ne pas les effrayer

même si elles nous font peur.

Que les créatures des bois
Vivent ensemble comme il se doit.

Mon Père, bénis et entends
Chaque oiseau et animal
Et surveille tendrement
Les petits êtres sans parole.

Prière traditionnelle

Mon Dieu,
Merci pour les fermiers
qui travaillent si dur pour garder
leurs animaux heureux et en bonne santé.

Mon Dieu,
Nous entendons les vaches beugler
et nous te remercions pour le lait qu'elles nous donnent.

Nous entendons les moutons bêler
et nous te remercions pour la laine qu'ils nous donnent.

Nous entendons les poules glousser
et nous te remercions pour les œufs qu'elles
  nous donnent.

Nous entendons tous les sons de la ferme
et nous te remercions pour les animaux.

grognement

rugissement

Bénis le lion affamé et son RUGISSEMENT
Bénis le gros ours brun et son GROGNEMENT
Bénis la hyène rusée et son effrayant RICANEMENT
Bénis les loups qui, au clair de lune, poussent
  des HURLEMENTS.

ricanement

hurlements

Des animaux multicolores
Avec des pois, des taches et des rayures,
Chacun d'eux est unique,
À aucun autre il n'est identique.

Mon Dieu,
Que notre chien soit loyal et obéissant,
doux et patient, gentil et amusant.
Que toute ma famille apprenne
à être comme ça.

Mon Dieu,

S'il te plaît bénis notre chat.

Qu'il soit assez sauvage pour s'en aller explorer.

Qu'il soit assez apprivoisé pour à la maison rentrer.

Lorsqu'un petit animal meurt
Et que le moment est venu de dire adieu
À un ami à fourrure que l'on a aimé,
Au ciel nous savons que Dieu
Se souviendra de lui avec amour :
Un amour qui ne se terminera jamais.

Si tu as entendu
Le chant d'un oiseau
Dans l'air frais du matin,
Tu sais alors
Que la musique des cieux
Te rendra toujours heureux.

Notre planète

Notre planète, notre maison,
Notre planète, notre terre,
Depuis notre naissance tu nous a bercés.

Notre planète, notre terre,
Notre planète, notre maison,
Dieu seul t'a créée.

Merci, mon Dieu,

Pour la bonne terre :
Je marche dessus.

Pour l'air pur :
Je le respire.

Pour l'eau pure :
Je la bois.

Pour le soleil ardent :
Il réchauffe la terre.

À l'aube et au crépuscule,
Le jour et la nuit,
Merci, mon Dieu,
Pour l'obscurité et pour
ce qui luit.

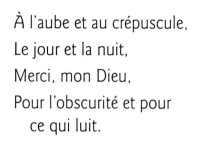

Mon Dieu,
Que les océans et les mers
restent comme ils sont,
Que les pluies et les rivières
restent comme elles sont,
Que les montagnes et les plaines
restent comme elles sont,
Pour que toutes les créatures aient
un endroit sûr où bâtir leur maison.

Dieu de l'océan,
Dieu de la mer,
Que les poissons nagent,
Forts, libres et fiers.

Dieu des vagues,
Dieu du rivage,
Protège-les
À tout jamais.

Les arbres poussent vers le bas,
dans la terre profondément,
ils existent depuis si longtemps.

Les arbres poussent vers le haut,
là-haut jusque dans le ciel,
là où soufflent les vents violents.

Les arbres se balancent,
ils se balancent dans le vent
et murmurent en chantant :

« Nous te remercions, mon Dieu,
de nous protéger
pour que l'on devienne forts et grands. »

Pour le soleil
et la pluie,
Pour les graines
et les fleurs,
Nous te remercions,
Ô Seigneur.

Les anges, au lever du jour,
Ouvrent les fleurs de l'été.
Et à la nuit tombée
Viennent les refermer.

Orange et roses sont les nuages du matin
Alors que le soleil se lève dans le ciel,
Et des nuages blancs flottent dans le bleu lointain
Quand à midi domine le soleil.
Le coucher de soleil est un mélange de pourpre
    et de mauve
Avec des teintes de violet, de rouge et de doré,
Et les anges me surveillent dans la nuit
Lorsque, dans mon lit, je me suis endormi.

93

Tout au long de l'année

Que la pluie tombe doucement,
sans provoquer d'inondation.
Que le vent souffle calmement,
sans entraîner d'orage.
Que le soleil brille vivement,
sans occasionner d'incendie.
Que la chaleur soit agréable,
jamais insupportable.

Dieu réveille la terre à nouveau
Le froid et le gel disparaissent.

Dieu réveille la terre à nouveau
De nouvelles feuilles vertes apparaissent.

Dieu réveille la terre à nouveau
Des vents chauds commencent à souffler.

Dieu réveille la terre à nouveau
Les fleurs du printemps commencent à pousser.

Hier
J'ai aimé la pluie,
Mais, mon Dieu,
S'il te plaît, fais qu'il ne
    pleuve pas aujourd'hui!

Dehors pendant l'été
Dehors sous le soleil
Merci, mon Dieu, pour l'été
Et pour tous ces bons moments passés.

Un jardin d'été
avec des arbres et des fleurs,
Le doux roucoulement d'une tourterelle,
Le bourdonnement d'une abeille,
Cela ne peut être qu'un aperçu
du paradis, juste au-dessus.

De baies de l'automne
rouges et rondes,
Par la main divine
Les oiseaux sont nourris.

Nuage gris, envoie ta pluie
au grain vert qui pousse.
Nuage blanc, éloigne-toi
de cette journée de moisson dorée.

Bottes d'hiver pour sauter dans les flaques
Bottes d'hiver pour jouer dans la neige
Bottes d'hiver pour tous les endroits boueux
où je vais.

Bonnet pour le temps froid
Bonnet pour les jours de tempête
Merci, mon Dieu, pour les vêtements d'hiver
qui aident à nous garder au chaud.

Les arbres en hiver
sont nus et gris.
Dieu leur donne
du givre d'argent comme habit.

Le printemps est vert et jaune
et l'été, rose et doré.
Le rouge de l'automne tournera bientôt au brun,
l'année est presque terminée.
L'hiver est bleu et blanc,
la glace est claire comme du cristal.
Toutes les couleurs se mettent à danser
autour du cercle de l'année.

Les moments tranquilles

Le regard levé vers le ciel
je me tiens sur la terre.
Je sais que Dieu, là-haut,
entendra mes prières.

Mon Dieu,
Es-tu si grand?
Es-tu vraiment saint?
Est-ce que j'ai le droit de t'approcher?

Car je ne suis pas si grand.
Je ne comprends pas vraiment la sainteté.
Mais je me sens par ton amour entouré.

Mon Dieu,
Aide-moi à bien grandir,
et montre-moi le chemin
que je dois suivre
pour arriver un jour au paradis
et m'y sentir bien accueilli.

Je suis assis
je réfléchis
je me pose des questions
je fais des souhaits
j'ai des rêves
et je prie.

Et j'espère
je rêve
et je crois vraiment
que Dieu entend
tout ce que je dis.

Mon Dieu,
Je demande dans mes prières
De profiter de tout ce que tu me donnes.

Mon Dieu,
Je te cherche dans ma vie.
Fais que je te trouve et que j'apprenne à vivre
comme ton ami.

Mon Dieu,
Je frappe à la porte du ciel.
Ouvre-moi la porte de ta maison céleste,
où je vivrai pour toujours comme ton ami.

Inspiré de Matthieu, chapitre 7, versets 7-8

Mon Dieu,
S'il te plaît écoute mes prières
Même si je ne trouve pas
Les bons mots pour m'exprimer.

Mon Dieu,
Je suis un explorateur courageux
Du monde que tu as créé.
Aide-moi à faire de belles découvertes
Et à grandir en sagesse.

Mon Dieu,
Tout ce que je vois sur la terre
M'indique qu'il y a un Créateur,
Et je suis sûr que ce Créateur, c'est toi.

Notre Père qui es aux cieux,
    Que ton nom soit sanctifié,
    Que ton règne vienne,
    Que ta volonté soit faite
Sur la terre comme au ciel.

Donne-nous aujourd'hui notre pain de ce jour.
    Pardonne-nous nos offenses,
    Comme nous pardonnons aussi
    À ceux qui nous ont offensés,
    Et ne nous soumets pas à la tentation,
    Mais délivre-nous du mal.

Car c'est à toi qu'appartiennent

Le règne, la puissance et la gloire,

Pour les siècles des siècles.

Amen.

Pour que tout aille mieux

Mon Dieu, je crois en la bonté,
Je sais que c'est mieux
   que la méchanceté.

Mon Dieu, je crois au bonheur,
Je sais que c'est mieux
   que la tristesse.

Mon Dieu,
Que ta belle terre
Prenne soin de nous.
Que nous prenions soin
De ta belle terre.

Mon Dieu,
Lorsqu'une bonne journée
Est gâchée,
Aide-nous
À arranger les choses.

Ils sont tellement moroses
Tellement tristes
Les jours
Où tout va mal.

J'espère toujours
Que Dieu au ciel
M'enveloppera
De son amour.

On se dit au revoir
En sachant que Dieu m'aime
Et que Dieu t'aime aussi.

On se dit au revoir
En sachant que Dieu ne m'oubliera pas
Et que Dieu ne t'oubliera pas non plus.

On se dit au revoir
En sachant que Dieu prendra soin de moi
Et que Dieu prendra aussi soin de toi.

Mon Dieu,
Lorsque les choses finissent tristement,
Permets-nous de les recommencer
  joyeusement.

Mon Dieu,
Je me sens malade,
Enveloppe-moi de douceur.

Mon Dieu,
Je me sens malade,
Enveloppe-moi de réconfort.

Mon Dieu,
Je me sens malade,
Enveloppe-moi de sommeil.

Mon Dieu,
Laisse-moi m'endormir,
Et au pays des rêves partir.

Mon Dieu,
Nous pensons à ceux qui sont malades
Et te demandons de les soulager.

Lorsqu'il faut partager quelque chose,
Apprends-moi à être juste.

Guéris les chagrins du monde
Sèche les larmes du monde
Calme les soucis du monde
Mets fin aux peurs du monde.

Mon Dieu,
Que tous les enfants du monde
Aient tout ce dont ils ont besoin
Pour bien grandir
Dans la joie et le bonheur.

Les jours
de fête

Pour chaque nouvelle année
Et pour tout ce qu'elle apporte,
Nous te remercions,
Ô mon Dieu.

Je compte les jours jusqu'à Noël
Et j'observe le ciel en soirée.
J'aimerais voir les anges
Vers Bethléem voler.

Je guette la venue des mages
Et de l'étoile brillante royale.
S'il te plaît, puis-je faire avec eux le voyage ?
Est-ce que l'étable est encore loin ?

Je compte les jours jusqu'à Noël
Tandis que l'on fait des achats, nettoie et cuisine.
Les lumières et les guirlandes scintillent,
Et moi, perdu dans mes rêves, j'imagine
Que lorsque l'on racontera l'histoire
Du Seigneur Jésus et de sa naissance,
La vie de tous les jours s'effacera
Et que le paradis sur terre arrivera.

Prière pour l'Avent

Très loin dans une étable, sans berceau pour couche,
Le petit Jésus posa sa tête.
Les étoiles du ciel de très loin regardaient,
Le petit Jésus dans la paille lové.

Les animaux chantent et l'enfant s'éveille,
Jésus ne pleure pas, il s'émerveille.
Je t'aime, petit Jésus! Protège-moi toujours,
Et reste avec moi, restes-y nuit et jour.

Près de toi, Jésus, je demande de rester
Près de moi toujours, je te prie de m'aimer.
Bénis tous les enfants et prends soin de moi,
Prépare-nous à vivre au ciel avec toi.

Chant traditionnel de Noël

Il y a une colline verte au loin,
À l'extérieur des murs de la ville,
Où le Seigneur a été crucifié
Lui qui est mort pour nous sauver.

Il est mort pour que nous soyons pardonnés,
Il est mort pour nous rendre bons ;
Pour qu'un jour au ciel nous allions,
Par son précieux sang sauvés.

Chant traditionnel pour le Vendredi saint,
paroles de Mme C. F. Alexander

Dans le jardin de Pâques
Les feuilles reverdissent ;
Dans le jardin de Pâques
Le Seigneur s'élève.

Dans le jardin de Pâques
Nous savons que Dieu
Nous ouvre les portes du ciel
Grâce à l'amour de Jésus.

Graine, germe, épi et grain

Qui poussent au soleil et sous la pluie.

Grain, farine, pâte et pain,

La récolte de Dieu nous nourrit.

Prière pour les récoltes

Les fleurs du pommier étaient roses et blanches
Les fruits de l'été étaient verts
Mais maintenant les pommes rouges et dorées
Sont trop lourdes pour que l'arbre puisse les porter :
Voici la bénédiction de Dieu pour les récoltes.

Prière pour les récoltes

Mon Dieu,

Lorsque la noirceur nous fait peur,

Ramène-nous vers la lumière

De ta bonté et de ton amour.

Prière pour la veille de la Toussaint

Mon Dieu,
Nous pensons aux personnes
Que nous connaissons aujourd'hui
Qui nous aident
À suivre Jésus.

Nous pensons aux personnes
Des jours passés
Dont les histoires nous ont aidés
À suivre Jésus.

Nous pensons à leurs sages paroles
Et à leurs bonnes actions
Et nous te demandons de nous aider
À suivre Jésus.

Prière pour la Toussaint

La journée est terminée

Bien blotti dans mon lit,
Je récite une petite prière
Pour toutes les personnes
  dans cette maison
Et pour les gens de la terre entière.

Sophie Piper

Les mains serrées, les yeux fermés,
Envoie ta prière à Dieu.
Que la nuit soit remplie de paix,
Que le jour soit rempli d'amour.

Sophie Piper

Maintenant je suis allongé dans mon lit,
Mon Dieu, protège ton enfant ;
Avec amour, protège-moi pendant la nuit
Et réveille-moi quand il fera jour.

Prière traditionnelle

Jésus, ami des petits enfants,
Sois mon ami ;
Prends-moi la main et garde-moi
Pour toujours près de toi.

Walter J. Mathams

Mon bon Jésus, conduis-moi
Tel un berger conduit ses brebis
Vers les verts pâturages
Et les eaux profondes endormies.
Protège-moi contre les dangers
Et les peurs qui viennent me hanter
Lorsqu'il fait noir pendant la nuit.
Dans ta bonté, amène-moi
Vers la lumière du paradis.

La lune brille,
Les étoiles scintillent
Avant le lever du jour ;
Dieu vous bénit tous,
Grands et petits à la fois,
Et vous envoie un jour
    rempli de joie.

Prière traditionnelle

Je vois la lune,
Et la lune me voit.
Mon Dieu, bénis la lune,
Et mon Dieu, bénis-moi.

Prière traditionnelle

L'ange des rêves
Est de bleu vêtu.
Un rêve pour moi
Et un rêve pour toi.

L'ange des rêves
Est de rose vêtu.
Doucement dans mon lit
Je me blottis.

L'ange des rêves
Est de blanc vêtu.
La journée est finie,
Alors bonne nuit.

Sophie Piper

Des nuages dans le ciel,
Des vagues sur la mer,
Des anges au paradis
Qui veillent sur nous la nuit.

Christina Goodings

Ferme les yeux,
Et sans crainte, endors-toi,
Les anges dans le ciel
Veilleront sur toi.

Sophie Piper

Premiers vers

EXPOSITORY PREACHING

EXPOSITORY PREACHING

The Art of
Preaching
Through a
Book of
the Bible

HAROLD T. BRYSON

BROADMAN
& HOLMAN
PUBLISHERS

Nashville, Tennessee

4221-16
0-8054-2116-5

Dewey Decimal Classification: 251
Subject Heading: Preaching\Sermons
Library of Congress Card Catalog Number: 94-35074

Unless otherwise noted, Scripture is from the New American Standard Bible, ©The Lockman Foundation, 1960, 1962, 1963, 1968, 1971, 1972, 1973, 1975, 1977, used by permission. Other versions are marked (KJV), the King James Version; (NIV) the Holy Bible, New International Version, copyright © 1973, 1978, 1984 by International Bible Society; and (RSV) the Revised Standard Version of the Bible, copyrighted 1946, 1952, © 1971, 1973.

Page design by Trina Hollister

Library of Congress Cataloging-in-Publication Data
Bryson, Harold T.
    Expository preaching : the art of preaching from a Bible book
/ by Harold T. Bryson.
        p.   cm.
    ISBN 0-8054-2116-5
    1. Preaching. 2. Bible—Homiletical use. I. Title.
    BV4211.2.B77   1995
    251—dc20
                                                            94-35074
                                                            CIP

Harold T. Bryson

to

Pat Brown

W. A. Hanberry

Jim Mathis

Jack Wolverton

Leroy Mullins

Ross King

F. Clark Sauls

—␉␉—␉␉—␉␉—␉␉—␉␉—

Seven laypersons
who have encouraged me
to study the Word,
to stay with the Word,
to serve the Word
so people can understand
and live the Word.

Contents

Introduction

Perhaps the most important imperative directed to a preacher came from the divinely inspired author of 2 Timothy 4:1–2. "I solemnly charge you in the presence of God and of Christ Jesus, who is to judge the living and the dead, and by his appearing and his kingdom: preach the word; be ready in season and out of season; reprove, rebuke, exhort, with great patience and instruction."

Five Imperatives

Five imperatives in these two verses make the setting seem like the crisp commands of a military officer.

Preach the Word!

The first imperative ("preach the Word") states the basis for the other four commands. The verb *preach* means "to herald" or "to announce a message." "The Word" probably referred to the good news about Jesus' life and ministry; it could also have alluded to the Old Testament Scriptures. Relating "the Word" to the Bible in today's world seems to fit the spirit of the imperative. The ancient imperative, "Preach the word," spoken in today's world could just as well be the admonition, "Preach the Bible!"

Be Ready!

The other four imperatives explain how the Word needs to be preached. The second imperative ("be ready in season and out of season") carries with it a picture of soldiers on duty, ready for combat at any moment. The imperative could allude to both the one who proclaims and to the one who hears the Word. If this imperative refers to the preacher, then the proclaimer of the Word needs to stay with the task of preaching whether he feels like it or not. If it refers to listeners, then the preacher must be faithful to preach the Word regardless of whether listeners welcome it, reject it, or ignore it.

Reprove!

The next three imperatives ("reprove, rebuke, exhort") apply respectively to the human reason, conscience, and will. Lawyers often used the verb translated "reprove" in cross-examining and questioning witnesses. In most cases, the verb means refuting something or proving something wrong. To reprove in preaching means to present the axioms of the Christian faith or to refute in a reasoned manner the errors marshaled against the faith.

Rebuke!

In the first century the verb translated "rebuke" referred to moral censure. Human beings err from the truth and often fall in sin. Preaching the Word sometimes requires confronting people with their errors.

Exhort!

The verb translated "exhort" had a double usage; it meant to comfort as well as to urge. Many persons are haunted by despair, disappointment, discouragement, and other hurts. To practice the imperative, "preach the Word," means to offer encouragement and to comfort the hurting. The verb *exhort* also means to urge or persuade. At times apathetic people must be urged to act. Preaching the Word means sharing the gospel in a reasonable manner, confronting errors in people's lives, comforting the hurting, and persuading people to act in obedience to God's agenda.

The expression, "with great patience and instruction," seems to refer to the last three imperatives. Preaching the Bible requires the divine endowments of personal patience and excellence in presentation. Preachers need patience to preach the Word because of people's apathy and resistance. The preacher could become disheartened and quit because of poor response. The preacher can ask for God's strength to help him remain faithful to preaching the Word. The word *instruction* probably refers to the preacher's painstaking care in sound content and capable presentation of the Word. Preaching the Word involves the combination of divine gifts and human endeavors for excellence in instruction.

Oddly enough, the command to preach the Word comes to the preacher from many sources. The Lord continues to command through the biblical references to be faithful expositors of the Bible. The indwelling Holy Spirit reminds the preacher constantly to preach God's Word. Deep within the being of every God-called preacher resides the conviction that the Bible must be the basis for sermons and the direction of ministry. Believers attend worship services expecting to receive a Word from God. As strange as it may seem, the imperative, "preach the Word," even comes from an unchurched world. The unsaved people recognize the uniqueness of Scripture and expect a preacher to have a Word from God.

Anyone desiring to be a preacher must hear the imperative, "Preach the Word!" and then begin to obey the mandate. Preaching the Word is the task of a born-again believer who has received a unique call of God. When God calls anyone to expound the Bible, he bestows the gift of expounding. God gives abilities to interpret, skills to communicate, and competence for speaking. But God's gifts do not come without human cooperation. The preacher must study the Bible, learn people's needs, develop communication skills, learn sermon organization skills, and develop constantly in the many areas of the preaching task. To preach the Word means to act as if everything in preaching depends on God and to work as if everything depends on the person. Preaching involves a pilgrimage full of glories, challenges, discouragements, delights, failures, improvements, and possibilities. I trust that this book—another book on preaching—will be received as a word of encouragement and instruction from one pilgrim to other pilgrims who want to work hard and allow God to help them strive for excellence in exposition.

The Unique Inspiration of the Word

The Bible was uniquely prepared in order for the world to have a Word from God. Long before the Bible came into existence, God spoke and acted. He revealed himself. God chose to make his character and his ways known to creation. Without the revelation of God, human beings could not have known about God. God has revealed himself in both general and special revelation. In general revelation, God lets himself be known in the hearts of every person and through the natural world. God has revealed even more of himself in special revelation. He disclosed himself in a special place, to a special people, and in a special history. This special revelation centers in the history of Israel, the life of Jesus Christ, and the work of the church.

Through the eras of God's special revelation of himself, God inspired human authors to keep records. The record of his revelation of himself became the Bible. God uniquely inspired over forty different authors over a period of approximately fifteen hundred years to write God's words and actions. The process of recording God's revelation is called *inspiration*. Even the writers of Scripture affirmed God's unique preparation for the Bible. "All Scripture is inspired by God and profitable for teaching, for reproof, for correction, for training in righteousness" (2 Tim. 3:16). The word for "inspired by God" is *theopneustos*, meaning "God-breathed." The idea is that Scripture owes its origin and uniqueness to God's miraculous preparation. The fact of inspiration seems to be more important than the process God used in inspiring writers. How God inspired authors to work with the record of God's revelation may never be known, but knowing the Bible came into being with God's control will always be known.

The Bible does not just represent a record of God's Word to people living in ancient times. God prepared the Bible to speak to people living at that time. The Word God spoke, the Word he inspired authors to write became God's Word for any time. The Bible had a word for then and has had a word for the world throughout history. The Bible also represents God's Word to our time. God continues to speak through the Scriptures. Evidently, God wanted his Word written and preserved so that people at all places and at different times could have a Word from Him.

Being convinced of the uniqueness of Scripture is absolutely essential to the preacher. The main word the preacher has to speak is God's Word. If God had not spoken, the preacher would have nothing to say. But God has spoken and his Word needs to be shared. With a Bible in hand, the preacher has the confidence that God has prepared that Word to share with others.

The Needed Exposition of the Word

The uniquely prepared Bible needs to be opened to others. Much of the Bible can be understood, but its real wealth of meaning comes as a result of spiritual insight rather than mental pursuit. "But a natural man does not accept the things of the Spirit of God; for they are foolishness to him, and he cannot understand them, because they are spiritually appraised" (1 Cor. 2:14). The Bible is a closed book that needs opening with God's help. God opens the Bible to every believer, for every Christian has the indwelling Holy Spirit to illuminate Scriptures.

The Bible draws a sharp distinction between God's truth, known to human beings on the level of their own thinking, and truth disclosed to them through an experience with God. Divine illumination does not exclude human reasoning. Illumination means understanding that comes primarily by divine insight rather than by human reasoning.

God has also chosen and gifted persons to open the Bible to others. "And he gave some as apostles, and some as prophets, and some as evangelists, and some as pastors and teachers" (Eph. 4:11). Many matters in Scriptures are not plain, and believers and nonbelievers alike need spiritually gifted persons to open these obscure matters. An example of the need for exposition of the Bible may be seen in Philip and the Ethiopian eunuch (see Acts 8). Seeing that the eunuch was reading from Isaiah, Philip asked if he understood what he was reading. The eunuch answered, "Well, how could I unless someone guides me?" Philip then sat with the eunuch and began to open the words of Scripture. God in his sovereign design has chosen some persons to open Scripture for other persons. These openers-of-the-Bible may be called expositors, for they expose the truth of God's Word.

One of the main reasons the Bible needs exposition is because of the cultural chasm that yawns wide and deep between the ancient world of the Bible and the contemporary world. God spoke his Word in an ancient world. Understanding the meaning of the Bible involves going back in time and place to that ancient world. It involves encountering a world which has long ceased to exist. Even modern translations of the Bible show a long past world. No one should detest studying the ancient world of the Bible, though, for the events of the Bible happened in history, and its word is a word of God put in classical hebrew, some Aramaic, and common Greek words. Reading the Bible reflects real life in the sense one encounters the Near East and the Greco-Roman world. Real historical happenings and cultural conditioning create the need for someone to help open a Bible that appears to be closed to many people.

Opening the Bible to others necessitates faithfulness to the biblical text of the ancient world. The preacher who wants to expose truth from a text needs to think back to the situation of the biblical writers in their history, geography, culture, and language. The ancient world cannot be ignored or neglected in opening the Scripture. Preachers cannot be slothful about working themselves back into the situation of the text. It would show contempt for the way God chose to speak. The worst mistake would be to read twentieth-century thoughts on the minds of ancient biblical writers. The authentic expositor brings out of Scripture what is there and does not put into the text what he thinks might be there.

The preacher who opens a biblical text to others must be sensitive to the needs of a modern world. God intended his Word spoken in ancient times and places to speak to all peoples in all ages and in every place. To know only the ancient text would make the preacher an exegete, or one who explained what the text meant. Certainly, the preacher is an exegete, but the preacher must move on to become an expositor who gives an exposition to people. Just as expositors think back into the ancient text, they also need to look around at their world. They will see human depravity, hear hundreds of human questions, feel the pain of people, and sense the disorientation and despair of many.

Opening a biblical text to others involves connecting what the text meant to the original author and readers with what the text means to contemporary hearers. In his book, *The hermeneutical Spiral: A Comprehensive Introduction to Biblical Interpretation,* Grant R. Osborne contends that preaching involves a spiral from text to context, from the original meaning of texts to their significance in people's lives today.[1] The exercise of exposing biblical truth involves making a hermeneutical arch. Fashioning the arch means studying the *then* of the text and moving to the *now* of the text. Exposition of the *then* of the ancient text involves only an exercise in antiquarianism. Exposition of a human need without using a biblical text

---

1. Grant R. Osborne, *The hermeneutical Spiral: A Comprehensive Introduction to Biblical Interpretation* (Downers Grove, Ill.: InterVarsity Press, 1991), 12.

makes an exertion in existentialism. The authentic expositor manages the past and the present simultaneously. he seeks to grasp what God *said* so he can open to others what God *says*.

The Diverse Presentations of God's Word

God spoke to many different people in many different places in many different ways about many different matters. In God's inspiration of Scriptures, the words had to be arranged in some type of understandable pattern. Inspired writers used many rhetorical shapes or genres to communicate God's message. God used no one fixed literary form to record the Word. Instead, he allowed many kinds of literary patterns to be used to communicate his Word. Observers of the Bible notice various general genres including narrative, poetry, wisdom, prophecy, Gospel, letter, and apocalyptic. Various literary patterns appear including law, parable, metaphor, simile, proverb, psalm, and hymn. The Bible contains diverse presentations of God's written Word.

When all of the books God intended to be used in the Bible came together, he continued to speak through the spoken Word based on the Bible. One of the primary ways God continues to speak is through a presentation known in today's world as a sermon. Sharing God's Word began with content rather than a form. As the good news of the gospel was shared, many spoken forms began to appear.

The art of preaching the Word began when a person interpreted a biblical text for other people. In about the year A.D. 115, Ignatius wrote a letter to Polycarp in which he referred to a word spoken to a congregation as a homily (*homilia*). Later, others began referring to biblical interpretations as homilies. The word *homilia* could have been a means of describing how the preacher's word said the same thing in another way as the words of a biblical text. The word *homilia* could have come from *homolego*, meaning "to say the same thing." Possibly the term *homily* referred more to the content than to the form.

God's Word is not restricted to any one spoken form. God spoke in many ways in the past, and he can get his Word across to others with many kinds of expositors and many styles of sermons. The form for sermons has never been fixed, nor will it ever be fixed. The *message* of preaching is far more important than the *method* of preaching. God uses many kinds of expositors to present his Word.

Some expositors use long texts; others use short. Some expositors employ a didactic offering while others utilize an inductive or narrative approach. Preachers select and arrange words in a sermon differently. They organize their thoughts with structural diversity. No one style of preacher and no one kind of sermon characterizes the preaching of the Word. A sermon is authentic when it brings the truth of a text in touch with contemporary needs.

Presenting God's Word in a sermon means an exposure. In a sermon, biblical truth is uncovered so that it can help with human existence. No sermon type ranks higher than another kind. Every sermon involves an exposure of God's Word. If biblical truth is not exposed during a preacher's speaking time, the exercise in no way deserves to be labeled a sermon. The issue in a sermon is not *how* God's truth is exposed but *if* God's truth is exposed. Biblical truth in a sermon can be exposed either explicitly with a deductive approach or implicitly with an inductive approach. *The manner does not matter but the message does.*

Sometimes expositors need to give extensive exposure to the Bible. Many different preaching methods have been used to preach the Word in an extensive manner. Some preachers choose to use a lectionary containing four selections of Scripture for each Sunday—an Old Testament reading, a psalm, a reading from an Epistle, and a reading from a Gospel. One popular method of exposing God's Word extensively is preaching a series of sermons from one Bible book. This book has been written to help expositors develop competency in planning, preparing, and preaching numerous sermons from one single book in the Bible.

The Enduring Expectation of God's Word

If one accepts the divine preparation of the Bible and assumes the role of an expositor, what can one expect to happen? The prophet gave a confident expectation of God's Word when he wrote, "For as the rain and the snow come down from heaven, and do not return there without watering the earth, and making it bear and sprout, and furnishing seed to the sower and bread to the eater; so shall My word be what goes forth from My mouth; it shall not return to Me empty, without accomplishing what I desire, and without succeeding in the matter for which I sent it" (Isa. 55:10–11). Three obvious results come from the decision to preach the Word.

Divine Proclamation

An expositor ought to expect divine proclamation. Exposition of Scripture represents much more than human words. The sermon serves as a means for God to speak his prepared Word through a chosen and gifted person. Karl Barth said, "Preaching is the attempt enjoined upon the church to serve God's own Word, through one who is called thereto, by expounding a biblical text in human words and making it relevant to contemporaries in intimation of what they have to hear from God himself."[2] When the prophets spoke, they were convinced they spoke God's Word. When the apostles preached, they used Scripture as the basis for their words. When the contemporary expositor preaches the Word, God continues to speak. Divine proclamations come repeatedly through the medium of preaching the Bible. This fact does not mean that the preacher is God, but God uses human beings to communicate his Word.

Divine Illumination

An expositor ought to expect divine illumination before, during, and after the preaching event. God's act of illumination permeates the process of getting his Word heard. he gave insight to biblical authors as they wrote the Word. he illumines preachers as they prepare sermons to speak the Word. As the sermon is being spoken, God works with listeners to convict, clarify, edify, explain, instruct, guide, and numerous other actions of illumination. The spoken Word represents a "theological happening." When God's Word is preached, people should expect various kinds of divine illumination. Something more than human reasoning is happening when a sermon is delivered.

Life Transformation

An expositor ought to expect life transformation as a result of preaching God's Word. Lives can be impacted and changed when God's Word is preached. Of course, transformation does not happen without human response. When the Word is preached, it needs to be heard. Just hearing the Word stops short. It needs to be obeyed. If God's Word is heard and heeded, life transformation

---

2. Karl Barth, *Homiletics*, trans. Geoffrey W. Bromiley and Donald E. Daniels (Louisville, Ky.: Westminster/John Knox Press, 1991), 44.

takes place. Each time a preacher preaches the Word, there should be the expectation that human lives will be transformed.

Preach the Word! The divine imperative needs human implementation. Preaching the Word involves a person willing to study the ancient biblical text and to be sensitive to contemporary human needs. Learning to study a Bible book in order to give extensive exposure to God's Word will help actualize the imperative.

CHAPTER 1

A Definition among
Definitions of Expository Preaching

Three Types of Definitions
    Etymological Definition
    Morphological Definition
    Substantive Definition
Misconceptions About Expository Preaching
    Exposition in the Homiletical Hierarchy
    Exposition as Exegetical Exposure
    Rigid Rules of Exposition
The Eclectic Emphases on Expository Preaching
    The Sermon Series
    The Sermon Content
    Free Form

Every discipline has its own vocabulary, and the art of preaching is no exception. Different homiletical terms have taken center stage throughout the history of Christian proclamation. Various emphases and needs have prompted people to preface the word *preaching* either with an adjective or as an adjectival phrase. Think for a moment of the descriptive words or phrases used to depict a particular type of preaching: *topical, textual, expository, doctrinal, inductive, deductive, biblical, biographical, life-situational,* and others.

Perhaps the most popular of these is the word *expository*. The unknown author of a thirteenth-century document entitled *Tractatus de Arte Praedicandi (A Treatise on the Art of Preaching)* distinguished three different kinds of preaching: topical, textual, and expository.[1] John A. Broadus popularized this threefold classification among Americans in *A Treatise on the Preparation and Delivery of Sermons* (1870). The influence of John A. Broadus, W. E. Sangster, T. H. Pattison, Austin Phelps, and others helped to establish these three categories. Preachers who classify their sermons as expository mean to verify the biblical nature of their messages.

Furthermore, laypersons have overheard the preachers' "shoptalk," and they express their expectation of preaching prefaced by the word *expository*. The laity like the term *expository* because of its ring of biblical authority. Many preachers affirm, "I am an expository preacher!" Christians who seek a pastor are often heard to say, "We want an expository preacher!"

Yet, if asked to define expository preaching, many preachers and laypersons give vague definitions. In 1870, Broadus understood expository preaching to be exposition of a biblical truth from a passage to a congregation. With the passing of years and with the numerous usages, however, the word *expository* became vague and relative.

So many definitions of *expository preaching* have developed through the years that writers on preaching have grouped the definitions into categories. Donald G. Miller gives four broad categories into which many definitions of expository preaching fall.[2]

Faris D. Whitesell establishes five broad categories of expository preaching. He lists ten statements of what expository preaching *is not*, then adds a sevenfold description of what expository preaching *is*.[3]

There is still no generally accepted definition of expository preaching. Many definitions have been constructed, but confusion still reigns.

---

1. Warren W. Wiersbe and Lloyd M. Perry, *The Wycliffe Handbook of Preaching and Preachers* (Chicago: Moody Press, 1984), 45.

2. Donald G. Miller, *The Way to Biblical Preaching* (Nashville: Abingdon Press, 1957), 20.

3. Faris D. Whitesell, *Power in Expository Preaching* (Westwood, N.J.: Fleming H. Revell Co., 1967), v–xvi.

Why this confusion? Why so little agreement about the meaning of such a widely used term? The answer may lie in the distinguishable difference between the meaning of the word and the usage of the word. Unfortunately, people get lured into the idea that words have one authoritative meaning and that these words can be defined clearly. Actually, words do have meanings, but their meanings can only be determined by their use in context. To put the matter simply, words do not have meanings, they have usages. Finding the word's usage helps arrive at its meaning. When St. Paul's Cathedral in London was finished in 1716, the king called it "amusing, awful, and artificial." Today we would think that the king had expressed a negative evaluation of the cathedral. But in those days *amusing* meant amazing, *awful* meant awe-inspiring, and *artificial* meant artistic.[4]

Words do not have authoritative meanings so much as they have relative usages. One person's usage of the term *expository preaching* may mean one thing, and another person's usage of the same term may presuppose an entirely different definition. Even Bible words have multiple, relative usages rather than single, authoritative meanings. For example, the Greek word *kosmos* which is translated "world" has several usages in the New Testament.

- "God so loved the world" (John 3:16). *Kosmos* here means the populated peoples of the earth.

- "Love not the world" (1 John 2:15). Here *kosmos* refers to a society of people opposing God.

What does *kosmos* mean? That has to be determined by its context.

Similarly, the term *expository* has taken on many meanings. No one knows exactly what the term *expository* first meant, and its meaning today comes from how people use it.

A young preacher received a visit from a pastoral search committee at a large, prestigious church. As the committee talked with this prospective pastor, they specified their expectations: leadership ability, interpersonal relationship skills with staff and church members, counseling ability, preaching skills, and numerous other pastoral responsibilities. The pastor felt reasonably secure with all

---

4. George F. Regas, *Kiss Yourself and Love the World: Keys to Authentic and Vital Living* (Waco, Tex.: Word Books Publishing, 1987), 90.

expectations until one member said, "Our church needs an expository preacher."

The term *expository* stayed in the preacher's mind even during conversation about other matters. The pastor had heard the word *expository* frequently while in seminary, but he had learned the professor's definition only to pass a test. He never thought the term would be an issue in his ministry.

Keeping in mind the maxim that words do not have authoritative meanings but relative usages, the cause for the confusion about expository preaching becomes apparent. The meaning of expository preaching comes from its usage by theorists and practitioners of preaching. Thus, a person's definition of the term depends largely on the books he has studied or the preacher he has revered.

Humpty Dumpty's conversation with Alice in Lewis Carroll's *Alice in Wonderland* offers some insight about word usage:

> "There's glory for you!" remarked Humpty Dumpty.
>
> "I don't know what you mean by 'glory,'" Alice said.
>
> "I mean there's a nice knockdown argument for you," he replied.
>
> "But glory doesn't mean a "nice knockdown argument,' " Alice objected.
>
> "When I use a word," Humpty said in a rather scornful tone, "it means just what I choose it to mean, nothing more or less."
>
> "The question is," said Alice, "whether you can make words mean different things."
>
> "The question is," said Humpty Dumpty, "which is to be master—that's all."[5]

The old, widely used homiletical term *expository preaching* needs to be and can be a prominent phrase in today's preaching vocabulary. The term needs to be retrieved from the homiletical museums. The expression does not have to be an antique phrase observed by theorists and replaced by different terminology. Learning how others used and still use the expression *expository preaching* could clarify the many emphases attached to it. The term may be vague and even disdained, but the phrase is too significant to be sacrificed by misunderstanding. Its meaning must be clarified.

---

5. Quoted in David H. C. Read, *Go and Make Disciples* (Nashville: Abingdon Press, 1978), 29–30.

This chapter presents the diverse definitions associated with expository preaching through the years, unmasks some myths associated with the term, and then presents a definition that I consider clear and practical.

Three Types of Definitions

No homiletical term has received as many definitions with an apparent authoritative definiteness than *expository preaching*. Each definition seems to be correct. Because of the variety of definitions, ambiguity abounds about a clear, authoritative, workable definition of expository preaching. Faris D. Whitesell and Donald G. Miller have divided the dozens of definitions into several broad categories.[6]

Will the bewildering variety of definitions motivate people to abandon the term? Can order and design be brought out of this confusion about such a meaningful homiletical term? The answers to these questions lie in the future after the reader has worked through the history of the term *expository preaching*. The pursuit begins with the origin of the word *expository* and continues with the presentations of the different definitions of expository preaching, both historical and contemporary.

Etymological Definition

A search for the meaning of a word begins with studying the form of the word and then investigating the various usages of the word. The first endeavor in searching for the meaning of *expository* involves studying its etymology. Words originated and developed by adding prefixes and/or suffixes to a root. The study of a root word and its prefixes or suffixes is called *etymology*. Therefore, to understand the word *expository*, we must examine its etymology. The root of *expository* seems to be the word *expose* which is a term derived from the Middle English word, *exposen*, which came from the Middle French word, *exposer*, derived from the Latin word *exponere*. In Latin the word *ponere* (the root) was combined with the prefix *ex* (out of, from), and the resultant meaning of *exponere* came to mean "to put on display."[7] In Late Latin (A.D. 180–600), the meaning of *exponere* came to mean "to interpret or explain." The

---

6. Miller, 20–21; Whitesell, viii–xiv.
7. *Cassells New Latin Dictionary*, 1968 ed., s.v. "expone."

related terms *exposition, expositor,* and *expository* came to the English language by way of French. All three terms came from the French word *expositus* which means "expounder." And *expository* is the adjectival form of exposition derived from the Medieval Latin *expositories.*[8]

In *Webster's Tenth New Collegiate Dictionary,* the noun *exposition* means "a setting forth of the meaning or purpose" and "a discourse or an example of it designed to convey information or explain what is difficult to understand." The noun *expositor* means "a person who explains," and the adjective *expository* is defined as "of, relating to, or containing exposition."[9] Paul D. Hugon placed the same emphasis on explanation when he used expository in relation to rhetoric. Exposition answered why and how in orderly detail. Hugon contended that exposition was unemotional explanation and appealed only to the intellect.[10] *Webster's New Dictionary of Synonyms* included a discussion of exposition:

> Exposition often implies a display of something . . . ; more often it implies a setting forth of something which is necessary for the elucidation or explanation of something else such as a theory, a dogma, or the law. . . . In a more general sense, especially in academic use, exposition applies to the type of writing which has explanation for its end or aim and is thereby distinguished from other types in which the aim is to describe, to narrate, or to prove a contention.[11]

Therefore, in both written and spoken discourse, explanation was the prominent and differentiating ingredient for exposition.

When the adjective *expository* prefaces the word *preaching,* it is modifying or ascribing some particular characteristic to the preaching. George M. Glasgow, with reference to public speech, said, "Exposition is the explanation of something, for example, a thing or a process, with the intention of making it clear."[12] If the basic etymological meaning of expository is followed, such preaching would

8. *A Comprehensive Etymological Dictionary of the English Language,* 1966, s.v. "expose."

9. *Webster's Tenth New Collegiate Dictionary,* 1993 ed., s.v. "exposition," "expositor," "expository."

10. Paul D. Hugon, *The Modern Word Finder* (New York: Grosset and Dunlap, 1934), 118.

11. *Webster's New Dictionary of Synonyms,* 1968 ed., s.v. "exposition."

12. George M. Glasgow, *Dynamic Public Speaking* (New York: Harper and Brothers Publishers, 1950), 80.

be proclamation that displayed or disclosed a view of the subject. If the spirit of the adjective's usage in written and spoken discourse is followed, expository preaching means etymologically a proclamation in which a subject is disclosed to view by means of explanation. Explanation is the dominant idea, and any other element such as interpretation, elucidation, declaration, description, or other element is subservient to the purpose of explanation. More than likely, the earliest usage of the adjective *expository* before the noun *preaching* meant an exposure or explanation of a Bible truth.

John Calvin (1509–64) used the term *exposition* in the sense of explaining Scripture. He seemed to consider an expositor to be one who explained a text by laying open the text to public view to set forth its meaning, explain what was difficult, and to make appropriate application. John H. Leith described Calvin's understanding of exposition:

> First of all, Calvin understood preaching to be the explication of Scripture. The words of Scripture are the source and content of preaching. As an expositor, Calvin brought to the task of preaching all the skills of a humanist scholar. As an interpreter, Calvin explicated the text, seeking its natural, its true, its scriptural meaning.... Preaching is not only the explication of Scripture, it is also the application of Scripture. Just as Calvin explicated Scripture word by word, so he applied the Scripture sentence by sentence to the life and experience of the congregation.[13]

John Calvin and other sixteenth-century preachers viewed preaching with the idea of exposing truth from a text. No complicated concepts of expository preaching seemed to exist in the sixteenth century. Basically, a definition of expository preaching at that time would have involved an etymological perspective of exposing truth by explanation and application in a verse-by-verse method of handling a Bible passage.

Over three hundred years after John Calvin and other sixteenth-century preachers, John A. Broadus continued to use the adjective *expository* in an etymological manner. In his 1870 work entitled, *A Treatise on the Preparation and Delivery of Sermons*, Broadus wrote:

> An expository discourse may be defined as one which is occupied mainly, or at any rate very largely, with the exposition of Scripture....

---

13. John H. Leith, "Calvin's Doctrine of the Proclamation of the Word and Its Significance for Today in the Light of Recent Research," *Review and Expositor* 86 (winter 1989): 33.

It may be devoted to a long passage, or to a very short one, even part of a sentence. It may be one of a series, or may stand by itself. We at once perceive that there is no broad line of distinction between expository preaching and common methods, but that one may pass almost insensible gradations from textual to expository sermons.[14]

Like Calvin, Broadus associated expository primarily with the explanation of Scripture. Merrill F. Unger, writing in 1955, continued to use the term *expository* in the etymological sense. Unger wrote: "No matter what the length of the portion explained may be, if it is handled in such a way that its real and essential meaning as it existed in the mind of the particular biblical writer and as it exists in the light of the over-all context of Scriptures is made plain and applied to the present-day needs of the hearers, it may be properly be said to be *expository preaching.*"[15]

The adjective *expository* seems to have first been attached to preaching to describe the exposure or explanation of biblical truth. As time passed, changes took place in the meaning of preaching terms. The simple, etymological usage of expository preaching developed into more complicated usages and meanings.

Morphological Definition

Some homileticians were not content with the etymological meaning of the adjective *expository* before the word *preaching.* As years passed different theories about expository preaching emerged. The term took on a more morphological usage that concentrated on the form of the sermon.

Definition by Length of Text. The most widely used morphological meaning defines expository preaching on the basis of the length of the text. Morphological theorists have classified sermons as topical, textual, and expository according to these criteria:

- Topical: a sermon built around an idea taken from the Bible or a subject outside the Bible taken to the Bible;

- Textual: a sermon based on one or two verses from the Bible;

- Expository: a sermon based on a text longer than two verses.

---

14. John A. Broadus, *A Treatise on the Preparation and Delivery of Sermons,* 7th ed. (New York: A. C. Armstrong and Son, 1891), 303.

15. Merrill F. Unger, *Principles of Expository Preaching* (Grand Rapids: Zondervan, 1955), 33.

Andrew W. Blackwood, professor of homiletics at Princeton during the 1940s, concretely attached the definition of the expository sermon to the length of the text. In *Preaching from the Bible*, Blackwood said, "In the broad sense, this sort of sermon is the unfolding of the truth contained in a passage longer than two or three consecutive verses."[16] In a later book, *Expository Preaching for Today: Case Studies of Bible Passages*, Blackwood again used the length of the text to define expository preaching. He said, "Expository preaching means that the light for any sermon comes mainly from a Bible passage longer than two or three consecutive verses."[17]

Andrew Blackwood's concept that expository preaching is based on the length of a text influenced other writers. Douglas M. White wrote, "In distinction to both the topical and textual sermon, the expository sermon is a treatment of a single extended passage of Scripture, a lengthy paragraph, a chapter, or more than a chapter, or even a whole book of the Bible."[18] T. H. Pattison agreed with Blackwood when he wrote, "The topical sermon, in which the theme is especially prominent; the textual sermon, in which more regard is paid to the words of the text; and the expository sermon, in which, as a rule, a longer portion of the Bible is taken as the basis for the discourse."[19] One of the most prominent morphological usages of expository preaching centered around the length of the text.

Definition as Connected Series of Sermons. Another morphological meaning was associated with the term expository preaching. Some people began to think of expository preaching as a connected series of sermons through a book of the Bible. William M. Taylor, in his Lyman Beechers Lecture on Preaching delivered in 1876, associated expository preaching with a series of sermons from a Bible book. Taylor stated: "By expository preaching, I mean that method

---

16. Andrew W. Blackwood, *Preaching from the Bible* (New York: Abingdon-Cokesbury Press, 1941), 38.

17. Andrew W. Blackwood, *Expository Preaching for Today: Case Studies of Bible Passages* (New York: Abingdon-Cokesbury Press, 1953), 13.

18. Douglas M. White, *He Expounded* (Chicago: Moody Press, 1952), 59.

19. T. H. Pattison, *The Making of the Sermon*, rev. (Philadelphia: American Baptist Publication Society, 1941), 53.

of pulpit discourse which consists in the consecutive interpretation, and practical enforcement, of a book of the sacred canon."[20]

F. B. Meyer also defined expository preaching along the lines of a series of sermons from a Bible book. Meyer said: "Expository preaching is the consecutive treatment of some book or extended portion of Scripture on which the preacher has concentrated head and heart, brain and brawn, over which he has thought and wept and prayed, until it has yielded up its inner secret, and the spirit of it has passed into his spirit."[21] Preaching a connected series of sermons from a Bible book developed as another idea associated with expository preaching.

Definition by Treatment of Text. Through the years, still another morphological meaning came to be associated with expository preaching. An expository sermon was defined by some on the basis of the homiletical treatment of a text. Such a slant of definition stressed that main points and even subpoints need to come from the text which was usually designated as longer than two or three verses. Charles W. Koller wrote that the expository sermon derived "its main points or the leading subhead under each main point from the particular paragraph or chapter or book of the Bible with which it deals."[22] Brown, Clinard, and Northcutt followed the same line when they wrote, "The expository sermon secures its major and first subpoints primarily from the text."[23] Nolan Howington thought an expository sermon was one that used the homiletical treatment of a text. Howington said, "An expository sermon is generally based upon a passage or unit of Scripture, and the theme with its divisions and development come from that passage."[24] Faris D. Whitesell presented a definition of expository preaching which included two morphological meanings: the length of the text and the homiletical treatment of the text. Whitesell wrote: "An expository sermon is based on a Bible passage, usually longer than a verse

---

20. William M. Taylor, *The Ministry of the Word* (New York: T. Nelson and Sons, 1876), 155.

21. F. B. Meyer, *Expository Preaching Plans and Methods* (New York: George H. Doran Co., 1912), 29.

22. Charles W. Koller, *Expository Preaching Without Notes* (Grand Rapids: Baker Book House, 1962), 21.

23. H. C. Brown, Jr., H. Gordon Clinard, and Jesse J. Northcutt, *Steps to the Sermon: A Plan for Sermon Preparation* (Nashville: Broadman Press, 1963), 54.

24. Nolan Howington, "Expository Preaching," *Review and Expositor* 56 (January 1959): 58.

or two; the theme, the thesis and the major and minor divisions coming from the passage; the whole sermon being an honest attempt to unfold the true grammatical-historical-contextual meaning of the passage, making it relevant to life today by proper organization, argument, illustrations, application, and appeal."[25]

Running Commentary. Still another form for expository preaching involves the association of a commentary format instead of a rhetorical or sermonic format. Discourses appear to be running commentaries from word to word and verse to verse without rhetorical unity, outline, and persuasive drive. David Breed in *Preparing to Preach* took issue with expository preaching as a running commentary when he wrote:

> The expository sermon is the product of exegesis, but it is in no sense its exhibition. It is not a running commentary upon some passage of Scripture in which its separate parts are taken up verbatim and explained, but, as its name implies, it is a piece of rhetoric: a sermon. It differs from the topical sermon in that it is all derived directly from the Scripture; and it differs from the textual sermon in that more of the details of the Scripture passage are employed.[26]

The morphology of the running commentary has had, and even continues to have, many users. In the history of preaching, some effective preachers employed the running-commentary method. John Chrysostom (ca. 347–407) used the commentary style in many of his oral presentations. Martin Luther, Ulrich Zwingli, and John Calvin also preached with a commentary format rather than the rhetorical sermon style. The Bible commentaries of both Luther and Calvin, which are still available, represent more of their style of preaching than study guides of Bible books. Today many preachers choose to preach through a book of the Bible going from verse to verse or from section to section of a passage with little concern for sermon structure.

With the association of many morphological meanings to the term *expository preaching*, confusion began to develop. The evolution of the various concepts of form around the adjective *expository* moved the simple etymological idea of exposing or explaining a biblical text to more complicated homiletical matters. Many ques-

---

25. Whitesell, vi–vii.

26. David R. Breed, *Preparing to Preach* (New York: George H. Doran Co., 1911), 387.

tions arose: How much should be exposed? In which way should a text be exposed? These became issues in the dialogue about expository preaching. Such definitions about length of text, series of sermons, treatment of a text, or format have confused expositors about the definition of expository preaching. Some people have become so confused over these morphological issues that they have dropped the use of the expression *expository preaching* entirely.

Still, closer study reveals many theorists and preachers through the years did not get obsessed with rigid forms and did not associate morphological meanings to expository preaching. Basically, they stayed with the etymological idea of exposing or explaining a Bible text. In our study, we started with the idea of expository as "exposing," but we have passed through such issues as the quantity and quality of exposure. Now we are ready to return to exposing or explaining a Bible text.

Substantive Definition

Through the years, many people have basically stuck with the idea that expository preaching exposes or explains a biblical text. Such an emphasis may be classified as substantive meaning. According to this emphasis, the substance of an expository sermon must be drawn from a Bible text, irrespective of how long or how short it is. The substantive category does not involve such criteria as length of passage, number of sermons, consecutive sermons in a series, homiletical treatment of a text, and other morphological matters. John A. Broadus advocated the substantive position when he wrote: "An expository discourse may be defined as one which is occupied mainly, or at any rate very largely, with the exposition of Scripture. It by no means excludes argument and exhortation as to the doctrines or lessons which this exposition develops. It may be devoted to a long passage, or a very short one, even part of a sentence. It may be one of a series, or may stand by itself."[27]

Austin Phelps, a significant author on the subject of preaching, wrote a year after Broadus that expository preaching was one type of explanatory preaching. Phelps argued that a sermon is expository if the text is the theme and if the chief object of the sermon is to explain the text by elaborate treatment with a view to persuasion.[28]

---

27. Broadus, 303.

These two classical homileticians—Broadus and Phelps—dismissed questions of form or morphology to define expository preaching from a substantive perspective. Both identified expository preaching with exposing and explaining a Bible truth.

A check with subsequent authors after Broadus and Phelps discloses a continuation with the concern for substance. Marvin R. Vincent, who is known primarily for his work *Word Studies in the New Testament*, wrote a work entitled *The Expositor in the Pulpit*. Vincent said that the phrase expository preaching properly covers all preaching. Exposition to Vincent was exposing the truth contained in God's Word. Vincent wrote, "Exposition is *exposing* the truth contained in God's word: laying it open; putting it forth where the people may get hold of it; and that is also preaching."[29] In 1910 Harry Jeffs wrote, "Exposition is the art of opening up the Scriptures, laying them out, reproducing their matter and their spirit in forms vitalized by the personality of the expositor."[30] Three decades after Jeffs, R. Ames Montgomery wrote:

> The expository preacher proposes above everything else to make clear the teaching and content of the Bible. The preacher seeks to bring the message of definite units of God's Word to his people. He discovers the main theme or constituent parts of a book's message as they were in the mind of the writer. These he unfolds step by step until he reaches the ultimate goal. He discovers the universal, organizing elements of thought in the book, and strives to set forth their essential relationship to contemporary life.[31]

Writing almost thirty years after R. Ames Montgomery, Faris D. Whitesell gave the following sevenfold concept of expository preaching:

1. It is based on a passage in the Bible, either short or long.

2. It seeks to learn the primary, basic meaning of that passage.

3. It relates that meaning to the context of the passage.

---

28. Austin Phelps, *Theory of Preaching* (New York: Charles Scribner's Sons, 1887), 21, 32.

29. Marvin R. Vincent, *The Expositor in the Pulpit* (New York: Anson D. F. Randolph and Company, 1884), 6.

30. Harry Jeffs, *The Art of Exposition* (London: James Clarke, 1910), 9.

31. R. Ames Montgomery, *Expository Preaching* (Westwood, N.J.: Fleming H. Revell Co., 1939), 42.

4. It digs down for the timeless, universal truths stemming out of the passage.

5. It organizes these truths tightly around one central theme.

6. It uses the rhetorical elements of explanation, argument, illustration, and application to bring the truth of the passage home to the hearer.

7. It seeks to persuade the listener to obey the truth of the passage discussed.[32]

Can you see some simple evolution in the substantive position? At first, writers simplified the substantive usage by emphasis on exposing or explaining a biblical text. With the passing of the years they added application and organizational matters to the explanation of biblical truth.

Homiletical developments took interesting turns. Writers on preaching began to add more morphological meanings to the term *expository preaching*. In 1957 Donald G. Miller reacted to the many forms being added to the art of explaining a Bible text. In his book *The Way to Biblical Preaching*, he contended that the adjective *expository* had been associated too closely with multiple divisions, length of text, and verse-by-verse commentaries. He felt that the expository sermon had been set off as a special type of sermon, "as one among many." Miller urged for a restoration of the word *expository* to its true significance. He wrote: "Truly biblical exposition is limited only by the broad principle that the substance of one's preaching should be drawn from the Bible. . . . Then it follows that all true preaching is expository preaching and that preaching which is not expository is not preaching."[33] Miller advocated that the limits of form hindered the act of preaching biblical sermons. He said: "Expository preaching is an act wherein the living truth of some portion of Holy Scripture, understood in the light of solid exegetical and historical study and made a living reality to the preacher by the Holy Spirit, comes alive to the hearer as he is confronted by God in Christ through the Holy Spirit in judgment and redemption."[34]

With Donald G. Miller, homiletical forms became subordinate to biblical substance. A variety of forms could be attached to biblical truth. Miller's conclusion was that all preaching was expository

---

32. Whitesell, xv.
33. Miller, 21.
34. Ibid., 26.

preaching, for the substance explained or exposed was more important than a homiletical form.

Many others have followed Miller's line of reasoning. Haddon Robinson, writing in 1980, proposed a substantive idea for expository preaching. Robinson said expository preaching was "the communication of a biblical concept, derived from and transmitted through a historical, grammatical, and literary study of a passage in its context, which the Holy Spirit first applies to the personality and experience of the preacher, then through him to his hearers."[35] According to this definition, expository preaching was more a philosophy than a method. The expositor's paramount concern was for the message of the text and how to communicate that message. In 1981 William Thompson rejected various morphological meanings in preference to a more substantive approach. Thompson sought to get substance from a biblical text by the processes of exegesis and interpretation.[36] In 1982 John R. W. Stott wrote about exposition: "It refers to the content of the sermon (biblical truth) rather than its style (a running commentary). To expound Scripture is to bring out of the text what is there and expose it to view."[37]

The substantive definition created some changes in the use of homiletical terminology. Some substantive advocates have decided to drop the term *expository* in preference for the word *biblical*. More than likely this use of the word *expository* represents a reaction to the many morphological concepts of the term. Other substantive advocates have chosen to retain the word *expository* to refer to all preaching. Such use of expository means that many homileticians stay basically with the etymological meaning of expository that all sermons expose biblical truth. With the three basic meanings of expository preaching in mind—etymological, morphological, and substantive—we are now ready to focus on the excessive emphases on the forms attached to expository preaching.

---

35. Haddon W. Robinson, *Biblical Preaching: The Development and Delivery of Expository Messages* (Grand Rapids: Baker Book House, 1980), 19.

36. William D. Thompson, *Preaching Biblically: Exegesis and Interpretation*, (Nashville: Abingdon, 1981), 9–10.

37. John R.W. Stott, *Between Two Worlds: The Art of Preaching in the Twentieth Century* (Grand Rapids: William B. Eerdman's, 1982), 125–26.

Misconceptions About Expository Preaching

Christian preaching originated with an authoritative message, not with an absolute technique. The New Testament preachers demonstrated more interest in telling the biblical truth than in developing some rigid forms for the messages. In fact, the first-century preachers used several forms to share their messages. One of the most prominent means of sharing God's Word originated in the synagogue service where Scripture passages were read and comments were made about the Scriptures. This form came to be known as the "homily" which probably originated from the Greek word *homologo* that means "to say the same thing." When a preacher delivered a homily in the synagogue, the same truth was said in the commentary that was true in the text. The word *homily* could have meant to confess currently what was true historically in the Old Testament text.

Soon after the New Testament era, biblical content began to use many forms. Greek and Roman rhetoric began to influence preachers, and sermons began to take on a more rhetorical form than commentary form. E. C. Dargan in *The Art of Preaching in the Light of Its History* examined the many forms sermons took from the first century to the nineteenth century. At various times the form of the sermon took more "center stage" than the content of the sermon. The wineskins (form) became more important than the wine (substance).

Over the years of Christian history some homileticians have become so obsessed with the form that many myths have been attached to the technique of making a sermon. No other area of homiletics has created more myths or personal feelings than expository preaching. These myths do not represent heresy or falsehood. Instead, these myths represent personal uses of the expression *expository preaching*. Perhaps, a homiletical demythologization needs to happen. In this section of a search for a definition of expository, some of the most prominent myths need to be challenged.

Misconception #1: Exposition in the Homiletical Hierarchy

Somewhere in the history of Christian preaching a classification of sermons developed. As early as the thirteenth century, sermons were classified as topical, textual, or expository. A topical sermon represents a message built around a subject taken from the Bible or a subject taken from life and related to a biblical truth. A textual sermon represents a message based on one or two verses from the

Bible with the main theme and the major division coming from the text. An expository sermon represents a message based on a Bible passage longer than two verses with the theme and major division coming directly from the text. As time progressed these classifications became more complicated as advocates spoke about topical/textual sermons and allowed an expository sermon to be based simply on a text longer than three verses without requiring major and minor divisions to come from the text.

From a simple classification of sermons by length of texts, the system grew into a complicated system of classifying sermons. The excessive emphasis on form drew away from the emphasis on the content of the sermons. A homiletical hierarchy of what was and was not biblical began to be associated with the three terms *topical, textual,* and *expository.* Generally, ranking began to develop as follows:

Topical sermon	Sometimes biblical but mostly nonbiblical
Textual sermon	Biblical but less biblical than expository
Expository sermon	Purely biblical

These rankings tended to exalt preachers who used long texts and disdained preachers who addressed a topic. Thus, a homiletical heresy or myth emerged which advocated that sermons based on longer texts were more biblical than sermons based on shorter texts or a topic taken from the Bible or a current topic taken to the Bible. Unfortunately, conversations emerged about biblical and nonbiblical preachers. This error raises some questions: How many verses does it take to make a sermon biblical? Is there such a thing as a nonbiblical sermon? If a message is not biblical, is it a sermon?

After seeing the myth in print and hearing advocates of this homiletical hierarchy, conscientious persons began to seek to demythologize the heresy. Donald G. Miller questioned the classifications from the standpoint that the length of a text does not determine biblical content. Miller said that both textual and expository sermons could have outlines worded from the text, but they might not really convey what that passage originally meant. In Miller's viewpoint a sermon might have a topical, textual, or expository form, but all three forms may miss the substance of a text.

Therefore, Miller disdained the ancient categories and sought to emphasize biblical content more than the form the sermon took.[38]

Clyde Fant rejected the myth which advocates that Christian proclamation occurs by an emphasis on an approach. He disdained the placing of terms such as *expository*, *textual*, or *topical* before preaching. Trying to distinguish biblical preaching from expository preaching or topical preaching represented a meaningless and intimidating exercise according to Fant. He said, "In fact it is not true that there is no 'biblical preaching,' there is only preaching."[39] Jay Adams shared Fant's sentiment about the terms *topical, textual,* and *expository.* Writing in the 1983 publication, *Essays on Biblical Preaching*, Adams described the distinctions between the three as "sheer nonsense," and serving "mainly to create confusion."[40] Adams claimed that each term was an indicator of an emphasis to be included in every sermon, though not always in the same proportion.[41]

John R. W. Stott also sought to demythologize the homiletic myth about different grades or levels of biblical preaching. He said,

> I know, of course, that some textbooks on homiletics supply a list of different kinds of preaching, one being "textual," another "topical," a third "expository," and sometimes others besides. . . . Whether one's text is a single word, a sentence, a verse, a paragraph, a chapter, or even a whole book, still the truly Christian preacher is an expositor, praying and thinking himself into and even under the text until it masters him, dominates his mind, sets his imagination alight and his heart aflame, so that when he preaches, God's Word sounds forth.[42]

Stott saw little value in the traditional classifications and scorned the idea that sermons could be ranked more biblical and less biblical.

William Thompson also sought to demythologize the tradition in which he was trained in classifying sermons topical, textual, and expository. Thompson preferred a substantive approach in which

---

38. Miller, 26–27, 35.

39. Clyde E. Fant, *Preaching for Today* , rev. ed. (New York: Harper and Row, 1975), 101.

40. Jay E. Adams, *Essays on Biblical Preaching* (Grand Rapids: Zondervan, 1983), 7.

41. Ibid., 10.

42. John R. W. Stott, "Biblical Preaching Is Expository Preaching," in *Evangelical Roots: A Tribute to Wilbur Smith*, ed. Kenneth S. Kantzer (New York: Rumas Nelson, 1978), 168.

the fundamental question is: How can one make sure the substance, the essence of the sermon, is biblical?[43] Thompson disliked the homiletical heresy that the length of a text determined whether the sermon was biblical. Thompson formulated the thesis that "biblical preaching occurs when listeners are enabled to see how their world, like the biblical world, is addressed by the word of God and are enabled to respond to the word."[44]

Miller, Fant, Adams, Stott, and Thompson represent conscientious attempts to challenge the myth that a sermon is made biblical by the length and exegetical treatment of a text. The questions sought by these writers and by this work are: What makes a sermon biblical? Does the number of verses make a sermon more or less biblical? Does the way one handles the text such as by detailed exegesis make a sermon more biblical? Leander Keck in his work *The Bible in the Pulpit* helped with these questions in his criteria for biblical preaching. Keck said, "Preaching is biblical when a) the Bible governs the content of the sermon and when b) the function of the sermon is analogous to the text."[45] Neil Richardson had a similar idea when he wrote, "Biblical preaching brings past and present into a creative unity, enabling those who listen to hear a word which illuminates their own situation."[46] Actually, a sermon cannot be a little or a lot biblical. If it is not biblical, then it is not classified as a Christian sermon but as a moral address or essay. In the opinion of this writer, a sermon is biblical when the original meaning of the text intersects with the contemporary meaning of the text, when what the text meant becomes what the text means, when the "now" of the text coincides with the "then." Assigning a length of text and a manner of treatment in order to label the sermon biblical or expository is a homiletical myth.

Misconception #2: Exposition as Exegetical Exposure

Another myth that has developed and continued about expository preaching is that the art is an exegetical exposure. Some have advocated and practiced a more didactic approach to preaching

---

43. Thompson, 9–10.

44. Ibid., 10.

45. Leander E. Keck, *The Bible in the Pulpit: The Renewal of Biblical Preaching* (Nashville: Abingdon, 1978), 26.

46. Neil Richardson, *Preaching from Scripture* (London: Epworth Press, 1983), 35.

rather than a rhetorical approach. To these advocates the cognitive details of a passage mean more than anything else. Such exegetical exposure involves detailed etymological analysis of Greek and Hebrew words. Syntactical arrangements and literary structures also become a primary part of the pursuit in this type of preaching. What is called a sermon resembles more of an exegetical exposure or a detailed commentary rather than a truth taken from a text and directed to people's needs. Doing detailed exegetical analysis may educate people in Greek and Hebrew nouns, verb tenses, and different genres, but such efforts often fall short of directing these truths to people's needs.

Challenging the myth that expository preaching involves exegetical exposure is necessary. But, the reader might see the challenge of the myth as an attempt to eliminate exegesis from a sermon. This challenge is not an attempt to eliminate exegesis but to propose the purpose and place of exegesis in preparing and delivering a sermon. Exegesis means to study the historical, grammatical, and theological background of a text in order to discover its meaning. After discovering the meaning of the text, the expositor tries to share in a sermon what the text means to people today. Preparing and delivering a sermon requires exegesis. Doing exegesis is not the myth; overly exposing the exegesis is the myth. Ideally, the detailed exegesis occurs educationally in the study and appears practically in the pulpit. David R. Breed presented this view: "The expository sermon is the product of exegesis, but it is in no sense its exhibition. It is not a running commentary upon some passage of Scripture in which its separate parts are taken up seriatim and explained, but, as its name implies, it is a piece of rhetoric: a sermon."[47] Jeff D. Ray also wrote that "exegesis draws out the hidden meaning; exposition places that meaning out in logical, appropriate, effective order. Exegesis is the task of the commentator; exposition is the task of the preacher."[48] Both Breed and Ray emphasized exegesis as a prelude to sermon preparation, but they warned against excessive exegetical information in the pulpit.

Exegesis is the prelude to preparing sermons. Walter Liefeld gave a good perspective of exegesis when he wrote "that careful exegesis should lead into exposition."[49] He also stressed the need

---

47. Breed, 387.
48. Jeff D. Ray, *Expository Preaching* (Grand Rapids: Zondervan, 1940), 71–72.

for a sermon not only to teach but to help and inspire.[50] How much exegesis appears in pulpit performance will vary from sermon to sermon. The amount of exegetical exposure which appears in a sermon does not make it biblical or expository. In fact, it does not even make it more biblical. Advocating that expository preaching is a continuous commentary on a Bible passage is a myth that needs to be demythologized. Irrespective of how much exegesis goes into preparation and how much exegesis appears in delivery, the authentic sermon is one which expounds or lays open the meaning of the Word of God.

Misconception #3: Rigid Rules of Exposition

When Christian proclamation first began, no rigid rules about techniques existed. The primary concern was to share the content of the gospel. First-century preachers chose varied forms to declare the content. As time passed, rules began to emerge about how preaching should take place. Perhaps the first formal set of rules appeared in the fourth century A.D. when Augustine wrote *De Doctrina Christiana*. This work was based on Aristotle's rules of speech in *Rhetoric*. After Augustine, numerous other homileticians added rules about the art of preaching. Many of these rules need to be demythologized. The content remains the same for preaching which is biblical truth, but ideas about technique or method for delivering sermons vary considerably. Principles or techniques need to be emphasized, but principles can develop into rigid rules. Such an overemphasis on technique can cause preoccupation with form rather than content. Homiletical rules are not to be arrogant masters but helpful friends for preparing and delivering biblical content.

Many theorists have proposed rules about expository preaching. Trying to follow rigid rules for expository preaching can be frustrating. Exposing and discussing all the rules attached to expository preaching is impossible, but some of the most prominent rules may be defined and demythologized.

Perhaps the most rigid of all rules about expository preaching centers on the length of the text. Many theorists have proposed

---

49. Walter L. Liefeld, *New Testament Exposition: From Text to Sermon* (Grand Rapids: Zondervan, 1984), 20.

50. Ibid., 21.

that expository preaching includes those sermons with a text longer than two or three consecutive verses. The length of a passage for a sermon seems to be irrelevant. The thought of the sermon should be controlled by the truth of the text. Whether the text is a single word, a phrase, a sentence, a verse, a paragraph, a chapter, or even the entire book, the sermon should expose a truth from the text directed to people's needs. Emphasizing the length of a text has lingered with the concept of expository preaching, and that rule needs to be deleted.

Rules tend to beget other rules. Establishing the length of a text for a sermon led to another rule—points and subpoints need to come directly from the text. Nothing is wrong with the points and subpoints coming from the text if the text merits it, but not all texts have the possibility of points and subpoints. Deriving points and subpoints from the text does not make a sermon more biblical. A sermon is biblical when the point, not necessarily the points and the subpoints, comes from the text. Trying to get major and minor points from a text could corrupt the meaning. The homiletical style of getting points and subpoints from the text has to be challenged.

In addition to the rigid rules about the length of the text and points and subpoints from the text, theorists have established ideas about sermons in a series from a Bible book. In the historical development of homiletics, the idea has emerged that expository preaching involves the consecutive treatment of some book in the Bible. Preaching a series of sermons from a Bible book is an excellent practice, but the rigid rules appear with coerced consecutivism. Having to treat every verse in a book in a consecutive manner appears to border on homiletical legalism. Less rigidity could be advocated by allowing selectivity of texts within a Bible book. Nonetheless, some theorists and practitioners insist on treating every verse in a book, beginning each week where the text stopped the previous Sunday and proceeding until the whole book is covered.

Numerous other rigid rules prevail about the legislation of expository preaching. No authoritative set of rules or definitions exists about expository preaching. Instead relative usages of the term abound, with many rules attached to their usage—preach expository sermons just on Sunday night; never try to preach through a Bible book morning and evening; do not interrupt the series of expository sermons for any reason; pick up the following

Sunday where you left off the previous Sunday. These rigid rules and many others exist, and they tend to put potential expositors in homiletical strait jackets.

No technique in homiletics should be infallible. Every theoretical proclamation idea needs to be questioned with regard to its validity and practicality. The demythologization process needs to be a constant practice. A homiletical hierarchy, an exegetical exposure, and the rigid rules have confused people too long. The time has come to look at expository preaching in a new way so the expression can be used with understanding, respect, and practicality.

The Eclectic Emphases on Expository Preaching

Because of the existence of the different definitions and the many myths, an honest examination needs to be made about clarifying or redefining expository preaching. The various usages that theorists and practitioners give to the term necessitate a close look at some options. What can be done with such an age-old, widely used, confusing term as expository preaching? At least four options seem to be available. First is the elimination option which entirely discards the adjective *expository* and substitutes the word *biblical.* Second is the elevation option which discards the adjectives *topical* and *textual* and retains only *expository.* Such an option calls for all sermons to explore a biblical truth and advocates calling all preaching expository. Third is the continuance option which perpetuates the classical concept that an expository sermon is one based on a text longer than two or three consecutive verses with the points and subpoints coming directly from the text. The fourth choice is the eclectic option which means to choose ideas from various sources and use them. Paul Scherer advocated the need for an eclectic approach to the sermon. Scherer listed the traditional types of sermons such as doctrinal, expository, ethical, and evangelistic. Then he said: "Let me say again that I have never preached or heard or read a sermon worthy of the name which was not to a greater or less degree all of these together."[51]

The eclectic option for defining expository preaching seems to be the best way to make the term understandable and practical for

51. Paul Scherer, *For We Have This Treasure* (New York: Harper and Brothers, 1944), 165.

today. Using ideas from etymological, morphological, and substantive meanings leads to a general definition that expository preaching involves the art of preaching a series of sermons either consecutively or selectively from a Bible book. Each sermon within the series needs to expose a biblical truth, and each sermon may also have different homiletical forms and any amount of Scripture for a text. Remember that a term's meaning is based on its usage; therefore, this concept of expository preaching does not declare all other ideas to be false and this one to be true. It represents only one definition among other definitions. Expository preaching seems to be distinguished from the expression *expository sermon*. Expository preaching refers to a series of sermons, and expository sermon refers to each sermon in the series. The sermons in the series expose truth regardless of the form they take. The eclectic emphasis, which becomes the emphasis of this book, will now be explained.

Eclectic Emphasis #1: The Sermon Series

The definition of expository preaching as a series of sermons, either consecutive or selective from a Bible book, begins the eclectic emphasis. However, the definition does not end with just a stress on a series of sermons. The emphasis on a series of sermons needs to be amplified with concern for content and with a freedom of form for each sermon in the series. By beginning with expository preaching as a series of sermons, the idea of an expository sermon becomes somewhat obsolete. The emphasis should not be on the length of a text or the source for major divisions and subpoints. Within the series of sermons from a Bible book, sermons may vary in the length of texts and in the structure of the sermons. Categorizing sermons within the series from a Bible book into topical, textual, or expository becomes a futile morphological task. The emphasis in each sermon in the series should be deriving a biblical truth from any size text, shaping the idea in an appropriate manner, and directing the biblical truth to people's needs. Thus, the emphasis is not on a single expository sermon but on a series of sermons from a Bible book.

Preaching a series of sermons from a Bible book does not mean rigid regulations about continuity. Many theorists think of expository preaching solely from the perspective of a consecutive series of sermons. This morphological perspective needs to be changed.

The series of sermons needs to be thought of as either a consecutive or a selective series. To be consecutive in the series means to treat every text in order from a Bible book. To be selective means to choose several texts from among the many texts in the book.

Some Bible books, because of the nature of their writing and the length of chapters, lend themselves more to a selective series. For example, preaching a series of sermons from Psalms, Proverbs, or one of the Gospels would be better for selected texts rather than consecutive texts. The nature of material in these and other books does not appear in consecutive order. Also, some books such as Jeremiah or Isaiah seem to be too lengthy for a consecutive series of sermons.

Preaching a series of sermons from such books as Amos, Philippians, James, and many other shorter books lend themselves to a consecutive series. Yet there is no rigid rule to forbid or to force either a consecutive or a selective treatment on any Bible book. The definition of expository preaching in this work allows for either a consecutive or selective series of sermons from a Bible book. A liberty exists in choosing texts for a series.

Eclectic Emphasis #2: The Sermon Content

After establishing the definition of expository preaching as an emphasis on a series from a Bible book, attention needs to be focused on the sermons in the series. Each sermon from the Bible book needs a preeminent concern for biblical content. Rather than concentrating on the length of text and the source for points and subpoints from the text, the concern for each text and sermon should focus on the text's original meaning and its meaning for today's hearers of the text. The emphasis on a series of sermons either consecutively or selectively comes from one of the morphological meanings of expository preaching, and the concern for content in each sermon in the series comes from both the etymological and substantive meaning of expository preaching.

The etymological meaning of expository mentioned earlier in this chapter is "to expose", or "lay open", the meaning of the Word of God in a particular text. The concern for content leads the expository preacher to find biblical truths in texts and then to expose them to contemporary hearers. In each sermon "listeners are enabled to see how their world, like the biblical world, is addressed by the word of God and are enabled to respond to that word."[52] Exposing truth from texts requires serious study of the text. Finding out what the text meant allows the preacher to expose what the text means. Donald G. Miller emphasized the concern for content when he wrote: "Expository preaching is an act wherein the living truth of some portion of Holy Scripture, understood in the light of solid exegetical and historical study, and made a living reality to the preacher by the Holy Spirit, comes alive to the hearers as he is confronted by God in Christ through the Holy Spirit in judgment and redemption."[53]

Harold E. Knott also wrote of expository preaching along the lines of content when he said, "The expository sermon is an effort to explain, illustrate, and apply the Scripture to life. . . . Its purpose is to help the hearers to find in the sacred writings the true interpretation of life."[54] Exposing truths from a text is no easy task; it takes discipline. What kind of study of the text is necessary for exposing truth? In the concern for context each text needs to be examined in the light of its historical background. Each text came from a historical event that involved both authors and readers, and these events and their historical environment need to be examined. Concern for content involves the disciplines of exegesis and interpretation. Simply stated now, but thoroughly studied later in this work, exegesis means to study words and word construction to see what the text meant to the original readers. Interpretation builds on exegesis and human experience to share what the text means today.

Sometimes in the morphological concept of expository preaching, a particular kind of form searches for content. In most cases in the etymological and substantive concepts, the content discovered by disciplined study of the text looks for a form to contain the content. In preparing individual sermons from a Bible book, the first concern should be the content. Every sermon in the series could be a treatment of a word, a phrase, a verse, a dozen verses, a chapter, or many chapters. Then the content is shaped into some form which leads us to discern the next aspect of the eclectic explanation of expository preaching. When biblical truth from a text has been

---

52. Thompson, 10.

53. Miller, 26.

54. Harold E. Knott, *How to Prepare an Expository Sermon* (Cincinnati: Standard, 1930), 11.

discovered by means of rigid study and by illumination of the Spirit, the truth must be shaped and shared.

Eclectic Emphasis #3: Free Form

The definition of expository preaching as a series of sermons either consecutive or selective from a Bible book goes beyond a mere series to a concern for content and an emphasis on freedom of form. More modifications may be needed in the area of form, especially in the length of the text and in the style of structure. Many definitions of expository preaching emphasize rigidity in these two areas. The definition of expository preaching proposed in this work continues to be eclectic. To preach effectively from a Bible book, freedom of form is necessary. No preacher needs to prepare for a series of sermons from a Bible book with the presupposition that for every sermon to be expository it must have a text longer than three verses. Nor does the preacher need to be handicapped with the presupposition that every sermon must have points and subpoints coming directly from each text.

Homiletical freedom allows the expository preacher to choose texts from a Bible book of various lengths. As previously stated, sermons from the series may be based on a word, a phrase, a verse, two or three verses, a short paragraph, a long paragraph, several paragraphs, a chapter, several chapters, or an entire Bible book. To make every sermon from a Bible book based on the same length of text seems to be too rigid, thus more freedom for different lengths needs to be considered. In plotting a series of sermons from a Bible book, several text lengths may appear. Generally speaking, the shape of a Bible book often determines the length of the texts. In some books long narratives involving several chapters may be the basis for a sermon, while in that same book one word or one sentence may be used as the text. For example, in a series from a Bible book, text lengths could range from words, phrases, sentences to small or long paragraphs. The predominant emphasis of this phase of the eclectic explanation of expository preaching is to be free to choose texts of various lengths.

For example, for a possible series of sermons from Psalms, you may preach consecutively from Psalm 1 to Psalm 150, or you may choose numerous psalms for a series. In selecting texts from Psalms, you may preach from a word, a phrase, a sentence, several sentences, or from an entire psalm. Also, in preaching from the

Psalms, a life experience may arise, and a text could be selected from the Psalms. Which choice seems to be the best way for selecting texts—using three verses for every sermon in the series or choosing texts of various lengths? The answer seems obvious. One method is binding and the other is liberating.

Not only does homiletical freedom exist in the choice of length of texts, but freedom exists in the homiletical form for the sermon. Taking to a text the principle that points and subpoints must come from the text seems much too rigid. Think for a moment about getting points from the text. At the outset of the discussion, settle the matter that getting points or outlines from the text represents a good way to develop an idea, but the problem comes when a homiletical rule tries to make every sermon have points coming from the text for it to be expository. Think more of the main idea or point coming from the text; then the points or outline may proceed from the point. The preacher tries to get across the point, which involves elaborating points or disclosing a plot. The actual divisions (points) of a sermon should be development of the main idea (point). Each part needs to be part of the theme. When the point of a passage is stated, the outline can be developed. At times, the points to develop the point may be contained in the text. At other times, the points for developing the point may not be found in the text. The guarantee that the sermon will be biblical lies in the point's being biblical. Do you detect a freedom with regard to form? The preacher should. The expositor goes to a text to get a point, and then by means of using that point, he may develop the point by dividing the text into parts or by elaborating on the biblical point.

In an attempt to make the popular term *expository preaching* more understandable, useable, and meaningful, an eclectic definition has been adopted. Excellent homiletical ideas have been examined and chosen from the etymological, morphological, and substantive emphases on expository preaching. In researching the subject of expository preaching, some homiletical rules have been included in the eclectic definition; and other rules have been studied and considered but discarded for the definitions of expository preaching. Such concepts as an emphasis on a series of sermons, an allowance in some cases for points coming directly from a text, and an emphasis on the explanation of Scripture have been retained with the feeling that these ideas make expository preaching a practical term. Yet other homiletical ideas, such as a consecutive series, the length of a text longer than two or three verses, and the absolute assertion that points must come from the text have been discarded with the feeling that these ideas represent too much vagueness and homiletical rigidity.

The eclectic definition primarily emphasizes that expository preaching is a collection of sermons rather than emphasizing the classification of individual sermons with the labels "topical," "textual," or "expository." The eclectic definition does not need to stop with the series. It needs to be expanded with a closer look at individual sermons within the series of sermons from a Bible book. The definition is expansive enough to allow sermons in the series to have different lengths of texts. The eclectic emphasis returns the etymological and substantive ideas with the emphasis that each sermon in the series must expose a truth in the text which will be directed to the people's needs today. In the eclectic definition of expository preaching, structural designs may vary from sermon to sermon or may have similar designs that depend on the shape of the text and the means of getting points from the point. Such an eclectic emphasis on expository preaching seems to make the term useable today.

Other sermons, other than those in a series from a Bible book, exist. These sermons, like those in a series from a Bible book, must expose a Bible truth and meet human needs. These sermons seemingly do not need to be classified as topical, textual, or expository but simply messages based on biblical truth prepared and preached to help people.

—⁓— —⁓— —⁓— —⁓— —⁓—

Expository preaching is the art of preaching a series of sermons, either consecutive or selective, from a Bible book. Subsequent chapters of this work emphasize the *art* of preaching sermons from a Bible book.

CHAPTER 2

Seven Disciplines Necessary for Preaching from a Bible Book

Preparing a Paper on the Historical Background of the Book
    Primary Purposes of the Paper
    Helpful Resources for the Paper
Making a Detailed Analysis of the Book
    Reasons for an Analysis
    Helpful Resources for an Analysis
Engaging in Extensive Exegesis of the Book
    The Appropriate Time for an Exegesis
    The Significant Usefulness of Exegesis
    Beneficial Resources for Exegesis
Initiating Interpretations of Each Text
    Valid Reasons for Interpretation
    Suggested Resources for Interpretation
Surveying the Variety of Literary Possibilities
    Preaching from Old Testament Books
    Preaching from New Testament Books
Plotting a Series of Sermons from the Book
    Unique Purposes of Plotting
    Helpful Resources for Plotting
Preparing Individual Sermons from the Book
    Advanced Planning of Sermons
    Weekly Preparation of Sermons

41

Any endeavor, whether recreational or occupational, requires rigid disciplines. Few people ever attain excellence in any area without long hours of dedicated devotion. Almost every profession or recreation requires work and continued discipline to be effective. To be a good tennis player, one has to learn about the game and must practice regularly. No golf game ever got better without learning stances, drives, and putts and working hard to implement the knowledge. If amateur athletic endeavors require such hard work, how much more discipline is required to be a professional athlete? Whatever goal a person pursues in life, whether professional or recreational, the endeavor requires the discipline of time and energy.

Preaching sermons involves both a theological event and human endeavor. God appears in the act of preaching, and he works diligently to make his Word known through the human act of preaching. If God works hard in Christian proclamation, the preacher needs to expend the necessary disciplines for making and delivering sermons. Every facet of the preaching task requires diligent work.

Certain disciplines are necessary in the human art of preaching. Getting one, two, or even three fresh, relevant, interesting biblical ideas each week requires a searching mind directed by God's Spirit. Preachers engage in homiletical hunting to have an idea processed and ready for Sunday. Finding a stimulating idea for a sermon is not the end of the work. Diligent labor has to be expended to discover human needs, study the text, find appropriate illustrations, shape the substance, and write a manuscript or make extensive notes.

Even after finding and structuring a sermon idea, the preaching task is not finished. The sermon has to be delivered. Delivering the sermon requires the preacher to use the voice properly and to keep the nonverbal behavior in conjunction with the verbal message. Oddly enough, the work of preaching does not end when gestures are gone, voices are silent, and benedictions are pronounced. Work continues with listening to the compliments and criticisms, dealing with the feelings about the sermon, and helping people put the message into practice. While evaluations and implementations occur, the preacher must work hard to begin the sermon routine again. Preaching effective sermons requires hard work.

If the routine task of preaching involves dedicated disciplines, how much more work is required in preaching a series of sermons from a Bible book? Deciding on Tuesday afternoon to begin a series of sermons from a Bible book on the following Sunday morning is not possible. Intensive advanced planning and preparation have to be done. Several months before delivering a sermon series, extensive academic and devotional study of the Bible book must be completed. Preparation involves concentrated study in the historical background, literary analysis, detailed exegesis, relevant interpretation, and homiletical plotting of the Bible book. Preachers contemplating the art of preaching such a series should count the costs because an enormous price must be paid for effective expository preaching.

In addition to the discipline of preliminary preparation, the discipline of intense concentration must be undertaken. For a number of weeks sermon topics and texts will come from the same book. Two questions need to be asked:

- Can I keep my interest in the series of sermons in one book over an extended period of time?
- Can the audience relate over several weeks to texts and topics coming from the same book?

Answering yes to both questions requires many disciplines including expending energies of creative exegesis, interpretation of texts to people's needs, variety in homiletical forms, and interesting and relevant illustrations. Should one choose to pay the price involved in both preliminary preparation and weekly intensive concentration, effective expository preaching can occur. The combination of expending the human disciplines and depending on the divine dynamic is necessary.

The purpose of this chapter is to give the specific costs or disciplines necessary for preparing and preaching a series of sermons from a Bible book. In subsequent chapters, each particular discipline will be explained and illustrated.

1. Preparing a Paper on the Historical Background of the Book (chap. 4).
2. Making a Detailed Analysis of the Book (chap. 5).
3. Engaging in Extensive Exegesis of the Book (chap. 6).
4. Initiating Interpretations of Each Text (chap. 7).
5. Surveying the Literary Possibilities in Old and New Testament Books (chap. 8–10).

6. Plotting a Series of Sermons from the Book (chap. 11).

7. Preparing Individual Sermons (chap. 12–14).

Exercising the disciplines necessary to preach from a Bible book with preciseness can result in sermons that are true to the biblical text and in tune with people's needs.

Preparing a Paper on the Historical Background of the Book

The first discipline involves preparing a paper on the historical background of the Bible book. About three to four months before the delivering the sermon series, the preacher should prepare a background paper. The paper needs to be a reconstruction of the author and readers, the occasion and purpose of the book, and insights about culture, history, politics, and other matters associated with the divine origin of the book. In studying the book's origin, no issue raised should be neglected. A background paper does not represent sermonic material which will be produced in sermon delivery. Instead, such a study provides the preacher a backdrop for every text studied in the Bible book. The background becomes foundational for the sermons in the series.

Primary Purposes of the Paper

Every book in the Bible has its place in history. God inspired human authors to write about real historical and human situations. A background paper represents research into the story behind the Bible book. Each book has an author or authors, readers, a time in history, an occasion and purpose, and other background matters.

By researching and studying detailed and complicated background matters, the preacher might fail to see the connection of the rather academic background paper with sermons. Authentic biblical sermons must consider to some extent the life situation of the Bible book from which a text comes. Otherwise, content could be used in a sermon that would not be the original intention of the text. A background paper does not represent academic hurdle to be leaped, or busywork to be endured to get to the main event of preparing sermons. Instead, each text used in the series will relate directly or indirectly to the original life situation.

Reconstruct the Story. Because a background paper requires such extensive work, questions may arise about the need for such a discipline. Some definitive purposes for the paper might need to be stated to defend its necessity. The primary purpose of the background paper is to help the preacher reconstruct the book's story. Each Bible book has its own unique historical happening. No book in the Bible is removed from human circumstances or devoid of meeting human needs. Human authors uniquely inspired by God addressed life situations. If biblical truth existed in the narrative within a historical framework, the life situation needs to be re-created with such clarity and power that the story lives again in human imagination.[1] Reconstructing this story requires information from Bible dictionaries, commentaries, atlases, encyclopedias, and other resources. But this reconstruction requires more than mere academic information. The interpreter must also have empathy and intuition to get into the experiences of the author and readers of a Bible book. The preparer of the background paper needs to feel he is there and that the circumstances surrounding the book happened to him and not just to the biblical people.[2]

Relate the Life Situation to Today's Life. Another purpose of the background paper involves connecting the original life situation with contemporary circumstances. Applications or interpretations of biblical texts need to coincide with the original life situation. Ignoring the life situations of the text could result in improper interpretations or applications of the text. Insights can be gained from a text without studying background matters first, but such insights need to be checked against the historical background. Studying the original life situation of a Bible book helps a person see what the book meant. Seeing what the book meant helps one to move naturally to what the book means. Authentic biblical sermons emerge when a book's message of then coincides with the message of the now. A background paper helps connect a Bible book's ancient message with today's message.

Unfortunately, some interpreters put texts in twentieth-century situations before they put the text in their original time and place. Such interpretation allows biblical texts to be subjected to the relativity of different cultures and of different times in history rather than subjecting texts to the objectivity of their original time and culture. For example, prooftexts from 1 Corinthians have been given for the silence of women in church, the length of a person's

---

1. Wayne E. Ward, *The Word Comes Alive* (Nashville: Abingdon Press, 1969), 16.

2. Ibid., 17.

hair, the covering for a woman's head in worship, and hasty church discipline. These texts have been used outside the historical and cultural context of first-century Corinth. Twentieth-century opinions should not be substantiated with different first-century situations. Understanding the original life situation of a Bible book furnishes a guide for applying ancient truths today. Beginners in the art of preaching from a Bible book often fail to see the value of a detailed paper on historical background. Yet those who exercise the discipline see the value and experience the satisfaction of discovering a Bible book's ancient story and relating that story to today's world.

Helpful Resources for the Paper

Obviously not all the data for the background paper comes from just the Bible book. Various resources need to be consulted to get pertinent background matters connected with the book. These resources include introductions to Old Testament and to New Testament books. These general works cover background matters and cultural issues. For example, before beginning the background paper, reading several articles in various introductions would help begin the process for reconstructing the book's original story.

Introductions. One-volume introductions could be valuable resources for the background paper. The following are helpful Old Testament introductions:

> W. S. Lasor, D. A. Hubbard and F. W. Busch, *Old Testament Survey*

> Robert L. Cate, *An Introduction to the Old Testament and Its Study*

> Roland K. Harrison, *Introduction to the Old Testament*

> Brevard S. Childs, *Introduction to the Old Testament as Scripture*

> Clyde T. Francisco, *Introducing the Old Testament* (Revised Edition)

> Gleason L. Archer, Jr., *A Survey of Old Testament Introduction*

> Edward J. Young, *An Introduction to the Old Testament*

The following are helpful New Testament introductions:

Joe Blair, *Introducing the New Testament*

D. A. Carson, Douglas J. Moo, and Leon Morris, *An Introduction to the New Testament*

Donald Guthrie, *New Testament Introduction*

Everett F. Harrison, *Introduction to the New Testament*

A. M. Hunter, *Introducing the New Testament*

Kirsopp Lake and Silva Lake, *An Introduction to the New Testament*

Introductions contain data about the author, readers, date, occasion, purpose, and contents of the book, as well as other critical matters. Reading different introductions will give diverse viewpoints about the Bible book.

Commentaries. In addition to introductions, Bible commentaries need to be consulted. Each commentary contains pertinent information about background matters. Generally speaking, commentaries are written from two basic philosophical stances. A critical commentary examines the book with the various critical problems associated with it. Some of these critical commentaries might be too technical for the average reader. Nonetheless, no issue should go unnoticed about any Bible book. A devotional commentary may mention critical problems but emphasizes practical issues. Every expository preacher should consult both critical commentaries and devotional commentaries. The preferred approach is to combine critical commentary study with devotional commentary study.

Commentaries on all the books of the Bible may be found in sets and in individual commentaries on Bible books. No person can tell another person the best set of commentaries. The individuality of each person allows different choices. The following commentaries might be consulted for background material of a Bible book:

Critical

The International Critical Commentary

The Interpreter's Bible

The Anchor Bible

Word Biblical Commentary

The Expositor's Greek Testament

The Old Testament Library

Hermeneia—A Critical and Historical Commentary on the Bible

Devotional/Critical

The Broadman Bible Commentary

New Century Bible

Carl F. Deil and Franz Dalitzsch, *A Commentary on the Old Testament*

Tyndale Old Testament Commentaries

Tyndale New Testament Commentaries

New American Commentary

The New International Commentary on the Old Testament

The New International Commentary on the New Testament

New Testament Commentary

Augsburg Commentary on the New Testament

Augsburg Old Testament Studies

Devotional

Daily Study Bible

The Communicator's Commentary

Interpretation: A Bible Commentary for Teaching and Preaching

Layman's Bible Book Commentary

Maclaren's Exposition of Holy Scripture

These commentaries offer a wide range of viewpoints; but, in the quest to gather background of a Bible book, no insight should go unnoticed whether agreeable or disagreeable to the interpreter.

Dictionaries and Biblical Backgrounds. In addition to general introductions and commentaries, background material may be gleaned from Bible dictionaries and other works related to biblical backgrounds. These works will furnish information about biographical, chronological, geographical, historical, and bibliographical matters. The following one-volume works will furnish brief, quick, useful information:

Holman Bible Dictionary

The Zondervan Pictorial Bible Dictionary

The New Bible Dictionary

Hastings' Dictionary of the Bible

Multivolume Bible dictionaries and encyclopedias furnish even more detailed information. Some of these works include the following:

The Interpreter's Dictionary of the Bible

The International Standard Bible Encyclopedia

Biblical Histories. Understanding original life situations of Bible books also involves fitting the book into various places in Bible history. Therefore, both histories of the Old Testament and the New Testament eras need to be consulted. Some helpful histories include:

Old Testament Histories

John Bright, *A History of Israel*

Ira Maurice Price, *The Dramatic Story of Old Testament History*

Martin Noth, *The History of Israel*

H. I. Hester, *The Heart of a Hebrew History: A Study of the Old Testament*

R. Paul House, *Old Testament Survey*

New Testament Histories

Joe Blair, *Introducing the New Testament*

F. F. Bruce, *New Testament History*

Floyd Filson, *New Testament History: The Story of the Emerging Church*

Bo Reicke, *The New Testament Era: The World of the Bible from 500 B.C. to A.D. 100*

H. I. Hester, *The Heart of the New Testament: A Study of the New Testament*

Abundant resources exist for gathering data for the background of a Bible book. These aids will help the interpreter know matters about the original life situation of a Bible book. The story can be reconstructed with the other relevant information. These aids help to know the *then* of the book so its *now* can be proclaimed.

Making a Detailed Analysis of the Book

While background material is gathered and organized, a detailed analysis of the Bible book needs to be projected. Work on an analysis needs to begin at least three or four months before the series of sermons begins. Analyzing a Bible book involves dividing the book into parts and giving attention to major themes or themes related to the major themes. An analysis is a detailed outline of the book and should be considered a study guide for the Bible book rather than sermon outlines from the book. The analysis serves as a means to understand the themes of the book with its various moves and structures. The analysis represents a valuable discipline necessary for preparing a series of sermons from a Bible book.

Reasons for an Analysis

Preparing sermons requires careful use of time. No one needs to spend time and energy on any homiletical exercise without knowing some of the valid reasons for the venture. Making a detailed analysis of a Bible book takes time and concentrated activity, but the process and the results pay enormous dividends.

Overview. Perhaps the foremost reason for preparing an analysis is getting to know the contents of a Bible book from beginning to end. The analysis gives the preacher a panorama of the book, revealing the literary plan of the work. Before examining and mastering microscopic matters, the general overview needs to be seen. Preparing an analysis helps one discover prominent themes, word patterns, and other literary matters. Constant readings of the book can help one see both the content and form of the book. With a comprehensive view of the book, one is better prepared to plot a series of sermons.

Guide for Exegesis. Either before preaching from a Bible book or while preaching from it, the preacher needs to engage in exegesis. An analysis furnishes a form for the exegetical work. Word meanings, relationships, contextual issues, and other exegetical matters must be placed within the overall flow of the Bible book. Most commentaries include an outline as the basis for exegetical studies. After making an analysis, the expository preacher will have a guide for organizing exegetical studies. This analysis could also be used as a teaching outline for the Bible book when such occasions arise. Teaching a book before preaching a series of sermons could help the preacher prepare in advance. Having an outline serves as both a homiletical and didactic resource.

Plotting the Series. Seeing the book from beginning to end with its themes and forms allows for advanced planning on the number of sermons in the series and on the theme of the messages. Completing a detailed analysis helps the preacher organize a continuous, consecutive exposition of the book. Seeing the flow of a book could prompt the preacher to select themes and texts from the book. At first glance, some might not recognize the value of a book analysis. But the more one does an analysis of a Bible book before planning the series, the more valuable the analysis will be viewed. Preparing a background paper and making an analysis should not be omitted. These disciplines require much time and much effort, but the results prove the worthiness of the pursuits.

Helpful Resources for an Analysis

Just as the background paper necessitated extensive use of resources, so does an analysis need some resources for its completion.

Original Languages. The most useful resource, of course, is the Bible book in its original language. No translation can reproduce with exactness the literary forms prevalent in the Greek or Hebrew.

Translations. Not all preachers can work with Greek or Hebrew, so the second most helpful resource for analysis is a translation of the book. Reading the book from several translations can help gain an analytical perspective on the book both in form and in content. Some helpful translations are:

> The King James Version
>
> The New King James Version
>
> The Revised Standard Version
>
> The New Revised Standard Version
>
> The New English Version
>
> The Today's English Version
>
> The New International Version
>
> New American Standard
>
> The Moffatt Translation of the Bible

Study Bibles. Some study Bibles such as the Master Study Bible, the Thompson Chain Reference Bible, the Harpers' Study Bible, the New International Version: Disciple's Study Bible, and other such works contain valuable background information and a suggested outline of each Bible book.

Outlines. In addition to the text from the Greek or Hebrew and translations, most commentaries contain outlines of the book. Seeing how other Bible scholars divide a book into parts can help others perform personal analysis of the Bible book. The analytical discipline must not be neglected by using another person's analysis. Making his own personal analysis can help a preacher get directly involved in the flow of the text and helps him produce his own analysis. Preparing a background paper and an analysis prepares a preacher to engage in an exegesis of the book.

Engaging in Extensive Exegesis of the Book

Both the background paper and the analysis should be completed before engaging in the exegesis of the book, for these materials influence the exegesis of every verse in the book. Completing an analysis can help the interpreter see the overall pattern of the book, and the analysis may be used in detailed exegesis. The discipline of exegesis refers to the historical, grammatical, and theological investigation of a Bible passage. Exegesis means to examine what the author meant by the words used and the form written in the time the passage was written. Anyone who preaches from a Bible passage stands in the present while interpreting ideas that came from the past. The student of the Bible needs to discover as much as possible about what each word and statement meant to the original writer and to the original readers. A comprehensive understanding of the text requires studying word meanings and usages, literary characteristics, grammatical relationships, stylistic matters, and other exegetical pursuits. Engaging in exegesis of a Bible book gives biblical substance or content that the preacher must interpret for the people.

The Appropriate Time for an Exegesis

Background study and analysis should begin at least three months before the series. The timing for engaging in exegesis may vary between two possibilities. First, the entire exegesis of a Bible book may be completed before the series of sermons begins. Such advance exegesis requires much work. Second, the exegesis may be attempted each week on the particular text selected. Most busy pastors choose this latter option. Both personal preference and personal time management will determine the appropriate time for exegesis.

Completing an exegesis of the entire Bible book before the sermon series begins can serve the purpose of teaching and preaching. The exegesis furnishes content or meaning for the messages in the series. Exegesis can be used as a resource for teaching the Bible book during a midweek Bible study. The analysis could be given to the participants. Several hours could be used to prepare an intensive exegesis, and the study could be shared in a didactic manner. Months later, the same book used in the midweek Bible study could become the source for a series of sermons. Having already prepared the exegesis and taught it, the discipline of exegesis for the sermon series would be completed. Additional study could then be given each week to embellish the completed exegesis.

A preacher might choose Romans for a Bible study on Wednesday evening. The analysis of Romans can be given to the participants. Over a period of three to six months, the preacher would teach Romans. During the Romans study, the pastor might tell the people that a series of sermons from Romans would be preached at a future time. Participants likely would not complain about redundancy because Romans should be treated in two different manners.

A complete exegesis before a series begins might be difficult unless the exegesis was used for teaching. Ideally, completing all the exegesis would provide a better perspective of the book as a whole and of how each part relates to the whole.

Another possibility is doing the exegesis in installments. A pastor could do about one fourth to one half of the exegesis on the book before beginning the sermon series and then complete the exegesis after beginning the series. For example, the preacher completes an exegesis of Romans 1–5. While preaching on those chapters, he completes the exegesis on Romans 6–16.

Another technique on the timing of the exegesis could be a weekly study of the text for the next Sunday. The preacher could analyze the Bible book and plot the possible texts. He could study the selected text exegetically. Suppose a preacher has plotted twenty-one texts from Romans for a series. On the week prior to the proposed text, study would be attempted. For example, if Romans 1:1–7 was the text for next Sunday, the pastor would complete the exegesis on that text. Then if the next text were Romans 1:8–17, the process would be duplicated until the series had been completed. Weekly exegesis would seem to free the preacher to be fresh on that text for the next Sunday. Because extensive exegesis on a text takes time, the discipline can often be neglected. Whatever the timing, all beforehand or partial, exegesis of a text involves a preeminent and necessary discipline in sermon preparation.

The Significant Usefulness of Exegesis

Engaging in both a scientific and devotional exegesis of a Bible passage greatly influences the homiletical outcome of a text. Responsible exegesis generally leads to authentic, biblical preaching. Unfortunately, many sermons have been proclaimed without allowing exegesis to influence the interpretation of the text. Exegesis and homiletics function as mutual friends. Exegesis helps get the authentic biblical message of the text, and the discipline of homiletics seeks to shape the message of the text into a sermon. Homiletics without exegesis often results in mere religious talk rather than the message of God's Word. Exegesis without homiletics may present a lot of exegetical information, but the end result might be deficient in communicating God's Word to people. Exegesis and homiletics belong together.

Engaging in exegesis of Bible passages greatly affects the content, theme, and structure of a sermon. Exegesis gets truth from a text. Word studies, grammatical relationships, different contexts, and other exegetical pursuits bring truths out of the text. The preacher who engages in responsible exegesis rarely lacks ideas for sermons or substance within a sermon.

Not only does exegesis provide substance and thoughts, exegesis also guides the theme and purpose of a sermon. The teaching of the text and its original purpose needs to coincide with the theme and purpose of the sermon. Casual readers may discover ideas in a text that the author did not wish to convey. Exegesis checks the meaning of the text with the meaning conveyed in a sermon. Sometimes the text of the sermon may have another truth; the truth of the sermon needs to be based on the truth of the text. Exegesis helps unite the text's biblical theme and purpose with the sermon's theme and purpose.

Exegesis also may influence the structure of the sermon. Often the shape of the text will affect the shape of the sermon. Doing an exegesis on a text always helps get the point of the sermon, but it also can help get points and subpoints from the text. These points and subpoints should be subservient to the point of the sermon, and getting structure from the text is an effective means of outlining a sermon. If exegesis affects the content, theme, and structure of a sermon, the discipline of exegesis needs to be respected and practiced.

Beneficial Resources for Exegesis

Resources for the background paper and analysis are also resources for exegesis. In exegesis, the preacher deals directly with the words, phrases, structure, and context of the Bible book. The preacher needs to consult additional resources more directly related to the text. The most important resource for exegesis is the text itself, primarily in the original languages and secondarily in translations. No other resource is as useful or important as the text itself. Helps in commentaries, dictionaries, atlases, and encyclopedias are secondary to the words of the Bible book.

The preacher will supplement study of the biblical text with other available resources. Lexicons, concordances, and theological dictionaries include helpful word studies. Lexicons contain articles on Hebrew and Greek words, giving special attention to the etymological makeup and varied usages of a word. William L. Holiday's English work, *A Concise Hebrew and Aramaic Lexicon of the Old Testament*, can help with Hebrew and Aramaic words. Joseph Henry Thayer's *A Greek-English Lexicon of the New Testament* can help with the Greek words. Concordances also contain the English words of the Bible with the places these words are used in the Bible. Robert Young's *Analytical Concordance of the Bible* is a helpful tool. Theological dictionaries provide Bible students with the scientific study of the Bible words. Two multivolumes of theological word studies are available. Gerhard Kittel and Gerhard Griedrich edited *Theological Dictionary of the Old Testament* and *Theological Dictionary of the New Testament*. These volumes represent an intensive study which would be more profitable for those knowledgeable in Hebrew and Greek. Colin Brown edited *The New International Dictionary of New Testament Theology*, a valuable theological study for those unfamiliar with the biblical languages.

Commentaries are helpful friends for exegesis. They have records of information and insights from other serious Bible students. In preparing for the discipline of exegesis on a Bible book, both critical and devotional commentaries need to be consulted. Sets of commentaries were listed on pages 47–49. Critical commentaries help with the preacher's cognitive information, while devotional commentaries help with the preacher's feelings about the text. A preacher should consider using three or four commentaries for the exegesis of a Bible book. He should select one extremely critical commentary, one less critical commentary, and two devotional commentaries. With primary consideration given to the text, with serious study given to the commentaries, and with the Holy Spirit's illumination, the meaning of texts within the Bible book should emerge.

Initiating Interpretations of Each Text

Exegesis and interpretation are related but distinct disciplines. William Thompson proposed that *exegesis* deals largely with questions about what the biblical writer meant and how that meaning was understood by those who first read it.[3] *Interpretation*, according to Thompson, deals primarily with the meaning of the biblical material to a contemporary audience.[4] Study of the text itself begins with exegesis, or what the text *meant* to the original readers. Study of the text continues with interpretation, or what the text *means* to contemporary readers.

Exegesis of a text does not go far enough: The student of a Bible book must also interpret the text. The past of the text must come alive and illumine the present with possibilities for personal and social transformation. Initiating interpretation on Bible passages means relating ancient times and events to today's events. Guidelines for exegesis abound, but in biblical studies the discipline of interpretation represents a newer emphasis; therefore, not many practical suggestions for interpretation prevail. Chapter 7 includes an in-depth investigation of interpretation. Along with the three previous disciplines—historical background, analysis, and exegesis—the expositor needs to institute the discipline of interpretation of every text written in the Bible book.

Valid Reasons for Interpretation

Interpretation is as necessary as historical background, analysis, and exegesis. Though interpretation occurs in the exegetical study of a text, a conscious effort needs to be made to interpret meanings in a Bible book in light of today's world. Interpretation helps move the preacher from text to sermon, from yesterday's message to today's meaning. The goal of preaching is not to disclose ancient history, geography, archaeology, or culture. The sermon is not just to inform people about Hebrew verbs, Greek forms, syntactical relationships, or literary stylistic designs. The discipline of interpretation builds on these exegetical matters, but interpreting means moving biblical information to relevant, sermonic thoughts.

---

3. William D. Thompson, *Preaching Biblically: Exegesis and Interpretation* (Nashville: Abingdon, 1981), 14.

4. Ibid., 15.

Closely akin to moving textual material to sermonic thoughts is the purpose of connecting biblical truth with people's needs. To accomplish this purpose the expositor must seek to know the biblical text and the needs of people and proceed to connect the two. F. Dean Lueking said: "Preaching the biblical word today cannot take on a peopleless monotone where such a story of people's stories is its authority. The Bible itself begs for, enables, provides, and commands that the truth of God be witnessed in word and deed by people for people in all their specific circumstances, gifts, weaknesses, hopes, failures, sin, and forgiveness."[5]

Interpretation helps the preacher be bifocal; it keeps his sights on the ancient past and on contemporary human needs. Interpretation exists as a discipline to keep the preacher's sight on applying the text to current issues and needs.

Suggested Resources for Interpretation

The disciplines of historical background, analysis, and exegesis require books for resources. While some books can be used to interpret a text, the primary resource for interpretation involves people. Lueking said, "Preaching barren of reference to people is preaching that is critically deficient."[6] He also said, "Preaching is for people, and the preacher must be with the people to reach and to relate to them effectively."[7] Thus, the preacher needs to study people just as much as the text. With study of the text and of people, a sermon can be connected with people. How does a preacher use people as a resource for interpreting a Bible text?

The Preacher. The first human resource for interpretation is the preacher. The preacher is a human being and experiences truths from the text. As expositors read texts from the Bible book, they need to ask what things in their own lives or in this world are like those of the people for whom the text was written. They might ask what changes they may make in their lives if they did what the passage proposes. More than likely, a person has not grasped the message of a text until a person has been grasped by it—until God's Word begins to accomplish a change. The preacher's practical

---

5. F. Dean Lueking, *Preaching: The Art of Connecting God and People* (Waco, Tex.: Word Books, 1985), 36.

6. Ibid., 21.

7. Ibid., 23.

application working cooperatively with the Holy Spirit's illumination becomes an incomparable resource for knowing the meaning of a text. So, the interpreter begins by asking, "What does this text mean to me?" This personal application can be prefaced by exegesis, or it can be followed by exegesis.

Encounters with People. Learning about people affords an excellent resource for biblical interpretation. But how do preachers study people? Listening to people and observing their behavior provides valuable insights. Movies, plays, and works on psychology and sociology also can help with human understanding, but nothing helps more than personal interaction with others. Therefore, pastoral visitation and informal personal communication are as essential for sermon preparation as hours locked in a study.

Practical Reflection. Thinking practically about how to use people as a resource for interpretation can add insight into this phase of the interpretation process. Suppose you were preaching a series of sermons from the Letter of James. The series begins with a message entitled "Facing Life's Trials" based on James 1:2–12. After personal interactions with the text, you listen and observe how the text and theme relate to the lives of people you encounter. You might solicit responses from people by asking, "What does James 1:2–12 mean to you?" "What are some prominent trials in your life?" "How have you found help when you faced trials?" Throughout the series of sermons, the interpretation process should continue with each text.

Preaching from a Bible book involves preparing a background paper and making an analysis of the book several months before the series begins. It also involves either advanced preparation of exegesis or weekly exegesis. Initiating interpretation should happen each week by personal encounter with the text and by hearing from others about the text.

Surveying the Variety of Literary Possibilities

A preliminary discipline necessary for preaching from Bible books also involves surveying the various literary possibilities. Failing to look at the many choices present in Scripture could limit the preacher's choice of Bible books. Both the Old and New Testaments need to be included. Within each Testament are various kinds of books that need to be considered. Present consideration will be given to a general survey of Bible books, and later in chapters 8, 9, and 10 specific consideration will be given to the various kinds of Bible books.

Preaching from Old Testament Books

Not one of the Old Testament's thirty-nine books should be neglected. Preachers and parishioners alike testify that the Old Testament books do not receive enough emphasis in sermon series. Though not in theory but in practice, some preachers have been followers of Marcion, the second-century heretic who taught that the church should jettison the Jewish Scriptures. In preparing to preach from Bible books, each of the Old Testament books deserves consideration. The next chapter includes a suggestion about how to preach annually from one Old Testament book and from one New Testament book. Using this method of selecting books reflects an important value system for Old Testament books.

Examining the books of the Old Testament reveals many prominent emphases. The Old Testament books include subjects such as beginnings, faithfulness, God in history, interpersonal relationships, covenant love, judgment, and redemption. Looking at the themes of Old Testament books can help a preacher choose a series appropriate to his congregation. If a congregation needs help in self-discipline and interpersonal relationships, the preacher might choose the Book of Proverbs. Varying themes of Old Testament books present a challenge to choose what is appropriate for the moment for a particular congregation.

The Old Testament has the general literary types: theological narration, legal codes, Hebrew poetry, wisdom literature, and prophetic literature. A particular genre will affect the sermons for a series. The preacher should strive for balance among the genres of Old Testament books. A balanced literary approach could be projected for five years as follows:

Year	Book	Genre
One	Genesis	A Pentateuchal Book with Narrative and Legal Codes
Two	Samuel	Theological, Historical Narration
Three	Psalms	Hebrew Poetry
Four	Job	Wisdom Literature
Five	Isaiah	Prophetic Literature

Surveying the Old Testament books and selecting the ones to include in a series could be influenced by a congregation's need, a lectionary plan, or a preacher's personal preferences.

In surveying Old Testament books for a possible series of sermons, consideration might be given to the length of the book. Some books are long; many are short. A preacher will want to think about whether the best plan would be to preach every chapter or verse in the book or to select various chapters or verses from the book for a series. For example, nothing prohibits a person from preaching consecutively through such books as Psalms, Jeremiah, Isaiah, and other lengthy books, but the series would last years. The preacher should consider his personal interest in the book and the parishioners' continuous weekly interest in the same book. A good procedure is to survey the length of books to decide whether to preach consecutively or selectively.

Preaching from New Testament Books

Most expository preachers base their series of sermons on New Testament books because these contain God's supreme revelation in Jesus Christ. Examining New Testament books reveals many prominent themes. The gospels contain the words and works of Jesus Christ, and His person and ministry constitute the main topic in the New Testament. The Book of Acts has the story of the church from Jerusalem to Rome, and the Epistles contain affirmations about the Christian faith, pastoral corrections of problems, and other matters. The New Testament books teach about Jesus Christ, the Holy Spirit, the church, revelation by faith, the Lord's return, and other doctrines. Choosing which particular New Testament book to use for a series of sermons depends on matching the theme or themes in the book with the needs of a congregation.

The New Testament has literary genres such as gospel, historical narration, epistle, and apocalypse. The way a book is written or its genre affects the sermons in the series. The effective expository preacher surveys the various literary types in the New Testament and selects various genres. A balanced literary approach could be projected for five years as follows:

Year	Book	Genre
One	Matthew	Gospel
Two	Acts	Historical Narration
Three	Galatians	Epistle
Four	James	Epistle
Five	Revelation	Apocalypse

Surveying New Testament books and selecting the ones for the series can depend greatly on the lectionary plan of the Christian year, the congregation's need, or a preacher's personal preference. With the various kinds of books in both the Old and New Testament in mind, the preacher can proceed to the discipline of plotting a series of sermons from a specific Bible book.

Plotting a Series of Sermons from the Book

The previous five disciplines discussed help prepare the preacher to develop a sixth discipline: plotting a Bible book for a series of sermons. Homiletical plotting is similar to real estate planning and development. The developer who buys five hundred acres of land for a housing development learns about the terrain, soil composition, trees, lakes, and rivers or streams on the land. She plots the entire five hundred acres by lots for houses, lakes, streets, and parks. The expository preacher must plot a Bible book. He projects texts and subjects from the book. Homiletical plotting usually happens during background study, analysis, and exegesis. Plotting helps the preacher see where he is going before starting the series.

Unique Purposes of Plotting

None of the disciplines necessary for preaching from a Bible book exist without reasons. The discipline of plotting is no exception. One primary purpose of plotting is to determine the number of sermons in the series. Rather than selecting a book and beginning to preach from it without advanced planning, the preacher should study the book, look at the possible texts, and plot a general direction for the series. Plotting in advance gives an overall plan for the series. This plan need not be rigid. Texts and topics can be added or deleted during the processes of preparation or proclamation.

Another purpose of plotting is to determine the parameters of texts within the series. Determining the parameters marks where a text can begin and end and yet offer a complete, meaningful thought. One should ask if the texts selected comprise a unit with its own integrity and therefore provide focus and restraint for the sermon. Fuzziness at the edges of a biblical text results in fuzziness at the edges of a sermon.[8] The text needs to be plotted in its analytical context, and the chances of violating context and the unit are reduced if the text has a definite beginning and ending. Texts do not need to be constructed with broken sentences and dangling thoughts.[9] The preacher must consider the borders of texts within the Bible book. Plotting parameters of texts within the book will give individual, complete units for sermon ideas.

Helpful Resources for Plotting

The most important resource for plotting is the text. Reading through the book in several translations can yield ideas for texts and topics. Reading one adopted translation many times can yield further insights into various topics and texts.

Another primary resource for plotting involves the analysis performed on the book. The analysis gives the flow of the book, and the preacher can use the analysis to plot parameters of texts and to determine subjects for sermons.

Yet another plotting resource is to study how other preachers treated a Bible book for a series of sermons. Seeing how others determined parameters of texts and selected subjects can help. In addition, looking at how many texts and topics other preachers treated in a series can help. Consulting these secondary resources should not lead to plagiarism but should serve only as an example of what other preachers have done.

Preparing Individual Sermons from the Book

The previous six disciplines lead to the last: preparing the individual sermons from a Bible book. Preparing individual sermons certainly involves weekly preparation; it also can involve preparing sermons several weeks in advance. Few preachers prepare large numbers of completed sermons in advance. Many project their

---

8. Fred Craddock, *Preaching* (Nashville: Abingdon Press, 1985), 110.
9. Ibid.

texts and topics but complete their sermons week by week. Chapters 12, 13, and 14 of this book treat individual sermon preparation. At this point, the expository preacher needs to have an overview of advanced and weekly preparation of sermons.

Advanced Planning of Sermons

Sermon ideas proceed from sustained study and serendipitous spontaneity. Studying the Bible and listening to people yield abundant ideas for sermons. Perhaps no greater means for advanced planning of sermons exists than preaching a series of messages from a Bible book. A background study, an analysis, an exegesis, and an interpretation can lead to abundant sermon thoughts. In most cases, the disciplined study of a Bible book produces more sermon ideas than can be used in a series. Some ideas will have to be eliminated because the series could get too lengthy. While studying a Bible book for a series of sermons, other sermons from other texts will come to mind. So, the disciplined study of a Bible book serves as a catalyst for advanced planning.

Weekly Preparation of Sermons

Advanced planning saves time and eliminates much of the tension expended in selecting a text and topic. Plotting topics and texts saves the preacher from searching for a text and a sermon idea each week. Instead he can concentrate time and energy on the sermon.

The Academic Routine. Weekly preparation of sermons from a Bible book requires a routine. No rigid schedule should be imposed on a preacher, but some general directions may be suggested for weekly sermon preparation. First, the preacher must work with the text. The energy in this description could be spent in exegetical pursuits with careful consideration given to the background of the book. Diligent work requires academic engagement with the text and commentaries.

The Pastoral Routine. While the exegesis takes place, the preacher would by various means take people to the text and interpret the meaning of the passage.

The Homiletical Routine. After determining what the text meant and what the text means, the theme would be shaped, content added, illustrations appropriated, and other homiletical necessities added. By Friday the weekly routine for sermon preparation could be concluded by writing the sermon for oral delivery.

Many preachers want to preach from a Bible book. They have chosen an ambitious goal with rewarding results. Before attempting the task, a preacher might want to consider the cost of the disciplines necessary for preaching from a Bible book. He should ask himself these questions:

1. Am I willing to study the technical matter of historical background? Would I be willing to prepare a thorough, academic paper relating to background matters?

2. Am I willing to read the book many, many times, to look carefully to examine its contents, and to make an analysis of it?

3. Will I really pay the price of engaging in thorough exegesis? Am I willing to struggle with detailed exegetical matters?

4. Do I want an academic investigation of the Bible book? Am I willing to look within myself and in the lives of others to see how the text connects with the lives of people?

5. Am I interested only in the Bible books that stimulate me? Am I willing to look into all the books of the Bible and to use more variety in the choice of books?

6. Do I want to know where I am going with a series of sermons? Am I willing to pursue with creativity a plot for a sermon series?

7. Am I willing to plan ahead for the sermons in the series? In individual sermon preparation, am I amenable to disciplined weekly study of individual texts in order to shape them into sermons?

CHAPTER 3

Homiletical Guidelines for Preaching from a Bible Book

Homiletical theories exist to help preachers understand the preaching task and to help make sermons applicable to listeners. The formal scientific term used to describe sermon construction and pulpit performance is *homiletics*. But the term *homiletics* does not exist for a theoretical purpose. It exists to help preachers prepare and deliver effective sermons.

Ideas of preaching may be read in books and heard in academic classrooms, but homiletical theories prove themselves true in the pulpit. Some principles of preaching sound logical as theories, but they have little or no usefulness. Some homiletical theories have excellent theoretical design, but they do not work in delivering a sermon. Theory and practice belong together. Practical, homiletical guidelines transform theory into technique.

The United States government once contracted Howard Hughes to design and build an amphibious airplane to carry seven hundred passengers. The eight-engine wooden plane had a wing span of 340 feet and a fuselage length of 220 feet. In 1947, Howard Hughes himself taxied off and the giant airplane rose seventy feet over the Long Beach, California, harbor and flew one mile before settling down again. The plane would not fly! Hughes had considered and followed sound principles, but his theory did not work out in practice. Sermons can also crash on the beach for the same reason.

Why have a theory or definition of expository preaching if it will not work? Every definition and concept of expository preaching must stand the pragmatic test. Now is the time to test the serviceability of the eclectic emphasis of expository preaching. In this definition or theory, expository preaching is the art of preaching a series of sermons from a Bible book. This definition seems to have some workable actions that proceed from the proposed principle. One such action is that the preacher does not have to classify sermons as topical, textual, or expository. Those classifications of individual sermons can be discarded. With the theory that expository preaching is a series of sermons from a Bible book, a preacher can realize that expository refers to a number of sermons in a series, not to a specific kind of individual sermon. This practical approach allows for sermons based on texts of various lengths.

Furthermore, this approach to expository preaching gets the main point from the text, rather than getting all of the points from the text. Some Scripture passages do not lend themselves to getting main divisions from the text, but all texts have the possibility of getting a biblical truth that can be related to people's needs. Using the term *expository* to mean that every sermon should expose biblical truth makes the expression more serviceable.

In addition, this definition allows both consecutive and selective order of texts in preaching from a Bible book. That preposition *from* allows both consecutive and selective exposition. Theories that require the preacher to expound every word of the Bible book do not pass the test of practicality.

The traditional, morphological definition of expository preaching has been weighed in the balances and found wanting. Theory has been placed on one side, and practicality has been placed on the other side. These theories about length of text, source for main divisions, and other principles weigh down heavily on the side of theory, but they are too light on the side of practice. Placing the principle of expository preaching as a series of sermons from a Bible book on the balances of homiletical theory and pastoral reality affords a balance of theory and practice. The best commendation of the eclective approach to expository preaching is this: It works!

So far we have examined *what* expository preaching is and *why* it is practical. Now let us move to the *how*. Some homiletical guidelines can make the theory serviceable. Our theory of expository preaching as a series of sermons from a Bible book raises some questions:

- How do I select a Bible book for a series?
- How many sermons should I include in a series?
- Can I interrupt the series?
- Should I preach the same series on Sunday morning or evening or both?
- Should I tie each sermon to the previous sermons in the series?
- Must I preach consecutively through every Bible book? Or can I be selective about texts?

These and many other questions arise when one chooses to preach a series of sermons from a Bible book.

Selecting the Bible Book

Suppose an expositor decides to adopt the theory of expository preaching as a series of sermons from a Bible book. Is the theory practical? How does the preacher get started? What is the first thing to do? Select the Bible book for the series. That seems simple. But choosing can be hard with sixty-six flavors to choose from. With so many excellent choices of Bible books available, the preacher faces a dilemma. Here are some guidelines to remember in making your selection.

Criteria for Choice

The process of selecting books needs to be prefaced and pursued by prayer and contemplation. Some preachers move from pastorate to pastorate, preaching from their two or three favorite books, or expounding their pet themes while neglecting everything else. The choice among Bible books must be made with earnest prayer and serious thinking. These disciplines need to be exercised throughout all the criteria suggested for choosing books for series of sermons.

Congregational Needs. All Bible books were divinely inspired to meet various personal and social human needs. The needs of people have remained the same since the beginning of the human race. Studying the prominent needs in a particular congregation and matching a Bible book which addresses those needs serves as an excellent basis for selecting a book for a series of sermons. Using such a criterion for choice requires the preacher to be bifocal.[1] The preacher needs to perform an exegesis of people to know their needs, and should study the Scripture systematically to find the particular book that relates to the congregation's needs. Suppose a congregation had problems with divisions, carnality, conflicts, or spiritual gifts. Seeing one or more of these needs would motivate the preacher to select 1 Corinthians. Or, think about a church needing help with religious heritage. They seek answers to important questions: How did the world begin? Who am I? Do I have an obligation to other people? The preacher could turn them to Genesis for answers to these and other serious questions.

Suffering prevails in many fellowships. Disease, accidents, and death evoke questions: Why does God allow suffering? Why do bad things happen to good people? or Why doesn't God reward the righteous? Observing human hurts and hearing these questions could turn the expositor to select Job or 1 Peter. Observing some congregations causes a preacher to see the need to apply faith to contemporary life situations. Seeing this need could prompt the preacher to choose Micah, Proverbs, or James. These books can help people apply faith to home, business, and various social issues. Illustrating how life situations could be matched with truth in Bible books could be endless. Whatever people need, whether personal or social, the Bible has a book suited especially for specific needs.

---

1. cf. James T. Cleland, *Preaching to Be Understood* (Nashville: Abingdon Press, 1965), 33–58.

Therefore, one of the best criteria for choosing a Bible book comes at the point of congregational need.

Lectionaries. Lectionaries contain four lections or choices of Scripture readings for each Sunday of the year and for special worship days such as Ash Wednesday, Christmas, and Good Friday. These readings include an Old Testament reading, a psalm, a reading from a Gospel, and a selection from an Epistle. These readings are arranged on a three-year cycle for the purpose of reading a large part of the Bible in worship and affirming the prominent themes of the Christian faith. The precedent for such a lectionary comes from the ancient Jewish synagogue, which divided the Hebrew Scripture into readings to be completed in three years. The Gospel readings influence the choice of other texts because of the emphasis of the Christian year from Advent to Pentecost. This time bears the title "the Lord's half" of the Christian year because it begins with preparation for the birth of Jesus and concludes with the coming of the Holy Spirit. Following Pentecost until Advent, extended readings are offered over large bodies of materials such as 1 Samuel or Isaiah. This time span is usually called "the church's half" of the Christian year.[2]

The three-year cycles are designated by the letters *A*, *B*, and *C*. One may determine which series (A, B, or C) to use by beginning the B series with Advent in a year whose last two digits are divided by three.[3] For example, 1996 calls for the B series to begin with the first Sunday of Advent. The C series would follow in 1997, and the sequence would begin with A in 1998. During the B series, the Gospel readings come from Mark. The C series contain readings from Luke, and the A series contain readings from Matthew. Readings from the Gospel of John are interspersed within the three-year cycle. The lectionary could be helpful for choosing which Gospel to choose for a series of sermons.

Other Bible books could be selected from the suggested lectionary readings of Scriptures. In addition to the Gospels, the lectionary has readings from various Old Testament passages, selected psalms, and readings from New Testament Epistles. An example of Bible readings may be observed in *Preaching the New Common*

---

2. Fred B. Craddock, *Preaching* (Nashville: Abingdon Press, 1985), 104.

3. James W. Cox, *A Guide to Biblical Preaching* (Nashville: Abingdon Press, 1976), 129.

Lectionary Year B: Advent, Christmas, Epiphany and *Preaching the New Common Lectionary Year B: Lent, Holy Week, Easter,* both edited by Fred B. Craddock:

14 readings from Mark

17 readings from John

15 readings from Isaiah

40 readings from Psalms

10 readings from 1 Corinthians

These readings come from a year of Scripture selections in the B cycle. A book or books could be selected for a series from the readings suggested. For example, in the readings mentioned above, the preacher could use the lectionary to select Isaiah, Psalms, Mark, John, and 1 Corinthians for one or two series of sermons during the year. The lectionary serves as an excellent means for choosing a book.

Preaching Through the Bible. Another criterion for choosing a Bible book involves a systematic attempt to preach through the Bible or through the Old or New Testament. Soon after W. A. Criswell became pastor of the First Baptist Church in Dallas, Texas, he began to preach through the Bible on March 3, 1946. He started with Genesis and completed the project on October 6, 1963. Criswell preached from every Bible book in a seventeen-year period. He preached extensively from some books and only slightly from other books. He selected Bible books on the basis of their order in the English translations.[4]

Harold J. Ockenga, former pastor of Park Street Church in Boston, Massachusetts, preached consecutively through the New Testament. He testified: "By the time I began my ministry in Park Street in 1936, I was primarily an expository preacher. Hence, I began at Matthew 1:1 and in twenty-one years have preached through the entire New Testament at my Sunday morning and Friday evening meetings."[5] Choosing Bible books in the order they appear in English translations is a legitimate means of selection, but it requires a long pastorate.

---

4. Harold T. Bryson, unpublished master's thesis, "The Expository Preaching of W. A. Criswell in His Sermons on the Revelation." New Orleans Baptist Theological Seminary, 1967, 20.

5. Clarence S. Roddy, *We Prepare and Preach* (Chicago: Moody Press, 1959), 115.

Several other criteria exist for selecting Bible books. People in the congregation may suggest their preference for a book. Also, some denominational emphases may provide bases for choosing a particular Bible book. Whatever the criteria, one needs to remember that behind any Bible book selection should be the Holy Spirit's leadership. The Spirit works within the logical methods mentioned, but sometimes the Spirit can lead to a selection which cannot be explained. Therefore, examine all the criterion for choices of a book and allow the Holy Spirit to help guide to the right book at the right time for a particular group of people.

Some Suggestions about Selection

The practical experiences with expository preaching do not end with the choice of a book or books. Other matters in the selective process need to be examined.

Preaching from Two Books Yearly—one from the Old Testament, the other from the New. Why select only two? Well, the disciplines necessary require a lot of time and energy, and two books appear to be all that a preacher could properly prepare. A further counsel about selecting two books is to preach from one Old Testament and one New Testament book. This suggestion can be adjusted at times for more than two books and more than one Old or New Testament selection. James W. Cox admonished, "Vary your preaching between Old and New Testament books."[6]

Preaching from One Bible Book at a Time. A book could be selected for Sunday mornings, Sunday evenings, or weeknight services such as Wednesday evenings. Only an exceptional preacher can have two or three Bible books going in a series of sermons and be able to prepare sufficiently and relate effectively to people. Preaching from one book at a time allows other worship services to be open to different kinds of sermon topics and techniques. Also, preaching from several Bible books at the same time can overload a congregation.

- Quite naturally, other questions arise about timing of the series: Should the series come on Sunday morning, Sunday evening, or at another time?

- Could the series just be morning, just evening, or could there be a series going morning and evening?

6. Cox, 129.

Answering these questions about timing seems to depend primarily on a preacher's personal preferences and a congregation's receptivity. One could choose to preach a series either in the morning or in the evening, or you could preach from a Bible book both in the morning and evening services. No rigid rules can govern the timing of the sermons in the series. Most expositors preach a series from a Bible book either in the morning or in the evening service.

Preaching from a Bible book requires guidelines for selection. Examine the criteria for choosing books from which to preach. Think about the suggestions given for number of books chosen and the timing for the series.

The Number of Sermons

Learning any art requires mastering practical techniques. If you want to be a golfer, you do more than study the rules of the game: you must master the skills of playing the game. Many of the procedures necessary for preaching from a Bible book seem simple, but proficiency results from following homiletical guidelines.

How many sermons should compose a series? This question troubles both the neophyte and the veteran. No hard rules are possible, but there are at least some issues that the preacher should consider.

The Variety of Series Lengths

No one can dogmatically declare a precise length for a sermon series. Over the years, Christian preachers have demonstrated diversity with the number of sermons from a Bible book. Some have preached years from one book; others have preached for a few weeks or a few months from the same book. To learn about guidelines for the number of sermons in a series, observations could be made into how other preachers handle the matter of series length. Effectiveness may be detected in extremely long series and in surprisingly short series.

Some preachers have chosen to preach many messages from a Bible book, making the series prolonged. Bernard of Clairvaux (1091–1153), a Frenchman, began a series of sermons from the Song of Solomon in 1135, and the series was cut short because of Clairvaux's death in 1153. For eighteen years and with few interruptions he preached from that book. He preached eighty-six sermons just on the first two chapters of the Song of Solomon.[7]

Donald Grey Barnhouse, former pastor of Tenth Street Presbyterian Church in Philadelphia, Pennsylvania, preached from the Book of Romans for three and a half years. He preached Romans exclusively in the morning services without a break for any other topic for over three years. Clarence S. Roddy reported excellent congregational response to the long series from Romans.[8]

D. Martin Lloyd-Jones, former pastor of Westminster Chapel in London, England, demonstrated a fondness for preaching many messages from one Bible book or a portion of a Bible book. He preached 60 sermons from the Sermon on the Mount in Matthew. On Friday evenings from October of 1955 until March of 1968, he preached from Romans 3:20–8:39 for a total of 161 sermons. Lloyd-Jones also preached 230 messages from Ephesians in the Sunday morning worship services.[9]

George D. Boardman, former pastor of First Baptist Church in Philadelphia, Pennsylvania, preached through the New Testament on successive Wednesday evenings. His series of 640 messages lasted more than ten years. Later, he began a similar kind of successive series from the Old Testament.[10]

W. A. Criswell began a series of sermons from Revelation in the First Baptist Church of Dallas, Texas, on January 6, 1961, and concluded on October 6, 1963, with a total of eighty-two sermons.[11] Criswell has demonstrated propensity for preaching lengthy series from other Bible books. He has preached 31 messages from Daniel, 21 from Galatians, and 128 messages from Acts.

Most preachers preach shorter series than these. Often the length of the Bible book does not determine the amount of sermons. Richard Halverson and Walter Luthi preached from the Book of Romans with twenty-four messages.[12] Warren Wiersbe

---

7. Edwin Charles Dargan, *A History of Preaching*, vol. 1, *From the Apostolic Fathers to the Great Reformers A.D. 70–1572* (New York: George H. Doran, 1905), 212.

8. Roddy, 33.

9. D. Martin Lloyd-Jones, *Romans: An Exposition of Romans 3:2–4:25 Atonement and Justification* (Grand Rapids: Zondervan, 1970), xi–xii.

10. M. Reu, *Homiletics* (Minneapolis: Augsburg, 1924), 319.

11. Bryson, 21–24.

12. cf. Richard C. Halverson, *The Gospel for the Whole of Life: A Concise Discussion of Romans—Its Application to Life Here and Now* (Grand Rapids: Zondervan, 1964) and Walter Luthi, *The Letter to the Romans: An Exposition*, trans. Kurt Schoenenberger (London: Oliver and Boyd, 1961).

used thirteen messages to preach from Romans,[13] and Harper Shannon used only seven messages to give the main theme of Romans.[14] John Huffman used seventeen sermons from Romans chapters 1–8.[15] So viewing the variety causes one to be amazed over the flexibility with regard to the number of messages in a series.

No one has to preach for years from a Bible book. John R. W. Stott, former pastor of All Soul's Church in London, England, preached nineteen sermons from Galatians, fourteen messages from the Sermon on the Mount found in Matthew 5–7, and thirteen sermons from Ephesians.[16] Who is right—D. Martin Lloyd-Jones with his 230 sermons from Ephesians or John R. W. Stott with his thirteen sermons from the same book? The answer is obvious. Neither a lengthy series nor a short number of sermons in a series serves as an authoritative model. Looking at the variety of series lengths has been used to show how variety abounds with amount of sermons. Some preachers excel in getting numerous sermons from a Bible book, and their congregations enjoy the long series. Other preachers choose shorter series, and their congregations prefer this method. This variety amazes us, and the flexibility encourages us. Instead of imitating the length of others' series, we should try to determine what factors weighed in designing the number of sermons in the series.

Factors Influencing Series Length

Three important factors weigh in determining the length of sermon series: the book's length, the preacher's personality, and the congregation's characteristics.

The Book's Length. Longer books—Genesis, Psalms, Isaiah, Jeremiah, Acts, and Revelation—seem to require longer series. Just to preach one sermon from each chapter of Genesis would require

---

13. Warren W. Wiersbe, *Be Right: An Expository Study of Romans* (Wheaton, Ill.: Victor Books, 1977).

14. Harper Shannon, *Riches in Romans* (Nashville: Broadman Press, 1969).

15. John Huffman, Jr., *Who's in Charge Here? Foundations of Faith from Romans 1–8* (Chappaqua, N.Y.: Christian Herald Books).

16. cf. John R. W. Stott, *The Message of Galatians* (Downers Grove, Ill.: InterVarsity Press, 1968); *The Message of the Sermon on the Mount* (Downers Grove, Ill.: InterVarsity Press, 1978); *The Message of Ephesians* (Downers Grove, Ill.: InterVarsity Press, 1979).

almost a year of Sunday mornings or evenings. To preach from one psalm each Sunday service would mean almost three years in the series. Twenty-two Bible books have twenty-four or more chapters, and just one sermon per chapter for one Sunday service demands a six-month series.

But lengthy Bible books just *appear* to necessitate protracted series. A lengthy Bible book can have either a long series of sermons or a short series. Charles Haddon Spurgeon covered all 150 Psalms while he preached at Metropolitan Tabernacle in London.[17] Leonard Griffith preached twenty-one selected psalms in one series and twenty psalms in a later series at City Temple Church in London.[18] Lloyd Ogilvie selected nineteen psalms for a series.[19] When James Montgomery Boice preached Genesis at Tenth Presbyterian Church in Philadelphia, Pennsylvania, he used 180 sermons.[20] In their separate churches Herschel Hobbs used ten texts for Genesis, and Jack Finnegan used twelve sermons in a series from Genesis.[21]

By the same obvious measurement used for long Bible books, it would appear that shorter Bible books such as Ruth, Jonah, Habakkuk, Malachi, Galatians, Philippians, James, and Jude would allow for a shorter series. What was illustrated in long and also short series from lengthy Bible books can also be demonstrated from shorter books. Cyril J. Barber preached nine sermons from Ruth while Warren Wiersbe chose twelve sermons.[22] William Elliot used sixteen sermons for a series on Philippians, and James Montgomery Boice chose forty-five sermons.[23] R. T. Kendall

17. Charles Haddon Spurgeon, *The Treasury of David*, 2 vols. (Grand Rapids: Kregel Publications, 1976).

18. Leonard Griffith, *God in Man's Experience: The Activity of God in the Psalms* (Waco, Tex.: Word Books, 1968) and *Reactions to God: Man's Response to God's Activity in the Psalms* (London: Hodder and Stoughton, 1979).

19. Lloyd John Ogilvie, *Falling into Greatness* (Nashville: Thomas Nelson, 1984).

20. James Montgomery Boice, *Genesis: An Expositional Commentary*, 3 vols. (Grand Rapids: Zondervan, 1982, 1985, 1987).

21. Herschel H. Hobbs, *The Origin of All Things: Studies in Genesis* (Waco, Tex.: Word Books, 1975); Jack Finnegan, *In the Beginning: A Journey Through Genesis* (New York: Harper and Brothers, 1962).

22. Cyril J. Barber, *Ruth: A Story of God's Grace* (Neptune, N.J.: Loizeaux Brothers, 1983); Warren W. Wiersbe, *Put Your Life Together: Stories in the Book of Ruth* (Wheaton, Ill.: Victor Books, 1985).

23. William M. Elliot, Jr., *Power to Master Life: The Message of Philippians for Today* (Nashville: Abingdon Press, 1964); James Montgomery Boice, *Philippians: An Expositional Commentary* (Grand Rapids: Zondervan, 1971).

preached twenty-two sermons from Jonah, and J. Hardee Kennedy used eight messages.[24]

The size of the Bible book influences but does not dictate series length. To preach *from* a book is different than preaching *through* a book. The expositor who preaches *from* a book does not choose every text in the book for a series. The expositor who preaches *through* a book chooses every verse. Preaching *through* a book requires a longer series than preaching *from* the book. To *cover* a book is to preach extensively from it. *Coverage* means to select texts and topics. Whatever the process—from, through, cover, coverage—either method has been an effective factor in deciding the series length.

The Preacher's Personality. Possessing the proclivity to preach for years from one Bible book does not make one a good or bad preacher, just different. Evidently, D. Martin Lloyd-Jones, James Montgomery Boice, W. A. Criswell, and a few others possess the ability to get many messages from a Bible book and to stay with the book for years. They seem comfortable with this approach. Because of their unique temperaments, other preachers choose to preach short series from Bible books, ranging from six to eighteen messages. They feel more comfortable with this system. A good maxim is to choose the number of sermons in a series on the basis of the expositor's personality, what the expositor feels comfortable doing, and what the expositor prefers rather than trying to imitate anyone else or trying to follow some homiletical rule.

The Congregation's Characteristics. Wise preachers know that collective groups take on temperaments or personalities, and a church is no exception. Some kind of mysterious makeup causes a congregation to prefer longer or shorter series. Some audiences become weary with month after month of sermons from the same Bible book. Other congregations listen to sermons for years on the same book. Expositors need to learn their congregation's characteristics and try to match the techniques of length with the congregation's temperament.

With a view of the variety of series lengths in mind and a knowledge of the influential factors for determining quantity, the discus-

---

24. R. T. Kendall, *Jonah: An Exposition* (Grand Rapids: Zondervan, 1978); James Hardee Kennedy, *Studies in the Book of Jonah* (Nashville: Broadman Press, 1956).

sion can become practical. Most preachers and congregations are comfortable with a series length of from six to twenty-four sermons. Exceptions will always exist with fewer than six or more than twenty-four in the series. Twenty-four sermons from one book requires almost six months of sermons for one series. More than twenty-four would have to be evaluated according to preacher and congregation. Whatever the size of a Bible book, a preacher can choose six to twenty-four sermons, depending on the technique of *through* or *from* or *cover* or *coverage*. A good general rule is this: Effective sermon series last from six weeks to six months.

The Individuality of Each Sermon

Homiletical guidelines exist to facilitate effective preaching. Expository preachers need directions for selecting a Bible book and determining the number of sermons in the series. In addition, they must maintain the individuality of each sermon in the series. The sermons in the collection should not run together, nor should they be bound inseparably. Each sermon needs its own individuality with independent texts, separate subjects, and particular relevance. Sermons in a series are interrelated, yet they must be prepared and proclaimed individually.

Impediments to Individuality

Some nonessential practices that slip into series preaching interfere with sermon individuality. These impediments need to be identified and eliminated for the sake of a sermon's singularity. One glaring impediment to sermon individuality happens with excessive announcements about the series. Printing the titles of the sermons in the series or announcing the series verbally on some occasions is needed. Hindrances occur when the preacher notifies the audience constantly of the series. People may not grow weary of a series from Romans, but they may get annoyed with the preacher's announcing for fifty Sundays, "I am in a series in the Book of Romans." A general guideline may be to announce the series at the beginning and only refer to the series occasionally. Such a technique should enhance the individuality of each sermon.

Another conspicuous impediment to a sermon's individuality comes with excessive review of previous sermons. The audience does not need to be brought up to date on previous sermons in the series. Each sermon should be designed for that particular day.

Picture the following scenario. The preacher says, "For the next nineteen Sundays, I am going to be preaching from the Letter of James." Nothing appears to be wrong with that predictive announcement. The problem comes with the following Sundays as the preacher seems compelled to review previous messages. He says, "Five Sundays ago, I started a series of sermons on James. On the first Sunday, I spoke about the lordship of Christ based on James 1:1. The second Sunday, I used James 1:2–12 to talk about facing life's trials. Do you remember how I told you in that sermon to expect trials, master trials, and profit from trials?" The scenario continues through three more sermon reviews, giving previous topics, tests, outlines, or even occasional illustrations before getting to the sixth sermon, which is the sermon intended for that day. Reviewing previous sermons is permissible only on rare occasions, but reiterations about previous messages is ridiculous and infringes on the territory of the sermon intended for that day.

The Interruption of Other Sermons

Can you interrupt a series for another message? Do you have to continue with the series? Sermons in series can be interrupted. No homiletical guidelines should force a preacher to deliver messages without any thought of interruption. The expositor needs to be flexible.

Why should a preacher interrupt a sermon series? At certain times of the year a preacher may break off the messages from the Bible book to preach seasonal sermons for several Sundays, then pick up the series again. At other times a preacher must break into a sermon series from the Bible book in order to deal with a crisis in the congregation. At other times a preacher may feel the need to stop the series for a while and proceed with other sermons, only to resume the series later.

The preacher begins by planning to preach the series without interruption. Yet no preacher should follow a plan rigidly. Valid reasons require preachers to break their sermon series. Sensitivity to the need for interruptions in a series gives preachers the unique opportunity to preach a needed sermon or sermons. Without this, congregations sometimes resist the series because they feel that other sermons are more timely than those from the Bible book. The expositor should plan the series for consecutive presentations as if nothing will interfere; however, if something influential happens, the preacher should consider an interlude with other sermons.

The Uniqueness of Each Sermon

Preaching from a Bible book should not lead to an excessive focus on the series. Continuous attention needs to be given to the individuality of each sermon and its uniqueness. Each sermon should have some distinctive characteristics.

Each sermon is a theological event. A sermon cannot be explained only by human homiletics; theological truths are needed to explain fully a sermon. Many writers describe preaching in terms of theology. Donald G. Miller said: "To preach the gospel, then, is not really to say words but to effect a deed. To preach is not merely to stand in a pulpit and speak, no matter how eloquently and effectively, not even to set forth a theology, no matter how clearly it is stated nor how worthy the theology. To preach is to become a part of a dynamic event wherein the living, redeeming God reproduces his act of redemption in a living encounter with man through the preacher."[25]

Clyde Fant compared the preaching event to the incarnation of Jesus. The human and the divine were combined in the historical Jesus. Likewise, each sermon should be an incarnational experience where both the human factors and the divine factors commingle. Fant said: "But preaching fails the dual purpose accorded it by theology—that it bears the eternal Word and that it touches the contemporary situation—when it betrays the wholeness of its calling by affirming part of its nature and denying the others. To the left, preaching becomes all human; to the right, all divine. To the left, there is nothing of God; to the right, there is nothing for humanhood."[26]

Many other writers consider God to be speaking in a sermon. The Second Helvitic Confession stated: *Praedictio verbi dei est verbum dei* or "the preaching of the Word is the Word of God which he himself has spoken." Gustaf Wingren said, "Preaching is not just talk about a Christ of the past, but a mouth through which the Christ of the present offers us life today."[27] Each single sermon

---

25. Donald G. Miller, *Fire in Thy Mouth* (Grand Rapids: Baker Book House, 1954), 17.

26. Clyde E. Fant, *Preaching for Today*, rev. ed. (New York: Harper and Row, 1975), 69.

27. Gustaf Wingren, *The Living Word* (Philadelphia: Fortress Press, 1960), 13.

needs to be regarded as a theological event where God gets involved in a sermon.

Each sermon is a unique congregational experience. Not only does God get involved in a sermon, but the preacher and the audience combine experientially for a unique involvement. The interaction of a preacher and listeners during the course of a sermon is a theological happening. God works with both the people and the preacher during a sermon. This kind of experience prohibits the real effects of a sermon being captured on video, cassette tape, or the printed page. Each sermon is a theological happening; therefore, each sermon needs to be distinct.

In the congregation's experience with a sermon, there is a uniqueness with each sermon. Settings for sermons may remain the same, and the participants in worship may vary little with those who do and do not attend. But no two meetings of a congregation are exactly the same. People bring different life experiences to the worship service. Differences can be found in the same basic group of people attending the same church each Sunday. The audience needs a unique, separate sermon for that particular Sunday.

Each sermon is homiletically distinct. A sermon series does not have to reproduce the same kind of sermons. Each message in a series needs to have a different text, theme, outline, content, illustration(s), and other homiletical matters. Each sermon in the series of sermons stands on its own as a separate entity. No sermon in a series needs to depend either on the previous sermon or on a subsequent sermon. Practicing this homiletical guideline could allow each sermon to be separate in that it could be proclaimed apart from the series at a different place and time.

Does the insistence on the individuality of each sermon in a series of sermons from a Bible book mean that the messages do not have any relationship with one another? Links do exist between the sermons. One obvious link is that each sermon has a text from the same Bible book. The background or life situation of the book will inevitably affect the content of each sermon. Another conspicuous connection exists because each sermon comes from the same literary distinctive and from a book with common forms and themes. Some preachers like to link a series of sermons from a Bible book with a general theme which covers all the sermons.

Successive or Selective Approaches for Choosing the Text

Whatever kind of preaching is chosen—whether individual messages or sermons in a series—selecting the text is always challenging. Preaching a series of sermons from the Bible book only appears to resolve the dilemma of choosing a text. Just looking at a Bible book filled with numerous possibilities for text selections causes frustration. Questions arise:

- Should I preach successively through the book?

- Am I allowed the option to survey many texts within a Bible book and then to choose a select number?

- Some homiletical guidelines would be helpful to learn how to preach from a Bible book, either successively or selectively.

The Successive Approach

The successive approach is a popular style of preaching from a Bible book. It involves selecting texts of sermons from a Bible book that follow each other in succeeding sequence. In the successive approach, no texts within the book are omitted. Often a preacher preaches from a Bible book using a commentary style for preparation and proclamation. Such preachers go from verse to verse explaining, applying, and illustrating various words, phrases, or clauses in the verses. Their main intention is to cover the entire book by using every verse and chapter.

Other preachers divide the book into paragraphs or textual units complete with a thought. The exact length of these parts or units varies, but they do come in successive order. Andrew W. Blackwood argued that the paragraph is the most frequent unit in the Bible.[28] Translations such as the *New International Version* and the *Revised Standard Version* clearly set off paragraph divisions. The paragraph unit has good possibilities for successive treatment of texts. Such textual selections can contain short or long units because paragraphs varies from one verse to numerous verses. No matter how small or large the units or paragraph, the successive approach uses each unit for sermons in the series.

---

28. Andrew W. Blackwood, *Preaching from the Bible* (Nashville: Abingdon Press, 1961), 94.

Most books in the Bible can be treated successively, either by the running commentary method or the paragraph system. But a few Bible books do not lend themselves to the consecutive use of texts.

- *Psalms* does not lend itself to the successive selective approach because it consists of a collection of individual psalms written by many people in different places and at different times. How the psalms came to be collected in the order in which they appear in the English Bible is a story in itself. The expository preacher might need to think more of successive order in some books such as Genesis or Romans, but consecutive treatment of the Psalms in the order of their appearance in the English Bible would be unnecessary. This, however, does not mean a preacher should not preach consecutively through the Psalms but that successive order presents difficulties in some Bible books.

- *Proverbs* is another collected book. It contains sayings and teachings collected over the years and later put in a scroll or book. The arrangement of the subjects has no distinguishable order. This makes preaching consecutively through the Proverbs difficult, though not impossible. Other Bible books because of their distinctive literary nature will be hard to approach consecutively.

- *Jeremiah* is not arranged chronologically, and selecting texts successively through Jeremiah presents problems.

- *Matthew, Mark, and Luke* contain pericopes, or groupings of material. The writers of these Synoptic Gospels did not try to arrange the materials in chronological order; therefore, following the successive approach of preaching through one of the Synoptic Gospels presents difficulties.

Any book of the Bible can be treated successively. Because of the nature of some books, various difficulties in the consecutive selection and treatment of texts may be encountered.

In the successive approach of selecting and using texts from Bible books, the length of individual texts may vary. Some expositors mark off short texts within the Bible book, and the series becomes lengthy. Other expositors designate longer texts within the book to make the series shorter. Two expositors preaching from Colossians demonstrate the possibilities of diversity in the number of texts chosen consecutively. Gary Demarest chose seven texts to preach successively through Colossians. His selections were:

1. What Does a Christian Look Like? 1:1–14
2. Something to Sing About, 1:15–23
3. Your Ministry: Choosing to Suffer, 1:24–2:5
4. Christ Is All You Need, 2:6–15
5. Living Beyond the Rules, 2:16–3:4
6. Off with the Old, On with the New, 3:5–17
7. Life As It's Meant to Be, 3:18–4:18 [29]

R. Kent Hughes chose twenty-one texts to preach consecutively through Colossians. His series was arranged as follows:

1. The Celebration of the Church, 1:1–8
2. The Prayer for the Church, 1:9–14
3. The Preeminent Christ, 1:15–18
4. The Supreme Reconciliation, 1:19–23
5. The Supreme Ministry, 1:24–29
6. The Supreme Concern, 2:1–5
7. The Supreme Charge, 2:6–7
8. A Safeguard against Seduction, 2:8–10
9. The Fullness in Christ, 2:11–15
10. The Guarding of Your Treasures, 2:16–23
11. The Seeking of Things Above, 3:1–4
12. The Putting Off, Putting On (I), 3:5–11
13. The Putting Off, Putting On (II), 3:12–14
14. The Fullness of His Peace, Word, and Name, 3:15–17
15. The Christian Family (I), 3:18–19
16. The Christian Family (II), 3:20–21
17. The Christian Family (III), 3:22–4:1
18. The Fullness in Communication, 4:2–6
19. The Fullness in Fellowship (I), 4:7–9
20. The Fullness in Fellowship (II), 4:10–14
21. The Fullness of Paul's Heart, 4:15–18[30]

---

29. Gary Demarest, *Colossians: The Mystery of Christ in Us* (Waco, Tex.: Word Books, 1979).

30. R. Kent Hughes, *Colossians and Philemon: The Supremacy of Christ in Preaching the Word* (Westchester, Ill.: Crossway Books, 1989).

Selecting texts successively usually depends on the gifts and personality of the preacher and the congregation's receptivity. The size of the Bible book does not have to determine the number of texts. Short books can have many texts or just a few texts, and the same thing is true for length of Bible books. Though Hughes had three times more sermons and texts than Demarest, both preachers used the successive approach for preaching from Colossians.

Choosing texts in a successive order is an effective way of preaching from a Bible book. Most expositors who choose this approach begin by reading and studying the Bible book; then they divide the book into units, parts, or paragraphs. Different preachers divide Scripture into different units of thought. Then each unit or part becomes a text for a sermon. Treating the Bible book in a running commentary approach may involve the division of the book into parts, but the predominant concern involves commentary from verse to verse, leaving off at the verse completed and picking up with the next verse for the next exposition. The successive approach of selecting and treating texts is one method of preaching from a book, but there is another option.

The Selective Approach

The selective approach of preaching from a Bible book involves choosing a collection of texts from a number of texts. Rather than treat every text in the Bible book, the preacher forms a systematic plan or makes a choice of texts. Using the selective approach gives the preacher greater freedom to determine how many texts to choose. No expositor has to treat a Bible book successively. In the selective approach, the preacher chooses a Bible book for a series of sermons, and then from that book the preacher specifies various texts in the book rather than all the texts in the book.

Bible Book of the Month. Choices of texts depend on the expositor's personal preferences and on the creative choice of the expositor. Lavonn D. Brown uses a unique, personal, selective technique for preaching from a Bible book. Periodically he chooses a Bible book for preaching all month during the Sunday evening services. He calls the emphasis, "The Bible Book of the Month." He challenges the audience to read the book during the month. The Sunday evening's text and sermon are taken from that book. Brown's selective selection of texts follows:

Sunday 1—A Book Sermon. On the first Sunday, Brown preaches from the entire book in one sermon. He acquaints the audience with the life situation of the book, its general flow, and one prominent theme in the book.

Sunday 2—A Biographical Sermon. In most books one or more personalities figure prominently. Brown chooses a character and preaches about him or her.

Sunday 3—A Chapter Sermon. Brown chooses one of the chapters from the book and uses it for a Sunday evening message.

Sunday 4—A Textual Sermon. In one of the Sunday evening messages, Brown chooses either a prominent verse or a prominent paragraph as the basis for a sermon.

Sermon 5—A Word or Theme Sermon. If the month has five Sundays, Brown chooses a significant word or theme from the book for a message.

Chapter by Chapter. Another selective method for choosing texts from a Bible book consists of choosing one text from each chapter of the book. This procedure does not mean that the entire chapter has to be used as a text, but one text in the chapter would be selected. For example, suppose a preacher chooses the Gospel of John for a series of sermons and does not want to use the successive approach because it would involve too many sermons and too lengthy a series. The selective process in John would involve getting several commentaries and studying all of John 1 early in the week. During the study of this chapter, some word, verse, or paragraph would emerge as the text to be preached. Admittedly, other verses would be omitted.

Early in the subsequent week the preacher would begin the study of John 2. Again the emerging text and theme in the chapter would be preached. Such a selective process would continue until one sermon from each of the twenty-one chapters has been preached. Many of the other texts and themes discovered in each week's study could be preached at another time. The preacher does not have to be absolutely rigid about the procedure. If two sermons must be preached from one chapter of John, no homiletical commandment has been broken. Many books, especially long Bible books, could be treated by one sermon from each chapter. Such a method allows for several alternatives in one chapter and prevents a series from being excessively long.

Preacher's Choice. Still another selective approach happens strictly by the personal choice of the preacher. When the expositor studies a Bible book and knows the audience, texts can be chosen by personal choice. More than likely most expositors cannot give rational explanations about their selection of texts. The choices are personal preference. Fred Wood did not choose to preach from all fifty-two chapters of Jeremiah. Instead, he chose twelve texts and themes from the book. His choices follow:

1. Fanning the Flame, 1:1–19
2. Can a Bride Forget? 2:1–4:4
3. Blow the Trumpet, 4:5–6:30
4. When the Bubble Bursts, 11:1–8; 11:18–12:6
5. What's Worse Than No Religion? 7:1–8:3; 26:1–24
6. While the Lights Are Still Burning, 13:1–7; 18:1–23; 19:1–20:18
7. The Dear Lord's Best Interpreters, 35:1–17
8. Better Had They Ne'er Been Born, 36:1–32
9. New Occasions Teach New Duties, Chapters 24, 29
10. But Thou, O Man of God, Chapter 28
11. A Correspondence Fixed with Heaven, 11:28–12:6; 18:18–23; 20:7–18; 15:10–21; 17:9–18; 21:1–14; 34:1–7; 37:1–10
12. New in My Father's Kingdom, 31:31–34[31]

Close examinations of Wood's choices disclose that he did not feel the necessity of choosing chapters in numerical order, and he used multiple texts from Jeremiah for one theme. As long as a preacher stays with the truth of the text, personal preference of selective text choices is a good way for the selective approach.

Great Personalities or Events. Still another angle of the selective approach involves the choice of personalities or events within the Bible book. Many Bible books have the content centered around characters. For example, an expositor could preach from Genesis by selecting texts and topics on the personalities. Such texts could be chosen on God, Adam, Cain, Abel, Enoch, Noah, Abraham, Lot, Sarah, Jacob, Rebekah, Laban, Joseph, and others. Jerry M. Self preached from the Gospel of John by choosing seventeen texts

---

31. Fred M. Wood, *Fire in My Bones* (Nashville: Broadman Press, 1959).

which contained seventeen personalities.[32] Numerous other books such as Judges, 1 Samuel, and Acts, could be chosen for texts involving Bible personalities. An expositor also could choose significant events in Bible books such as Exodus or Joshua. The unique nature of many Bible books provides many unique possibilities about selective choices of texts and topics.

Great Sentences. Another selective approach could be the choice of great sentences from a Bible book. These sentences could be declarative, imperative, or interrogative. The expositor could choose a dozen or more imperative statements from many Bible books. Roger Lovette in *Questions Jesus Raised* chose twenty-one questions Jesus asked that are recorded in John.[33] Choosing one or several kinds of significant sentences from a Bible book is an effective method of preaching from a Bible book.

Word Studies. Still another selective approach involves choosing significant words used throughout a Bible book. The expositor could preach from Romans by choosing texts which have an emphasis on the words *gospel, faith, sin, righteousness, wrath, justification, grace, condemnation,* or *sanctification.* Or the expositor could choose texts from 1 John with the phrases *word of life, advocate, light, righteousness, know, love,* or *commandment.*

Expositors can choose any one of the selective approaches, or they can use a combination of several approaches. If an expositor chooses to preach from a book using some paragraphs, a few narratives, several personal choices of texts, or a number of words, no homiletical rule has been violated. The basic principle or homiletical guideline of the selective approach emphasizes flexibility and creativity.

—⁓——⁓——⁓——⁓——⁓—

Homiletical rules should never dominate the expositor, but the prospective expository should consider the practicality of the following four guidelines.

1. Preach series from one Old Testament and one New Testament book each year.

---

32. Jerry M. Self, *Men and Women in John's Gospel* (Nashville: Broadman Press, 1974).

33. Roger Lovette, *Questions Jesus Raised* (Nashville: Broadman Press, 1986).

2. Preach not less than six, nor more than twenty-four sermons in each series. Ponder this issue before accepting this guideline. Can your audience handle a year or more of sermons from one Bible book?

3. Give attention to the individuality of each sermon. Make each sermon in the series a self-contained message not dependent on preceding or subsequent sermons.

4. Think carefully about your approach in selecting texts. Choose deliberately between the successive and selective approaches.

These guidelines can help you start preparing to preach a series of sermons from a Bible book. But as you develop this art, other regulations will emerge out of personal involvement. Homiletical guidelines should be your helpful friends but not your arrogant masters.

The Life Situation of a Bible Book

Each book in the Bible has both a human and a divine dimension. The *divine dimension* gives each Bible book unique characteristics of divine inspiration. God spoke through humans to people in many circumstances. The essential substance of every Bible book is God's Word to people in an ancient situation, and this substance has been God's Word to people throughout the centuries. The content of Scripture continues to be God's Word to people today.

Each Bible book also has a *human dimension*. A book is human because the words were written by people to people in a particular life situation or what many biblical scholars call the *Sitz im Leben*. The content for every Bible book came as a result of human realities. Inspired authors used common literary types. Bible books arose out of historical situations, possessed the influence of human environmental conditions, and bore the traits of composition by human authors. We should study Bible books with bifocal vision, watching for both the human and the divine.

The Bible differs from all other religious books. Other religious literary works contain meditations, mystical reflections, instructions for cultic rituals, moral codes, sayings, or laws. All of these matters can be found to a limited extent in the Bible. But when there is a mystical reflection, a law code, or a description of a religious ritual, it is rooted in a particular historical event in which God revealed the truth to people. Bible books and their content are rooted in actual historical events. Biblical statements or practices are easily misunderstood when studied without regard for these historical events.[1]

Every Bible book resulted from God's interaction with humans. The Lord observed human situations and inspired authors to give His word for human circumstances. Each book bears the distinctive of divine inspiration, but it also possesses the trait of historical times, particular places, and human needs.

Because God spoke in actual historical events, the only way to hear again what God said is to recover the reality of those events at the deepest possible level. Because those events took place in history, we must recover the historical setting. Studying the life situation of a Bible book helps the expositor see the background for every text selected from the book. What the Bible book *meant* yesterday influences what the book *means* today. What the original writer or writers *said* to ancient readers affects what expository preachers *say* to modern audiences. Preachers carefully study a book's background before preaching a series of sermons from a Bible book. They study then-and-there situations in order to

---

1. Wayne E. Ward, *The Word Comes Alive* (Nashville: Abingdon Press 1969), 15.

address here-and-now situations. Each text must be interpreted in light of its life situation.

Ringling Brothers, Barnum & Bailey Circus came to my hometown every year. My parents often took me. Performances took place under a large tent called the "big top." Bleachers for the spectators and three rings, or areas, for the circus shows were all under the big top. Tents, trailers, and booths outside the big top had other spectacles—the two-headed calf, the world's strongest man, the world's fattest woman, and . . . a burlesque show. When I asked my parents to let me go to one of these shows, they assured me that these were sideshows. They were just parasites but didn't really belong to the circus. My parents guaranteed me that only what took place under the big top was the circus.

Every text in the Bible book comes under the big top of historical background. Interpreting a text without regard to its historical background turns the text (and sermon) into a sideshow. Studying biblical background helps the preacher show the overall cover for each text in the Bible book. Studying these life situations is hard work, but the careful expositor knows that it is worth the effort because it pays off in authentic biblical sermons.

The Book within Bible History

The Bible records the story of God's speaking and working in human history. Each Bible book is a small piece that fits into the larger puzzle. The Old Testament records the history of Israel—the people of God. The center of Scripture is Jesus—his life, death, and resurrection. In the period following Jesus' resurrection, the New Testament narrates the ongoing life of the church. Every Bible book needs to be studied and interpreted within the context of particular historical events.

Periods of Bible History

Every biblical preacher should know the broad outline of Bible history. The preacher constantly reviews the periods of Bible history, especially the period related to the book selected for a series of sermons. Putting the Bible book within the context of its place in Bible history helps the preacher retell the book's story or stories. The following outline of Bible history is a framework for relating Bible books to their historical setting.

1. Beginnings. This period extended from the beginning of the world to the time of Abraham, somewhere near the year 2000 B.C. The biblical account of this period is found in Genesis 1–11. The great events in this period are the creation of the universe and the human race, the fall of humankind, the murder of Abel, the flood, the beginning of a new civilization from the descendants of Noah, and the confusion of tongues resulting in the dispersion of people.

2. Patriarchs. Hebrew history began with the call of Abraham. The Bible records more than a record of events. It describes "salvation history," known commonly by theologians with the German term *Heilsgeschichte.* The patriarchal period included the times of Abraham, Isaac, Jacob, and Joseph. The times are recorded in Genesis 12–50.

3. Sojourn, Exodus, and Wilderness Wanderings. The time of the sojourn includes Jacob and his family going into Egypt as refugees from famine. They stayed for about four hundred years and became slaves to the Egyptians. Later, God delivered Israel through Moses with an exodus from Egypt. This time involved giving the covenant at Sinai and the experience of wandering in the wilderness before arriving at Canaan. This period is recorded in Exodus, Leviticus, Numbers, and Deuteronomy.

4. Conquest of Canaan. Following Moses' death, Joshua led the people in the conquest of Canaan. Joshua divided the land among the twelve tribes of Israel. This period is found in the Book of Joshua.

5. Judges. Joshua's leadership was followed by a succession of judges, who were part military and part religious leaders. The record of this period is found in Judges and Ruth.

6. United Monarchy. Samuel, the last and greatest of the judges, established a kingdom and anointed Saul to be king. Three kings (Saul, David, and Solomon) reigned, each of them about forty years. This period and three subsequent periods are recorded in 1 and 2 Samuel; 1 and 2 Kings; and 1 and 2 Chronicles.

7. Two Kingdoms. Following Solomon's death in about 931 B.C., the northern tribes established a kingdom separate from the two southern tribes. After the separation, the Northern Kingdom was called Israel, and the Southern Kingdom was called Judah. The Northern Kingdom came to an end with the assault of Assyria in 722 B.C. In addition to the historical books of Kings and Chronicles, the works of Amos, Micah, Hosea, and Isaiah furnish historical details of the era. Judah continued to exist as a separate nation for more than a century. Kings, Chronicles, Isaiah, Jeremiah, Ezekiel, Micah, Habakkuk, and Nahum have historical details for the period. With the fall of Jerusalem to the Babylonians in 586 B.C., the Hebrew practice of kingship ended. The leaders and many people were taken to Babylon as captives.

8. Exile and Restoration. During the exile, Israel dwelled in Babylon. After defeating the Babylonians in 539 B.C., the Medo-Persian king Cyrus allowed the exiles to return to Canaan. A large group returned to Jerusalem to rebuild the temple and the city walls. Records of this period are found in Ezra, Nehemiah, and Esther. Information about the period is also found in Haggai and Zechariah.

9. Intertestamental Period. The Old Testament closes with the restoration of the people from exile and the reestablishment of the people in Palestine. A period of about four hundred years passed before the writing of any New Testament books. To understand many ideas and practices found in the New Testament books, this period needs to be studied.

10. The Period of Jesus' Life and Ministry. John the Baptist broke the silence of the four hundreds years. He prepared the way for Jesus. In a brief span of thirty-three years, Jesus lived on earth and began his ministry. The record of these decades is found in Matthew, Mark, Luke, and John.

11. The Period of the Early Church. After the resurrection and ascension of the Lord recorded in the Gospels is the account of the spread of the gospel in Acts and the Epistles.

The careful expositor studies each Bible book in light of its historical background in order to understand its message. Preaching without a knowledge of this history is doomed to failure. Each Bible book originated in its own time and world with geography and history as its setting. When the book is placed in that historical setting, its people are better seen as real people and its content as a living word.[2]

---

2. Robert L. Cate, *An Introduction to the Old Testament and Its Study* (Nashville: Broadman Press, 1987), 15.

Fitting the Text into Bible History

After selecting a book for a series of sermons, the expositor studies the book in light of its story. Using the periods of Bible history, the expositor reconstructs the story and relives the feelings of the author and readers of the book. Knowing Bible history helps the preacher get into the shoes of the writer and the people of the Bible book.

A Bible book may be set in one historical period but written in a later period. These two periods may be separated by many years. For example, the events recorded in the Gospels happened in the first three decades while the writing about those events took place three or more decades later. One set of circumstances prevailed during Jesus' life; another set of circumstances prevailed when the Gospels were written. Careful Bible students think about both sets of circumstances. Two stories need to be matched to reconstruct the story found in the Gospels. Such reconstruction of two historical periods applies to many other Bible books.

Fitting the Bible book into its life situation may seem elementary, but it is essential to understanding the book. Study the book to learn about the events it describes; then try to discover the circumstances when the book was written. Events in the Book of Joshua, for example, occurred in the period of the conquest, but the book might have been written later. The Book of Judges took place in the period of Israel's judges, but the writing of the book came later. The book tells a story, but the circumstances surrounding the writing of the book are yet another story. Reconstructing every possible fact about both narratives helps determine the Bible book's original life situation.

After reconstructing the historical setting of a book, the expositor can then get involved with the feelings associated with the book. Getting into the feelings of the circumstances, conditions, environment, and times of the book involves another method of using Bible history. The expositor needs to become a participant in the events in the book. Because truth in a Bible book is often taught through a story and in the account of an event in history, it is necessary to re-create that situation with such clarity and power that it lives again in the expositor's imagination.[3] Entering into the feelings of the happenings in a Bible book requires getting into the historical facts, but it also requires the gift of empathetic insight and

---

3. Ward, 16.

intuitive feeling to get into the feelings of others. The best expositors get the facts of the story, then portray the events as happening to ancient people and to people today. Getting into the feelings helps to understand the *Sitz im Leben* as much as gathering historical facts about the book.

How does an expositor get into the feelings in a Bible book?

- *The expositor reads and rereads the book.* At last every detail of the narrative is fixed in the mind. Even reading the book aloud can help.

- *The expositor researches the biblical background.* A good commentary or Bible dictionary helps put the Bible book in its historical setting. Reading the book and researching historical facts surrounding the book gives the expositor a feel for the circumstances of the narrative surrounding the book.

- *The expositor tries to relive the experiences described in the book.* The ideal is to enter the shoes of the Bible characters and the original readers. This exercise seeks to put the story of the Bible book in the expositor's mind so the expositor can communicate truths in the story to others.

- *The expositor asks God to illuminate the listeners.* The same God who inspired the Bible book can illuminate others about the facts and feelings of the story.

The prophet Micah prophesied during the period of the separated kingdoms. He spoke specifically to Judah, the Southern Kingdom, in the eighth century B.C. (see Mic. 1:1). Leaders in Jerusalem were practicing injustices toward humans. These facts help explain the deep feelings expressed in Micah's prophecy. Reading and rereading the Book of Micah and studying the circumstances from commentaries can help bring out feelings in the book. Micah was incensed by the greed of people who spent nights plotting their next business moves to exploit their helpless neighbors. He was angered by prophets who preached for more money and attacked those who did not pay them. Micah could foresee only one possible end for such a society. Punishment had to come—Judah would go into exile. The expositor who understands Micah's situation can retell Micah's messages with corresponding feelings.[4] The

---

4. Ronald J. Allen, *Contemporary Biblical Interpretation for Preaching* (Valley Forge, Pa.: Judson Press, 1984), 31.

study of fact and feelings together creates what Wayne Ward called the *you-are-there sensation.*[5] The events in Micah did not just happen to Micah and to the residents of Judah. The events must also happen to the expositor.

The first stage in knowing the life situation of any Bible book is to reconstruct the facts and feelings of its story. Getting the historical picture in focus allows the expositor to move on to other details. Not one sermon should be planned or preached without knowing how the text of the sermon fits in the historical situation of the Bible book.

The Book's Setting

After focusing attention on the story of the Bible book, consideration needs to be directed to historical surroundings. Bernard Ramm wrote: "Whatever men wrote they wrote from out of their cultural backdrop. Their culture modifies, determines, guides, colors, or influences the manner in which they express themselves. . . . Therefore a study of culture is indispensable in Biblical interpretation."[6] Information about historical surroundings includes geographical, political, cultural, and theological factors. Since each Bible book originated in a historical context, it can only be understood accurately and completely when those surroundings have been considered.

The Geographical Setting

Geographical factors influenced the author's thought, language, and illustrations. The expositor of any Bible book needs to understand the geography of the biblical world, the native country of the original author and readers. The geography will have to be studied from the perspective of changes. Because many historical events occurred, the geography of the biblical world changed. Geographical factors changed throughout the various periods of Bible history, and often some changes took place within the period. Geographical factors in Abraham's time were not the same during Paul's life. Some cities that existed in 2000 B.C. no longer existed in A.D. 50. Through the years the boundaries of nations changed.

---

5. Ward, 15–31.

6. Bernard Ramm, *Protestant Biblical Interpretation: A Textbook of Hermeneutics* (Grand Rapids: Baker Book House, 1970), 152.

Every expositor needs to be acquainted with Palestine, the cross-roads of the Near East. Great leaders of world empires marched through the land. An expositor needs an overall perspective of the topography of the land with a view to mountains and valleys, lakes and rivers, cities and villages, highways and plains, populated and desolate places. When an expositor becomes aware of such things, the message and the history become real. The plains, the deserts, the Sea of Galilee, the Mediterranean, the rivers, the Dead Sea, the hills, the mountains, the roads, the boundaries, the cities, the villages, and many other factors figure into the geographical surroundings. In addition to these topographical matters, an expositor also needs to understand something about the Palestinian seasons, the prevailing winds, and the temperature variance.

To get an even better picture of the geographical surroundings, an expositor needs to know about the trees, shrubs, and flowers of Palestine as well as its animal life, grains, vegetables, and fruits. How could an expositor explain the poet's statement the "dew of Hermon, coming down upon the mountain of Zion" (Ps. 133:3) without being familiar with the effect of Mount Hermon's snow-clad peak on the mists that are constantly rising from the ravines at its base? How can an expositor explain such expressions as "the glory of Lebanon" and "the excellency of Carmel and Sharon" without a knowledge of its luxuriant vegetation and surpassing beauty? How can an expositor explain how David eluded Saul without understanding the countryside?[7] Only familiarity with the seasons enables an expositor to explain "the early and later rains" in James 5:7. Knowing about the sirocco, the scorching wind blowing in from the Arabian Desert, helps to interpret James 1:11. These examples point to the need of being acquainted with the physical features of Palestine.

Geographical factors explain some essential features of some Bible books. Knowing the lay of the land affects comprehension of the Book of Joshua. How could an expositor preach from that book without knowing the parts of the land of Canaan and how they are laid out in relation to other parts of Canaan? Or how does an expositor interpret the Gospels without a geographical understanding of Judea, Samaria, and Galilee? No expositor needs to preach

---

7. Louis Berkhoff, *Principles of Biblical Hermeneutics* (Grand Rapids: Baker Book House, 1970), 121.

from any Bible book without a thorough understanding of the geographical features and layout of the land of Palestine.

Understanding the countries surrounding Palestine is also important. How can an expositor preach from Exodus without knowing the geographical relationship of Palestine to Egypt? To preach from the historical books of Samuel, Kings, and Chronicles, an expositor needs to know about Syria, Assyria, Babylon, and other ancient powers. Preaching from most of the prophets also requires an investigation of the geographical location of other nations. No preacher could preach effectively from the Book of Acts without knowledge of Palestine, Syria, Assyria, Macedonia, Achaia, and Italy.

Does the expositor need to know geography to preach from Paul's Letter to the Philippians? To get the full historical picture, the preacher needs to know that Philippi was a prominent city located in the region of Macedonia, which Paul visited on his second missionary journey. Philippi was a strategic city on the East-West travel route, and it enjoyed an interesting history. Its status had been elevated to a Roman colony. Knowing these geographical factors figures prominently in getting the full picture behind the Book of Philippians and in examining the truths in sermons from the book.

The Political Setting

Expositors need to study carefully the history of Israel and its relationship with other nations. Political conditions varied greatly from the period of the patriarchs to the period of the exile and restoration; and God's people changed from the time of the restoration to the time of Christ. Bible books came out of diverse political situations, and these circumstances shed meaning on many texts in the books. How can an expositor preach intelligently from 1 Samuel without knowing the political transition from a judge to a king? How can an expositor preach effectively from Psalm 137 without understanding something about the situation when it was written? How can an expositor understand and explain Jesus' conversation with the woman at the well of Sychar without knowing about the longstanding conflict between Jews and Samaritans? Explaining the political realities within Israel helps clarify the surroundings of many Bible books.

International politics shaped Israel's internal politics. Serious Bible students try to reconstruct ancient international affairs. Preaching from Isaiah 7–10 requires information about the situation in Judah under King Ahaz, the situation in the Northern Kingdom of Israel under Pekah, the circumstances of Syria under Rezin, and even the situation of Assyria.

The expositor of Mark, 1 Peter, or Revelation needs to understand the politics of the Roman Empire. Throughout the first century, the *pax Romana*, or the Roman peace, prevailed. The events in Mark, which constituted the life and ministry of Jesus Christ, occurred in a time when the Roman peace ruled the world. But when the Gospel of Mark was written, the Romans had launched persecutions against the Christians. Christians had everything but peace. The author of Mark, 1 Peter, and Revelation wrote out of the circumstances of suffering. The Romans were persecuting the Christians.

Bible books which are rooted and grounded in history cannot ignore the political factors. A historical understanding of the political surroundings is not a superfluity that an expositor can neglect. To leave out political matters would divorce the biblical text from the processes out of which they were born.

The Cultural Setting

Each Bible book also originated out of a cultural context. The expositor needs to study what Bernard Ramm called "biblical culture."[8] Anthropologists divide human culture into material culture and social culture. Material culture refers to all things such as tools, household furnishings, dwellings, weapons, garments, and other material matters that people use in the maintenance of life. Social culture refers to all the customs, practices, rites, social relationships, and other aspects in life.[9]

Each Bible book has its own unique material and social cultural surroundings. Most standard Bible dictionaries contain material on the various cultural factors. Some rather obvious examples of material culture include:

- Occupations in biblical times such as sheep raising, vinedressing, farming, fishing, and merchants;

---

8. Ramm, 155.
9. Ibid.

- Foods and drinks;
- Types of dwellings throughout biblical history including tents and simple homes;
- Furnishings found in the dwellings;
- Business methods of measures, weights, and currency.

An expositor will encounter many evidences of material culture studying a Bible book. These evidences provide abundant insight for understanding and explaining texts in the Bible book.

Various social cultures appear through biblical history. In studying a specific Bible book, the careful expositor seeks to uncover the specific social culture behind the book or passage in the book. The expositor of Genesis studies the background of Mesopotamia and Egypt. The expositor of Exodus investigates Egyptian social culture. Before preaching from Acts or from a Pauline letter, the careful expositor studies Graeco-Roman culture.

Research sheds light on cultural practices of Bible lands:

- Marriage rites
- Puberty rites
- Burial rites
- Legal systems
- Political structures
- Family systems
- Farm practices
- Business practices
- Methods of warfare
- Slavery
- Monetary system
- Economic system
- Religious practices

In searching the background of the Book of Ruth, the expositor discovers that ancient legal transactions often took place at the city gate. In studying to preach from Colossians, the same expositor learns about philosophical-religious ideas that prevailed in the Lycus Valley.

Studying cultural elements gives the original usage of language and enables the interpreter to know the literal and socially designated meaning of a word, a phrase, or a custom. Words, sentences, and expressions become meaningful at the original level of culture. The primary purpose for studying the cultural elements in a Bible book is to aid the interpreter in knowing what the original elements are which are referred to in Scripture. They are indispensable for the accurate understanding of the Bible.[10] For example, in studying the Gospels, the reader sees such words and expressions as *alms, coals of fire, devouring widows' houses, proclaiming on the housetops, a sabbath day's journey,* and many others. Interpreting these expressions requires the expositor to study the social cultures from which the language emerged.

The Theological Setting

Because each Bible book originated in human history, it has geographical, political, cultural, and other human factors. But a Bible book is only incidentally language and history. It has a greater surrounding which is its theological purpose. Each book in Scripture originated out of the reality that a gracious God acted in history. No part of Scripture originated in a theological vacuum. The Bible is a book of faith—Israel's faith in the Old Testament and the churches' faith in the New Testament. In studying a Bible book, the expositor investigates these theological surroundings.

Understanding the life situation of a Bible book requires movement from the historical data to the study of what God was saying and doing at that point in human history. The biblical writers did not just describe historical events. Instead, they were involved in the events, and they remembered and interpreted those events. Events fused with interpretation; Bible writers were confronted and overwhelmed by the reality of an encounter with God amidst historical surroundings. For example, the Hebrews who crossed the Red Sea from Egypt remembered the event and reported it as God's action.[11]

Time passed between the biblical events and writing about those events. James Luther Mays in *Exegesis as a Theological Discipline* told how the Bible came as the result of a complex process of shaping and growth. The interval between event and writing was not

---

10. Ibid., 157.

11. John Newport, "Interpreting the Bible" in *The Broadman Bible Commentary*, Vol. 1, rev. (Nashville: Broadman Press, 1973), 30.

dormant or vacant. The biblical events were told and retold, and the events gained a new dynamic contemporaneity. The continued witness confirmed and deepened theological understanding and insight into the event. Every Bible book came out of this theological context of events: telling/retelling, and writing.

Expositors must delve behind the literary and historical surroundings of a Bible book to understand the theology that produced it. Expositors need to discover the theology that moved the writer to choose the words and make the observations. Such a theological approach is not a violation of sound principles of knowing a Bible book. Historical and grammatical study should examine the theological surroundings of a Bible book. For example, in preaching from 1 Corinthians, an expositor needs to know the directives Paul gave to the Corinthians and the theology that moved Paul to give these directives.[12]

Theology motivated every biblical writer. Because the Bible originated with people of faith, the contemporary interpreter must also be a person of faith. Rational study of history and grammar is not enough to explain a Bible book. Each Bible book yields its meaning best to persons who have a personal experience with God through Jesus Christ and who are indwelled by the Spirit of God.

The Book's Special Features

After placing the Bible book in its particular historical setting and examining its historical surroundings, expositors need to examine specific historical situations of the book. Expositors need to come to a clear understanding of the historical situation that prompted the writing of the book. Knowing the historical situations aims at understanding precisely what the biblical writers meant at the time when they wrote for their particular public. Such knowledge comes by asking pointed questions about the book:

- Who wrote the book?
- Who were the original readers of the book?
- What occasion prompted the book and gave it purpose?
- Why did the book take the literary shape it did?
- How have the historical traditions affected the understanding of the book?

---

12. Ibid., 31.

Texts used from the Bible book should be interpreted in light of the specific historical situations.

The Author or Authors

Probably the first question to seek an answer to is, Who wrote the book? Every author leaves personal characteristics on a book. Even though each Bible book was divinely inspired, the book retains uniquely human impressions of its author. Adequate interpretation of what was written cannot be divorced from considerations about the author. Interestingly enough, though the author or authors seem to be an important factor to consider, not every Bible student has been interested in investigating the author or authors of a book. Students of Scripture with an excessive fixation on the divine origin and nature of the Bible sometimes give little or no attention to studying authorship. Such students consider historical background irrelevant. When the critical study of Scripture began over a century ago, the first important matter considered was, Who wrote the words? Many critical scholars such as Julius Wellhausen and F. C. Bauer challenged traditional authorship of Bible books, and many Bible students rejected these challenges. Some refused to investigate the question of who wrote a book. Over the years biblical criticism has helped expositors with the questions about authorship and how the author or authors affected the words used in the Bible book.

Biblical critics such as Rudolph Bultman and others minimized the importance of authorship. These critics thought the writers took on the role of mere compilers or editors of the units of tradition, not the role of an author creating language. Such views obviously disclaimed the personal contribution of the author. The impersonal side of these Bible critics led to the development of a redaction criticism with a renewed emphasis on the importance of the book's author. Recent biblical scholarship attaches more significance to the human author or authors of a Bible book.

Identifying the author of a Bible book often involves diligent pursuit. Sometimes the task is easy, and sometimes the task is difficult. Some Bible books contain direct implications about authorship. In these kinds of books the individual's name is given at the beginning of a book, and students associate the name with authorship. For example, in most of the prophetic books of the Old Testament, a name appears in an opening superscription along with other historical information. Thirteen New Testament books open with the salutation of Paul. Since the name appears, some Bible scholars associate Paul with the authorship of the book. Other Bible scholars present reasons other than identification of authorship for why the name appears.

Some Bible books do not have names at the beginning, but they have standing traditions about authorship associated with the book. Ancient writers not too many years distanced from the writing of Bible books have been proposed or named authors of some Bible books. For example, through hundreds of years the name Moses has been associated with the Pentateuch, and the name of David has long been associated with the Psalms. Likewise, longstanding reputable traditions have associated Paul as author of the Pastoral Letters. Critics in the past hundred years have challenged traditional authorship, presenting alternate ideas about authorship. Generally speaking, tradition has been rather reliable for examining authorship of some books.

In addition to people's names in the beginning of the book and the strong external traditions, some Bible students associate the name of the book with the author. Actually proper names came to be associated with books from a hero or heroine in the book. Few Bible scholars name Ruth as the author of the book. The Book of Joshua was also named after Joshua, the heroic leader in the book. But the Book of Joshua was not necessarily written by Joshua. These books and others bear the names of individuals, but the expositor might need to search elsewhere for the identification of the author.

Searching for the identity of a biblical author presents a stimulating challenge. This search often passes through three phases.

First, the student investigates the internal evidence. The Bible book contains clues about who wrote it. Such internal evidences as the appearance of a name, stylistic matters, historical data, and other matters give clues about authorship.

Second, the student investigates external evidences. What do ancient writers and writings outside the Bible say about the book's authorship? Putting internal and external evidences together can help determine who wrote the book.

Third, the student constructs an author profile. The student looks for the author's personal characteristics, mental habits, distinctive views, and heritage of ideas. What was the author's immediate environment? These factors influenced what the author said and helped determine the significance of what was written.[13] The most important factor is learning about the personhood of the author, especially the kind of person the author was at the time of writing the book. Such knowledge helps expositors understand what was said and why it was said.

The Readers

Who were the book's first readers? The more data expositors can learn about the original recipients of the book, the more the language, circumstances, and style of the book can be understood. The heritage of ideas of the first readers, their character, their mental habits, and their environment determined the manner in which an author addressed them, and influenced the ideas and terminology used to convey the thoughts.

Just as the quest for authorship involves investigating internal and external data, so does the pursuit about recipients involve these same matters. Many Bible books do not contain internal information about the readers. None of the pentateuchal books have a clue about original readers; therefore, we would have to surmise that these books were addressed to the believing community of Israel at some time in their history. Other books such as 1 John, Hebrews, and the Gospels contain no explicit reference to the original readers. When no explicit references about original recipients appear in the book, an expositor has to work with the assumption that the book was written to help some believing community. Searching for the particular time and place of that faith community requires diligent investigation.

Most Bible books give us internal evidence about the original recipients. The recipients of many Bible books are mentioned: "The vision of Isaiah the son of Amoz, concerning Judah and Jerusalem which he saw during the reigns of Uzziah, Jotham, Ahaz, and Hezekiah, kings of Judah" (Isa. 1:1). "Paul and Timothy, bond-servants of Christ Jesus, to all the saints in Christ Jesus who are in Philippi, including the overseers and deacons" (Phil. 1:1). The superscription of prophetic books and the salutation of New Testament letters yield a clue about the original readers.

---

13. H. C. Brown, Jr., H. Gordon Clinard, and Jesse J. Northcutt, *Steps to the Sermon: A Plan for Sermon Preparation* (Nashville: Broadman Press, 1963), 54.

Geographical study can help expositors find information about the original readers of a Bible book. Donald Guthrie stressed the discipline of getting to know the geographical location of the readers.[14] The location where the readers lived and the environmental surroundings of that place affected the lives of the readers and their needs.

Expositors also need to study the character of the readers. Expositors need to decide which statements in the book refer to the particular situation of the readers and which references are of a general significance. The Corinthian correspondences provide a case in point. Some of the advice given by Paul regarding women in 1 Corinthians may be due to some local background. Assuming that Paul laid down a general principle might be questionable, though extracting some general teaching from the specific example is possible. Without a doubt the readers influenced the ideas and language found in a Bible book. Investigating the identity of the readers can help complete the specific historical situation of the Bible book.

The Date

While searching for information about the author and the original readers, expositors inevitably encounter matters about when the book was written. Arriving at the precise time is not always possible, and it is not always essential to understanding the book. Douglas Stuart offered suggestions about dating Old Testament books: "If the passage is a historical narrative, seek the date for the events described. If it is a prophetic oracle, seek the date when it might have been delivered by the prophet. If it is poetry, or some other sort, try to determine when it might have been composed."[15] Stuart suggested further ideas about setting boundaries for the dating of a Bible book: "If you cannot suggest a specific date, at least suggest the date before which the passage could not have occurred or been composed (*terminus a quo*) and the date by which the passage surely must have already taken place or been composed (*terminus ad quem*)."[16]

---

14. Donald Guthrie, "Questions of Introduction" in *New Testament Interpretation: Essays on Principles and Methods* (Grand Rapids: William B. Eerdmans, 1977), 105–16.

15. Douglas Stuart, *Old Testament Exegesis: A Primer for Students and Pastors* (Philadelphia: Westminster Press, 1980), 29.

16. Ibid.

Arriving at the precise date of Old Testament books presents a problem because of the hundreds of years of Hebrew history. Also, many Old Testament books have a relationship with the dates—one when the events in the book happened and another when the events were written.

Dating New Testament books presents fewer problems than dating Old Testament books. New Testament history (excluding the intertestamental period) covered less than one hundred years, and dating any New Testament book falls within a time frame of about fifty years. Most New Testament scholars put all the books of the New Testament in a period from A.D. 49 to A.D. 95 with most books being written before A.D. 70.

Just as some principles prevail for the study of authorship and readers, so some principles exist for dating Bible books. The first guideline for seeking a book's date would be putting the events in the book within the context of history. Expositors should seek to identify the times in which the events in the book happened. The second guideline for dating a Bible book involves searching for evidences of when the book was written. The various surroundings and content of the book (including vocabulary and literary type) help identify a time of writing. Dating a Bible book can be done adequately only with a sense of an overall view of Bible history to which the expositor can relate the times with the book and the time of writing the book.

The Occasion and Purpose

Studying the author, readers, and date of a Bible book begins the process of divulging the occasion and purpose of the book. No Bible book originated without a reason for being. Some human situation prompted God to inspire an author to write. The readers had needs that needed to be addressed. Thus, the author had a valid reason for writing. To know the occasion and purpose of the Bible book puts an expositor at the vantage point of understanding.

Several factors help us understand why a Bible book came to be. Studying a book's author and readers often reveals the book's occasion and purpose. Also, reading the book can yield many internal clues the author gave for writing the book. Sometimes explicit statements may be seen about the author's reason for writing. For example, in Luke 1:1–4 and Acts 1:1, the author gave the purpose for presenting the material that followed. The fourth Gospel clearly states its purpose in John 20:31: to witness to Christ so people might believe. The tenfold repetition of the expression "these are the generations of" in the Book of Genesis suggests the book's purpose: to record developments of the human race as the prelude to making a nation of faith. In 1 Peter, the author encouraged the leaders to stand fast amid persecution. Such an encouragement would suggest an occasion of hardship and a purpose of ministry to suffering believers. Thus, an author's explicit statement or repetition of certain phrases represents one way to determine an author's purpose.[17]

The occasion and purpose of a Bible book could be seen by observing the parenthetical parts. These blocks of material often give important clues about the author's intention. The Book of Hebrews, for example, is interspersed with exhortations and warnings, so there is little doubt that the author's purpose was to persuade persecuted Jewish believers not to return to Judaism but to stay true to their new profession of faith (see Heb. 10:19–23, 32–35; 12:1–3). Many of Paul's letters have theological facts followed by "therefore" and an exhortation. These exhortations often reveal why Paul wrote the book.[18]

The author's selection of material also helps reveal the purpose of a Bible book. Henry A. Virkler suggested that the Bible student "observe points that are omitted or issues that are focused on."[19] For example, the writer of 1 and 2 Chronicles did not give a complete history of all national events during Solomon's reign and the kings in the separated kingdoms. The writer under the leadership of God's Spirit selected only those events which illustrated that Israel could endure only as she remained faithful to God's covenant. The phrase "did what was evil (or right) in the sight of the Lord" occurs frequently.[20]

Writers of the four Gospels had access to much material about Jesus' life and ministry, but they did not intend to give a sequential biographical account of Jesus. Their selections emphasized certain aspects of Jesus' life and ministry to address the needs of their par-

---

17. Henry A. Virkler, *Hermeneutics: Principle and Process of Biblical Interpretation* (Grand Rapids: Baker Book House, 1981), 83.
18. Ibid.
19. Ibid.
20. Ibid., 83–84.

ticular readers. To know the occasion and purpose of any Bible book as well as the author's reason for writing helps clarify the text.

The Literary Character

God led authors to use a variety of literary types or genres. Different literary forms existed at different stages within the Bible's composition. The Bible contains many general genres including law, theological narration, wisdom literature, poetry, prophetic books, gospels, epistles, and apocalyptic. All of these genres embody characteristic literary patterns common to the literature of the culture in which the Bible arose.

The historical-critical study of Scripture has led to the truth that Bible books did not just appear. They did not just express disembodied and timeless truths apart from particular historical circumstances. Thomas G. Long said, "Biblical texts are written by particular people employing particular resources in particular circumstances and for particular purposes."[21] Bible books use various literary techniques to present historical situations. Many recent Bible scholars insist on identifying the general genre of a Bible book. James M. Efird said about genre study, "Naturally, much merit can be found in such an approach, for it is obviously true that these books are literary creations, wholistic units, and should be understood as such when interpreted."[22] This study of literary characteristics avoids the pitfalls of prooftexting, a method which often looks only at bits and pieces of the material.

A literary approach to Scripture also avoids the existentialist approach, which only accepts as valid those passages which speak "to me." Understanding how a particular literary form emerged and was used, the intentions of persons who wrote in these forms, and the message conveyed by the literary form help the expositor discover the intent and meaning of the Bible book. Sermons from Bible books will be influenced not only in content but also in form by what the text says and how the text's literary form says it. Therefore, the general literary characteristic of a Bible book needs to be taken into account in preparing sermons from the book. After identifying the general genre and its particular qualities, the complete

---

21. Thomas G. Long, *Preaching and the Literary Forms of the Bible* (Philadelphia: Fortress Press, 1989), 23.

22. James M. Efird, *How to Interpret the Bible* (Atlanta: John Knox Press, 1984), 8.

picture of the historical situations of the Bible book can be put together.

Each Bible book is a historical document. It must be understood historically, which means in terms of its own time, place, and culture. In re-creating the historical situation a preacher tries to answer basic questions:

- Who wrote this book?
- To whom was this book written?
- When was the book written?
- From where was the book written?
- What literary genre did the book follow?

Careful historical investigation places the Bible book in its own cultural, religious, political, and literary environment and helps clarify original intent of the message. The words of a Bible book came to its audience addressed to the audience's situation. By uncovering that specific historical situation, expositors can see what God's Word said and is still saying today.

Techniques of Historical and Literary Study

Seeking to understand the life situations of a Bible book involves both devotional and scientific studies. Through the years the Bible has proved to be a word from beyond to be encountered and an object on earth to be studied. The expositor should allow each book in the Bible to be an object to be studied scientifically and a subject to be encountered devotionally. Truth will be encountered either by simple, Spirit-directed reading or by disciplined academic study of Scripture known as "biblical criticism." The expositor should not choose only one but both the devotional and critical study of a Bible book. Some areas of biblical criticism help an expositor with some insights into the life situations of the Bible book.

Historical Criticism

Sometimes the term *historical criticism* is used as a synonym for the whole field of biblical criticism.[23] Yet in most cases the term *historical criticism* refers to the field of scientific biblical research which

---

23. R. N. Soulen, *Handbook of Biblical Criticism*, 2d ed. (Atlanta: John Knox Press, 1981), 78.

seeks to investigate the historical context of a text, establish its date, and determine the circumstances surrounding the writing of the text.[24] Historical criticism takes seriously the idea that God has shaped the people in history and that he has formed the Bible through a historical process. Any book in Scripture can be studied in the light of scientific historical evidence.

In historical criticism an expositor needs to know the identity of the writer, when and where the author wrote the book, to whom it was written, and the reason or reasons for its composition. The expositor needs to know how the words came to be recorded, handed down through the centuries, and finally placed in the Bible. Answers to these inquiries come by scientific examination of internal evidences from the Bible book and from external comments of various writers about the book.

Historical criticism developed for two reasons. First, historical criticism casts light on the meaning of the text. This helps to determine more precisely the nature of the text and the truths in it. Meanings of various statements within a Bible book become apparent when they are placed in their historical context. For example, without seeking to understand scientifically the religious, political, and cultural contexts of Revelation, an expositor cannot get in position to understand the problems being addressed by the author. Failure to grasp these matters can lead to fanciful, humanistic speculation without the necessary historical, objective checks and balances provided by the background of Revelation. According to G. B. Caird, missing these checks and balances may lead an interpreter to "penetrate to a meaning more ultimate than the ones the writer intended."[25] Mixtures of historical matters may be used to illumine the meaning which the author intended to be grasped by the original readers.

Second, historical criticism substantiates the historical accuracy of what purports to be a historical account. The method of substantiation consists of applying historical science to Bible study. This process consists of the careful scrutiny of a Bible book and of comparisons with other sources that might shed light on it. Good historians possess a reasonable knowledge of all the sources which might

---

24. Ibid.
25. G. B. Caird, *The Language and Imagery of the Bible* (Philadelphia: Westminster Press, 1980), 1.

be relevant. To substantiate a text's reliability means to probe into what is historically probable and to form a historical hypothesis which coincides with the sources. Too often the sources are fragmentary and opaque; too often the original events are too complex for any source to reproduce them fully; too often several reconstructions of what happened are possible. Nonetheless, an expositor can use historical criticism to substantiate historical accuracy in the text. For example, years ago Sir William M. Ramsey began research in the Book of Acts with the assumption that Acts was a second-century document. The archaeological evidence he investigated led him to the verdict that Luke was a first-class, first-century historian. Ramsey devoted his life to research to find confirmatory evidence for the historical truth in Bible books.[26]

Form Criticism

Research into the historical life situations leads naturally to form criticism. Such a scientific study of Scripture presses beyond the book itself to the situation or conditions in the religious community that gave rise to the written text. This discipline is more concerned with the text's oral history rather than its literary characteristics. Biblical scholars in recent years have given increasing attention to the period of oral tradition—the period between the event and its final literary appearance in the written text. Form criticism attempts to classify the various Bible books according to their literary genre and to analyze the smaller units of material according to the "form" or "shape" they possessed during the oral period. The form critic seeks to identify those various conditions that gave rise to the use of certain concepts. This careful study of the *Sitz im Leben* (life situation) of the text helps critics appreciate how the concept conveyed in the text related to the life situation of the religious community. Form critics ask how a passage came to be formed in a certain way. They seek to learn about these historical conditions which produced the form.

Psalms was one of the first books to be analyzed from a form-critical perspective. The Psalms were classified into distinct literary groups: laments (personal and community), thanksgivings (personal

---

26. I. Howard Marshall, "Historical Criticism" in *New Testament Interpretation: Essays on Principles and Methods* (Grand Rapids: William B. Eerdmans, 1977), 126–27.

and community), and hymns. Other groupings were also recognized. In each type of psalm were clearly defined patterns of content, mood, and structure. The psalms have come to be associated with many "life settings" in the community and worship of Israel. In the psalms we can see how form critics connect the literary, historical, and sociological dimensions.[27]

Many of the New Testament writings have been investigated from the form-critical perspective. First, the Gospels were studied from this perspective, and later the Letters. Investigation of the Gospels uncovered miracle stories, parables, birth narratives, and many other blocks of material. The Epistles also revealed a wide variety of smaller genres such as hymns, prayers, and speeches. The faith and life of the early church became visible in an unprecedented fashion. The great contribution of form criticism has been to make Bible students aware that a message is shaped by its hearers and its authors. Students have realized that there is much more to the question of how a Bible book came into existence than simply asking who wrote it. Applying form criticism helps relate the passage to the life setting that gave it birth.

Redaction Criticism

Another scientific study of a Bible book related to its life situation is called redaction criticism. This method of study "seeks to lay bare the theological perspectives of a biblical writer by analyzing the writer's editorial (redactional) and compositional techniques and interpretations, unshaping and framing the written and/or oral traditions at hand."[28]

Form criticism sometimes leaves Bible students with the impression that the writer of a Bible book was little more than an editor who collected sources and put them together. Redaction critics recognize that the author had a more active role and a more intense interest in collecting and shaping the material. Redaction criticism seeks to identify the author's theological purpose for selecting materials and resources.

Bible books have at least three life situations. First is the setting of when the events happened in the book. Second is the setting of

---

27. John H. Hayes and Carl R. Holladay, *Biblical Exegesis: A Beginner's Handbook* (Atlanta: John Knox Press, 1982), 78.

28. Soulen, 165.

the oral transmission of the events. The third setting is the author's understanding and environment at the time of writing. Redaction critics look carefully at the third setting. They look carefully for editorial comments of the author, summaries at the end of sections, and more specifically, the materials selected.

—⁂——⁂——⁂——⁂——⁂—

Critical studies exist to help people understand and proclaim the Bible with confidence. Historical criticism, form criticism, and redaction criticism do not represent attempts to discredit or to destroy the Bible. Instead, these critical disciplines, which relate to a text's life situation, help illuminate and substantiate truths in the text. All of these disciplines have the common purpose of trying to understand a Bible book or a text in the light of its own time and in relation to its place in history, literature, and tradition.

Preaching a series of sermons from a Bible book begins with the tedious task of examining background data. The expositor needs to prepare a background paper in order to understand as much as possible about the book's author, date, readers, occasion, purpose, and literary genre. This study should result in some type of narrative about the book's beginning. The narrative can be embellished with subjects of geographical, political, social, and theological interest. Throughout the process of preparing a background paper, an expositor needs to consider such scientific studies as historical, form, and redaction criticisms. The academic disciplines of the background data or paper might not produce sermons directly, but they can produce a "big top" under which texts can be studied. Hopefully these disciplines can keep sermons from Bible books from being "side shows." Knowing the life situation of the Bible book provides a narrative, or story, from which all other texts and stories in the book need to fit.

The Analysis of a Bible Book

Each book in the Bible possesses its own unique content and its own distinctive arrangement of content. God uniquely inspired human authors to record a word from the Lord. These authors used human words from their own cultures and environments to communicate God's Word both in content and in form. The authors arranged the words so that readers could follow the flow. Studying how divine inspiration worked with human word selection and arrangement helps the expository preacher better know and use a Bible book. If anyone is to understand a Bible book and use it for a series of sermons, that person needs to learn as much as possible about how the author arranged the contents.

Learning about the arrangement or the outline of a Bible book involves a homiletical discipline known as the analysis. An analysis may be defined as the art of resolving a Bible book into its constituent elements or compound parts. It involves a detailed consideration of the separate parts of a Bible book and their relationship to each other. The analysis may be called the outline of the Bible book, the arrangement of the Bible book, the flow of the Bible book, or any other synonymous term. Whatever the term used, the purpose remains the same: to look at the various parts of the book and see how they relate to each other.

Through the years Bible students have attempted to understand and to delineate the arrangement of materials within a Bible book. From the earliest times people have sought to break down the material into small portions. Hebrew manuscripts of the Old Testament contained indications of where the major divisions of the text began and ended. Because these Old Testament selections were sometimes long, someone would make marks of some sort in the margins. Little is known about these markings in Hebrew manuscripts. They might have been added for the guidance of the reader in the synagogue to suggest points where reading might begin and end. Early manuscripts of the New Testament also marked sections. These sections were shorter than the present chapter divisions, but they were longer than the present verse divisions. Maybe the markings represent early attempts to block off units of material that contained a dominant theme.

More noticeable arrangement or analysis of Bible books came with the creation of chapters and verses. The chapter divisions are usually attributed to Stephen Langston, Archbishop of Canterbury, in England. Langston died in 1228. Cardinal Hugo, who died in 1263, used these chapter divisions in a concordance which he prepared for use with the Latin Vulgate. Chapter divisions are found in Wycliffe's version of the New Testament (1382) and in all subsequent English versions. Langston's chapter divisions proved so convenient that Jewish scholars incorporated them in their editions of Hebrew Scripture. The present-day Hebrew Old Testament has the same chapter divisions as the English Old Testament. Chapter divisions help readers locate Scripture selections and group units of thought.

Further need for dissolving material into smaller parts came with the dividing of chapters in Bible books into verses. Many authorities hold that the verse divisions for the Old Testament were devised by a person known as Rabbi Nathan in 1448. A Greek New Testament, which was published in 1551 by Robert Stephanus, a printer in Paris, contains the same verse divisions and numbers which we now have in the New Testament. Stephanus' Latin version of Old and New Testaments published in 1551 was the first complete Bible to contain the verse arrangements currently in English versions. The first English Bible to contain the verses proposed by Stephanus was the Geneva Bible, published in 1560. Since then, all English Bibles have contained the same configuration of verses.

Even after dividing Bible books into chapters and verses, other attempts have been made for additional analysis. Some Bible translators in the twentieth century have arranged the Bible into paragraphs. The *American Standard Version* of 1901 and its revision in the *Revised Standard Version* (1946, 1952) and *New Revised Standard Version* (1990) divide most Bible books into paragraphs. Other recent translations such as the *New English Bible* (1970 and 1989), *New International Version* (1978), and *New American Standard Bible* (1977) divide most Bible books into paragraphs. The *New International Version, New American Standard Bible*, and *New English Bible* translators modified the paragraphs in the *American Standard* of 1901 and the other two revised versions, and added headings to the main sections where the paragraphs begin. Paragraph designations help all readers, especially preachers seeking the parameters of texts. Andrew Blackwood explains, "In preaching from the Bible the most frequent unit is the paragraph."[1] The paragraph helps the potential expositor see a Bible book's content in parts.

Further help in analysis other than chapters, verses, and paragraphs comes at the point of dividing poetical material into poetical lines and separate stanzas. Translators of the *New International Version, New American Standard Bible*, and *New English Bible* designate poetical passages with indented lines and spaces between stanzas or strophes. The stanzas or strophes resemble paragraph divisions. The designation of biblical poetry helps the expositor not only to observe different kinds of material but to help analyze any Bible book containing poetry. These various attempts at breaking Bible

---

1. Andrew W. Blackwood, *Preaching from the Bible* (Nashville: Abingdon Press, 1941), 94.

books into parts such as chapters, verses, paragraphs, poetical lines, and strophes serve as resources for the expositor's analysis of the book.

The effective expositor must understand the flow of the Bible book from beginning to end. Each book which is being prepared for a series of sermons needs to be seen in its totality and in its individual parts. Ordinarily, the discipline of analyzing a Bible comes alongside and after the discipline of background study. Studying background matters usually furnishes insight into why and how the author arranged the content as well as the reasoning behind the genre used. Background study leads to analysis. Later, one will observe how analysis leads to exegetical study and homiletical plotting, and how exegesis leads to interpretation and to individual sermon building. Actually, the disciplines suggested for preaching from a Bible book do not represent sequential steps as much as the confluence of exercises.

Few books either in biblical interpretation or in homiletics contain discussions about analyzing a book in the Bible. Writers in the area of biblical studies treat genre types, literary forms, grammar, syntactical arrangements, and structure or form. But little help comes from Bible scholars about how to make an outline of a Bible book. Most Bible commentaries contain some sort of outline, but there is no help on the technique of making an outline. Writers in the area of homiletics occasionally mention the necessity of knowing the arrangements of a Bible book, but here again no help comes with the art of analyzing a book. This chapter attempts to offer some practical discussions on the matter of making an analysis of a Bible book.

Reasons for Analyzing the Bible Book

Analyzing a Bible book analysis is not busywork. This section points out some of the most important reasons why the expositor should carefully engage in this analysis.

Reason #1: To Gain a Perspective of the Book

Making an outline of a Bible book before the series of sermons begins helps to give perspective. Have you ever heard the expression, "He can't see the forest for the trees"? He cannot see the general outline of the group of trees because he is too focused on individual trees. Unfortunately, some expository preachers try to look at a Bible passage with a microscope before they look at it with a telescope. Such a procedure leads to a failure to see how the passage fits into the total content and arrangement of the book. Getting a telescopic view of a Bible book helps prepare for the detailed, microscopic investigation. Expositors can look so pointedly and specifically at a part of a Bible book that they cannot see the view of the whole and the relationship of the part to the whole. In the haste to preach a series of sermons, texts within the book could be chosen and the series started without seeing how these texts fit into the general plan of the book. Failing to take time to look at the book's overall arrangement could lead to frustration soon after the series begins as well as to ambiguity about how the texts and sermons relate to the overall structure of the book.

Reason #2: To Guide in Exegeting the Book

Preparing an analysis of a Bible book helps the expositor get ready for the exercise of exegesis. Having an analysis or a telescopic view of a book serves as a guide for making a microscopic examination of a book. To preach a series of sermons from a Bible book involves serious exegesis of each text within the book. The analysis affects how the exegesis needs to be accomplished; thus the discipline of analysis precedes the task of exegesis.

Preparing an analysis means to furnish a guide for the tedious task of exegesis. Having an outline or analysis is like having a map which serves as a guide for exegetical travels through the text. Performing an exegesis involves complicated investigation into the etymology of words, usage of words, context, syntactical relationships, and other exegetical involvements. None of these studies need to be separated from the whole. The analysis serves as a map, a means of organizing all of the exegetical endeavors. Without having some sense of organization the exegesis might be hard to comprehend. The exegesis follows the direction of the analysis, and exegetical matters are viewed in relationship to the flow of the book.

Most Bible commentaries follow an outline. The expository preacher needs to follow much the same kind of practice. The analysis needs to serve as the guide for exegesis. Actually, the analysis can be used as a private exegetical guide for the preacher, and it can also be used as a visual aid for a teaching experience of the Bible book. Some expository preachers such as Charles R. Swindoll give their audiences an outline of the Bible book so their hearers will have an overall picture and can follow the preacher as sermons come weekly from the book. The analysis can be a guide for exegesis as well as a visual aid for audiences.

Reason #3: To Help Plot Texts and Topics

An analysis not only helps in giving a perspective of a Bible book and in furnishing a guide for exegesis, but it also helps the preacher to plot the direction of a series of sermons. In looking at an analysis, one sees a Bible book divided into parts. Having an analysis enables an expositor to observe the parameters of many texts within the book. Seeing the outline of a Bible book will furnish a guide for choosing texts for the series. Usually the analysis will help to determine how many texts and topics will be used in the series. The analysis can also help to determine whether the series of sermons will be consecutive or selective with texts and topics. The analysis helps to determine what texts and topics will be included and what texts and topics will be omitted.

Effective preaching of a series of sermons from a Bible book depends greatly on preliminary preparation. Both background data and an analysis of the book are necessities. Background helps to get to the book, and analysis helps to get through the book. Careful consideration needs to be given to the discipline of analyzing a Bible book. While the analysis is being done, all of the profits may not be seen immediately, but ultimately an analysis will prove to be enormously valuable. The expositor with an outline of the book will have an overall view of the book, a guide for exegesis, and a periscope for selecting texts and topics.

Special Types of Bible Books

The Bible is a large and complex work; it is a collection of smaller individual works. Actually the word *Bible* means "little books" and hints at what is a fact, namely, that the Bible is a library of Hebrew-Christian writings that has been produced under the inspiration of God by numerous writers over a span of hundreds of years. The expositor knows that the Bible is a collection of different works with various literary types but seeks to treat each literary type distinctly.

Although the Bible contains a collection of diverse works, it must also be regarded as a unified whole. There is unity of national authorship: every book except Luke and Acts is written by a Jew.

There is a unity of subject matter: God's dealings with his people is the theme of the whole Bible. There is a unity of worldview and general theological outlook from book to book. The unifying purpose of the Bible is to reveal God to people so they might know how to order their lives.

While keeping the unity amid diversity in mind, the expositor needs to recognize the Bible's diverse literary forms. Knowing the chosen text's literary form will help with the theological interpretation and with the practical application. The kind of literary form a Bible book takes determines to a great extent how the book will be analyzed. Because each genre or literary type has its distinctive features, each one will have its own procedures for analysis. Generally speaking, three broad categories of literature affect the manner of analyzing a book. These categories are sequential books, collection books, and epistolary books. The diversity of these books requires different approaches in making an analysis.

Sequential Books

Narratives and discourses make up a series having continuity, connection, and uniformity. The sequential books possess single or diverse literary types that are generally united by a predominant theme. The Bible contains many books which are characterized by a type of literature known as *narrative*. If a Bible book is comprised largely of narration, the method of outlining the book will be to follow the sequence of the events in the narrative. For example, over 40 percent of the Old Testament is narrative.[2] Since the Old Testament constitutes three-fourths of the Bible, it is not surprising that the single most common type of literature is narrative. The following Old Testament books are largely or entirely composed of narration: Genesis, Joshua, Judges, Ruth, Samuel, Kings, Chronicles, Ezra, Nehemiah, Esther, Daniel, and Jonah. Also, Exodus, Numbers, Jeremiah, Ezekiel, and Isaiah contain substantial narrative portions. In the New Testament, the Gospels are predominantly narrative and all of the Book of Acts contain narration.

Anyone who studies the historical-narrative units of Scripture needs to recognize the purpose of the narration. The history was written interpretively, giving the readers a theological perspective,

---

2. Leland Ryken, *How to Read the Bible as Literature* (Grand Rapids: Zondervan Publishing House, 1984), 35.

and they represent the author's witness to a faith in God. The sequential-historical or narrative books contain much theological information. They tell the reader what God is like, about his purposes in the world, and about the responses which God expects from his creatures. The reader who studies God's involvement in history encounters God in a real and personal sense. The Christian faith is not based on a system of thought or upon a writer's dreams or visions; it is based on historical happenings. The genre of theological narration builds on three basic ingredients: setting, character, and plot. Reading, studying, and analyzing narrative books involves paying close attention to the interaction of those three elements.[3] This distinctive of theological narrative sets the Bible apart from other religious writings.

Making an analysis of sequential books is an easy way to outline. It means to follow the flow of the narrative. For example, think about doing an analysis of Genesis. Immediately, the analyzer will recognize that Genesis predominantly contains narration. Reading, studying, and observing how others outline Genesis will disclose two large divisions: the narratives of primeval history (chapters 1–11) and the narratives of patriarchal history (chapters 12–50). Closer analysis of Genesis chapters 1–11 will cause the analyzer to see creation accounts, the story of man and woman, the story of Cain and Abel, the account of the flood, the story of Babel, and the beginning of Abraham's story. Upon a careful look into Genesis chapters 12–50, the expositor can see stories centering around Abraham, Isaac, Jacob, and Joseph. Making the analysis of Genesis merely means following the order of events in the narrative. As one follows the flow of events, a predominant theme of all the material will emerge, and then specific themes for each narration within the book will become obvious.

Collection Books

Not all Bible books arrange their content sequentially. A few Bible books simply collect or assemble diverse materials. Of course many of the narrative books contain materials from different sources, but they have been arranged in a sequential fashion. The most prominent books of the collection variety include Psalms,

---

3. Leland Ryken, *Words of Life: A Literary Introduction to the New Testament* (Grand Rapids: Baker Book House, 1987), 90.

Proverbs, and the Gospels. The materials in these Bible books represent happenings and sayings in history. They have a story behind them, but various materials were collected, and they were not arranged according to any sequential narrative pattern.

The Book of Psalms is a collection of inspired Hebrew prayers and hymns. The psalms were used as worship resources when the Israelites worshiped privately or corporately. The psalms were eventually collected into five groupings called "books." There are five such books:

Book I, Psalms 1–41

Book II, Psalms 42–72

Book III, Psalms 73–89

Book IV, Psalms 90–106

Book V, Psalms 107–150

Many different types of psalms are scattered throughout the collection. Only rarely would the expositor want to make an analysis of the entire Book of Psalms. In preaching a series of sermons from Psalms, the best procedure is to make an analysis of each particular psalm selected. The psalm would be divided into its separate parts, noticing carefully how each part of the psalm fits into the overall theme of the particular psalm.

The Book of Proverbs also fits into a literary category of collection materials. Proverbs contains collections of material from the wisdom of Israel. The proverbs or sayings grew out of the religious and daily life of the Israelites. The proverbs were used as wisdom sayings for the various dimensions of living. Many of these proverbs were collected in a literary book known as the Book of Proverbs. People could use these rules, regulations, and maxims to help them live responsible lives. As far as arrangement of material goes, there are some clusters of proverbs on a single subject. There is a coherent section in chapters 1–9 of instructions unified by a common theme of wisdom. Yet beyond this section the material is miscellaneous, and the unity is virtually nonexistent. So, any attempt to make a sequential analysis of the Book of Proverbs would not be easy. Probably the best way to make an outline of Proverbs would be to group the proverbs under general topics. It is relatively easy to arrange the Book of Proverbs into topics such as wisdom, work, money, marriage, and parenting.

The four Gospels also fall into the collection category. It is generally claimed that the Gospels represent a unique literary form, and there is no model with which they can be adequately compared. The Gospels combine historical narrative, dialogue, oration, address, sayings, proverbs, teaching sections, and other nuances of genre. The Gospels are loosely chronological. The general pattern consists of a movement from Jesus' birth to his resurrection. Within the general chronological framework, the individual Gospel writers arranged their material to fit their specific thematic and narrative purpose. Making an outline of an entire Gospel may be much easier than outlining Psalms or Proverbs, for there is a general chronological pattern in the background of the collection of material. In analyzing a Gospel, the expositor keeps in mind the general chronology of Jesus' life and ministry, fits the encounters, miracles, parables, and teachings into the chronology of Jesus' life as well as the theme and purpose of the Gospel writer. An analysis of a Gospel will be arranged according to sequence and theme.

The Book of James is another collection. Martin Dibelius characterizes the work as a paraenesis which represents a collection of ethical maxims and exhortations which cannot be related to a single Christian community or a unified Christian situation.[4] Paraenetic literature set ethical maxims on a variety of subjects side by side without emphasis on their mutual relationship. Paraenetic literature is difficult to outline in a manner which demonstrates sequential development of thought. Probably the best way to analyze the Book of James would be to identify the topics within the book and then to divide the subject section into parts.

Epistolary Books

About four-fifths of the New Testament books use the epistolary form. The epistolary form is generally conceded to be present when one or more of the following features is present: a formula of greeting, the name of the sender, the identity of the recipient, a thanksgiving to God, and a personal greeting at the close of the document. New Testament Epistles follow the broad outline of their Hellenistic counterparts. All these Epistles convey information and maintain personal acquaintances. New Testament Epistles,

---

4. Martin Dibelius, *James: A Commentary on the Epistle of James*, rev. Heinrich Grieven and trans. Michael A. Williams (Philadelphia: Fortress Press, 1976), 3.

however, have a special content: a word from God to individuals and churches.

Within the broad category of epistolary books, a distinction can be made between an epistle and a letter. Both utilize the same general format, but an epistle is less confidential in tone and directed to a wider circle of readers. The difference can be illustrated by comparing Romans with Philemon. The forms are similar, but tone and content make it clear that the Epistle to the Romans is intended for a wide circle of readers while the Letter to Philemon is more like a private correspondence. Although a rigid distinction cannot be drawn between the categories of letter and epistle, there are useful designations for indicating one aspect of literary character. From this perspective, Ephesians and Romans seem to be more epistolary than 1 Corinthians, which discusses specific problems of a particular Christian community. The Corinthian correspondence stands closer to the category of a letter than an epistle.

The epistolary form requires different activities for making an analysis than narrative or collection books. The flow of a letter or epistle is generally topical and logical. It needs to be real and studied as a literary whole. An epistle is best outlined by topics, noting how one argument or idea leads logically to the next thought. Gordon Fee and Douglas Stuart advise the expositor to "think paragraphs" when reading, studying, or outlining a New Testament epistle.[5] The New Testament epistle or letter follows the normal form of salutation, body, and conclusion. When the forms have been identified, the readers need to observe how the writers incorporated small literary genres into overall letter form. So, the art of analyzing an epistle involves seeing the general structure of salutation, body, and conclusion; "thinking paragraphs" within the body; and being sensitive to various literary patterns within the book.

The main determinant for analyzing a Bible book involves identifying the particular literary characteristic. The way the author patterned the book definitely affects the way it is outlined. Because many books follow a sequential pattern, the best procedure for analysis is to pursue the continuity, connection, and the uniformity of the events as they are presented. Outlining the collection books involves looking at sections of books such as Psalms, Proverbs, and

---

5. Gordon Fee and Douglas Stuart, *How to Read the Bible for All Its Worth: A Guide to Understanding the Bible* (Grand Rapids: Baker Book House, 1979), 22.

the Gospels. While one may analyze all of Proverbs and one of the Gospels, the entire Book of Psalms would not be analyzed. The twenty-one epistolary books of the New Testament represent relatively easy books to outline, for they are generally structured with a common form, possessed with paragraphs, and contain a predominant theme or purpose repeated throughout the book.

Procedures for Making an Analysis

Just having resources and knowing theories will not make an analysis. Learning how to use resources and to actualize theories is what really matters. While a person who desires to preach a series of sermons from a Bible book learns concepts about reasons for analysis, determinants of analysis, and resources for analysis, perhaps more insight is needed in practical suggestions about how to make an analysis of a Bible book. The books which give directions about how to preach from a Bible book are few, and hardly any homiletics books mention the necessity of making an outline of the entire book before doing a series on it. Consequently, expositors find little help in making an outline for themselves on a Bible book. Three procedures may be used in creating an analysis.

Reading the Book Again and Again

Talk abounds about how to study a Bible book, but little is said about reading it. Elton Trueblood, a renowned Quaker scholar, urged students of Scripture to spend lots of time reading the Bible before plunging into technical study or sermon preparation. Preachers often begin sermon preparation with the study of the text before reading the text to see what it has to say.[6] Study of the commentaries might precede the conscientious reading to "hear the book." Intensive, in-depth Bible study profits greatly, but Bible study begins with Bible reading. The technical and sermonic study of texts will be enhanced and buttressed by repeated readings of the book. Analysis begins with the words of the book itself and then proceeds to the commentaries and other study aids.

Scripture reading requires discipline. Bible reading is an art, just like Bible study. Effective reading engages the reader's mind with the author's mind. Reading Scriptures means much more than reading

---

6. Quoted in a chapel service by Elton Trueblood at New Orleans Baptist Theological Seminary (n.d.).

a classic or contemporary novel. Reading the Bible means hearing what God spoke to ancient readers and what God is saying to contemporary readers. The same Holy Spirit who inspired the original writing helps us read today. To read the Bible means much more than normal observation of words for information. It means to read with disciplined concentration, contemplation, reflection, motivation, and inspiration. As you read a Bible book, concentrate on the words. Try to put everything out of your mind except the words and the thoughts behind the words from Scripture. With the mind focused on the biblical text, think about what is being said. In reading the book, the thought of the biblical writer could emerge, as well as the way the author organized the thoughts could become obvious. Repeated readings could help to crystallize these thoughts along with the manner in which they were presented.

As you read a Bible book, pause often to think and reflect upon what has been said. Disciplined, contemplative reading will help you understand Bible truths. Remember that the Holy Spirit will lead you into truths and discernible patterns of the text. Because the same Holy Spirit inspired original authors, the readers who seek the direction of the Spirit will be enlightened in a mystical manner. Contemplative and Spirit-illumined reading of a Bible book will require disciplined dedication. Such readings are not automatic, nor are they effortless. Working on reading a Bible book with the Spirit's direction and with careful, disciplined listening will be a great beginning for a creative analysis.

Read the book from many translations. Perhaps the best practice is to adopt one translation as a primary text and to use other translations to compare with the adopted text. Choosing one primary translation means that more of the repeated readings will come from it. You might adopt the *New American Standard Bible* as the dominant translation. You would read and reread the Bible book from this translation. Probably no less than twelve readings would suffice. Then other translations could be used to compare with the *New American Standard Bible*. Reading from one dominant translation repeatedly leads to a thorough familiarity with the book. It could even lead to memorization of many verses within the book. Repeated readings of one translation help also to grasp content and to observe structural designs.

Many expositors acknowledge the importance of reading the book several times before beginning the series. G. Campbell

Morgan was the minister of Westminster Chapel in London for twenty-two years. In preparing for a series, Morgan read through the selected book forty to fifty times. These repeated readings helped Morgan to discern the flow of the book, to dissect the book into its parts, and to muster the contents of the work.[7]

Don't skip over the admonition to read the book repeatedly. Begin the analysis with contemplative reading and rereading. Reading the Bible book many times helps us digest the work and allow it to become a part of our intellectual and spiritual digestive system. Maybe most contemporary expositors will not read a Bible book through fifty times, but think about reading it through at least twelve times in a primary translation and ten times in other translations. Repeated readings of the Bible book involve the first and primary procedure for making an analysis. These readings beget other procedures.

Examining the Book's Literary Characteristics

Analyzing a Bible book is not a logical, sequential process that follows step one, step two, and step three. It is more dynamic than methodical. Instead, analysis arises from repeated readings and resultant observations from the readings. While careful and continuous readings take place, literary patterns become obvious. Books in Scripture fit into genre categories and possess their own literary characteristics. These literary qualities need to be observed carefully for the analysis to take shape. To help with the practical procedure of observing literary distinctives, consideration will be given briefly to the general genre of the book and then to specific literary characteristics within the general genre.

Consider briefly the general genre of a Bible book. Each book in the Bible fits into a broad type of literary distinctive or genre. Bible scholars usually identify the basic literary types to be historical-theological narration, poetry, wisdom books, prophetic books, Gospels, epistles, and apocalyptic. Identifying the general genre determines how the analysis will be made.

The Book of 1 Samuel fits into the general category of historical-theological narration. It would be outlined as most books in this category in a sequential fashion. The readers would follow the flow

---

7. Faris D. Whitesell, *Power in Expository Preaching* (Old Tappan, N.J.: Fleming H. Revell Co., 1967), 20.

of the inspired author. The Book of Proverbs would be outlined around subjects because the literary form fits the style of a collection of material on timely topics. Then the Letter of Romans would be analyzed differently from 1 Samuel and Proverbs. Romans fits into the genre of an epistle or letter, and the reader would need to follow the thought patterns of the author where one could gain insight into the content and form of Romans. The kind of genre affects how a Bible book will be analyzed; therefore review carefully the matter of literary characteristics.

Also, while reading a Bible book the expositor needs to become sensitive to specific genre qualities within the book. Every literary genre has distinctive literary features through which the message is written, and it achieves its effect on readers or hearers. Thus, after identifying the general genre, the expositor should examine particular literary features and isolate elements by which to understand these matters. For the expositor who wants to make an analysis of a Bible book, at last four literary qualities need to be anticipated: repetition, syntax, parallelism, and narrative patterns. Of course, no one should assume that these types exhaust the subjects of literary qualities within Bible books. These literary qualities have been selected from many other choices for the purpose of illustrating how literary patterns affect the way a book is outlined.

Repetition of words, phrases, and sentences throughout the book should alert readers to the importance of content and to manners of design. For example, if one is preparing to preach a series of sermons from Genesis, continuous readings will disclose many repetitious sentences, one of which is "these are the generations." Eleven times and at strategic places throughout the book these sentences appear (2:4; 5:1; 6:9; 10:1; 11:10, 27; 25:12, 19; 36:1, 9; 37:2).[8] More than likely, these repetitious expressions help to divide the Book of Genesis into parts. Some Old Testament scholars build outlines of the entire Book of Genesis from these repeated sentences.

Frequently used words and phrases help with the understanding of the message of a book as well as discerning the pattern of the book. Even casual readers of 1 John will notice the frequent use of key words such as *abide, light, righteous,* and *love.* Some scholars outline

---

8. Derek Kidner, *Genesis: An Introduction and Commentary* in Tyndale Old Testament Commentaries (Downers Grove, Ill.: 1967), 59.

1 John around three words: light, righteous, and love. Robert Law in his study *The Tests of Life* divided 1 John into five sections: an introduction, a section on light, a section on righteous, a section on love, and a conclusion. Law's analysis was based on repetitious use of words in 1 John.[9] While reading repeatedly a Bible book and thinking about preparing an analysis, the expositor should look carefully for frequently used words, phrases, and sentences.

Syntax is another important factor in analyzing a Bible book. Syntax is the sentence structure within the book. While the readings of a book take place, some prominent questions need to be asked: What are the main clauses and the subordinate clauses? What are the modifiers? What are the parts of speech and their relationship with each other? Merrill Tenney showed the importance of syntax in outlining Galatians.[10] Tenney encouraged the expositor to list main clauses; then under these main clauses, he listed subordinate clauses and modifying phrases. Walter Liefeld followed Tenney's method in analyzing Colossians 1:15–20. He uses the syntactical arrangement of main clauses and subordinate clauses.

1:15 He is the image of the invisible God, the firstborn of all creation.

1:16 For by him all things were created: things in heaven (etc.) . . .

1:17 He is before all things and in him all things hold together.

1:18 And he is the head of the body, the church; he is the beginning the firstborn from among the dead, so that in everything he might have the supremacy.

For God was pleased to have all his fullness dwell in him, and through him to reconcile. . .all things. . . . [11]

In the Scripture passage there are several affirmations about Christ expressed primarily in main clauses. The large section of the analysis could come from three main clauses that depict Christ's relation to God, to the universe, and to the church. The syntactical

---

9. Robert Law, *The Tests of Life: A Study of the First Epistle of St. John* (Grand Rapids: Baker Book House, 1968).

10. Merril C. Tenney, *Galatians: The Charter of Christian Liberty*, rev. and enl. ed. (Grand Rapids: William B. Eerdmans, 1950), 165–85.

11. Walter Liefeld, *From Text to Sermon: New Testament Exposition* (Grand Rapids: Zondervan Publishing House, 1984), 47.

arrangement of main and subordinate clauses helps the reader to discern the form and context of the text.

Studying syntax within a book often yields analytical insights. Identifying parts of speech and their relationship with each other can denote changes in thought patterns. Coordinating conjunctions such as *and, but, therefore, moreover,* and *however* indicate changes in subjects. Also, subordinating conjunctions such as *because, although, whether, since, which, when, until,* and *where* could lend a clue to transitions of thought. Many other observations of words and their relationship to each other will help the preacher see the flow or direction of an author's thought.

In addition to repetition and syntax, the literary trait of *parallelism* needs to be noticed. Many different kinds of parallels exist. Readers of a Bible book need to notice where lines within a book have similarity, comparison, or antithesis with other lines. Peter Rhea Jones analyzed 1 John with fifteen notations of antithetical parallels. Studying these parallels led to the analysis of the entire book. Jones detected four patterns of parallels: "if we say" (1:5–10); "the one saying" (2:4–11); "everyone who" (2:23–3:12; 4:7–11); and "the one" (4:12–5:12). He arranged most of the analysis of 1 John on the basis of these parallels. [12]

The Bible contains numerous parallel constructions, especially in the Book of Psalms, in the Prophets, and in the Gospels. Psalm 1, for example, revolves around the contract of the righteous person (1:1–3) with the ungodly person (1:4–6). This contrasting pattern may also be seen in Romans 5:12–19 where Adam and Christ are contrasted. Also, Galatians 5:19–26 contains the contrast of the works of the flesh and the fruit of the Spirit. While reading Bible books, expositors need to pay close attention to synonymous and antithetical parallel expressions.

The biblical culture had different ways of telling stories. The study of narrative patterns in biblical genre may be too technical for this work, but some awareness needs to be cultivated of certain conventional patterns followed in narration. Only a few examples will help with the analytical process with narration. Perhaps the primary pattern which needs to be observed would be the normal sequential flow of events. For example, if an analysis of Genesis was

---

12. Peter Rhea Jones, "A Structural Analysis of I John," *Review and Expositor,* 67, no. 4. (fall, 1970): 440–44.

being made, chapters 12–50 could be outlined around Abraham (12:1–25:18), Jacob (25:19–36:43), and Joseph (37:1–50:26). Then attention could be focused on the series of smaller stories within the larger stories. There are many smaller stories contained in the larger stories of Abraham, Jacob, and Joseph. Then, after getting the sequential patterns of narration, a helpful exercise would be *discourse evaluation* which is the study of the conversations of characters within the narration. The patterns of conversation comprise a vital part of the inspired text; they help one understand the dynamics of the circumstances and the theological and personal issues involved.

In addition to following the sequential flow of the narration and studying conversations of characters, the expositor might need to become aware of *structural analysis.* Structural critics contend that human consciousness expresses itself in only a few basic patterns or structures. These patterns underlie written forms of expressions much as the floor plans of a house underlie its construction.[13] Structural study seeks to show how and why a text moves from one place to another. As a way of conducting structural analysis, Ronald J. Allen suggests the following formula:

1. Note the situation at the beginning of the text.

2. Note the situation at the end of the text.

3. Note the transformation that takes place as the text moves from beginning to end.[14]

Numerous other literary qualities within a Bible book exist. Scholarly works on word studies, form criticism, structuralism, and other genre studies would help with the analysis of a book. The expositor is not seeking to engage solely in literary analysis. Instead, the expositor seeks to identify the general genre of the book and to recognize some specific literary qualities within each genre. With repeated readings taking place and literary qualities under observation, the expositor can use the procedures as a process in making an analysis of a book.

---

13. Ronald J. Allen, *Contemporary Biblical Interpretation for Preaching* (Valley Forge, Pa.: Judson Press, 1984), 71–81.

14. Ibid., 77.

Dividing the Book into Parts

All the procedures discussed should lead to a practical analysis of a Bible book. This analysis will attempt to get an overview of the book, a guide for an exegesis, and a plot plan for a series of sermons. Three primary analytical procedures are general overview, specific resolution, and detailed division.

Step #1: Gaining an overview. A general perspective comes from repeated readings and observation of other outlines of a book. The general overview involves dividing the book into its broadest or largest parts. Let's look at the previous examples of Genesis, 1 Samuel, Galatians, and James for general overviews. The Book of Genesis falls into two large sections: the primeval history in chapters 1–11 and the patriarchal history in chapters 12–50.

The book of 1 Samuel may be arranged in a general overview around several personalities: Samuel (chaps. 1–7), Saul (chaps. 8–18), and David/Saul (chaps. 16–31). The Letter of Galatians falls into three general categories: personal insights (chaps. 1–2), theological insights (chaps. 3–4), and practical insights (chaps. 5–6). Because of the paraenetic nature of the Letter of James, fifteen subjects comprise the letter's overview:

1. The Salutation 1:1

2. Facing Trials 1:2–12

3. Confronting Temptations 1:13–18

4. Living the Word 1:19–27

5. Treating People Fairly 2:1–13

6. Putting Faith to Work 2:14–26

7. Using Correct Speech 3:1–12

8. Choosing Godly Wisdom 3:13–18

9. Struggling with Selfishness 4:1–10

10. Warnings against Criticism 4:11–12

11. Planning for the Future 4:13–17

12. Cautions against Social Injustice 5:1–6

13. Waiting for the Lord's Return 5:7–12

14. Learning to Pray 5:13–18

15. Restoring Erring Believers 5:19–20

Most Bible books can be divided into major sections, and a general overview may be observed. Of course one major exception involves the Book of Psalms. In the case of Psalms, individual psalms can be put through the same procedures an expositor would put a book. A general overview of the psalm would be made; then specific breakdowns of the major divisions could be made, and finally detailed divisions of the psalm could be detected. Seeing the larger sections of the Bible book and even a psalm provides a telescopic overview. With generalities observed, specific sections of the book can then be analyzed.

Step 2: Resolving General Divisions into Specific Sections. The small sections proceed directly from the larger divisions. With the detailed resolution, the analysis of a Bible book really begins to take shape. Let's illustrate the specific sections resolved from the larger sections of Genesis, 1 Samuel, Galatians, and James. Examine the analysis of Genesis.

The Primeval History (chapters 1–11)

    A. The Story of Creation, 1:1–2:3
    B. The Nature and Fall of Man, 2:4–3:24
    C. The Life of Sin and Death, 4:1–6:8
    D. The World under Judgment, 6:9–8:14
    E. The Renewal and Repopulation of the Human Race, 8:15–10:32
    F. The Story of Babel, 11:1–9
    G. The Genealogy of Shem, 11:10–32

From the general outline of 1 Samuel, one specific resolution may be noticed.

1 Sam. 1:1–7:17

    A. The Birth of Samuel, 1:1–2:11
    B. Samuel and the House of Eli, 2:12–36
    C. The Call of Samuel, 3:1–4:1
    D. The Philistines and the Ark, 4:1–6:8
    E. The Journey of the Ark, 5:1–7:1
    F. The Ministry of Samuel, 7:2–17

More specific resolutions may be seen of the general sections of Galatians and James.

Personal Insights (Gal. 1:1–2:21)

    A. Greetings, 1:1–5

B. No Other Gospel, 1:6–10
C. God's Revelation to Paul, 1:11–17
D. Paul's First Visit to Jerusalem, 1:18–24
E. Paul's Second Visit to Jerusalem, 2:1–10
F. Confrontation with Peter, 2:11–14
G. No Justification through the Law, 2:15–21

Facing Trials (James 1:2–12)

A. The Attitudes toward Trials, 1:2a
B. The Variety of Trials, 1:2b
C. The Results of Trials, 1:3–4
D. The Need for Wisdom, 1:5–8
E. Two Specific Trials, 1:9–11
F. The Beatitudes about Understanding Trials, 1:12

Each of these examples cited illustrates how large, major divisions of a Bible book may be divided into smaller sections. With major divisions resolved into specific sections, the analysis takes on more form. But with the next analytical procedure the analysis will assume more divisions, and the process will be complete.

Step 3: Making a Detailed Analysis of the Specific Sections. Detailed division of the text becomes microscopic where every possible detail can be outlined from the smaller sections. Consideration of these detailed divisions need to be given to the way the text flows and to the manner in which the details relate to the sections. Again, the procedure will be illustrated with examples. Go back to the telescopic view of the larger sections and to the more detailed smaller sections. Then notice the detailed divisions from Genesis, 1 Samuel, Galatians, and James.

The Primeval History (Gen. chapters 1–11)

A. The Story of Creation, 1:1–23
   1. The Source of All Creation, 1:1
   2. The Condition of the Earth, 1:2
   3. The Development of Heaven and Earth, 1:3–25
      a. The Creation of Light and Darkness, 1:3–5
      b. The Creation of the Sea and Sky, 1:6–8
      c. The Creation of Land and Sea, 1:9–10
      d. The Creation of Trees and Vegetation, 1:11–13
      e. The Creation of Heavenly Bodies, 1:14–19
      f. The Creation of Creatures from the Sea and the Sky, 1:20–23

g. The Creation of Land Creatures, 1:24–25
4. The Creation of Mankind, 1:26–31
   a. The Image of God, 1:26–27
   b. The Dominion of Mankind, 1:28–30
5. The Rest from Creation, 2:1–4

1 Samuel (1 Sam. 1:1–7:7)

A. The Birth of Samuel, 1:1–2:11
   1. The Family of Samuel, 1:1–2
   2. The Barrenness of Hannah, 1:3–8
   3. The Vow of Hannah, 1:9–11
   4. The Blessing of Eli on Hannah, 1:12–18
   5. The Conception and Birth of Samuel, 1:19–20
   6. The Dedication of Samuel, 1:21–28
   7. The Prayer of Hannah, 2:1–11

Personal Insights (Gal. 1:1–2:21)

A. Greetings, 1:1–5
   1. The Author, 1:1
      a. No Apostle by Human Authorship, 1:1a
      b. An Apostle by Jesus Christ, 1:1b
   2. The Readers, 1:2
      a. The Companions with Paul, 1:2a
      b. The Churches of Galatia, 1:2b
   3. The Greeting, 1:3
   4. The Work of Christ, 1:4–5

Facing Trials (James 1:2–12)

A. The Attitude Toward Trials, 1:2a
   1. The Making of a Mind, 1:2a
   2. The Meaning of Joy, 1:2a
B. The Variety of Trials, 1:2b
   1. The Surprise of Trials, 1:2b
   2. The Various Kinds of Trials, 1:2b
C. The Results of Trials, 1:3–4
   1. The Experience of Trials, 1:3a
   2. The Result of Patience, 1:3b
   3. The Mature Christian, 1:4
D. The Need for Wisdom, 1:5–8
   1. The Lack of Wisdom, 1:5a
   2. The Request for Wisdom, 1:5b

3. The Person of Faith, 1:6–8

E. Two Specific Trials, 1:9–11

  1. The Trial of Poverty, 1:9

  2. The Trial of Riches, 1:10–11

F. The Beatitude about Understanding Trials, 1:12

  1. The Blessed Person, 1:12a

  2. The Crown of Life, 1:12b

—⁊⁊— —⁊⁊— —⁊⁊— —⁊⁊— —⁊⁊—

Analyzing a Bible book is an excellent preparation for a series of sermons. Making an analysis helps an expositor see the book from beginning to end so that sermon texts and topics can be plotted. Making an analysis moves the expository preacher on to the next process: doing an exegesis of the book. Not every book can be analyzed in the same way. Materials in the book may come as a result of collections, proceed in a sequential narrative fashion, or bear the structure of first-century letters or epistles. Actually the expositor will not find great difficulty in doing an analysis. Reading the book repeatedly and observing literary features will help get an outline in view. When the book is divided with general overviews, specific sections, and detailed divisions, the analysis will evolve. With the discipline of analysis completed, the description of exegesis can begin.

CHAPTER 6

The Exegesis of a Bible Book

Seven Complexities of Exegesis
    The Third-Party Perspective
    The Language Barrier
    Cultural Diversity
    Historical Distance
    Collective Growth
    Multiple Texts
    The Interpreter's Perspective
Exegesis and Interpretation
    Exegesis
    Hermeneutics
    Interpretation: The Interaction of Exegesis and Hermeneutics
Initial Contacts with the Text
    Selecting the Text
    Establishing Boundaries of the Text
    Translating or Paraphrasing the Text
Text and Context
    Book Context
    Sectional Context
    Immediate Context
    Parallel Contexts
Literary Factors
    Types of Biblical Literature
    Figurative Language
    Literary Forms in a Bible Book
    Figures of Speech in a Textual Unit
Word Study
Syntactical Study

Exegesis is the investigation of a text, whereby the researcher, using a variety of tools, tries to determine the author's meaning for the original readers.[1] The word *exegesis* comes from a transliterated Greek verb *exegeomai* meaning "to lead out of." The basis or root meaning is "to bring out the meaning." Exegesis seeks to bridge the centuries between the time of the text and the present.

Exegesis begins with a careful, critical examination of the text in its historical context, paying special attention to the political, cultural, religious, and philosophical milieu. It also investigates the text's language. Grammatical, syntactical, and lexical considerations figure significantly in exegesis. Therefore, the task of exegesis can be defined as a careful, critical, historical investigation of a text, where the text is examined historically, contextually, grammatically, syntactically, and lexically. The descriptive term to cover this approach is the grammatico-historical method of *exegesis*.[2]

Seven Complexities of Exegesis

Bridging the centuries between texts within a Bible book and today's context is a complex task. John H. Hayes and Carl R. Holladay, in their valuable work *Biblical Exegesis: A Beginner's Handbook*, discuss factors that make the exegesis of a biblical text complex.

Complexity #1: The Third-Party Perspective

The expositor does not know the primary or original parties in the text. The interpreter is neither the sender nor the receiver but is a third party who observes the original process. Hayes and Holladay call this *"the third-party perspective."* No Bible book was addressed to anyone in the twentieth century. Genesis was not addressed to contemporary scientists. The Psalms were composed for ancient Hebrew audiences. Paul's letters were written to believers in Galatia, Rome, Philippi, Corinth, and other people and places. The interpreter has to seek to understand the Bible book by identifying with both the original sender and receiver.[3]

---

1. A. Malherbe, "An Introduction: The Task and Method of Exegesis," *Restoration Quarterly* 5 (1961): 169–78.

2. Ian A. Fair, "Disciplines Related to Biblical Interpretation," in *Biblical Interpretation: Principles and Practice*, ed. F. Furman Kearley, Edward P. Myers, and Timothy D. Hadley (Grand Rapids: Baker Book House, 1986), 35–36.

3. John H. Hayes and Carl R. Holladay, *Biblical Exegesis: A Beginner's Handbook* (Atlanta: John Knox Press, 1982), 8–9.

Complexity #2: The Language Barrier

A second complexity in exegesis is the *language barrier.* Bible books exist in a language completely different from the exegete's language. English exegetes must acquire enough knowledge of Greek or Hebrew to read the text, or they must resort to translators who have overcome the language barrier. Since the biblical languages have their own grammatical features, vocabulary nuances, and distinctive structures, an outsider often finds acquiring the proficiency needed in these languages difficult. Translations of Bible books are interpretations, not exact transferences of thoughts from one language to another. Expositors should be grateful for translations because translations help with the language barrier, but they can never completely relate meanings. The expositor has to search constantly for language meanings, making the task of exegesis complex.[4]

Complexity #3: Cultural Diversity

Bible books written in one cultural context and explained in another pose significant problems to the interpreter. Bible books explicitly mention, describe, or allude to special ideas, practices, and customs which likely were understood clearly by the original readers but may baffle readers in subsequent cultures. Modern readers have difficulty reading Bible books for ideas, concepts, and worldviews which existed in the original readers' minds. Furthermore, authors from other cultures expressed ideas differently from the way modern readers write about concepts or events. Any expositor has difficulty living in one culture and encountering a culture of another era.[5]

Complexity #4: Historical Distance

Today's expositor is separated chronologically from yesterday's world when the Bible book was produced. Historical facts and features anchored in the ancient past have to be explained to the living present. The distance between original readers of Bible books and today's readers ranges from two thousand to three thousand years. The exegete encounters persons and places, practices and perspectives, and other matters different from today.[6]

---

4. Ibid., 9–10.
5. Ibid.
6. Ibid., 10–11.

Complexity #5: Collective Growth

Bible books often were written by more than one author or were written in more than one time period. In the ancient world some works were the product of collective growth.[7]

Complexity #6: Multiple Texts

Bible books have been copied and recopied many times as they were circulated to other readers. When these documents were copied by hand, words were often omitted, misspelled, or repeated. Consequently, several copies of Bible books existed. Unfortunately, at present no original manuscripts of Bible books exist. Expositors must become aware of these textual variants and decide what appears to be the authorial form. Copies of texts will often need to be compared to discover the most likely reading.[8]

Complexity #7: The Interpreter's Perspective

The primary purpose of any expositor is to explain as clearly as possible the author's meaning. The interpreter must represent the text, not his or her own prejudices, feelings, judgments, or concerns. To indulge in personal projection on the text means to engage in *eisegesis*, "reading into" a text what the interpreter wants it to say. *Eisegesis* is the opposite of *exegesis*. Exegesis is bringing truth of the text out of its life situation. Eisegesis is the interpreter's projection of ideas into the text. Separating one's self-imposed ideas from biblical interpretation is one of the greatest complexities of exegesis.[9]

Authentically biblical sermons allow the text to serve as the leading force in shaping content and purpose for the sermon. Leander Keck's concept of biblical preaching was that (1) the Bible governs the content of the sermon and (2) the function of the sermon is analogous to the text.[10] Speaking to the needs of people in today's world begins by listening and learning about how God addressed human needs in the biblical world. Exegesis of a Bible book produces abundant substance for sermons. What was *said* becomes the

---

7. Ibid., 11–12.

8. Ibid., 12–13.

9. Ibid., 13–14.

10. Leander E. Keck, *The Bible in the Pulpit: The Renewal of Biblical Preaching* (Nashville: Abingdon, 1978), 106.

basis for what the contemporary expositor *says*. Exegesis prevents preachers from being so relative and tends to give them more authority. Human opinions and conclusions can be checked with truth of the text. What the text *meant then* becomes the basis for what the text *means now*.

Exegesis involves one of the most important disciplines for preaching a series of sermons from a Bible book. Exegesis can be done on the entire book before the series begins, or it can be done weekly on the text for the next message. The disciplines involved in exegesis need to be studied carefully.

Exegesis and Interpretation

The words *exegesis, hermeneutics,* and *interpretation* are used to refer to biblical studies. Dialogue abounds concerning which particular term should be used to describe the search for meaning of the ancient biblical text. Some insist that the term *exegesis* should be used. James Smart in the book *The Past, Present, and Future of Biblical Theology* calls the task of understanding a text's ancient past "exegesis." Smart argues that exegesis involves a dialogue between the *then* and the *now*. On the other hand, James Sanders in an article in *The Interpreter's Dictionary of the Bible: Supplementary Volume* called the search for meaning in ancient texts "hermeneutics." This section investigates the words *exegesis, hermeneutics,* and *interpretation*.

Exegesis

Earlier in this chapter the word *exegesis* was seen to have come from the Greek verb *exegeomai* which means "to lead out of." The term *exegesis* needs to understood in concept and in the New Testament usages more than in etymology. Exegesis as a concept means to inquire what the original authors of a biblical text meant. The exegete seeks to bridge the centuries between the past and the present. The exegete must get involved with linguistics, or the study of the meaning and usages of words. The process also involves philological skills, or the process of analyzing genre forms. Exegesis includes the task of understanding biblical context and theology. No one can perform exegesis without analyzing in detail the grammar, vocabulary, and stylistic matters in a biblical text. Through the process the exegete seeks to understand what the text meant when it was written. The exegete performs the role of historian, grammarian, literary analyst, philologist, and theologian. The exegete begins at the beginning, working process by process to understand what precipitated the writing of a Bible book. The exegete strives to understand why Genesis was written, what events were taking place between Paul and the Corinthians, or what was occurring with John's readers when he wrote from Patmos. Such scientific search to see what a text meant may be called exegesis.

Exegesis is the discipline in which the interpreter searches for the historical meaning of the text. Having established this historical meaning through exegesis, the interpreter then seeks to explain the significance or application of the historical meaning to the contemporary context. The goal of exegesis is never to stop with the historical meaning of a text. No part of the Bible exists merely as a relic to be studied and admired. The Bible is a book by which God spoke and by which He continues to speak. Exegesis leads to interpretation. Exegesis generally precedes hermeneutics, and even when it does not, interpretation should proceed to exegesis. Exegesis must always precede and govern homiletics, or proclamation.

Hermeneutics

Our word *hermeneutics* is derived from the Greek word *hermeneus* which means "to translate, interpret, or explain."[11] The word is reported to have had its origin in the name Hermes, the Greek god who served as messenger for the other gods. In the technical meaning, hermeneutics is often defined as the art of interpreting a text in its meaning for contemporary audiences. Scholars who write under the rubric of hermeneutics seem more interested in the meaning of a Bible passage for people living in today's world. For many years scholars using the academic disciplines of biblical criticism studied the Bible as an object. The Bible became little more than an object under scientific investigation. Generally speaking, such studies functioned under the label of exegesis. But biblical scholarship led by Gerhard Ebeling and Ernst Fuchs discussed something they called "The New Hermeneutic."[12] One of the most prominent ideas to emerge from the rather complicated movement known as "The New Hermeneutic" is this: People do not interpret the Bible as much as the Bible interprets people.

---

11. Fair, 31.

12. See James M. Robinson and John B. Cobb, Jr., *The New Hermeneutic* (New York: Harper and Row, 1964).

Professor Merrill Abbey has applied the discussions of the new hermeneutics to Christian proclamation. In his book *The Word Interprets Us* Abbey writes, "Exegesis asks: What does the text *say?* But hermeneutics delves deeper: In the light of our whole approach to the Scriptures, what does the text mean "[13] Abbey contends that a two-way dialogue needs to take place with every text. The expositor must perform diligent exegetical-critical work, but must also examine contemporary life.[14] First the expositor exegetes; then the Bible interprets the expositor and the world around him. John Knox said that true preaching must always be one elliptical reality drawn around two foci: one in the world and one in the text. Knox said the text was first spoken to a human situation and cannot be understood unless it was approached through a life situation in which the expositor is experientially involved.[15]

Hermeneutics addresses contemporary implications of a biblical text; it involves analogy or application of the text. The expositor, while studying a text, seeks to determine what conditions or considerations in the contemporary context might be applicable to the biblical message. The meaning and significance of the historical message confronts situations which are analogous to contemporary conditions. Thus, the revelation of God and His will in the Bible is understood by exegesis and brought forward and interpreted to contemporary situations.

Interpretation: The Interaction of Exegesis and Hermeneutics

Exegesis and interpretation do not exist in unrelated, individualistic isolation from one another. Exegesis without interpretation leads to a disclosure of ancient truth without contemporary relevance. Interpretation without exegesis leads to human subjectivity about biblical texts. Discovering truth from the historical past helps us understand contemporary human needs. What value, for example, is exegetical information about how Jews traveled between Judea and Galilee by avoiding the land of Samaria? The expositor learns from the historical, exegetical study of John 4 about the disdain of the Jews for the Samaritans. But exegesis does not go far

---

13. Merrill Abbey, *The Word Interprets Us* (Nashville: Abingdon Press, 1967), 15.

14. Ibid., 20–26.

15. John Knox, *The Integrity of Preaching* (Nashville: Abingdon Press, 1957), 22.

enough. The expositor needs to relate how people in today's world disdain and avoid each other. Exegesis (studying what the text meant) exists to interpret what the text means.

Which should come first: exegesis or interpretation? The answer is either one. If exegesis of a text begins the process of Bible study, the expositor needs to see what the ancient words and events in the text meant to the original readers. Then the expositor can proceed from the exegesis to see what God is saying to people today from the text. Should interpretation, or what a text means to an expositor, come to mind as the first process of Bible study, the task of exegesis needs to come next to see that what the text means coincides with what the text meant. What a text means to a person should be compared with what the text meant to the original readers. If there is a great discrepancy between interpretation and exegesis, the idea or ideas need to be abandoned. On many occasions God illumines his Word to the expositor before any exegesis occurs. Yet on all occasions what the text meant should coincide and interact with what the text means.

Exegesis and interpretation involve proclamation in two time zones: the past and the present. The exegetical task involves reconstructing the ancient past of the text to get clues about how it might have been understood by the original readers. The hermeneutical task involves interpreting the text for contemporaries. Walter Wink said the purpose of these tasks is "To interpret the Scriptures so that the past becomes alive and illumines our present with new possibilities for personal and social transformation."[16] Discussions of exegesis and interpretation belong in a work on expository preaching. Exegesis exposes the truth of the text, and interpretation exposes the meaning of the truth for today's world. *Hermeneutics* is the broad word that covers both exegesis and interpretation.

Initial Contacts with the Text

Preachers can begin sermon preparation either with the experiences of people or with a text. When preparation begins with the needs of people, these matters must be taken to an appropriate text. When the sermon preparation begins with the truth of a text, it needs to be taken to the needs of people. Generally speaking, when

---

16. Walter Wink, *The Bible in Human Transformation* (Philadelphia: Fortress Press, 1973), 2.

someone preaches a series of sermons from a Bible book, the point of beginning is with the text. The expositor begins immediately with involvement with the text. Before tedious exegesis begins, the expositor needs some preliminary contacts with the text such as selecting texts, marking parameters, and settling on a translation.

Selecting the Text

Experienced preachers constantly wrestle with choosing a text. What will be my text for next Sunday? Texts are numerous, and finding the best text for the day often poses a problem. Text selection through the years has occurred in two ways: by the personal choice of the preacher or by following the lectionary. When the text selection comes by the preacher's choice, several patterns may emerge: random choices influenced by personal or pastoral factors; choices dictated by issues or occasions; choices dictated by the program of the church; or a series of texts for messages from a Bible book. Many preachers choose to use random selection of texts for sermons. Those who attempt this method usually speak of the need to be relevant and to meet needs as they arise—needs that cannot be known in advance. Planning to preach a series of sermons from a Bible book moves toward more advanced planning for the selection of texts. It helps relieve the pressure of what text to select.

Using a lectionary is another way to relieve the pressure of text selection. A lectionary is a carefully prepared three-year cycle of Scripture selections arranged to cover the major events of Israel, the major Christian doctrines, and the seasons of the Christian year. Lectionaries contain four lections, or readings, for each Sunday and special worship days such as Ash Wednesday, Christmas, and Good Friday. The four lections include an Old Testament reading, a psalm, a reading from an Epistle, and one from a Gospel. The three-year program is designed to guarantee public reading of the biblical texts affirming the central themes of the Christian faith. Using the lectionary is a good system of selecting texts on a week-to-week basis.

Both methods of text selection, personal and lectionary, can be used to choose texts in a series from a Bible book. Generally speaking, the texts in the Bible book prescribed by the lectionary have already been selected. No unpardonable homiletical rule has been violated if an expositor wants to modify these text selections in the lectionary readings from a Bible book.

Selecting texts from a personal perspective takes more effort. Choosing a book for a series does not mean that texts are selected automatically. Two primary personal procedures exist for the choice of texts: *lectio continua* and *lectio selectia*. Many expositors choose the *lectio continua* procedure which is the continuous treatment of texts in a Bible book. This process involves treating every verse and paragraph in a consecutive fashion. For example, a *lectio continua* treatment of the Letter of James means choosing every verse such as "Servanthood," 1:1; "Facing Life's Trials," 1:2–12; "Dealing with Temptation," 1:13–18; "Using the Bible Correctly," 1:19–27; and so forth. Textual selection in the *lectio continua* procedure involves a consecutive treatment of James with every verse or verses selected as texts.

Instead of a continuous selection of texts, the *lectio selectia* method involves the expositor choosing several texts from many texts. Not all the texts in a Bible book will be chosen, but only those texts which are the personal preference of the expositor. For example, a *lectio selectia* treatment of the Letter of James could mean choosing only eight texts for a series of sermons such as "Facing Life's Trials," 1:2–12; "Using God's Word Correctly," 1:19–27; "Saving Faith," 2:14–26; "A Course in Speech," 3:1–12; "Proper Planning," 3:13–17; "The Malady of Me-ism," 4:1–10; "The Lord's Return," 5:7–11; "Learning to Pray," 5:13–18.

Generally speaking, the *lectio continua* procedure seems to be the most popular method for choosing texts when preaching from a Bible book. In the cases of lengthy Bible books such as Isaiah, Jeremiah, Acts, and others, the *lectio continua* method could lead to a long series of sermons; therefore, the expositor might choose to use the *lectio selectia* method. Both methods have their advantages and disadvantages. Each expositor will weigh personal preference and audience receptivity and decide the best way to select texts from a Bible book.

Establishing Boundaries of the Text

The action of text selection coincides simultaneously with determining the parameters of the various texts in a Bible book. Determining the parameters of texts involves marking where a particular text begins and ends. These designations are human creations; the Bible did not come in designated text sizes. A text taken from a Bible book resembles a small piece cut from a roll of cloth with a large pattern. Once a small piece is removed, one may no longer be able to see how the small piece fits the overall design.[17] Therefore, care needs to be exercised in determining the parameters of texts.

Texts need to be designated where they begin and end. The expositor needs to be confident that the passages chosen from texts represent genuine, self-contained units. These are sometimes called *pericopes.*[18] The expositor needs to examine closely what comes before the text chosen and what follows it to see if the surgical incision has occurred at a responsible place. Every text relates to the other texts in the book. The parameter of a text involves one that can stand as a reasonable coherent unit of thought.

Ordinarily, locating the beginning and ending of texts in the Bible books is not too difficult. Reading the book and checking the commentaries can help give the preacher various units of thought in the book. Generally speaking, the preacher may look for clues for the beginnings and endings of texts. Fred Craddock designated two clues, namely thematic and literary.[19] A single theme makes 2 Samuel 11:1–27, James 2:14–26, and 1 Corinthians 13:1–13 each a unit. Only casual reading discloses these themes to be the sin of David with Bathsheba, the relationship of faith and works, and Christian love. While marking off texts in Bible books, units need to be designated which have single themes.

Literary clues in the Bible book also may provide beginnings and endings for texts. Some books have brief introductions to units of material such as Jeremiah's words, "The word which came to Jeremiah from the Lord, saying." Other units of material can be seen by the author's designation of time such as "the next day" (John 1:29), "again the next day" (John 1:35), and "the next day" (John 1:43); or in designations of place such as Matthew 8:28, "and when He had come to the other side into the country of the Gadarenes;" or notations about occasions such as "after these things there was a feast of the Jews, and Jesus went up to Jerusalem" (John 5:1). Often writers closed units with summary statements: "so the churches were being strengthened in the faith, and were increasing in num-

---

17. Thomas G. Long, *The Witness of Preaching* (Louisville, Ky.: Westminster/ John Knox Press, 1989), 64.

18. Douglas Stuart, *Old Testament Exegesis: A Primer for Students and Pastors* (Philadelphia: Westminster Press, 1980), 22.

19. Fred Craddock, *Preaching* (Nashville: Abingdon Press, 1985), 111–12.

ber daily" (Acts 16:5). Sometimes connecting word phrases serve as literary devices for closing one thought and moving to another.

Some commonsense questions help the reader determine the parameters of a text.

- Does the passage have a recognizable, obvious beginning and end?
- Does the length of text chosen have some sort of cohesive, meaningful content that is easily observed?

Douglas Stuart advises expositors to check decisions about parameters of texts with the biblical languages when possible and with modern translations.[20] The preacher is looking for a text that stands as a reasonably coherent unit of thought. Initial contact with a Bible book may yield a tentative decision about parameters of texts in the book, but subsequent extensive exegesis may cause the expositor to make changes.[21]

Translating or Paraphrasing the Text

Initial contact with a Bible book not only involves selecting and designating parameters of texts, it also involves a check of the translation of the text. Nothing substitutes for contact and involvement with the words of Scripture. The best contact with the text, obviously, is to work with the original language of the text, examining the textual variants and comparing personal translation or paraphrase with other established translations and paraphrases.

If an expositor cannot translate from the original languages, the next best contact with the text should involve selecting a reliable, modern translation such as the *New American Standard Bible* and comparing the wording in it with two or three other reliable translations.[22] Reginald H. Fuller suggested that each preacher, after checking with the original language and/or translation, should make a personal paraphrase of each text selected. Such an exercise allows the expositor to give a restatement of a text by giving the meaning in another form. Fuller contended that the paraphrase of a text is the beginning interpretation of a text. Further steps in exegesis, according to Fuller, would be intended to correct or modify

---

20. Stuart, 22.
21. Long, 64–65.
22. Ibid., 65.

the paraphrase.[23] Making a paraphrase has many benefits. It can help the expositor notice the passage's structure, its grammatical features, and some aspects of its theology. Furthermore, making a paraphrase can help put truth in the vocabulary of the expositor and in the language of people in the congregation.

Translating, reading from translations, or paraphrasing texts necessitates checking into significant textual issues. Simply stated, studying translations of texts involves checking for any variant or alternate words or phrases in the text. Variant readings have to do with disagreements among the manuscripts from which translations are derived. Footnotes in Old Testament translations may occasionally read, "Meaning of the Hebrew construction here," "Text obscure here," or may simply provide the Hebrew word translated in the text so a reader who so desires can work at other ways to translate the word. Considering textual variants is primarily a New Testament matter, for over five thousand whole or fragmentary Greek manuscripts exist.[24] Fortunately, the contemporary preacher has abundant resources from the scholars to help with the translations of the text. The definitive work for the New Testament is *A Textual Commentary on the Greek New Testament* by Bruce M. Metzger. The book lists and presents briefly the evidence for most significant textual variants in the New Testament.

After translating and/or paraphrasing the text, the preacher should read the individual text silently or even the entire book many times, and at least once aloud. The initial reading should be naive, spontaneous engagements with the text; it is the time to listen, feel, think, imagine, and ask without concern for what one should think or say in the sermon. During the initial reading, the preacher is internalizing the text's message and identifying in relation to parishioners. After the initial reading of the text, the preacher should consult secondary resources.

Text and Context

Good exegetical procedures dictate that the details within a text be viewed in light of the total context of the text. When texts have been selected and parameters have been set, these individual texts

---

23. Reginald H. Fuller, *The Use of the Bible in Preaching* (Philadelphia: Fortress Press, 1981), 21.

24. Craddock, 107.

in Bible books cannot be atomized or fragmented with words, phrases, sentences, or even paragraphs in isolation from surrounding Scriptures. The word *context* comes from the Latin word *contexus* (*con* "together," and *texere* "to weave"), which means "woven together." Context then refers to the connection of thought that runs through a passage, those links that weave it into one piece.[25] Considering contextual data in exegesis involves examining Scripture which precedes and follows the text being considered. The thought in a text is usually expressed in a series of related ideas so that the meaning of any word, phrase, sentence, or paragraph is almost always determined by what precedes or follows. In considering contextual data the areas which need study are book, sectional, immediate, and parallel contexts.

Book Context

The book context means to compare a text with the overall plan and purpose of the Bible book. Historical background and analysis help put a text in its frame of reference. Sometimes texts in a book not only need to be studied from the viewpoint of the book it is in but also from the perspective of the total teachings of Scripture. Another contextual study involves the sectional relationships, or connections.

Sectional Context

Conducting an analysis of the Bible book helps locate the slightly exposed seams which mark off specific sections of the book. Walter C. Kaiser, Jr., gives some clues for locating sections in a Bible book:

1. A repeated term, phrase, clause, or sentence may act as a heading for a section or to conclude a section.

2. Grammatical clues such as transitional conjunctions and adverbs; for example, "then, therefore, wherefore, but, nevertheless, or meanwhile may designate a section."

3. A rhetorical question could signal a switch to a new idea.

4. A change in time, location, and setting often indicates a new theme in narrative materials.

---

25. Fair, 36–37.

5. A vocative form of address deliberately showing a shift from one group to another constitutes one of the most frequent devices.[26]

From the study of the connection of the parts in a Bible book, the unity and purpose of texts may be known and used properly.

Immediate Context

Still another area of contextual data involves the immediate surroundings of a text. When studying a particular text, the student of Scripture needs to study the words immediately before the text and the words immediately after the text. Newer translations break the biblical material into paragraphs to indicate the natural thought units of the author. These paragraphs are helpful for the immediate context because chapter and verse numberings often confuse rather than help the Bible student. Immediate contexts help the expositor see it in its framework and meaning. For example, 1 Corinthians 13 fits the context of a discussion of spiritual gifts in chapters 12 and 14. Paul stressed the supremacy of love with regard to the use of spiritual gifts. Failing to see this immediate context could lead to misuse of 1 Corinthians 13. Another example of the importance of observing the immediate context comes from Galatians 5:4: "You have fallen from grace." This verse could be used to teach apostasy, but closer study of verses preceding this text and following it discloses that Paul spoke of people falling away from the grace way of Christian growth.

Parallel Contexts

In some parts of the Bible are various sorts of terse statements for which the expositor receives little or no help from verses which precede or follow it. For example, much of Proverbs consists of individual units or statements which are complete within themselves. These isolated texts need to be studied in comparison to parallel passages. The parallel passages consist of similar texts in the same Bible book or parallel passages from other books.

Placing a text within contextual data begins the exegesis process correctly; it brings an understanding of the underlying thought of the passage. Contextual data helps the exegete put the passage in

---

26. Walter C. Kaiser, Jr., *Toward an Exegetical Theology: Biblical Exegesis for Teaching and Preaching* (Grand Rapids: Baker Book House, 1981), 71.

the time and place originally spoken and written. Generally, basic thoughts exist in a series of ideas, and a study of the context enables the exegete to see the connection of thought as it goes into, through, and away from the text.

Literary Factors

The process of exegesis also includes investigating various dimensions of literary data. The literary forms associated with a text affect the meaning of its words and sentences. Three basic areas or circles of literary data exist, beginning with the largest area and moving to the most detailed. These areas are: (1) the genre type of the whole book; (2) major genre forms found in a textual unit such as parable, allegory, and other major literary forms; and (3) figures of speech of a smaller dimension.

Types of Biblical Literature

Scholars differ about the number of literary categories, but to help the expository preacher with the process of exegesis six major forms will be identified.

1. Narrative. Narrative materials comprise a large part of the Bible. These books may be prose in their entirety or a narrative contained in a larger work. Entire books such as 1 and 2 Samuel, 1 and 2 Kings and Acts involve historical narration with only brief contents of other literary types. Nonetheless, prose or historical narrative is not hard for the expositor to identify. Prose may be descriptive, explanatory, or emotive. It may have speeches, prayers, records of laws, genealogies, letters, or rituals, as well as historical narratives. In preparing sermons from a primary narrative book, the expositor needs to keep two things in mind: First, the narrative must not be read as matter-of-fact details but theological interpretations of events. Second, the narration must not be allegorized or spiritualized. Knowing that a Bible book falls into a narrative category helps the exegesis proceed in the proper direction.

2. Poetry. One-third or more of the Old Testament consists of poetry marked by semantic parallelism. Two or more lines in a text may express the same idea, contrast ideas, or build a flood of ideas. All of the Book of Psalms, most of the Book of Proverbs, and much material in the Prophets consist of Hebrew poetry.

3. Wisdom. Wisdom literature appears in Job, Proverbs, Ecclesiastes, Song of Solomon, and James. Within wisdom books are varied literary forms, the most common being the proverb, together with epic and didactic material.[27] Wisdom books sought to bridge the gap between the Torah (the law) and everyday life. They brought religion into the practical areas of human existence. Two practical types of wisdom material originated: (1) prudential wisdom, which includes admonitions and wise sayings for a happy life (such as Prov. 1–9, Pss. 1; 37); (2) reflective wisdom, which takes a philosophical approach to the meaning and significance of life (such as in Ecclesiastes or the Song of Solomon). Trying to apply the maxims of wisdom universally creates difficulty; therefore, the expositor needs to understand the setting of the particular wisdom book.

4. Gospels. Separate from narrative books stands a different literary category known as gospels. The apostles and others told the story of Jesus orally for about thirty years before anyone wrote the story. Later, inspired writers selected incidents from the life and ministry of Jesus and arranged them in pericopes, or blocks of material with a common theme. When preaching from a Gospel, expositors need to know they are dealing with books that are collections of materials arranged to tell a particular writer's witness to the life and ministry of Jesus Christ.

5. Epistles. A major portion of the New Testament consists of epistles and letters. At least twenty-one books may be classified as epistles or personal letters. Generally, Epistles may be those books such as Romans, Hebrews, and Ephesians where the life situation of a church does not govern the themes and events. Other books such as 1 and 2 Corinthians, Galatians, Philippians, Colossians, and 1 and 2 Peter speak to specific problems in a church. Personal letters such as 1 and 2 Timothy, Philemon, Titus, and 2 and 3 John deal with relationships between individuals. Epistles and letters need to be considered in their distinctions, and the words and sentences in them are affected by the epistolary form.

6. Apocalypse. The Book of Revelation is an apocalypse, and parts of Daniel, Isaiah, Ezekiel, Joel, Zechariah, Mark, Matthew, and Luke contain apocalyptic literature. In preaching from apocalyptic books, care is needed in observing their unusual characteristics.

---

27. Walter M. Dunnett, *The Interpretation of Holy Scriptures* (Nashville: Thomas Nelson Publishers, 1984), 107.

Basic rules of grammar and syntax still apply, but the meaning of the symbols needs to be sought.

Figurative Language

After looking at the literary form of a complete Bible book, the expositor needs to examine major figures of speech found in a Bible book. A figure of speech represents an author's conscious departure from the natural laws of grammar and a departure from the normal use of words for special purposes. The Bible contains many figures of speech; thus, the expositor needs to distinguish between the literal and figurative language. Figurative language does not lessen the force or significance of thought. Instead, it adds force to biblical truth in a different way. Edward P. Myers gives valuable help in identifying when language is figurative.

1. The sense of the expression will usually indicate figurative speech. In Psalm 23:1 the sense is obvious that the Lord is not a shepherd. It is a figurative expression.

2. An expression would be interpreted figuratively when the literal meaning involved an impossibility. For example, when Jesus said, "Let the dead bury their own dead" (Matt. 8:22, NIV), he used language that involved an impossibility if understood literally.

3. An expression is figurative if it requires what is ethically wrong or prohibits that which is right. For example, to have Jesus requiring a person to amputate a hand or to pluck out an eye lies beyond what he meant.

4. Some texts in their context disclose that they are figurative. Jesus said, "Destroy this temple, and in three days I will raise it up" (John 2:19). He was not speaking of the literal temple but the "temple of His body" (v. 21).

5. A passage is figurative if a literal view would conflict with another passage that is clearly understood. Thus, there is no contradiction between "shall never die" (John 11:26) and "for as in Adam all die" (1 Cor. 15:22). One is to be understood literally and the other figuratively.

6. Statements that are made to ridicule or mock are generally understood as figurative. When Jesus referred to Herod as a "fox," He was referring to Herod's craftiness.

7. In many cases, common sense will suggest that the language is figurative. For example, when Jesus spoke with the woman at the well, he spoke of living water that people could drink and never be thirsty again. He was speaking of water in a figurative sense.[28]

Literary Forms in a Bible Book

No exegetical endeavor could be complete without an investigation of the major figures of speech found in a Bible book. Seven prominent examples of major figures will be examined to help the expositor perform exegesis of a Bible book.

1. Proverb. Proverbs are short, sagacious sayings. A. Berkeley Mickelson speaks of personal proverbs, interpersonal proverbs, proverbs referring to God, proverbs referring to possessions, and proverbs referring to moral principles.[29] Charles T. Fritsch explains: "Proverbs is written in a poetic style. That is, each verse is characterized by the parallelism of its members or stichs, and by a certain number of beats or accents usually three or four in those stichs. Paronomasia (a play upon words which sound alike but usually have a different sense) also plays an important role in the literary structure of the book. The couplet, composed of two stichs, is the most common form of the proverb."[30]

Once an expositor recognizes the poetic nature of proverbs, some sound exegetical principles can be practiced. Figures of speech in the proverb need to be identified. Then expositors need to check the context into which the editor placed the proverb and see if a grouping of proverbs produces a common theme. In most cases these will be obscure. Most proverbs express common wisdom. They originated from historical experiences, and they may or may not be universally applicable.

2. Parable. A parable is one of the oldest and most common figures of speech. It is often a story in which something real in life is used as a means of presenting moral or spiritual truth. The charac-

---

28. Edward P. Meyers, "Interpreting Figurative Language," in *Biblical Interpretation: Principles and Practice* edited by F. Furman Kearly, Edward P. Myers, and Timothy G. Hadley (Grand Rapids: Baker Book House, 1986), 92–93.

29. A. Berkeley Mickelson, *Interpreting the Bible* (Grand Rapids: William B. Eerdmans Publishing Company, 1977), 334.

30. Charles T. Fritsch, "The Book of Proverbs," *The Interpretor's Bible*, IV, 776.

ters in parables are believable persons who do nothing which cannot be done in real life. A parable is often an extended form of the simile; for example, "the kingdom of heaven is like." Some parables appear in the Old Testament, but they are most obvious in the teachings of Jesus.

When expositors encounter a parable in a text, they need to remember some general principles. Usually most parables have one primary point, and the expositor needs to study the parable to find its point. Parables were used as language events to call for decisions; therefore, the interpreter needs to look for what the parable is trying to get hearers to do. Parables contain the components of daily life; thus, the expositor needs to learn about the details and what they contribute to the story. Of course, the expositor must not forget to examine the parable in its historical setting and its textual context. With these principles in mind the interpreter is more adept at applying the parable to modern life.

3. Allegory. An allegory presents meaning symbolically through an extended story or picture. The allegory is put together with several points of comparison. In one Old Testament allegory, Israel is portrayed as a vine from Egypt (Ps. 80:8–15). In the New Testament, the weapons of Christian armor are described in Ephesians 6:11–17. Allegory is generally a longer figure of speech involving a narrative that teaches some spiritual or moral truth.[31]

Allegory and parable are easily confused. A parable keeps the story distinct from its interpretation or application, but an allegory intertwines the story and its meaning. An allegory will have several points of comparison, whereas a parable will usually have one main comparison.

G. B. Caird distinguishes between allegory and allegorization. In an allegory, the author tells a story to convey a hidden meaning. It is correctly interpreted when that intended meaning is perceived. But allegorization occurs when one imposes hidden meanings that the story's author did not intend.[32]

4. Fable. A fable is a fictional story meant to teach a moral lesson. Usually the characters are members of the animal or vegetable realm whose actions, being contrary to natural activities of animals or

---

31. Ibid., 71–72.

32. G. B. Caird, *The Language and Imagery of the Bible* (Philadelphia: Westminster Press, 1980), 165.

plants, depict the vagaries, emotions, and failures of human beings. The most obvious biblical fable is Jotham's fable found in Judges 9:8–15 and Jehoash's fable found in 2 Kings 14:9. Expositors need to keep two general exegetical principles in mind when interpreting fables. First, they should understand as much as possible the situation in which the fable was spoken. Second, they should observe the message of the fable and its intended influence on the hearers.

5. Riddle. A riddle is a question, statement, or description designed to test ingenuity or amuse the hearer or reader. It is an enigmatic saying usually intended to perplex or sometimes entertain. The best-known riddles in the Bible come from Samson (see Judg. 14:12–20).

6. Type. In typology the exegete finds one or more correspondences between a person, event, or thing in the Old Testament and a person, event, or thing close to or contemporaneous with a New Testament writer. Correspondence is the basic idea of typology. This correspondence is within the historical framework of divine revelation, as opposed to allegorism, which is concerned with hidden meanings beneath the primary and ordinary meanings and which shows little or no regard for a historical base. Milton S. Terry lists four classes of types: (1) Persons: Adam, Elijah, Abraham, Melchizedek, (2) Institutions: Sabbath, Passover, (3) Offices: prophets, priests, kings, (4) Actions: Moses lifting up the serpent.[33]

When the exegete encounters typology in a text, the specific point or points of correspondence need to be noted. These two correspondences should be examined carefully in the light of the historical context of both. Also, expositors need to keep in mind the biblical emphasis on God's involvement with his people in history.

7. Symbol. A symbol recalls something else that has similar qualities or that is associated with it in fact or thought. Any person seeking the meaning of a symbol in a text needs to understand the cultural situation in which the symbol appeared. Many symbols appear in the apocalyptic texts, especially Daniel and Revelation. Numbers, colors, and precious stones abound in symbolic use. Also actions symbolize or suggest a truth beyond the action. Ezekiel and

---

33. Milton S. Terry, *Biblical Hermeneutics* reprint, (Grand Rapids: Zondervan, 1974), 255–56.

John ate a scroll to show that God's message was essential to their lives.

Symbols point to something different from themselves, directing one to a lesson or truth. The expositor needs to study carefully the qualities of the literal object denoted by the symbol and discover what the writer was trying to say by using the symbol. Objects do not always have symbolic meaning. For example, "well" in John 4:6 referred to a literal place to get water, but in John 4:14 it was a symbol for the life-giving provisions Jesus offered. Again, the names of Babylon and Egypt were commonly used in the Bible for physical locations, but in Revelation 18:2 Babylon symbolized Rome, and in Revelation 11:8 Egypt symbolized the place of crucifixion.

In pursuing the process of examining literary data, two genres or literary categories have been discussed—the genre of the whole book and the major figures of speech in a textual unit. Without trying to be exhaustive, discussion will now center on some common figures of speech which could appear in a text. Walter M. Dunnett gave eight examples.[34]

Figures of Speech in a Textual Unit

1. Metaphor. Metaphor is a literary device which uses comparison by direct assertion in which the speaker or writer describes one thing in terms of something else. Metaphor resembles a simile in that both draw a correspondence between two things. A simile uses the explicit words "like" or "as", whereas a metaphor adopts a bolder strategy. It omits the comparative words and asserts that A is B. "The Lord is my shepherd" (Ps. 23:1); "their throat is an open grave" (Ps. 5:9).

2. Simile. A simile is an explicitly stated comparison employing the words "like" and "as." A simile has a reference to a person or to a thing with explicit correspondence to what is being discussed. "All flesh is like grass" (1 Pet. 1:24); "Thou dost surround him with favor as with a shield" (Ps. 5:12).

3. Hyperbole. A hyperbole is a conscious exaggeration by a writer to gain effect. "And their camels were without number, as numerous as the sand on the seashore" (Judg. 7:12b). A hyperbole is not

---

34. Dunnett, 114.

expected to be believed. Instead, it adds emphasis to the real message.

4. *Synecdoche.* A synecdoche uses a part for a whole or a whole for a part. An individual may be used for a class or a class for an individual. A singular may be used for a plural and a plural for a singular. For example, "And afterwards I shall see his face" (Gen. 32:20, RSV). A part in this passage was named to represent the whole. "That all the world should be enrolled" (Luke 2:1, RSV). The whole is given to represent a part. "In the day when the keepers of the house tremble" (Eccl. 12:3, RSV). The singular day stands for an extended, particular period of time.

5. *Metonymy.* Metonymy is the substitution of the name of one thing for another thing. "And beginning with Moses and with all the prophets" (Luke 24:27). Jesus referred to the writing of the Old Testament.

6. *Irony.* In irony a speaker uses words to denote the exact opposite of what the language declares. It is a simulated adoption of an opposite or different tendency, an adoption of another point of view or laudatory tone for the purpose of ridicule. "You have a fine way of rejecting the commandment of God, in order to keep your tradition!" (Mark 7:9, RSV).

7. *Litotes.* In this figure of speech a negative statement is used to declare an affirmative truth. A milder form is found where simple understatement heightens the action which is being described. "I am the least of the apostles, who am not fit to be called an apostle, because I persecuted the church of God" (1 Cor. 15:9). Litotes is the exact opposite of hyperbole.

8. *Euphemism.* In euphemism a word or phrase which is less direct is substituted because the writer believes that the direct form would be distasteful, offensive, or unnecessarily harsh. "From which Judas turned aside to go to his own place" (Acts 1:25). The expression "his own place" was a euphemism for the final destruction of Judas.

In many cases, especially in the Old Testament, euphemisms were used about personal or sexual matters. Writers substituted mild, vague, and even roundabout expressions for personal matters. Elijah's mocking words about Baal "he has gone aside" (1 Kings 18:27, RSV) speak of a personal matter as well as the euphemism of one "relieving himself" in Judges 3:24. For a man to "know" his wife was to have sexual relations with her (Gen. 4:1, RSV).

This discussion on literary data has repeatedly stressed the importance of determining the literary form in which a passage is cast. Failure to consider this process carefully and correctly can cause considerable confusion in determining the divinely intended meaning. The expositor needs to take the words in a passage either in their literal or figurative sense with primary consideration to the meaning conveyed by the language.

Word Study

This study pertains to the words or the vocabulary of the biblical languages. Lexical data should precede syntactical data because words need to be studied individually before they are studied with relationship to grammar or construction. Words are the building blocks for constructing sentences. The task of the exegete involves discovering the meaning of a word, not determining its meaning. The meaning that the word had in a biblical text rests on the meaning it had for the author.

The Bible student may use several disciplines in doing a word study. One of these disciplines is etymology: the study of where words came from. To know the etymology or root of a word, however interesting it may be, almost never tells us anything about its meaning in a given context. Henry A. Virkler points out two problems with etymological studies. First, the historical roots of Bible words are mainly unknown and are often quite conjectural. Second, the meaning of a word changes radically with the passage of time so that little or no apparent connection remains between the original meaning of the root word and its meaning many years later.[35]

Any exegesis that depends heavily on etymological derivations possesses questionable validity. Words change in all languages, including Hebrew, Greek, and English. In the 1800s the English word *enthusiasm* meant "possessed by God" and was so used. The French phrase *dent de lion* originally meant a "lion's tooth," but today it means a flower (dandelion). The English word *spinster* meant one who spun wool with her hands, but today the word means an unmarried woman. Years ago English dictionaries listed the word *manufacture* with the meaning "to make with hands," but

---

35. Henry A. Virkley, *Hermeneutics: Principles and Processes of Biblical Interpretation* (Grand Rapids: Baker Book House, 1981), 100.

today few items are manufactured by hand. These are only a few examples of the changing meanings of words.

In addition to etymological studies, students should also study how Bible words were used in ancient literature outside the Bible. Such a procedure is done more on Greek words rather than Hebrew words. Knowing how the word was used outside the usage of biblical writers helps to know more about meaning.

Words also need to be studied in their usage in various biblical references. Concordances can help us at this point. Hebrew and Greek concordances contain listings of every occurrence of a given word. An English concordance lists all the passages in which various Hebrew and Greek words were translated into a given English word. To define a word in a given context, one should observe how the word was used elsewhere by the same author, subsequently moving to consider the usage by other authors. To understand a Bible text, one needs to be acquainted with the significations which the words acquired in the course of time and with the sense in which the biblical authors used them.

Lexicons or dictionaries that list the meaning of Hebrew and Greek words help. Brown, Driver, and Briggs' Hebrew lexicon includes word etymologies and usages from different historical periods. The lexicon of Liddell and Scott gives extensive examples of various meanings of Greek words during the classical and *koiné* periods. *A Greek-English Lexicon of the New Testament and Other Early Christian Literature* by Walter Bauer, edited and translated by W. F. Arndt, F. W. Gingrich, and F. W. Danker, lists Greek words and their meanings from the time of the Septuagint to early Christian literature. These listings indicate when a word had certain meanings. Greek and Hebrew lexicons help with word meanings because they include studies of etymology and the usage of the word throughout a period of history.

In addition to etymological and historical word study, the Bible student must examine the word in the particular sentence in which it is used. This expositor should ask some questions about this procedure: Does the author use the word as other authors used the word? Does the author give the word a theological meaning? These questions must be answered in light of the immediate context. The exegete should have recorded a summary of the earliest discovered use of the word and its development up to and into the sentence under investigation.

To illustrate the fact that word meaning is determined by usage, look at the various references of the word *sarx* or *flesh*. At least three usages of this word could be noted. In John 6:53 where Christ talks about his own flesh, the word denotes a symbolic representation of the will of God. Paul used the word *flesh* in 1 Corinthians 15:39 to refer to the human body, and in Colossians 2:18 the same author used the word *flesh* to refer to the sensuous nature of a human being. Words in the Bible do not have authoritative meanings as much as they have relative usages. The task of the exegete is to pursue lexical data to discover the way a word was used; hence, to know how it was used will yield its meaning.

Syntactical Study

Syntax studies how words, phrases, and clauses relate to each other. As important as lexical data or word study is, it profits little in understanding Scripture without putting word meanings in the syntactical context. People do not think, talk, or write in disconnected words. They express themselves with words put together in phrases, clauses, and sentences. Studying the relationships of words, phrases, and clauses helps us understand the biblical text. The same sort of resources used to understand words also helps understand grammatical or lexical data.

Word order sometimes offers a guide to meaning. In English texts, nouns generally precede verbs, which normally precede direct objects or predicate nominatives or adjectives. Hebrew is also an analytic language, though less so than English. Greek, in contrast to Hebrew, is a synthetic language, and meaning often comes by how the words are arranged in their order. An English reader should select a fairly literal translation to observe the sentence flow. The *Revised Standard Version* and the *New American Standard Bible* are the most helpful for corresponding word order in the Hebrew and Greek text. As another alternative resource for word order the expositor might want to consult an interlinear.

Identifying parts of speech is another helpful discipline for the exegete. Students of the original languages can study carefully the Hebrew and Greek verbs, nouns, pronouns, adjectives, adverbs, conjunctions, and prepositions. More than likely most expository preachers will deal with the English text, but even so, the parts of speech need to be identified and studied in the English translations.

The expositor should be able to recognize at least these six parts of a sentence:

1. The subject. A subject might be a noun, a pronoun, a phrase, or a clause. It is used to identify the actor, or with the passive verb the person or object acted upon. The subject may identify anything or anyone about whom a statement is made or a question is raised.

2. The verb. A verb expresses action or existence. It may occur in a simple word or a verbal phrase and may include modifiers or coordinating participles. The verb not only indicates action or existence, it may also indicate a kind of action, the time of action, or the nature of the subject.

3. The object. The object may be a noun, a pronoun, or a clause, along with its modifiers. It identifies the person or object acted upon, and thus can be a direct object. It may also identify something or someone who benefited from the action; thus, it can be an indirect object.

4. The adjective. The adjective may be a word, a phrase, or a clause which describes either the subject or the object. It usually tells which one or what kind.

5. The adverb. The adverb may also be a word, a phrase, or a clause which modifies the verb and usually tells how, when, where, why, or how much. Both adjectives and adverbs come under the classification of modifiers.

6. The connectors. The connectors are usually short words identified as prepositions, relative pronouns, and conjunctions. They serve to indicate coordination or subordination.

With word order observed and the parts of speech identified, the third syntactical discipline can be pursued—the discipline of determining relationships which words have to each other. It involves the observation of modifiers. Diagramming a sentence helps the exegete see syntactical relationships. To diagram a sentence one needs to begin with the subject and predicate of the noun clause and continue diagramming with the coordinating elements placed under each other and identifying subordinate or modifying elements. Suggestions about diagramming sentences follow:

1. Begin on the left side of the paper with the subject, predicate, and object of the first main clause. In most cases rearrangement of the word order into subject-verb-object will be helpful.

"Man is blessed" (Ps. 1:1) for "Blessed is the man."

2. Continue the diagram with subordinates by indentation. The exegete needs to subordinate by indentation of all adverbial modifiers, participial phrases, adjective clauses, and noun clauses.

Man is blessed

    does not walk in the counsel of the wicked

    nor stand in the path of sinners

    nor sit in the seat of scoffers

3. Coordinate the sentence diagram by observing coordinate clauses, phrases, words, or balanced pairs or contrasts by lining them up directly under each other.

We speak wisdom (1 Cor. 2:6)

We speak wisdom (1 Cor. 2:7)

Notice the coordination of the phrases "of this age" and the conjunctions in 1 Corinthians 2:6.

wisdom

not of this age

nor of the rulers of this age

4. Mark connectors and transitions within the sentence. Conjunctions, participles, relative pronouns, and sometimes demonstrative pronouns serve as structural signals. These need to be underlined in the diagram and related to the preceding word or word group it coordinates or subordinates. Notice the connector in 1 Corinthians 2:6:

We speak wisdom

among the mature

but

These four brief hints for the diagramming of a sentence move the expositor to closer observation of sentence structure, modifiers, and connectives. Excellence in exegesis means detailed study of syntactical data.

To get a better grasp of the process of performing an exegesis of a Bible book or of an individual passage, review a summary of the essential tasks.

- Use the analysis of the Bible book as a guide for the exegesis. Fit context, genre, word study, and syntactical investigation into the framework of the analysis.
- Survey the broad and immediate contexts of a passage. See how the passage fits into the Bible book, the paragraph, the preceding sentences, and even the entire Bible.
- Identify the genre factors about the passage. These identifications involve studying the general genre of the Bible book and examining specific genre matters in the book.
- Plunge into the study of words. Learn the etymology of a word and the various usages of the word.
- Diagram the sentences in each text. Identify parts of speech and their relationship with each other.

Karl Barth on the event of his formal farewell to his students in Bonn, before his expulsion from Germany in 1935, said: "And now the end has come. So listen to my last piece of advice: exegesis, exegesis and yet more exegesis! Keep to the Word, to the Scripture that has been given us."[36] To preach a series of sermons from a Bible book a preacher must engage in extensive exegesis. The resources for exegesis are plentiful and the rewards are profitable. With the scientific task of exegesis performed, a preacher can then turn to the world and interpret the Word of God for people in today's world.

---

36. Quoted in Eberhard Busch, *Karl Barth: His Life from Letters and Autobiographical Text*, trans. John Bowden (Philadelphia: Fortress Press, 1976), 259.

The Interpretation of a Bible Book

Expository preaching is both ancient and modern. Contemporary expositors study a biblical text so that the past will come alive and illumine people's lives. A true sermon has two poles: the past meaning of the text and the present meaning of the text. All preaching—topical, textual, expository, life-situational, ethical, doctrinal, biographical—should draw from what the text meant to the original readers in order to apply that meaning to contemporary audiences. Emphasizing one dimension of the text while neglecting the other dimension results in unbalanced proclamation.

Preaching from a Bible book requires the disciplines of exegesis and interpretation. Exegesis studies what the text *meant* when it was written, and interpretation strives to understand what the text *means* to contemporary audiences. Some persons mistakenly believe that expository preaching deals exclusively with what the text meant. They have the idea that expository preachers only decline Greek nouns, parse Greek verbs, share Hebrew and Greek syntactical arrangements, and expose facts of Bible history.

These exegetical investigations are necessary, but exegesis alone is not enough; it needs to proceed to interpretation to establish what the text means to today's world. One person asked, "What do a bunch of camel drivers have to say to me in the jet age?"[1] Studying the Bible as mere history puts the Scriptures in a category with Homer and Herodotus. Exegetical research establishes one pole from which to proceed to the next pole—establishing what the text *meant* to what the text *means* in current human experiences.

Perhaps the most neglected pole in expository preaching is the interpretation of individual texts within a Bible book. Some preachers appear more skilled at understanding the ancient Hebrews than today's Americans. Interpretation and exegesis should be inseparable. Exegesis protects interpretation from excessive subjectivism. To deal only with a person's existential experience with a text could turn a well-intended sermon into a psychological session, a sociological lecture, or a philosophical adventure. Sermons may have psychological, sociological, or philosophical insights, but the sermon must be woven from the truth of the text where it originated. The hermeneutical task is this: to interpret the *now* of the text in light of the *then* of the text.

Every expository sermon builds a bridge from the then to the now or from the now to the then. Sermons can begin with the ancient biblical truth and then move to the present needs of people; or sermons can begin with a contemporary need and proceed to the ancient biblical truth. Wherever the sermon idea starts, both poles

---

1. Roy L. Honeycutt, *Crisis and Response* (Nashville: Abingdon Press, 1965), 105.

must be connected, and they must be congruent.[2] This process of connecting exegesis and interpretation could be described as building "the hermeneutical arch." Most preachers begin with exegesis, then proceed to interpretation. Some preachers have the gift of discerning meaning from a text, and then they engage in exegesis to see if the meaning matches or coincides with what the text meant. Movement needs to take place both in sermon preparation and delivery between the poles of the past and the present.

A Perspective on Interpretation

Biblical scholars have used the terms *exegesis* and *interpretation* in different ways. Most biblical scholars have used the term *exegesis* to describe the concern for what a biblical writer meant and how that meaning was perceived by those who first read it. Somewhere in the process of studying Scripture, biblical scholars also began to use the word *hermeneutics*. On one hand, the word *hermeneutics* was used in the broad sense of studying Scripture which would include both exegesis and interpretation. On the other hand, the word *hermeneutics* came to be associated in the narrow task of understanding what the text means after studying what the text meant.[3] When encountering the word *hermeneutics*, readers should determine whether the term is used in the general sense or in its narrower understanding. In this book, the word *hermeneutics* is used as a general term referring to both exegesis and interpretation. The term *exegesis* will be used to describe what a text meant, and the term *interpretation* will be used to discover what a text means.

The Origin of the Term

The precise time of the narrower use of the term *hermeneutic* or *interpretation* cannot easily be determined. But some clues about its origin can be discovered. The influence of rationalism and the scientific study of Scripture, which began over one hundred years ago, drastically changed the approach that some made to the study of the Bible. Near the end of the nineteenth century and throughout most of the twentieth century, many Bible scholars treated Scripture as an object. Consequently, truth could be discovered, they

---

2. John R. W. Stott, *Between Two Worlds: The Art of Preaching in the Twentieth Century* (Grand Rapids: William B. Eerdmans, 1982), 135–79.

3. A. Malherbe, "An Introduction: The Task and Method of Exegesis," *Restoration Quarterly* 5 (1961): 166–78.

reasoned, by scientific procedures. Scripture, according to some, could be mastered with textual criticism, literary criticism, historical criticism, source criticism, redaction criticism, and other scientific approaches. The basic stance of such a scientific approach is to study a Bible book as any other book, thinking the truth of the text emerges only as a result of scientific investigation.

Some scholars began to recognize and to declare the inadequacy of the scientific approach to biblical studies. In 1973, Walter Wink shocked the world of biblical scholarship by declaring that "historical biblical criticism is bankrupt."[4] In 1980, James Luther Mays underscored the decline of the critical approach. Mays said, "The dominance of historical-critical exegesis seems to be on the wane."[5] Neither Wink nor Mays disdained the scientific study of Scripture, nor did they perceive the Bible as a nonhistorical book, yet they saw the need to move from pure investigation of what the text meant to look for what the text means. With Wink and Mays, the Bible continued to be an object to be studied, but it also needed to become a subject that interprets people.

Biblical scholarship began to be influenced in the 1960s by a movement called the New Hermeneutic led by Gerhard Ebeling, Ernst Fuchs, Walter Wink, and others. According to the New Hermeneutic, the language of Scripture ceases to be mere language with its own fixed cognitive meaning and becomes instead a dynamic language event that creates faith and meaning for the hearer-interpreter. The New Hermeneutic helped move the study of Scripture away from pure objective reasoning to a more subjective experience for the interpreter. James Robinson explains, "The flow of the traditional relation between subject and object, in which the subject interrogates the object . . . has been significantly reversed. For now it is the object—which should henceforth be called the subject matter—that puts the subject in question."[6]

According to writers in the New Hermeneutic, subjective presuppositions influence the meaning of the text as much as the interpreter is influenced by the text. Movements such as the New

---

4. Walter Wink, *The Bible in Human Transformation: Toward a New Paradigm for Bible Study* (Philadelphia: Fortress Press, 1973), 1.

5. James Luther Mays, "Editorial," *Interpretation: A Journal of Bible and Theology*, (April 1980), 182.

6. James M. Robinson, "Hermeneutics Since Barth," in *The New Hermeneutic*, (New York: Harper and Row, 1964), 23–24.

Hermeneutic have heightened tension between objective, historical study of the Bible and the interpreter's subjective reasoning. Although a few enthusiasts have neglected the historical dimension, the New Hermeneutic has helped Bible students recognize the importance of their own experience in understanding the text.

Interpretation does not need to treat the text from a subjective stance only. No interpreter can penetrate the meaning without studying what the original author intended. The dynamic relationship between text and contemporary application, where the objectivity of the text and the subjectivity of the interpreter are both preserved, can be maintained only when Bible study moves from the historical interpretation toward the subjective context of the interpreter.

Values of the Process of Interpretation

The discipline of interpretation has become a valuable addition to Bible study. The emphasis on interpretation has helped preachers understand and preach more effectively from the Bible. The biblical message becomes God's Word to any hearer or interpreter when it enters the mind and speaks with inner authority by showing the real self in the mirror of divine encounter. It has created what Merrill Abbey, in *The Word Interprets Us*, called the Word interpreting us or biblical preaching in the present tense. Communicating truth from the Bible involves much more than learning facts from an objective endeavor. It involves personal experience with the text, and it involves both interpreting the text and allowing the text to interpret the interpreter.

Interpretation involves dialogue with the text. Preaching to be understood holds the text and experience together in their interacting, interpretive roles. This is sometimes called "the hermeneutical circle" because interpretation flows from subject to object and from object to subject. Two questions interact:

- What was the writer trying to say to ancient readers?
- What is God saying to me and to us who hear this text?

Engaging with the *then* and *now* of the text helps us see the continuity of human nature and experience. God inspired ancient authors to write Scripture. They had a different understanding of the cosmos; a different interpretation of human happenings; and numerous other cultural, social, and political differences. Perhaps some really were camel drivers! Yet they are kin to us in the jet age because of the similarity in human nature and experience, despite our social or cultural differences. Engaging in the experience of the ancient culture and the contemporary helps us understand and apply biblical texts. Gerhard Ebeling says the purpose of a sermon is to let "the text become God's word again."[7] James T. Cleveland says that "a Word of God is always the Good News (or an aspect of it) immersed in a Contemporary Situation."[8]

Ernst Fuchs and Gerhard Ebeling refer to our encounter with the biblical text as a "language event."[9] This term stresses that the Word of God comes from beyond human searching, for God confronts people by his Word. Words cease to be mere words and become a language event. The study of hermeneutics or interpretation can help us see that preaching is a word event that brings faith to life. When the truth of a text is proclaimed, God's engaging, saving Word comes into action.

Assumptions of Interpretation

Our personal presuppositions affect everything we read and hear. Human minds collect attitudes, emotions, beliefs, prejudices, myths, and interests. Our presuppositions influence our Bible study. When we seek to interpret a biblical text, we bring our cultural, political, social, and other personal conditioning to the process. Rudolph Bultman insists that "there cannot be any such thing as presuppositionless exegesis."[10] Even if persons try to divest themselves of their traditions, total avoidance of presuppositions cannot occur. The Word of God never comes to a blank-tablet mind.

The process of interpretation falls an easy prey to the subjective element. Exegesis establishes checks and balances against excessive subjectivism, but exegesis is not enough. The Holy Spirit breaks into our lives to apply the biblical text, giving basis for a rational, theological understanding of the text. Some basic presuppositions or assumptions are the basis for interpretation.

---

7. Gerhard Ebeling, *Word and Faith* (Philadelphia: Fortress Press, 1963), 329.

8. James T. Cleveland, *Preaching to Be Understood* (Nashville: Abingdon Press, 1965), 44.

9. Merrill Abbey, *The Word Interprets Us* (Nashville: Abingdon Press, 1967), 66.

10. Rudolph Bultman, *Existence and Faith* (London: Hodder and Stoughton, 1961), 343–44

Assumption #1: The Reality of God

All other assumptions rest in the expository preacher's understanding of God. This is the expositor's primary assumption: the *theological assumption.* Any appropriate and applicable study of Scripture begins with a person who affirms the reality of the existence of God. Belief in God is essential—God who is real, changeless, eternal, and loving, the same in the present and future as he has been in the past. Expository preachers must assume that God still functions as he always has—creatively and redemptively. God is not capricious; if he were, no one else could trust the Bible. William Thompson writes, "While God may surface in unexpected places and at times we cannot predict and in ways we would never have guessed possible, his nature and activity are constant and eternal and good. That is the first presupposition upon which we build."[11] Preachers need to build on the assumption that God will continue to be and continue to act as he promised. He will forgive sins when people repent; he will be with people through testing and trouble; and he will take his own to eternity with him when death comes.

Assumption #2: The Continuity of Human Nature and Experience

The biblical interpreter must assume the continuity of human nature and experience. This is the *psychological assumption.* One of the prominent emphases of scholars in interpretation is the kinship of ancient and modern human beings. Cultural differences make people express themselves differently, but the basic nature and experience of human beings remain the same. If a radical distinction existed between human nature and experience of people in the Bible and people today, study of the Scripture would be fruitless.

Humans have always rebelled against God—from Old Testament times right up to our own day. Sin marks every human being. God created every person in his own image, yet every person has "sinned and fall short of the glory of God" (Rom. 3:23). People are sinners, whether they live in a bedouin's tent or a high-rise. Leander Keck writes, "Certain perversion of life and of Christian faith are perennial, paradigmatic; indeed one may call them archetypal."[12] Human

---

11. William D. Thompson, *Preaching Biblically: Exegesis and Interpretation* (Nashville: Abingdon Press, 1981), 41.

nature has remained the same throughout the centuries. Each person has chosen to rebel against God and to run life his or her own way.

Not only does continuity exist in human nature, but kinship may also be seen in human experience. Though people live at different places and in different times, they experience life in much the same way. They search for the meaning and significance of life; they seek to live in healthy, happy relationships; they want forgiveness for their sins, ease for their guilt; they suffer from disease, natural disasters, and divorce; they dread and experience death. No one can understand the meaning of the biblical text or preach from it apart from the assumption of the continuity of human nature and experience through the years and throughout the culture.

Assumption #3: The Bible as God's Word

Expositors also must make a *biblical assumption*. They need to base their sermons on the Bible because they believe it is the Word of God. The Bible is a unique book that contains the historical tradition of Jews and Christians. Furthermore, the Christians' experience with the Bible authenticates it as the Word of God. It continues to be the place to go for information about God and guidance for living.

Three words describe the nature of the Bible: *revelation, inspiration*, and *authority*. The word *revelation* literally means an unveiling of something that was formerly hidden. In one sense, revelation describes the act of imparting information about God. The Bible records the account of God's action unveiling his essential hiddenness and offering himself in fellowship.

Inspiration is another word describing an assumption about the Bible. It describes God's unique way of having the Bible written. Debates have raged and continue to rage about the method of inspiration. The method God used does not matter. What really matters in the biblical assumption of the preacher is that God brought the Scriptures into being and that they are authoritative for the Christian faith.

Authority is another word associated with the preacher's presupposition about the Bible. Revelation denotes the content of God's

---

12. Leander E. Keck, *The Bible in the Pulpit* (Nashville: Abingdon Press, 1978), 117.

message in the Bible; authority denotes its value, power, and influence. People generally do not like to be under authority. Nonetheless, when a preacher chooses a biblical text for preaching, the choice and usage of the text carry the force of authority or high value. The Bible's authority must undergird the preacher's enterprise of preaching.[13]

Assumption #4: The Experience of God

The final presupposition a preacher uses in the process of interpretation is personal experience with the text. This is the *experiential assumption*. Any person can derive benefit from reading the Bible. The Bible has literary value, and it can be understood by most readers. A preacher cannot function as an authoritative interpreter without a personal experience of redemption in Jesus Christ. A preacher then cooperates with and relates to the Spirit who produced, preserved, and illumines the Scripture.

Expository preachers need more than expertise in exegesis; they need skills in interpretation. They need to experience the Lord—the Lord who abides in the interpreter wrote the Bible, and the indwelling Spirit will lead the expositor to understand the Bible. The truth confirmed and authenticated by centuries of Christian tradition is that only the preacher who knows the Lord in an experiential way can communicate that experience with power and lasting effect.

Interactions in Interpretation

Life exists on both sides of biblical interpretation. The interpreter is alive, but the text is also alive with the Spirit's power and direction. Effective interpretation occurs when the interpreter and the text interact. To say that the text comes alive when interpretation of it turns into *its* interpretation of the interpreter is not to rob it of its own objective authority.[14] Without a doubt the preacher interacts with a text by means of objective exegesis. From such pursuits, the preacher learns about the historical past of the text. Exegesis constitutes an exciting involvement with a text, but the preacher should remember that exegesis is only one side of the involvement.

---

13. Thompson, 42–43.
14. Abbey, 41.

Another side of the interaction happens when the text interacts with both the interpreter and the people addressed by the interpreter. The text does more than read out of the interpreter what is in the interpreter. It contributes to the understanding of life as oriented by events and insights which have an unyielding objectivity. The text searches, judges, and changes the interpreter.

The Text Interprets the Preacher

In most cases, the preacher will begin with exegesis, then move on to interpretation. Gerhard Ebeling explains, "In dealing with the text, *its* being interpreted by us turns into *our* being interpreted by the text."[15] While the preacher studies a text, interaction begins and continues from the life in the text. The text begins to affect the thoughts, feelings, and actions of the interpreter. In the exercise of exegesis, the preacher had asked repeatedly, "What did the text say to the people who heard it for the first time?" Later the preacher poses the other question, "What is God trying to say to me in this text?" When the preacher studies the text exegetically and encounters it experientially, that preacher is ready to expose biblical truth to people's needs.

No systematic methodology can be construed for programming the text's effect on the preacher. The text is alive and functions dynamically. Yet some personal disciplines can be considered with the expectation of the text's interpreting the interpreter. Think seriously about considering all and engaging some of these disciplines. Consider these disciplines as interactive processes happening during the course of exegesis—during personal meditation, research, pastoral visitation, or other occasions.

Hearing. The first discipline to exercise in letting the text speak to the preacher involves disciplined hearing of the text. Originally, every text in Scripture involved God inspiring a human author to write a message. The message of the divinely inspired had to be heard; therefore, there was a hearing. Every encounter with the Scripture should be a similar speaking and hearing experience. God still speaks by means of biblical texts, and preachers need to give special attention to what the Lord is saying.[16]

---

15. Quoted by Robinson, "Hermeneutics Since Barth," 68.

16. Elizabeth Achtemeier, *Creative Preaching: Finding the Words* (Nashville: Abingdon Press, 1980), 52–56.

Frequently people think that the process of hearing just happens. They think it is a mere physiological process. Though hearing may happen on some occasions, it involves in most cases a disciplined activity. Charles Bartow observes, "The talk is only half, and it is the least important half. The other half and the most important is listening."[17] Hearing what a text says does not just happen because the text is God's Word. Listening to a text requires active physical, emotional, and mental engagement. Hearers need to understand, summarize, apply, question, agree, or disagree with what the text is saying. Allowing the text to speak to the preacher includes the emotional involvement of empathetic imagination to hear from the biblical writer's perspective. The preacher who studies a text should assume a position of listening until the message uncovered in reading and exegetical study becomes the acting Word on the life of the exegete.

Hearing the truth of the biblical text needs to precede the telling of the truth from the text. How can a person declare truth from a text which that person has not heard? Maybe preachers get so preoccupied with the question, What shall I say? that they have neglected to ask, What is God saying to *me* in the text? A good position for the expository preacher to assume with a text is the stance Eli told Samuel to adopt, "Speak, Lord, for Thy servant is listening" (1 Sam. 3:9). God continues to speak through his Word, and preachers need to listen.

Questioning. Listening and questioning are kindred arts—the two processes belong together. They are not necessarily sequential steps but simultaneous happenings. Raising questions to ideas within the text creates the possibility of the text interpreting the preacher. While reading and studying a text, questions arise both naturally and intentionally. Thomas G. Long calls us to interrogate the text. He cites the theological tradition of the preacher, the contemporary situation, and puzzling aspects of the text as the source of the questions. Long cites a case study of interrogating a text from Amos 5:21, 24 (RSV).

I hate, I despise your feasts,

and I take no delight in your solemn assemblies.

But let justice roll down like waters,

and righteousness like an everflowing stream.

---

17. Charles Bartow, *The Preaching Moment* (Nashville: Abingdon Press, 1980), 13.

The preacher may ask some questions:

- Is the text claiming that God rejects all religious assemblies, feasts and ceremonies, or is there a more complex dynamic at work? If so, what is it?

- Theologically, are justice and righteousness two separate qualities, or are they two faces of the same issue?

- Is there anything about our worship that God "hates"? What would it be? Why?

- Are there places in our religious life where church and civil government become cozy co-conspirators against the needy as they did in Amos' day?

- Is the empty ceremony of the church the only target of the text, or are there other "sanctuaries" in the culture where ceremonies take place that undermine justice and righteousness? If so, where are they?

- Can justice be infused with justice? Can justice be infused with worship? What would these look like?

- This text sounds like bad news. When is bad news "good news"? Can it be bad news and good news at the same time? For the same people?

- What about those people in the congregation who are hanging on to their church life by a thread—people who approach worship and the Christian faith warily, wondering if there is anything here for them? Is there a word in Amos' prophecy for them? A word against them? No word at all?[18]

Interrogating any text does not mean the preacher takes the same question to every text. The uniqueness of each preacher, each text, and each situation demands a different set of questions. Thomas Long raises his questions from his own perspective on the text of Amos. No preacher needs to use another person's questions, and no two texts need to have the same set of questions. Asking questions to a text helps establish interaction and rapport so the text can interpret the preacher.

Paraphrasing. Along with listening and questioning, the act of paraphrasing can also enhance humanly the text's ability to speak to

---

18. Thomas G. Long, *The Witness of Preaching* (Louisville, Ky.: Westminster/ John Knox Press, 1989), 66–67.

the interpreter. Paraphrasing is the interpreter's attempt to rephrase the words of the text in the interpreter's language. Repeated readings and careful exegesis of a text yield truths from the text. These truths need to be expressed in today's language. The truth will not be altered, but the language will vary. Hearing the truths of a text in other words will open the possibility for the text to interpret the preacher.

Empathizing. So far the discussion has centered on actions which could help the text interpret the interpreter. Listening carefully, questioning probingly, and rephrasing practically have been the focus. Another action to help the text interpret the preacher involves imaginative empathizing. It means to crawl into the situation (as much as possible) of the biblical writer and the original readers. Imaginative empathizing involves projecting oneself into the need and to hear the Word of God again. The tedious task of exegesis enhances the preacher's act of empathy to have a greater sense of biblical accuracy rather than mere human speculation.

Meditating. The text is in action during the processes of listening, questioning, paraphrasing, and empathizing. Related to all the actions is another process which enhances the text to interpret the preacher—meaningful meditation. In the quiet moments, in times of reflection, God's Spirit illumines truth from the Word. Such a process cannot be programmed or predicted, but it can be checked with exegesis. The preacher can be assured that God will illumine in a text what he inspired to the text. Experience with Scripture attests to the reality that when one broods on what the Spirit wrote, the same Spirit will illumine the contemporary interpreter.

These five processes or personal disciplines cannot be viewed as sequential steps. Instead, they are actions built into the lifestyle of the expository preacher. They happen at various times. Sometimes one or more of these may happen as the preacher engages in serious exegesis. At other times they may happen during a casual reading of the text. Then again, the text can interpret a person during the routine of living. The best advice is for the exegete to study the text as a scholar and expect the text to interpret the exegete as he or she experiences the text. When the text interprets the preacher, then the truth is ready to be shaped in a sermon so the truth of the text can interpret the audience.

The Text Interprets the People

Interaction occurs when the text interprets the preacher; interaction also occurs when the text interprets the audience by means of the preacher. During the preaching moment, the Holy Spirit who illumined the preacher in preparation illumines the hearers, and the truth of the text interacts with the people. Each text in a series of sermons from a Bible book will pass through the personality of the preacher and interpret truths as people listen. Biblical texts originated as a result of God addressing the needs of people. A preacher serves a text best when that preacher allows and helps the text to interpret people with their various needs.

Just as no systematic methodology could be proposed for the text to interpret the preacher, no foolproof system can help the text interpret the people. Nonetheless, some procedures can be practiced to help listeners make contact with the text.

Knowing the People. One helpful procedure is for the preacher to know people. Knowing people involves the process of cognitive understanding. Truths within a text had people for their destination, and these same truths need to be addressed to people in today's world. Fred Craddock said that "in both the text and the congregation there are real issues of life and death and purpose which reach out to each other, resonating with each other asking help of each other."[19] All listeners represent creatures made in the image of God. In every person, God's image has become marred. Yet every person has the potential in Christ to become more what God intended that individual to be. Human beings of all cultures and races share the same experience of love and hate, trust and suspicion, evil and good, guilt and forgiveness, tragedies and triumphs. Such cognitive knowledge of human nature and experience should help the preacher connect the text with the people.

Sharing with People. In addition to cognitive knowledge about human beings, knowledge can be gained by experience with people. Most preachers who preach a series of sermons from a Bible book function as a pastor, which allows them to have personal contact with people. The pastor hears about joys and sorrows, ambitions and disappointments, successes and failures. The pastor sees people at their best and their worst. The more a pastor relates experientially with people, the more the possibility increases of connecting

19. Fred B. Craddock, *Preaching* (Nashville: Abingdon Press, 1985), 86.

the text with people. Understanding experientially enables the preacher to hold a text before the lives of people. Fred Craddock said: "If the listeners can leave the service with no sense of having been put down; if their self-worth has been affirmed or restored; if God's love and grace are seen as available realities; if they are convinced that repentance and trust are acceptable to God; if there is more awareness of other persons and more hunger for covenanted life; even then strangers will likely say to the preacher, 'You understood us well.'"[20]

Emphathizing with People. The effective expositor seeks to empathize with people in the audience. Craddock calls this "empathetic imagination."[21] This is the capacity to achieve a large measure of understanding about another person without having had that person's experience. Craddock suggests that preachers take a blank sheet of paper and write at the top, "What's It Like to Be?" Beneath the heading he writes a phrase that describes some human experience: facing surgery, losing a mate by death, living alone, going through a divorce, loss of wealth, instant riches, fired from a job, sixteen years old, unable to read, being poor.[22] Going through such empathetic imaginations can enable the preacher to know people and to relate the sermon text to their lives.

Relating the Text to Their Lives. Another procedure useful in helping the text connect and interpret people involves touching the truth of the text to their lives. Two different focuses are needed in studying a text: one on the world of the biblical text and the other on the world of the listeners. The biblical world has its contexts: historical, theological, grammatical, and literary. The listeners also have their contexts: personal, domestic, social, political, and economic. The gap between these two worlds is generally called distance. Factors of time, language, worldview, and circumstances created the distance. The preacher needs to know both worlds so he will have a better chance of touching the then and now in the act of preaching.[23]

Working for Discovery. The effective expositor strives to present the truth of the text so that people can discover the truths of the text as the preacher discovered the truths. Sermon preparation

---

20. Ibid., 90.
21. Ibid., 95.
22. Ibid., 96.
23. Ernest Best, *From Text to Sermon* (Atlanta: John Knox Press, 1978), 11–53.

should not just involve the preacher finding truth and delivering truths to audiences as edicts and ultimatums to be accepted and obeyed by docile listeners. Truth needs to be discovered by the preacher, but it also needs to be communicated so that listeners can get in on the process of discovering truth. Sometimes preachers may be dictators of orders, but in many cases preachers may be facilitators or leaders in exploration. After the preacher's "eureka!" the action needs to be to help the listeners come to their "eureka!"

Principles of Interpretation

Exegesis and interpretation are kindred disciplines, but they differ in theory and practice. Through exegesis, the expositor uses rather established scientific guidelines, but there are not scientific guidelines for interpretation. The exegete studies texts rather scientifically and arrives somewhat objectively at what the text meant. The interpreter builds or refers back to exegesis in helping determine and communicate what the text means. We can bake a cake by a recipe, assemble a bicycle from instructions, and play golf by a rule book; but interpreting texts cannot come from a rule book. The Bible contains dynamic possibilities found by human discovery and intriguing illuminations brought by the Holy Spirit; therefore, prescribed procedures cannot be fully applied to the discipline of interpretation.

Principles of performing interpretation of a text are not as prominent among biblical scholars and writers on homiletics as the guideline for performing exegesis. Perhaps the reason for such a deficiency exists because exegesis and interpretation have not been treated as separate disciplines for many years. In his book *Preaching Biblically: Exegesis and Interpretation,* William D. Thompson distinguishes between the tasks of exegesis and interpretation. In exegesis the preacher seeks to get at what the text *said* and in interpretation the preacher seeks to get at what the text *says.*[24] Thompson gives guidelines for completing exegesis and then blazes a new trail by giving some guidelines for engaging in interpretation. To be an expository preacher, the truth of a text needs to be exposed and related to the needs of people. Drawing from many of the ideas of William D. Thompson, six general principles will be discussed to help the preacher interpret or relate the text to people in today's world.

---

24. Thompson, 15.

Interpretive Principle #1: Observe the Obvious

The starting point for the interpretation of a text begins with the observations of the clear, plain, obvious meaning of a passage. John Calvin said: "Let us know, then, that the true meaning of Scripture is the natural and obvious meaning; and let us embrace and abide by it resolutely. Let us not neglect as doubtful, but boldly set aside as deadly corruptions, those pretended expositions which lead us away from the intended meaning."[25] Mere human sensibility about a text needs to be applied before attempting to discover some deeper meaning.

Most texts in the Bible can be grasped with a simple, thoughtful reading. Think of the obvious meanings in a few selected passages. "And the Word became flesh, and dwelt among us, and we beheld His glory, glory as of the only begotten from the Father, full of grace and truth" (John 1:14). Obviously, this text means that the eternal God became a human being. The Word lived among people, and they were able to see God's glory in the incarnate Christ. Though the theology is quite profound, the interpretation of the text is obvious.

Consider two other passages. "And He went a little beyond them" (Matt. 26:39a). The simple meaning of the passage seems to be that Jesus went geographically further into the garden of Gethsemane away from the disciples. But some have interpreted the passage to mean that Jesus went beyond his disciples in dedication. That latter is certainly true, but was not the truth of that particular text. Another passage often taken beyond the obvious meaning is: Jesus said, "Put out into the deep water" (Luke 5:4a). Some expositors interpret this passage as an exhortation to go deeper with God. While going deeper with God is a legitimate demand, Jesus was obviously telling Simon Peter to go deeper in water for fishing.

Discerning the simple meaning of a text helps guard against the widespread allegorization. Allegorizing a text involves deriving meaning other than the author's intended meaning. Allegorizing a text cuts it loose from the moorings of time, place, and historical circumstance and gives it a timeless, spiritual meaning. For example, Jesus' parable of the woman seeking the lost coin (see Luke 15:8–10) has been interpreted allegorically so that the woman

---

25. John Calvin, *Commentaries on the Epistles of Paul to the Galatians and Ephesians* (Edinburgh: Calvin Translation Society, 1854), 136.

lighting a lamp became a reference to the doctrine of the church. The lamp represents the church, the wick is the Scripture, the oil is prayer, and the flame is the Holy Spirit. Such allegorical assertions depart drastically from the simple, obvious teaching that Jesus seeks the lost and rejoices when he finds them.

Observing the obvious meaning of a text does not mean that an interpreter fails to consider both literal and figurative language. Examples of texts where literal language prevails might be helpful. "But I say to you, love your enemies, and pray for those who perse- cute you" (Matt. 5:44). "And beyond all these things put on love, which is the perfect bond of unity" (Col. 3:14). The meaning of these words from Jesus and Paul obviously should be taken literally. Jesus wanted his followers to love their enemies, and Paul wanted believers to put God's kind of love into their lives. Those meanings are quite obvious, and nothing unrelated to those meanings should be read into the passage.

In figurative passages, interpreters need to be careful about the literal language. Consider these two texts as an example. "If anyone comes to Me, and does not hate his own father and mother and wife and children and brothers and sisters, yes, and even his own life, he cannot be My disciple" (Luke 14:26). "And if your right eye makes you stumble, tear it out" (Matt. 5:29a). Obviously Jesus did not teach people to hate family members or to tear out their eyes. Jesus used hyperbole, or exaggeration for effect, to describe the pri- ority of commitment to him and to depict the removal of lust. The best action involves the exercise of common sense.

Interpretive Principle #2: Probe for the Purpose

Interpreting a text does not build on a foundation separate from exegesis. Performing exegesis on a passage rests heavily on the his- torical background; interpretation also builds on the text's original background. Every passage in a Bible book was included there for some reason. No book in the Bible just happened. God inspired Bible books to meet human needs, and his words have a lasting rel- evancy to people. The interpreter's task is to probe for the original purpose of a passage. This has been called "the pursuit of intentionality."[26]

---

26. Thompson, 26.

Discovering the intentionality of a text does not come as easily as observing the obvious meaning of a text. Knowing the purpose of a passage requires skillful and persistent probing. Intentionality in a text results from the exercise of exegesis where one studies the life situation *(Sitz im Leben)* of a Bible book. Some circumstance motivated the author to write the book—a gathering for worship, a severe persecution, a doctrinal error, an unruly church, or a rebellious nation. Each specific text needs to be studied, giving serious consideration of the overall purpose of the Bible book and the relation of the text to that purpose.

Probing the overall purpose of a Bible book prevents taking the text out of its original intentionality. Consider a passage from Colossians 2:21 (KJV): "Touch not; taste not; handle not." Sometimes this text has been used as a basis to fight the use of drugs and alcohol. Paul was writing against false doctrine. He warned the Colossians against the heretics' food and drink ordinances. Sermons against alcohol and drug addiction are necessary, but they need to be based on texts that call Christians to self-control and warn against addiction.

Intentionality begins to emerge when an interpreter takes time to overhear Israel's kings and prophets or to hear Paul's discussion with Christians in various congregations. Books were addressed to specific persons, in specific places, and in specific circumstances. Colossians 1:2a is an example: "To the saints and faithful brethren in Christ who are at Colossae." As the interpreter probes the ancient past and the specific situation of a text, distances of time, place, and culture fade as ancient issues of faith, morality, failure, forgiveness, orthodoxy, family, government, and death begin to sound remarkably current. Searching for the author's intention often leads the interpreter to the current application of biblical truth.

Interpretive Principle #3: Build the Bridge

The whole interpretation process involves connecting the biblical world with the contemporary world. The preacher needs to see and to help others see how God's Word to an ancient people becomes a word to contemporary people. Using the fruits of exegesis, the preacher needs to conduct a diligent search between the Word spoken then and the meaning of that Word now. John R. W.

Stott gave the graphic metaphor of a bridge to illustrate the essential nature of preaching. Stott wrote:

> Now a bridge is a means of communication between two places which would otherwise be cut off from one another by a river or ravine. It makes possible a flow of traffic which without it would be impossible. What, then, does the gorge or chasm represent? And what is the bridge which spans it? The chasm is the deep rift between the biblical world and the modern world. . . . It is across the broad and deep divide of two thousand years of changing culture . . . that Christian communicators have to throw bridges. Our task is to enable God's revealed truth to flow out of the Scripture into the lives of men and women of today.[27]

Writers on interpretation use various terms for bridge building such as correspondence, correlation, historical continuity, similarity, equivalency, identification, transference, parallelism, linkage, analogy, resemblance, paradigm, or comparability.[28] Though the terminology varies, the pursuit remains the same—moving from the past to the present. Leander Keck said, "The preacher must identify what today's hearers share with the author's original hearers so that the text confronts them both."[29]

Crossing the chasm between the biblical world and the modern world is sometimes easy. God spoke to Moses about leading the children out of Egyptian bondage. Moses responded with reluctance because of the enormity of the task. God made a promise to Moses: "Certainly I will be with you" (Ex. 3:12). God assured Moses that He would be with him as he led the Israelites from Goshen to Canaan. In the text, building the bridge comprises no real difficulty. Any person responding to God's bidding can be assured of the reality of God's presence.

Building a bridge from the historical context of James 5:1–6 to today's world is not difficult. James addressed a specific historical situation where some wealthy landowners had cheated common laborers. Parallels can be easily made and bridges built from that first-century economic injustice to twentieth-century economic injustices.

In other texts, the art of giving an analogy and building a bridge is more difficult. Ernest Best in his book *From Text to Sermon: Responsible Use of the New Testament in Preaching* discusses three fac-

---

27. Stott, 137–38.
28. Thompson, 51.
29. Keck, 117.

tors that widen the chasm between the past and the present: situations, culture, and worldviews. Some ancient situations correspond little with modern culture. Among the churches of Galatia, people known as Judaizers insisted that Gentile converts to Christianity had to be circumcised and had to observe other Jewish laws. This specific situation does not exist today. Making the correlation and building a bridge from Galatians to today take creative work. Though groups known as Judaizers do not exist today, people with stress on what one should and should not do prevail. Thus, correspondence can be established from the specific Galatians situation to contemporary legalistic situations. The situations may differ in specifics, but analogy can be established.

Ernest Best also wrote about how culture separates the ancient world from the contemporary world, making correlation of the two difficult. One of the clearest examples of differences between the cultures is in the biblical understanding of personality. The Hebraic mind-set thought of persons as a whole being. The Greek-dominated culture of the New Testament thought persons were separated into body and soul. The Greek view of dividing persons made possible the heresy that one's soul could be saved while the body enjoyed whatever pleasures it would. Also, some cultural ideas were common to both Greeks and Jews. Because ancients were not so fascinated as we moderns with "laws of nature," ancients believed in miracles more easily than moderns. Many today seek scientific explanations for everything.

In addition to situations and culture, Best specified worldview as another significant separation of the ancient and contemporary worlds. Within the Greek world, one could find the Epicurean, the Stoic, the Gnostic, and many other worldviews. Judaism produced several worldviews with the zealots, the legalists, the apocalypticists, and others. The Christian stance prevailed against these two worldviews.

Crossing the chasms created by situations, cultures, and worldviews involves vicarious projection. Learning the ancient languages, archaeology, history, and anthropology helps the interpreter crawl into the skin of the ancients.

Another consideration helps with the correspondence of the biblical world and today's world: the continuity of human nature and human experience in all cultures. Every person in every culture shares in the image of God, the fall, and the yearning for a relationship with God. Furthermore, Christians today share the experience of a redeeming relationship with the God of Abraham, Isaac, and Jacob.

The chasm is wide. A preacher cannot afford to have one stance either in the past or in the present. Though the distance is difficult, bridges can be built from the ancient to today.

Interpretive Principle #4: Learn About the Language

Learning about the nature and use of the language helps discern meaning. The New Hermeneutic movement gave a new slant on work when they spoke about "language event." Gerhard Ebeling thought of language not as "mere speech" but "an event in which God himself is communicated."[30] Ebeling's concern was not that people use terms such as *reconciliation* to speak about God's past and continuing action. He was concerned that the words *create* reconciliation. The power of language did not originate with the New Hermeneutic movement. The starting place for the action is the Bible itself with its language format of power. "And God said" constitutes words spoken and actions occurring.

Learning the language of a text involves understanding the elements of language and observing the action intended behind the text. William D. Thompson points out four elements that inform the interpreter of what constitutes language: words, grammar and syntax, abstraction, and figures of speech.

- Discovering the meaning of words holds a high priority in exegesis, and learning and disclosing the meaning of words overlap and figure prominently in the interpretation process.

- Grammar and syntax comprise a large part of exegesis, and the process needs to be continued in interpretation.

- Abstraction is another element in language. To learn the use of language, communicators need to move from the abstract to the concrete.

- Figures of speech help the preacher make language come alive.[31]

---

30. Gerhard Ebeling, *The Nature of Faith* (Philadelphia: Fortress Press, 1968), 183.

31. Thompson, 66–70.

Learning language also involves the action intended behind the text. Fred Craddock suggested that the interpreter ask, What is the text doing?[32] When words of the Bible were inspired and written, those words were doing something. They were informing, correcting, encouraging, persuading, confirming, comforting, or many other actions. Words of the text never consisted of mere words but words intended to do something. These words have not died. They continue to do something, and the task of the interpreter is to get at what the text is doing. What a text is doing usually proceeds from the historical and literary contents or from the form of the text.[33]

Interpretive Principle #5: Ask for the Analogy

Closely akin to the principles of probing and building the bridge is the principle of asking for the analogy. The task of the interpreter involves finding where there is correspondence of the ancient text and current human needs. William Thompson writes, "The basic interpretative process involves correspondence between the biblical and contemporary worlds."[34] Writers on interpretation describe the relationship as correlation, historical continuity, similarity, identification, transference, parallelism, linkage, analogy, resemblance, paradigm, or comparability.[35] The basic idea is to take a truth or an event of the ancient past and relate it to the contemporary world or to take a current life situation and find analogy with the biblical world.

James Sanders in his book, *God Has a Story Too*, clarifies some thoughts about analogy. Sanders warned against using texts as maxims for morality rather than mirrors for identity. According to Sanders, the preacher does not study texts to find lessons, but the preacher identifies with biblical characters and situations to find analogy. The interpretative technique that seeks to discover, classify, and apply propositions to life resembles "a box of jewels of wisdom forever of static value." Application in this perspective tends to view an audience as passive people who have come to learn lessons about God and put them in practice.[36]

---

32. Craddock, 123.

33. Ibid.

34. Thompson, 50.

35. Ibid., 51.

36. James Sanders, *God Has a Story Too* (Philadelphia: Fortress Press, 1979), 134.

Sanders gave another technique for application which he called "dynamic analogy." God's Word is not mere record; it is dynamic and alive. The biblical story continues to happen. Therefore, a congregation is not listening to lessons but identifying with people and situations in the biblical text. Asking for the analogy involves such questions as: Where do I see myself in this text's truth or story? Where do people to whom I preach fit into the story or truth? Discovering the meaning of a passage often occurs when a person places himself or herself in the text. Such projection prompts a person to ask what the text meant to the original audience and what the text means to hearers today.

Helmut Thielicke set his little son in front of a large mirror. At first the boy did not recognize himself. The boy smiled at the image. He made movements and watched the image in the mirror. After a while the expression on the boy's face changed as he recognized the familiarity of the motions, and he seemed to say, "That's me!"[37]

The same thing happens when any interpreter places himself or herself in the truth of the story of the text. Making an analogy involves bringing an ancient text in contact with people's needs in today's world in such a way that the two relate. Making an analogy is a process that relates biblical truths so hearers not only understand how these truths affect change in their lives but also feel obligated and even eager to implement these changes. To ask for the analogy means to ask where and how the ancient past of a passage throws light on people living in today's world.

Interpretive Principle #6: Interpret by Illustration

In the process of exegesis and interpretation, a vital process in helping with meaning is illumining the passage of Scripture. Finding meaning in a text comes when the interpreter illumines the truths found in a text. Quite often illustrations have been restricted solely to the field of homiletics, but actually illustrations can fit securely in the field of hermeneutics when someone searches for meaning in a passage. To illustrate means to illumine, to throw light on a subject. Illustrations transform the abstract into the concrete, the ancient into the modern, the unfamiliar into the familiar,

---

37. Helmut Thielicke, *The Waiting Father: Sermons on the Parables of Jesus*, trans. John W. Doberstein (London: James Clarke and Company, 1959), 17–18.

the general into the particular, the vague into the precise, the unreal into the real, and the invisible into the visible. The truly interpretative expositor turns hearers' ears into eyes and helps them see what is being said.[38]

The task of biblical interpretation needs to include the process of illustration. The biblical writers used parables, similes, metaphors, and other illustrative techniques to illumine their axioms and admonitions. A frequent expression in Jesus' ministry was "The kingdom of heaven is like," and then the analogy was given. Instead of using abstract language to explain the Kingdom, Jesus used picture language. Paul often interpreted abstractions such as the conflict between good and evil with an illustration from the equipment of a Roman soldier (Eph. 6:10–20). He interpreted the invisible by a visible illustration.

To illumine truth in a text requires imagination. Henry Ward Beecher defined imagination as "that power of the mind by which it conceives of invisible things, and is able to present them as though they were visible to others."[39] Paul referred to his preaching of the cross to the Galatians as a "public portrayal" before their eyes of Jesus Christ as the one who had been crucified (see Gal. 3:1). The crucifixion occurred twenty years previously, and none of Paul's Galatian readers had been present to witness it. Yet, by his varied imagination, Paul brought the past event into the present, out of hearsay into a dramatic visual image. Such is the purpose of interpreting by illustration, to stimulate people's imaginations and to help them to see truths and ancient events clearly in their minds.

—⁂——⁂——⁂——⁂——⁂—

The expository preacher looks both at what a Bible book *meant* and what a Bible book *means*. Each of these perspectives requires a different set of principles. Using the exercises for exegesis and the guidelines for interpretation together helps the expositor see what was *said* and what the text is *saying*. No expositor should neglect either exegesis or interpretation, especially in the process of preaching from a Bible book. Exegesis helps the expositor understand what happened in the past, and interpretation helps use the discoveries in exegesis and relate biblical truth to the present.

---

38. Stott, 239.

39. Henry Ward Beecher, *Yale Lectures on Preaching* (New York: J. B. Ford and Company, 1872), 134.

Preaching from Old Testament Books (Pentateuch, History, and Poetry)

Effective expositors must select and preach systematically from both Old Testament and New Testament books. Most contemporary preachers have few problems in choosing New Testament books. But some careful observers believe the Old Testament is a neglected resource for expository preaching.[1] An expositor needs to acknowledge all sixty-six books as the canon; thus, any one of these

---

1. Neil Richardson, *Preaching the Scriptures* (London: Epworth Press, 1983), 79.

197

inspired books could become the resource for a series of sermons. Preaching the whole counsel of God involves preaching both Old and New Testament books. The suggestion has already been made in this work that the expositor preach a series of sermons from one Old Testament book and from one New Testament book each year.

According to Elizabeth Achtemeier, "Many preachers rarely, if ever, preach from the Old Testament."[2] They prefer texts either from the Gospels or the Epistles. In practice, if not in theory, many preachers have become followers of Marcion, the second-century Christian who suggested that the church should get rid of the Hebrew Scriptures. Fortunately, most of Marcion's fellow Christians thought otherwise. Ever since, two testaments have formed the Christian Bible. Because both testaments are divinely inspired, historically substantiated, theologically informative, and providentially preserved, the contemporary preacher should not neglect any Bible book either for an individual sermon or for a series of sermons.

Although few today are followers of Marcion, much contemporary preaching neglects the Old Testament. Achtemeier says, "It is fair to say that the Old Testament is largely a lost book in many parts of the U.S. church."[3] Achtemeier also observes that when preachers do preach from the Old Testament, most of the text selections come from the Ten Commandments, some stories used as moral lessons, a few psalms, and some of the noble sayings of the prophets.[4] Beyond these few selections, "the Old Testament is unknown and unimportant to them, an unopened antique book from the distant past that can safely be left with the other antiques on the curio shelf."[5]

Donald E. Gowan in his book, *Reclaiming the Old Testament for the Christian Pulpit*, gives a possible reason for the neglect of the Old Testament in the Christian pulpit and a possible solution for reclaiming the Old Testament. Gowan thinks the neglect is caused by the allegorization of Old Testament texts throughout Christian history. Preachers like Bernard of Clairvaux, who preached eighty-six allegorical sermons on the Song of Solomon, could conscribe all

---

2. Elizabeth Achtemeier, *Preaching from the Old Testament* (Louisville, Ky.: Westminster/John Knox Press, 1989), 21.

3. Ibid.

4. Ibid.

5. Ibid.

kinds of doctrines from the Old Testament texts. Gowan's hope for reclaiming the Old Testament for the Christian pulpit rests with the historical-critical approach to the Scriptures. Serious and scientific study of the Old Testament has put allegorical and typological interpretation out of favor. Gowan believes that the Old Testament could be reclaimed for the Christian pulpit by serious study of life situations of Old Testament books, the language found in the Old Testament books, and other exegetical studies.[6]

Books of the Bible may be grouped into literary categories. These categories make a difference in the kind of sermons created from a Bible book in the category. To preach effectively and systematically from Old Testament books, the expositor should become acquainted with five general divisions:

- pentateuchal books
- historical books
- poetical books
- wisdom books
- prophetic books

During a lifetime of ministry, the expositor should preach at least one series of sermons from each of these five categories.

The Pentateuchal Books

The first five books of the Old Testament (Genesis, Exodus, Leviticus, Numbers, and Deuteronomy) made up the first section of the Hebrew Scriptures. These were accepted as authoritative for the life of the religious community. These books have been grouped in titles such as the Law, Books of Moses, and Pentateuch. To many Jews these books were known as *Torah*, which is the Hebrew word for *law*. The Jewish people accepted these books as having more authority than other books. In some circles these five books were called the Books of Moses primarily because Moses was the central figure in most of the books and because many associated Moses with the authorship of the books. Early in the Christian tradition, these books came under the category or title of the Pentateuch. The word comes from two Greek words, *pente* (five) and *teuchos* (volume) which simply referred to a five-

6. Donald E. Gowan, *Reclaiming the Old Testament for the Christian Pulpit* (Atlanta: John Knox Press, 1980), v–vi.

volume work.[7] Abundant literary varieties exist in these five books. Expositors will encounter historical narration, law, poetry, and many other literary forms. Though these first five books come under a common title, each book in the Pentateuch possesses its own uniqueness, unity, and message.[8]

General Information About the Pentateuchal Books

To preach effectively from any Old Testament book, information needs to be secured about the general genre. A thorough study of the Pentateuch is helpful, though some expositors consider the issues tedious and unrewarding. This work is not intended to be an extensive study in pentateuchal issues, but some studies will be mentioned so expositors can pursue these matters.

Authorship. For over sixteen hundred years, Christians generally held that Moses was the author of the Pentateuch. In 1753, a French physician, Jean Astruc, published a work that encouraged source criticism of the Pentateuch. Astruc saw two documents in Genesis. He distinguished passages using the name Elohim (God) from those using the name Yahweh (Lord). Astruc separated the Pentateuch into different documents, but he continued to argue that Moses was the author. This research at first seemed like harmless speculation, but it launched the beginning of scholarly research in the authorship of the Pentateuch.

Later scholars in pentateuchal studies proposed that four principal sources were used to compose the Pentateuch, all of which claimed to have been completed after the time of Moses. The first source was known as J. It was dated in the tenth century B.C. and was written in Judah. Yahweh was the name used for deity. The second source was labeled E, dated in the eighth century B.C., and was written in Ephraim. The prominent name for deity was Elohim. The third source was called D from the deuteronomic historians. It was dated about 621 B.C. The fourth source was known as P from a priestly group of writers about 500 B.C. It consisted mainly of legal sections and the history bound up with the laws. Julius Wellhausen's source criticism concluded that four main documents

---

7. Robert L. Cate, *An Introduction to the Old Testament and Its Study* (Nashville: Broadman Press, 1987), 115–16.

8. James M. Efird, *How to Interpret the Bible* (Atlanta: John Knox Press, 1984), 19.

stand behind the Pentateuch. His theory became known as the Documentary Hypothesis.[9]

The Documentary Hypothesis flourished for a while among Old Testament scholars. Commentators spent much time trying to identify sources in the material in the Pentateuch. Yet more recent pentateuchal scholarship has turned away from the Documentary Hypothesis. Scholars such as Umberto Cassuto have challenged every argument upon which the hypothesis rests. Though Cassuto and other scholars have struck at the foundations of the documentary hypothesis, some scholars still refuse to desert the theory entirely, but they are busy remodeling the interior.

Competent conservative Old Testament scholars hold to the idea that Moses wrote the first five books of the Bible. Writers such as Edward J. Young, Allen P. Ross, and Derek Kidner named Moses as the author, and they also allowed that other authors could have been used to write parts of the Pentateuch. Convictions about Moses as the author of the Pentateuch are presented with both internal and external evidences. Any serious study of authorship of the Pentateuch must deal with some internal evidences of Moses as the author (see Exod. 17:14; 24:4; 34:27; Num. 33:1–2; Deut. 31:9, 22). Other references in Scripture associate Moses with the Pentateuch. For centuries the tradition has existed that Moses wrote most of the Pentateuch.

The essential issue about the authorship of the Pentateuch rests on inspiration and reliability, not the precise identification of sources. The materials in the Pentateuch deserve a series of sermons because they are God-breathed, related to life in ancient Israel, and pertinent to life today. Questions about human authorship will probably go unanswered, but affirmation about divine authorship has already been settled.

Literary Limits. In the Hebrew canon, the Torah is made up of the first five books. However, for over one hundred years, some Old Testament scholars have called attention to the fact that the material in Genesis through Numbers is different from Deuteronomy. Thus, they called the first four books the Tetrateuch (meaning four).

Other Old Testament scholars have cited similarities between the material in Joshua and the material in Genesis through Num-

---

9. Clyde T. Francisco, "Genesis," in *The Broadman Bible Commentary*, Vol. 1, rev. (Nashville: Broadman Press, 1973), 103.

bers. Thus, these scholars propose the literary unit extends from Genesis through Joshua, and it should be called a Hexateuch (meaning six).

Still other scholars pointed out the relationship of Deuteronomy and the material in Joshua, Judges, 1 and 2 Samuel, and 1 and 2 Kings. Scholars now call this block of books the Deuteronomic History.

All of these literary groups have proposed plausible units. But the reality an expositor faces is that from the earliest days of the Hebrew Canon, the basic literary unit was the Torah—Genesis through Deuteronomy.[10]

Relation to Other Ancient Literature. Some kind of similarity exists between the biblical material in the Pentateuch and other materials found in the Near East of which Israel was a part. Some creation accounts such as the Babylonian account Enuma Elish show affinity to the Genesis account. Some flood narratives such as the Gilgamesh Epic—a Babylonian flood account—also show similarities. Law codes of other nations of the Near East show degrees of similarity to the Pentateuch. Three possible explanations could be presented. First, Israel borrowed from other sources. Second, other sources borrowed from Israel. Or, a third explanation is that all borrowed from an unknown source.

Robert L. Cate has suggested a good possibility about reconciling the relationship of literary relationships. Cate argues that the Israelites could have taken ancient narratives of other people and used them to explain the nature and action of the true and living God.[11]

Numerous other issues exist regarding pentateuchal material. As an expositor studies the first five books, references can be noted about polygamous marriages, substitution of handmaidens for barren wives, birthrights, family blessings, long life spans, and numerous other matters. Preaching from any one of the five pentateuchal books requires investigation of such material. The expositor will be informed about these matters, though not all of this study will come before the congregation.

---

10. Cate, 116–17.
11. Ibid.

Individual Investigation of the Pentateuchal Books

Genesis. Though the first five books of the Bible have been classified in a larger unit called the Pentateuch, an expositor needs to examine each book to see which one needs proclamation. The name for the Book of Genesis comes from the Greek Septuagint through the Latin Vulgate and carries with it the idea of origin or beginnings. Genesis is truly a book of beginnings; it relates the beginning of God's redemptive work. It also relates the beginning of the nations and the Hebrew people in particular. The rabbis called the first of the biblical books *Bereshith*, which is translated "in beginning."

The key to the structure of Genesis begins in the Hebrew word *toledhoth*, which is translated in most cases "generation." The word *toledhoth* was a word used to introduce sections of history. The ten usages of *toledhoth* are preceded by an introductory passage (1:1–2:3). The other ten divisions are the *toledhoth* of the heavens and the earth (2:4–4:26), of Adam (5:1–6:8), of Noah (6:9–9:29), of the sons of Noah (10:1–11:9), of Shem (11:10–26), of Terah (11:27–25:11), of Ishmael (25:12–18), of Isaac (25:19–35:29), of Esau (36:1–37:1), and of Jacob (37:2–50:26). Genesis may be seen in two main parts, the first being the primeval history in chapters 1–11 and the second being the patriarchal history in chapters 12–50.

Abundant preaching themes prevail in Genesis. In Genesis 1–11 such ideas as the creation of the universe, the creation of human beings, the fall of human beings, the redemptive promise for human beings, the interpersonal problems, the judgment of God with a flood, and the mob mentality of wanting to exalt human accomplishment. Also, preaching themes abound in Genesis 12–50 with insights and truths found in and around the lives of Abraham, Isaac, Jacob, and Joseph.

Exodus. The name for Exodus comes from a Latinized form of the Greek word *exodus*. It also came to the English Bible through the Septuagint and the Vulgate. The Jews called the book by its first words, "And these are the names." The Book of Exodus continues the story of Genesis. Exodus has both a historical and theological purpose. Historically, one can see how the people of Israel were delivered from Egypt and brought to Sinai. Theologically, we can see the sovereign power of God. The Book of Exodus has as its theme the revelation of God's power and lordship over history, nature, and human beings. The book contains the record of God's people in Egypt, their deliverance, and their sustenance in the wilderness. Roy L. Honeycutt in emphasizing the historical and theological aspects of Exodus used the following analyses:

1. Yahweh, Lord of History, 1:1–7:13

2. Yahweh, Lord of Creation, 7:14–18:27

3. Yahweh, Lord of Man, 19:1–24:14

4. Yahweh, Lord of Worship, 25:15–40:38[12]

Even a casual reading of Exodus reveals that the Lord is in control of everything.

In light of the message of Exodus and the historical happenings in Exodus, many preaching possibilities exist. God working in ancient history could be related to his work in the world today. Preaching from Exodus could portray the providence of God in events from Exodus to Sinai and then to the wilderness. Many theological themes from Exodus relate to life today.

Leviticus. The Book of Leviticus is named after the tribe of Levi. The Levites were responsible for the ceremonial functions of Hebrew religion. The Book of Leviticus has to do more with the priests than with the tribe of Levi. Not all Levites were priests, but each priest had to be a Levite. The Book of Leviticus contains codes and regulations regarding priesthood and worship. The Book of Leviticus was written to teach people how to worship and to encourage God's people to be holy because he is holy. Of the five books of the Pentateuch, Leviticus is the one most consistently described as Law. Its contents consist almost entirely of laws and regulations with only a few intervening narratives. The contents are as follows:

1. The instructions for sacrifice, 1:1–7:38

2. The ministry of the priests, 8:1–10:20

3. The regulations regarding purity, 11:1–15:33

4. The great day of atonement, 16:1–34

5. The laws of holiness, 17:1–26:46

6. The laws about oaths and gifts, 27:1–34[13]

---

12. Roy L. Honeycutt, "Exodus," in *The Broadman Bible Commentary*, vol. 2 (Nashville: Broadman Press, 1973), 299.

13. Ronald E. Clements, "Leviticus," in *The Broadman Bible Commentary*, vol. 2 (Nashville: Broadman Press, 1970), 7.

Numbers. The fourth book of the Pentateuch takes its title from the Septuagint. The title apparently originated because of the three recorded numberings of the children of Israel (see Num. 1; 4; 26). The Hebrew title *bemidhbar* which means "in the wilderness" fits more appropriately to the actual content of the book. The Book of Numbers serves as a bridge between the legislation of Leviticus and Israel's preparation for entering into the land of Canaan. Numbers begins with a large block of statistical and legislative material, then proceeds to narrative material about Israel's travel from Sinai to Kadesh and thirty-eight years of wanderings until they reach Moab, a land on the threshold of Canaan. The Book of Numbers flows as follows:

1. At Sinai, 1:1–10:10

2. From Sinai to Paran, 13:1–21:35

3. Murmurings in the Wilderness of Paran, 13:1–21:35

4. Camping at Moab, 22:1–36:13[14]

Preaching from Numbers presents some real challenges. The book contains census lists, descriptions of territorial boundaries, cultic material, festival calendars, narration, poetry, prophetic oracles, and reports of divination. The first section of the book contains statistical and legal material that are rarely used as sermon texts. The next three sections of Numbers contain many items of sermonic interest such as Moses and his father-in-law; the complaining people; the complaint of Miriam and Aaron over Moses; the investigation and report of the twelve spies; the rebellion of Korah, Dothan, and Abraham; the budding of Aaron's rod; Moses striking the rock; the fiery serpents; the victory over Sihon; the Balaam incident; the commission of Joshua; the instruction about vows; and the review of the journey. The book not only records events but also interprets the events by seeing God's leading his chosen people, meeting their needs, keeping his covenant, extending grace during times of rebellion, and exercising discipline when necessary.[15]

---

14. J. J. Owens, "Numbers," in *The Broadman Bible Commentary*, vol. 2 (Nashville: Broadman Press, 1970), 80–82.

15. Clyde T. Francisco, *Introducing the Old Testament*, rev. ed. (Nashville: Broadman Press, 1977), 87.

Deuteronomy. The title of the fifth pentateuchal book came from a mistranslation of Deuteronomy 17:18, "a copy of the law." Instead, the expression was rendered "this second law." Though the translation was not the best, the title fits the book, for it is a repetition of the legislation found in the preceding books. The Jews called Deuteronomy *ellah haddevarim* which involves the first two words in the Hebrew, meaning "these are the words."

The Book of Deuteronomy is composed primarily of speeches. It contains a series of three discourses delivered by Moses to the Israelites on the plains of Moab at the close of the wilderness wanderings and just prior to the entrance into Canaan. The themes for these discourses are God's gracious dealings with Israel and his appeals to Israel for a response of love and loyalty. The first discourse (1:1–4:43) outlines the journey from Horab to Moab. Moses exhorted the Israelites to be loyal to the Lord and to renounce idolatry. The second discourse (4:44–26:19) contains exhortations and legislative material. This section summarizes civil, moral, and religious laws and stresses the idea of holiness. The third discourse (27:1–31:30) contains the blessings and curses, the blessings of obedience and the curses of disobedience. Following these discourses are three appendages: Moses' song (32:1–52), Moses' blessing (33:1–29), and Moses' death and burial (34:1–12).

Proclamation possibility abounds in Deuteronomy, though the book contains some difficult explanations, including the commands for holy war. Jesus used Deuteronomy as a resource when he was tempted (see Matt. 4:4, 7, 10); when he answered the question about the greatest commandment (see Matt. 22:37–38); and when he gave the Sermon on the Mount (see Matt. 5:33–34). From the addresses, historical episodes, exhortations, warnings, and even some of the legislation, an expositor could preach a series of relevant sermons from Deuteronomy. Any series from Deuteronomy could not avoid emphasizing God's providence on his people and God's expectations of his people. Whether it was the original audience who first read Deuteronomy or people in the twentieth century, the truth is the same: Obeying God results in his blessings, and disobeying God leads to his curses.

Sermon Methods with the Pentateuchal Books

The expositor must consider the Pentateuch's wide variety of literary styles. Probably no other larger unit of Scripture contains such diversity. The pentateuchal books have historical happenings; theological narratives; parables; fables; census lists; cultic and ritualistic material; civil, moral, and religious laws; poetry; prophetic oracles; oratorical addresses; and other literary devices. We will confine our attention to law and narrative.

Law. The Books of Exodus, Leviticus, Numbers, and Deuteronomy contain over six hundred laws which the Israelites were expected to keep. Though other kinds of literary material may be found in these four books, the primary content is law. Genesis, which does not contain law as such, is traditionally classified with the Law. Nonetheless, in most instances when "the Law" is mentioned, it refers to the body of material beginning at Exodus 20 to the end of Deuteronomy. Most of content from Exodus 20 is legal material. To preach intelligently from Exodus, Leviticus, Numbers, and Deuteronomy, some understanding of Old Testament law is necessary.

The Old Testament maintains God gave the law to Israel through the mediation of Moses. Law or *Torah* is God's teaching about how to live. The basic meaning of *Torah* is "teaching" or "to point the finger" conveying the idea, "This is the way to live." Seemingly, God gave the law for Israel to order society and to conduct life; he wanted Israel to be a society different from other peoples. Israel cannot be understood on the basis of blood, soil, or sociology. Israel was to live a life ruled by God.[16]

Most of the material found in the Torah has to do with laws and ritualistic/cultic regulations. Israel was to be governed by rules and principles that would distinguish it from other peoples. The most famous of the code of laws found in the Pentateuch is the Ten Commandments, or the Decalogue. These commandments were guidelines for relationship with God and with human beings. Most of the remainder of law materials in Exodus, Leviticus, Numbers, and Deuteronomy established civil, moral, dietary, and modes of behavior that were to characterize God's people. Many people today wonder about the relevance of the laws to their lives. Those who preach from these books need some guidelines for their work.

Guideline 1: Some pentateuchal laws cannot be directly applied to today's society. God gave these laws to the Israel which existed between approximately 1400–400 B.C. The cultic and societal laws

---

16. Achtemeier, 94–96.

applied to Israel during these years. Most of these cultic, societal, and dietary laws no longer apply.[17] For example, American Christians do not practice a sacrificial system of worship or have Israel's type of court system. American Christians do not have Israel's family life, commerce, landholding, or warfare. Israel had laws regulating all of those matters. Such laws applied only to citizens of ancient Israel, and no one today is a citizen of ancient Israel. In thinking about preaching on the laws recorded in the Pentateuch, the expositor needs to remember that some stipulations of the Old Covenant have clearly not been renewed in the New Covenant.[18]

Guideline 2: Seek the intention behind Israel's laws. Achtemeier says that the clues to preaching the legal material lies in the intention of those laws.[19] Perhaps one of the best guidelines for understanding the law material can be seen in the "Holiness Code" found in Leviticus 17–26. "You shall be holy, for I the Lord your God am holy" (Lev. 19:2). The word holy means "other than." Anyone or anything which is holy is different, set apart, special. God is "other than" human beings. God's people also are to be "other than" the peoples of the earth. The laws were given with the intention of making God's people holy or different. For example, the eating of pork was forbidden. The question of why this particular meat was forbidden is open for discussion. Was it because the Canaanites ate pork? Or were pigs used in the worship of Baal? Or was it because people who ate pork became seriously ill? The reason for the prohibition has been lost, but the principle is clear: God wanted his people to be different. They must not be associated with pagan practice. They must not do anything to harm their health.[20]

Guideline 3: Relate pentateuchal laws to the Christian faith. Achtemeier suggests that preachers show how the Old Testament background has passed into the Christian faith. The Law lays much of the basis for an understanding of the New Testament. With the sacrifices and the priestly system, the expositor can relate to the sacrifice of Christ on the cross. The Passover can help Christians understand the Lord's Supper. Christian congregations need to be

---

17. Ibid., 105.
18. Ibid.
19. Ibid.
20. Efird, 33–34.

taught about the priesthood and how those regulations relate to the priesthood of all believers, namely lives of purity and goodness.[21]

Guideline 4: Some pentateuchal laws can be applied to the lives of Christians. No one obeys the laws to gain acceptance by God, but Christians share with Israel the glad duty of responding to God's love by obedience to his commandments. Obedience grows out of a relationship with the Lord, and the Law discloses who the Lord is and what he wants.[22] God's commandments are gracious guidelines for believers. The Lord loves his people; therefore, he instructed them with laws about how they may live life to the fullest. The laws were never given as a means of establishing a relationship.

Keeping the matters of the Law in mind when preparing a series of sermons from Exodus, Leviticus, Numbers, and Deuteronomy will be helpful. Heeding these matters could prevent mistaken interpretations of Israel's laws. The informed expositor should preach from legal material in order to disclose who God is, who God's people are, and what God wants in principle for his people.

Narrative. Only a casual observation discloses the many narratives found in the Pentateuch. These narratives may be grouped into stories from the primeval history, the patriarchal history, and the wilderness wanderings. Think for a moment about the stories in the primeval period: creation, Adam and Eve, Cain and Abel, the flood, and the building of a tower. Move from these stories to think about the four main patriarchal figures: Abraham, Isaac, Jacob, and Joseph. Within each of these bigger stories are numerous other smaller stories.

Consider next the numerous narratives found from Exodus to Deuteronomy, the record of Israel's movement from Egypt to Sinai and finally to Moab, the land on the edge of Canaan. Preaching a series of sermons from the books of the Pentateuch, with the exception of Leviticus, will reveal an abundance of narratives. The principles for preaching narrative literature are found in the following section on historical books.

The Historical Books

Several Old Testament books come under the category of history: Joshua, Judges, Ruth, 1 and 2 Samuel, 1 and 2 Kings, 1 and 2

---

21. Achtemeier, 106.
22. Ibid., 106–7.

Chronicles, Ezra, Nehemiah, and Esther. These books need to be considered for a series of sermons because they contain both historical information and theological interpretation of historical happenings. These biblical writers believed that history came under the control of the God who was working out his plan and purposes through the historical process. Preaching from the historical books does much more than relate happenings in history; it also relates the theological interpretations of what God did in that history.

General Observations about the Historical Books

The Hebrew Old Testament does not categorize any books as histories. The Hebrew Old Testament offered the three categories of Law, Prophets, and Writings. In the Hebrew canon, Joshua, Judges, 1 and 2 Samuel, and 1 and 2 Kings come under the category of Former Prophets. Another grouping called the Latter Prophets included those books which are usually associated with biblical prophecy: Isaiah, Jeremiah, and the twelve Minor Prophets. More than likely, the title "Former" refers to the placement in the canon.

The Hebrew people attached great importance to their history. First orally, later in writing, they told what happened from the time of the exodus to the settlement in the land, the monarchy, the divided kingdom, the captivity, and the restoration. The Israelites not only told and wrote their history but also explained what God was doing in these historical events. What was important to Israel was not so much the events, but the significance of these events. Ruth, Esther, 1 and 2 Chronicles, Ezra, and Nehemiah are classified in the Writings in the Hebrew canon, but Christians often classify these as the historical books because of their narrative nature.

The Former Prophets have an interesting relationship with the Pentateuch. Some scholars argue that the Book of Joshua needs to be included with the first five books; thus, the category would be a Hexateuch (six books). Other scholars suggest that Deuteronomy differed so much from the other five books of the Pentateuch that it was moved to another section; thus, there would be a Tetrateuch (four books). Such scholars associate Deuteronomy as an introduction to the Former Prophets. Martin Noth and Gerhard von Rad, two reputable scholars, proposed that Joshua, Judges, 1 and 2 Samuel, and 1 and 2 Kings were written, edited, and collected by a group of people known as "deuteronomic historians."[23]

Many Old Testament scholars have proposed that God used the deuteronomic historians to compose many historical books. Joshua through Samuel, according to these Old Testament scholars, were probably written by one person and later edited by deuteronomic historians. The Books of 1 and 2 Kings appear to have been compiled from earlier materials with editing from students of the deuteronomic tradition. The six books (Joshua, Judges, 1 and 2 Samuel, and 1 and 2 Kings) of the Former Prophets have come to be called the Deuteronomic Histories.

Any study of a Bible book or group of Bible books involves observation about authorship. Traditionally, the individual books in the copies of historical books have been studied in isolation with the authorship determined for each book. Yet, in the past two hundred years, many such theories have emerged, and the matter of authorship of these books now centers around redactors. Just as with the pentateuchal books, the primary consideration is not the human author but the divine inspiration of the authors. God inspired people to write theological narratives and interpret the times from the death of Moses to the time of restoration after the Babylonian Captivity.

Most Old Testament scholars date the historical books before the exile (586 B.C.). Since Ezra and Nehemiah record events after the exile, they were undoubtedly written later; 1 and 2 Chronicles also were likely written later.

Individual Investigation of the Historical Books

Though six books are classified as the Former Prophets and five books belong to the category of the Writings, all eleven will be investigated under the historical category because of their narrative nature. Like the other books of the Bible, these historical books belong to the Word of God. A word addressed to historical situations also can be addressed to contemporary situations. Balanced expository preaching includes all literary categories, and this balance would include the historical books.

Joshua. The Book of Joshua continues the history of Israel after the death of Moses. It relates Israel's entrance into Canaan, the mil-

---

23. Cate, 200–201.

itary campaigns led by Joshua, and the divisions of the land into tribal allotments. The title of the book in both Hebrew and the Septuagint comes from the name of its champion, Joshua. The flow of the book may be seen as recording the conquest of Canaan (chaps. 1–11), the allotment of the land (chaps. 12–21), and a conclusion (chaps. 22–24). Closer study of these historical situations reveals a theological purpose. The primary witness found in the Book of Joshua is that obedience to God leads to blessing, whereas disobedience leads to judgment. Therefore, preaching a series of sermons from Joshua must deal with more than the location of cities, descriptions of battles, and the disclosure of persons. Instead, sermons from the book must relate theological purpose to the historical incidents in order to apply them in today's world.

Judges. The name for the Book of Judges comes from the persons God raised up to help Israel in times of crises. The book relates how Israel rebelled against God, how they got in trouble, how they called on God to help, and how God delivered them. After an account of the completion of the conquest (1:1–3:6), the writer relates the story of thirteen judges or leaders (3:7–16:31). The writer closed the book with two incidents illustrating the period before the monarchy (17:1–21:25). The Book of Judges contains obsolete matters from an ancient culture and an old covenant, but there are eternal verities in the creative expression of the faith of early Israel. Judges belongs to God's revelation and deserves consideration for a series of sermons.

Ruth. Though the Book of Ruth belongs to the Writings in the Hebrew canon, the Christian canon places it among the historical books because it contains a narrative which happened during the days of the judges. The story relates the personal tragedies and ultimate victory of Naomi. The Book of Ruth discloses God's sovereign love that works in human lives even when human beings do not know about his action. The story has at least five turns: (1) sojourn in Moab, 1:1–5; (2) return of Naomi and Ruth to Bethlehem, 1:6–22; (3) struggle with poverty relieved by Boaz, 2:1–23; (4) Ruth's bold act, 3:1–18; and (5) redemption of Naomi's property and the marriage of Ruth, 4:1–22. God's care and control operate behind the historical events. Sermons from Ruth must tell about more than the Moabites, grain fields, threshing floors, and village gates. Instead, sermons from Ruth must communicate God's care over his people during the tragedies of life.

1 and 2 Samuel. Originally the two Books of Samuel, like the two Books of Kings, formed one book (scroll). They were probably divided for the sake of convenience. First Samuel opens with the birth of Samuel, and 2 Samuel closes with the last days of David. These books relate Israel's development during the days of Samuel, Solomon, and David. These books reveal how Israel changed from a loose tribal confederation to a thriving monarchy. These books may be divided into five major sections with the primary consideration centered around these men.

1. The birth and work of Samuel, 1 Samuel 1:1–7:17

2. The birth and work of Saul, 1 Samuel 8:1–14:52

3. The birth and work of David, 1 Samuel 15:1–2 Samuel 11:27

4. The fall of David, 2 Samuel 12:1–26

5. Appendages, 2 Samuel 21:1–24:26

The ancient Hebrews recorded their history not just to inform the intellect of posterity but to disclose insights into the nature of God's relationship with his people. Those who preach from Samuel will see that the unity of God's people rests in their common faith in a living, reigning Lord. God can be seen working through the historical events to carry out his plans. Many narratives filled with theological truths await the preacher who preaches from Samuel.

1 and 2 Kings. Like the Books of Samuel, 1 and 2 Kings originally existed as one book. Second Samuel ends with the last words of David, and 1 Kings opens with David's death. The Samuel and Kings books could have been a single volume at one time. The Kings material contains interpretations of Israel's history from the death of David to the last days in the land of Judah. Kings may be divided as follows:

1 Kings

1. The reign of Solomon, 1–11

2. The kingdom divided, 12–22

2 Kings

1. Israel and Judah until the fall of Samaria, 11–17

2. History of Judah until the destruction of Jerusalem, 18–25

A student of 1 and 2 Kings can see that more than Israel's history is being related. Present in 1 and 2 Kings is the message that the Lord was the true king and that nothing can thwart the rule of God among his people. Preaching from the Kings material will take on new meaning when the messages move beyond mere history to theological insights.

Ezra and Nehemiah. Though the events in Ezra and Nehemiah follow the events in the Chronicles, the Chronicles and Ezra-Nehemiah come last in the Hebrew Bible. Little doubt exists that the Books of Ezra and Nehemiah were originally one book. They contain one continuous story and appear in the Septuagint as one book. The books furnish information about the Hebrew people after the exile. The Book of Ezra begins with the decree of Cyrus for the return of the Jews, then traces the return under Zerubbabel and the attempt to rebuild the temple. Ezra sought to bring reform, but the attempt ended in failure. The Book of Ezra closes with failure, and the Book of Nehemiah opens when Nehemiah returns to Judah to rebuild the city walls. After the wall was completed, Ezra read the law to the people. The books may be seen as follows:

Ezra

1. The return of Zerubbabel, 1–6

2. The return of Ezra, 7–10

Nehemiah

1. Nehemiah's return to Jerusalem, 1:1–6:19

2. The people's renewal, 7:1–13:3

3. Nehemiah's second return to Jerusalem, 13:4–31

1 and 2 Chronicles. Chronicles means "the events of the days." Chronicles was written much later than Kings. The writer of Chronicles evidently wanted to write part of Israel's history at a later time, probably in the Persian Period, from a priestly perspective. The writer was definitely a theologian, emphasizing God's intervention in history in response to Israel's prayer and repentance. The writer demonstrated interest in worship activities.

The writer of Chronicles compiled a history of the Hebrew people from Adam to David through a genealogy. The writer also wrote about the people of God who lived in Judah and whose lives revolved around the temple. He focused on the Southern Kingdom. The Northern Kingdom was never mentioned after the division. Few kings of Judah were mentioned, and only those kings who had special connections with the temple were discussed. The books may be divided as follows:

1 Chronicles

1. The genealogies of the tribes of Israel, 1–9

2. The reign of David, 10–29

2 Chronicles

1. The reign of Solomon, 1–9

2. The history of Judah to the fall of Jerusalem, 10–36

Again, as other historical books, Chronicles must not be viewed as mere history but as theological narration. Preaching from Chronicles and staying true to the texts can produce sermons about the sovereignty of God and how all nations and individuals are responsible to him for their actions.

Esther. The Book of Esther contains historical material, but it falls in the category of the Writings in the Hebrew canon. The book is essentially about how Esther rose to the queenship during the Persian domination of the Hebrew people. It contains the story of Haman, the Persian ruler, who plotted against the Jewish people. The book closes with the story of deliverance. To preach from Esther the expositor must face the problem of the absence of God's name in the book and questions some historians have about the historicity of the work. Just as the book is read today at the Jewish Feast of Purim, the Book of Esther can be the focus of a series of sermons for people in today's world.

Sermon Methods with the Historical Books

The Bible contains more narrative material than any other literary type. Over 40 percent of the Old Testament is narrative, and most of the material is found in the historical books. The Bible narratives relate events that happened, but not just any events. The writers used narration to show what God was doing in history among his people. These narratives glorify God, help readers understand and worship him, and give people disclosures of his providence and protection.[24] To preach effectively from the

---

24. Gordon Fee and Douglas Stuart, *How to Read the Bible for All Its Worth: A Guide to Understanding the Bible* (Grand Rapids: Baker Book House, 1979), 74.

historical books, the literary nature and the theological purposes need to be kept in mind.

Preaching a series of sermons from any one of the historical books requires study of some basic principles about narration. First, preaching biblical narratives involves more than the disclosure of people, places, and events. The narratives contain incidents about what God did through his people. Characters, events, developments, plots, and climaxes all occurred; but behind the historical happening, God is the decisive character.[25]

Preparing sermons from historical books also involves the reading *of* the stories rather than reading *into* the stories. An indispensable principle for preaching from biblical narrative involves exegesis of the story rather than an eisegesis of the story. Old Testament narratives for the most part are not allegories or narratives filled with deeper, hidden meanings. The narratives are records of literal historical happenings in which God was involved. The task of the expositor is to perform exegesis of narration.

The effective expositor of Old Testament history must live empathetically through the events and experiences recorded in the book. Most of the historical books do not have explicit teachings; they relate events that happened and the teachings come implicitly. For example, in the narrative of David's adultery with Bathsheba (see 2 Sam. 11), no explicit teaching may be found such as, "In committing adultery, David did wrong." The narrative only relates the act of adultery and the results that came from the adultery.

In preaching from biblical narratives, the expositor should put minor narratives in the context of major narratives. Fee and Stuart described three levels of narration. The top level is the broad story of God's redemptive plan for his creation. The middle level includes God's redemptive work through Israel and includes the main stories such as the call of Abraham, the deliverance from Egyptian bondage, the destruction of Israel and Judah, and the restoration of God's people after the exile. The bottom level of narration includes stories of God's work through many individuals. These hundreds of individual stories at level three fit into what is going on at levels one and two. Expositors who preach from the historical books should keep all three levels of narration in mind.[26]

---

25. Ibid., 74–75.
26. Ibid.

The Poetical Books

Twenty percent of the Old Testament was written as Hebrew poetry. Much of the prophetic books contain poetry, and poetry is the form for all 150 psalms. Our discussion of Hebrew poetry will focus on the Book of Psalms. Most of the information given on Hebrew poetry in this section will apply to the poetical forms in other parts of the Old Testament.

The Book of Psalms differs from most other Bible books because of its exclusive poetical nature. The Book of Psalms is the longest book in the Bible, containing 150 psalms inspired, collected, and used in various ways among the Hebrew people. It contains an anthology of hymns, prayers, and laments composed from approximately the tenth to the third century B.C. The Psalms grew from the aspirations, vissitudes, humiliations, and hopes of people. The Psalms are rich in theological and devotional truths, giving insights into the presence and power of God in diverse human experience. Like any other literary type, the poetical style of the Psalms needs careful study if effective sermons are to be preached from the Psalms.

The Distinctive Nature of Hebrew Poetry

Before preaching from the Psalms, serious consideration needs to be given to the distinctive nature of Hebrew poetry. Most people consider poetry as the rhyme of sounds—words at the end of lines rhyme with words at the end of other lines. While that particular style may fit English poetry, it does not follow Hebrew poetry. Hebrew poetry does not rhyme with sounds; instead it has a parallelism of ideas. Parallelism is a literary device in which a single thought is expressed in one line, and then the same, opposite, or related idea is expressed in the next line in a different way. The second line is like an answer of the first line, but it is an answer in idea rather than sound. In 1753, Robert Lowth became the first person to present a systematic treatment of the formal elements of Hebrew poetry. Lowth's exposition of the parallelistic structure of Hebrew poetry has been followed by many Old Testament scholars.

Hebrew poetry includes three styles of parallelism: synonymous, antithetic, and synthetic. *Synonymous parallelism* uses two lines to say the same thing. The author expresses something, then repeats the same thought with similar words in the next line. Consider two examples:

> For He has founded it upon the seas,
> And established it upon the rivers. (Ps. 24:2)
> Day to day pours forth speech,
> And night to night reveals knowledge. (Ps. 19:2)

Antithetic parallelism uses the second line to contrast what has been stated in the first line. Following are some examples:

> For the Lord knows the way of the righteous,
> But the way of the wicked will perish. (Ps. 1:6)
> They have bowed down and fallen;
> But we have risen and stood upright. (Ps. 20:8)

Synthetic parallelism states an idea in the first line, then adds further information in the second line.

> "But as for me, I have installed My King upon Zion,
> My holy mountain." (Ps. 2:6)

On some occasions the lines following the first line show a degree of difference:

> For a day in Thy courts is better than a thousand outside.
> I would rather stand at the threshold of the house of my God,
> Than dwell in the tents of wickedness. (Ps. 84:10)

Sometimes in synthetic parallelism a second line may state a reason for what was said in the first line.

> But there is forgiveness with Thee,
> That Thou mayest be feared. (Ps. 130:4)

At times after the first line, a series of lines amplify the thought expressed in the first line.

> How blessed is the man who does
> not walk in the counsel of the wicked,
> Nor stand in the path of sinners,
> Nor sit in the seat of scoffers! (Ps. 1:1)

Recognizing parallelism will help the expositor interpret Hebrew poetry. The Hebrews used poetic technique to stress their ideas. They also used parallelism as an aid to memory. Even today, words from songs can be recalled much more easily than sentences from books or speeches. Israelites used poetry to enhance their memory and their meaning.

The General Nature of the Book of Psalms

In addition to the study of parallelism in Hebrew poetry, the expositor needs to take a general look at the Book of Psalms before preaching a series. With as much investigation as possible, consideration needs to be given to the historical context of each psalm selected. God inspired some author at a particular point in history to write the psalm. According to Artur Weiser, "exegesis of the psalms has always had to face the difficulty that most of them are for us just pictures without a frame, as we are still in the dark about the details of their origin and use."[27] Each psalm was composed at a special time in the life of Israel and was related to a specific incident. The psalms themselves contain the only clues in learning the historical context of a psalm's composition. Therefore, careful exposition of each psalm can yield insights into the historical background.

Any attempt to outline the 150 psalms would be as futile as trying to outline a contemporary hymnal. English Bibles divide the Psalms into five sections: 1–41; 42–72; 73–89; 90–106; and 107–150. Each of these sections ends with a doxology (see 41:13; 72:18–20; 89:52; 106:48; 149:9b). Psalm 1 is generally considered as an introduction to the Psalter, and Psalm 150 is a closing doxology for the work. Scholars have noted the different uses of the names for God in these fivefold divisions. In books 1, 4, and 5, *Yahweh* is used more frequently than *Elohim*, and the reverse is true about book 2. The names *Elohim* and *Yahweh* are fairly distributed with *Elohim* slightly predominant. These five sections apparently had a separate existence, and later they were united in one book. Scholars have conjectured that *Yahweh* was the name for God preferred in Jerusalem and Judah, while *Elohim* was the name preferred among the Northern Kingdom. If this conjecture is correct, book 2 was the hymnbook for the northern tribes, and books 1, 4, and 5 were used in Judah. Book 3 probably was collected and used after Israel fell and the refugees from Israel took part in worship in the Northern Kingdom.[28]

Many English translations have titles for some of the psalms. These titles were added after the psalms were written. They give

27. Artur Weiser, *The Psalms: A Commentary in the Old Testament Library* (Philadelphia: Westminster Press, 1962), 9.

28. Cate, 441–42.

some ideas about possible authorship, musical direction, and historical circumstances. One hundred psalms have the name of an individual or a group of individuals in the title. Seventy-three titles contain the name of David; twelve have the name of Asaph (50; 73–83); eleven, the sons of Korah (42; 44–49; 84–85; 87–88); two the name of Solomon (72; 127); one Moses (90); and one Ethan (89).

Many musical terms and directions are found in the title of the psalms. Such terms regulated the use of psalms in worship. The exact meaning of most of these terms is obscure, especially the term *Selah*.

The titles of Psalms 18; 51–52; 54; 56–57; 59–60; and 63 contain information about the historical background of the psalms. Titles bearing the historical occasion usually are associated with David.

Herman Gunkel, a writer in the early part of the twentieth century, classified the Psalms with major forms. He divided the Psalter into the major forms of hymns, national laments, individual laments, individual songs of thanksgiving, and royal psalms. Gunkel also saw four minor types of psalms: songs of pilgrimage, communal thanksgiving, wisdom psalms, and liturgies. Clyde T. Francisco classified the Psalms on the basis of content: nature psalms, character psalms, penitential psalms, psalms of the Word of God, psalms concerning worship, psalms of suffering, psalms of assurance, psalms of praise, and messianic psalms.[29] Studying the psalms from the perspective of content and form will yield many themes for a series of sermons.

Sermon Methods with the Book of Psalms

Those who do not preach from a prescribed lectionary which includes extensive selections from Psalms should develop a personal lectionary with either occasional sermons from the Psalms or an extended series from the Psalms. More than likely, the preferable plan for preaching from the Book of Psalms would be selective rather than consecutive. However, nothing is wrong with a consecutive series of sermons from Psalms. One good method is to group eight to twelve psalms together and use them as a series.

The expositor then needs to make an intensive study of each psalm selected for a series of sermons. Such matters as title (if one is used), content classification, form classification, and the domi-

---

29. Francisco, *Introducing the Old Testament*, 237–53.

nant theme or themes need careful consideration. Each psalm also needs structural investigation. Most psalms have strophes, or stanzas, where ideas are blocked together. At times one theme runs through a psalm, and the strophes help develop a theme. At other times, different themes appear in the strophes in the same psalm. Each psalm needs to be studied as a literary unit. It is to be treated in a holistic manner, not atomized in single verses so a verse is used out of context. If an expositor chooses to use a simple verse from a psalm for a text, the verse needs to be investigated from the viewpoint of its relationship to the whole.

In some of the Psalms, expositors need to know the writer's use of acrostics. In this pattern, the author began each first word in the next line with different letters of the Hebrew alphabet. Being aware of original acrostic forms helps the expositor with the study of a psalm. Psalm 119 is an acrostic.

In preaching from the Psalms, the expositor needs to keep in mind that the Psalms are not plain prose but descriptive Hebrew poems. The exalted language of Hebrew poetry declares both metaphorically and memorably. It is important to listen to the poetical language and hear what it means. It is important not to compress poetical language too literally. For example, in the Psalms, mountains skip like rams (114:4), and enemies spew out words from their lips (59:7), and God is often portrayed as a shepherd, a fortress, and a rock. An ability to appreciate the style of Hebrew poetry and to translate symbolic notions into actual fact could lead the preacher to preach more effectively from the Psalms.

CHAPTER 9

Preaching from Old Testament Books (Wisdom and Prophetic)

The Wisdom Books
    The Meaning of Wisdom in the Wisdom Books
    The Literary Nature of the Wisdom Books
    Sermon Methods with the Wisdom Books
The Prophetic Books
    The Nature and Character of Old Testament Prophets
    Literary Forms in the Prophetic Books
    Historical Contexts of Prophetic Books

Proverbs, Job, and Ecclesiastes are known as the wisdom books of the Old Testament. Few expositors preach series of sermons from these books. Some preachers choose short, random texts, but these are often isolated from their biblical context. Wisdom books originated from situations in life; these books helped interpret God's creation and helped God's people enjoy life as he intended it. Preaching from any one of these three wisdom books will help people live in today's world with God's guidance and help.

Perhaps the Old Testament prophetic books are abused books in the Bible. Prophecy flourished for three hundred years, from the eighth to the fifth century B.C. The prophets spoke primarily to their times, and they occasionally alluded to the future. Today some expositors preach from prophetic books by reading current events into prophetic texts to predict the future. Like any other Bible book, the prophetic books need to be interpreted in light of their historical setting to see what they *meant* so the contemporary expositor may proclaim what they *mean*. Careful study of the prophetic writings can yield sermons that come from the past but which intersect with the present and the future.

The Wisdom Books

Wisdom movements flourished in the ancient worlds, especially in Egypt and Mesopotamia. It was probably not until the time of David and Solomon that the wise man became a part of the Hebrew societal structure. Wisdom literature represents the quest to understand the world and to learn how to cope with life in the world. Wisdom literature often took the direction of practical teachings given by a parent or a teacher to students. Most wisdom literature was designed to teach basic principles for living in order to help the reader find success, prosperity, or happiness. Those who rejected wise counsel would be afflicted with problems and unhappiness.[1]

The Old Testament wisdom books are distinct because they were shaped by the uniqueness of the biblical faith and divine inspiration. The preacher who desires to preach sermons from wisdom books must try to comprehend the nature of wisdom in Israel and the faith of Israel.

The Meaning of Wisdom in the Wisdom Books

Many Old Testament scholars accept the term *wisdom books* as a convenient designation for Proverbs, Job, and Ecclesiastes. These three books use the term *wisdom (hokmah)* and possess certain characteristics of wisdom books.[2] The Greeks thought of wisdom as the search for the real or the cunning craftiness or cleverness that enabled a person to be successful. Hebrew wisdom was different. A primary meaning of *hokmah* in the Old Testament was "moral discernment." Solomon prayed for the ability to "discern between good and evil," and God answered, "I have given you a wise and discerning heart" (1 Kings 3:9, 12). Hebrew wisdom meant more

---

1. James M. Efird, *How to Interpret the Bible* (Atlanta: John Knox Press, 1984), 61.

2. Roland E. Murphy, "Wisdom Literature and Psalms," in *Interpreting Biblical Texts* (Nashville: Abingdon Press, 1983), 14.

than success; it meant doing that which is right according to God's way.

Wisdom also described the Hebrews' reverence and obedience to the Lord. Wisdom required a fear of the Lord. "The fear of the Lord is the beginning of knowledge" (Prov. 1:7, 9–10). The expression "the beginning" means both the starting point and the foundation for a happy life. The focus in this use of wisdom is on God as the source of wisdom and practical interaction on how to worship and obey him.

In addition to moral discernment, reverence, and obedience to God, wisdom was also associated with intellectual acumen. Solomon's wisdom was illustrated in 1 Kings 4:29–34 by reference to his 3,000 proverbs and 1,005 songs. Wise men valued study, training, and knowledge; yet the Hebrews did not overly exalt intellect. The Hebrew wise man was advised to get wisdom and with all the wisdom to get understanding. In other words, intellect did not stand alone; it was followed by the ability to know how to use intellectual information.

Often wisdom was used in the Old Testament to denote technical skill and dexterity. The word describes the skill of the craftsman in constructing the tent of meeting and the utensils for the worship of Yahweh (see Ex. 31:3). Sometimes the word meant craftiness, not craftsmanship—cunning or simple cleverness, not competence. Second Samuel 14:2 describes Joab as using "a wise woman" of Tekoa to persuade David to allow the exiled Absalom to return. The word *wise* in this usage means shrewdness or cleverness. On the basis of the word *wisdom (hokmah)*, the axiom "Words do not have meanings but usages" is helpful. While the word *wisdom* can describe skill or manual dexterity, cleverness or shrewdness, or intellectual acumen, the wisdom books more often use it to refer to discernment and reverence to God with the intent of keeping his commandments.

The wisdom books focus on people and their behavior, how successful they were in analyzing God's truths, and whether they learned from the experiences they had. Hebrew wisdom contains descriptions of conclusions learned by personal experiences and by faith in God. The wisdom books approach wisdom from various vantage points. The Book of Proverbs usually reaches conclusions about life from a prudential and pragmatic perspective: following God's rules seems to guarantee results. Job and Ecclesiastes approach conclusions about life from a different perspective: The person who obeys God's laws may not get what he or she deserves. That seems to be the viewpoint of Job and Ecclesiastes. In these two books a more philosophical dimension to wisdom appears. Verbal wrestlings occur in the books about the fairness of life, justice in the world, and the search for meaning in life.

The Literary Nature of the Wisdom Books

The wisdom books, like all of the Psalms and most of the prophetic books, contain the predominant literary style of Hebrew poetry. Like the Psalms, the two lines of a proverb relate to each other in one of the three types of parallelism: synonymous, antithetical, or synthetic. These three forms have been discussed in the section dealing with the Book of Psalms, but insights for interpreting the parallelism in the Book of Proverbs would be enhanced by observing illustrations of parallel constructions in the Proverbs. Observe the following *synonymous parallelism* in a proverb:

> Pride goes before destruction,
> And a haughty spirit before stumbling. (Prov. 16:18)

Antithetical parallelism may be seen as follows:

> Righteousness exalts a nation,
> But sin is a disgrace to any people. (Prov. 14:34)
> A gentle answer turns away wrath,
> But a harsh word stirs up anger. (Prov. 15:1)

Notice the following examples of *synthetic parallelism* where the second line accentuates and elaborates the first line:

> As a ring of gold in a swine's snout,
> So is a beautiful woman who lacks discretion. (Prov. 11:22)
> The beginning of strife is like letting out water,
> So abandon the quarrel before it breaks out. (Prov. 17:14)
> Wine is a mocker, strong drink a brawler,
> And whoever is intoxicated by it is not wise. (Prov. 20:1)

Closely akin to synthetic parallelism is the *two line verse of comparison*. These lines usually appear in the form of "better this than that." This form is frequent throughout the Book of Proverbs. Consider a couple of examples:

> Better is he who is lightly esteemed and has a servant,
> Than he who honors himself and lacks bread. (Prov. 12:9)

> It is better to live in a desert land,
> Than with a contentious and vexing woman. (Prov. 21:19)

In addition to the parallels mentioned above, the Book of Proverbs has numerous parallel comparisons, especially in chapters 25–27. In this literary form one thing is said to be like another thing. Consider two examples:

> Like apples of gold in settings of silver
> Is a word spoken in right circumstances. (Prov. 25:11)
> Like an earthen vessel overlaid with silver dross
> Are burning lips and a wicked heart. (Prov. 26:23)

In preaching from the Book of Proverbs, the nature of numerous sayings needs to be studied in addition to the parallels. The Book of Proverbs has three types of sayings. A proverb may be in the form of a simple observation: "Pride goes before destruction" (Prov. 16:18a). Or a proverb may be in the form of an admonition: "My son, give attention to my words" (Prov. 4:20a). A third kind of proverb is the paradoxical statement: "He who spares the rod hates his son" (Prov. 13:24a).

Most of the Book of Proverbs contains two-line parallel constructions, but there are several exceptions. One exception may be found in chapters 1–9, which contain a collection of lengthy didactic poems about wisdom and folly and the advantages or disadvantages of embracing one or the other. Another kind of didactic poem in the Book of Proverbs is the enumerative sayings. This type of poem lists a number of things, one of which is not customarily thought of as belonging with the others. Consider this enumerative saying:

> There are six things which the Lord hates,
> Yes, seven which are an abomination to Him:
> Haughty eyes, a lying tongue,
> And hands that shed innocent blood,
> A heart that devises wicked plans,
> Feet that run rapidly to evil,
> A false witness who utters lies,
> And one who spreads strife among brothers. (Prov. 6:16–19)

The enumerative sayings usually have a common denominator with one saying having a quixotic element of an uncommon factor.

The allegory, a story in which every aspect has a transferable application, may be found in Proverbs and Ecclesiastes. The form of Proverbs 5:15–23 appears in the style of an allegory, but its admonition concerning marital fidelity is unmistakably clear. The allegorical poems of Proverbs chapters 1 and 8, which contrast wisdom and folly, represent examples of allegory in wisdom writings. Ecclesiastes 12 contains an allegory which was used to describe the enfeebling of the human body in old age.

The Book of Job has a literary quality of dramatic dialogue. In this work, conversations exist between persons and God and between persons. The dialogues provide a convenient method for overhearing the different interpretations about the meaning of life.

To preach individual sermons or a series of sermons from the wisdom books, expositors need to observe the literary notice of the wisdom books. The forms of wisdom expressions range from the two-line proverb to the long didactic poem, numerical saying, dialogue, ridicule, fable, and allegory. In this literary diversity, one common ingredient is found—a reportorial statement of conclusion about life reached after extensive experience.[3]

Sermon Methods with the Wisdom Books

Old Testament wisdom books are distinct within themselves. They were shaped by the uniqueness of faith in the Lord, and expositors must try to comprehend the thought and bases of Israelite wisdom before using texts from these books. Otherwise the results could be an exposure of views of modern psychology rather than the biblical faith.[4]

Proverbs. Preachers should consider a series of sermons from the Book of Proverbs. The title of the book comes from the Hebrew word *mashal* which means "to be like." At first the word referred to the short sayings, but it grew to include any kind of wisdom material. The Book of Proverbs contains a collection of divinely inspired material. More than likely, the book was compiled in post-exilic times by teachers in schools for moral instruction of Jewish young people. It represents a wide variety of sources and periods of time; the four main sections are designated in the text itself with its own introductory title. The title in 1:1 serves as an introduction to the section (1:1–9:18) and also to the entire book. The other three sec-

---

3. L. D. Johnson, *Israel's Wisdom: Learn and Live* (Nashville: Broadman Press, 1975), 23.

4. Elizabeth Achtemeier, *Preaching from the Old Testament* (Louisville, Ky.: Westminster/John Knox Press, 1989), 165.

tions are 10:1–22:16; 22:17–24:34; and 25:1–29:27. Also, four smaller pieces serve as postscripts and are found at the end of the book—30:1–9; 30:10–33; 31:1–9; 31:10–31.[5]

The Book of Proverbs may be outlined as follows:

1. The discourses in praise of wisdom, 1:1–9:18

2. The proverbs of Solomon, 10:1–22:16

3. The collection of teachings from the wise, 22:17–24:34

4. Additional proverbs of Solomon, 25:1–29:27

5. The proverbs of Agur, 30:1–33

6. The proverbs of Lemuel, 31:1–9

7. An acrostic poem on the good wife, 31:10–31

Studying each of these sections with its time of composition, literary style, and themes can help the preacher plan a series of messages from Proverbs. Other than the identification of the major situations, further outlining of Proverbs is difficult.

Any series of sermons from the Book of Proverbs needs to be planned in accordance with the purpose of the book. The proverbs assume an absolute order of reward and retribution that provides a reliable structure for life. According to Proverbs, life is arranged with predictable results of behavior. The basic overall concern of Proverbs is living the good life. Its major emphasis directs attention to the contrast between the wise person and the fool. Many subjects may be detected in Proverbs: laziness, speech, alcohol, the treatment of enemies, pride, parenting, relationships of children to parents, sex, business, women, and numerous other timeless topics.[6]

Gordon Fee and Douglas Stuart gave some helpful principles for interpreting the Book of Proverbs:

1. Proverbs are often parabolic and figurative, pointing beyond the language.

2. Proverbs are intended to be practical, not theoretically theological.

3. Proverbs are worded to be memorable, not technically pure.

4. Proverbs are reflections of ancient culture, and they need to be translated.

---

5. Johnson, 31.

6. Clyde Francisco, *Introducing the Old Testament*, rev. ed. (Nashville: Broadman Press, 1977), 266.

5. Proverbs are not guarantees from God, but poetical guidelines for good behavior.

6. Proverbs can be used wrongly to support a materialistic lifestyle.[7]

Studying and reading these principles will help expositors deliver authentic biblical sermons from the Book of Proverbs.

Job. The Book of Job is a classic of world literature. It possesses the capacity for reliant messages directed to common human experiences. No other book of the Bible is so highly stylized as Job. In the prose prologue (1:1–2:13), the scene shifts back and forth from heaven to earth. This section is followed by a long poetical section of dialogue between Job and God and Job and his three friends. Three cycles of speeches between Job and his friends follow the prologue (4:1–31:40). With each friend's speech and each response by Job, the problems grow more acute. The three friends discuss the problem of human suffering and present the leading explanations of suffering. A young bystander named Elihu listens to the dialogue and offers his insight (32:1–37:24), but Elihu really doesn't add anything new. After human wisdom speaks about suffering, God speaks (38:1–42:6). The book closes with a prose epilogue (42:7–17).

Expositors who desire to preach from Job need to study its dialogical style and its overall purpose. The book does not contain the answer to suffering, but it does explore the various thoughts about suffering, especially as suffering relates to the righteous. Satan proposed that Job served God for personal reward. He asked, "Does Job fear God for nothing?" (Job 1:9). God decided to prove that one man served Him whether or not he prospered. The Book of Job silences the satanic lie that religious people serve God for personal reward. Preaching from Job requires consideration of this theme and the caution against taking verses out of context. The speeches of Eliphaz, Bildad, Zophar, and Elihu need to be seen as reflections of human wisdom. Sermon texts from their speeches need to be placed in their context.

Ecclesiastes. Another literary outgrowth produced as a result of Israel's interest in wisdom is Ecclesiastes. Apparently the book originated when diverse meanings of life flourished. The author identi-

---

7. Gordon Fee and Douglas Stuart, *How to Read the Bible for All Its Worth: A Guide to Understanding the Bible* (Grand Rapids: Baker Book House, 1979), 203.

fied himself as *Koheleth* in the first line of the book. This word or title comes from a Hebrew root that means "to call" or "to assemble." Various meanings have been proposed for the word *Koheleth*. Some say it represents one who assembles an audience, such as a preacher or lecturer. Others say *Koheleth* referred to a debater or discusser. Still others give the word the force of one who is a collector of truth.

Koheleth wanted to discover the highest good in life. He tried wisdom, wealth, and pleasure but found them empty. A recurring line throughout the book testifies to the meaninglessness of many pursuits. "Vanity of vanities," says the Preacher, "Vanity of vanities. All is vanity" (Eccl. 1:2). Throughout the book, Koheleth questioned, speculated, challenged tradition, and refused to accept unsubstantiated dogma. He knew worldly wisdom and grew weary with it. The searcher came to a conclusion: "The conclusion, when all has been heard, is: fear God and keep His commandments, because this applies to every person" (Eccl. 12:13). Koheleth concluded that wisdom, pleasure, or work could not explain the meaning of life. The foundation for life's true meaning, according to Koheleth, was located outside a person. Only God could give meaning to life. Today people are still searching for satisfaction, and this should challenge the expositor to preach from Ecclesiastes.

An outline of Ecclesiastes can help an expositor plan and prepare messages from the book. James M. Efird offers the following outline:

1. Introduction, 1:1–11

2. The search for meaning in life, 1:12–3:15

3. Observations about life, 3:16–9:12

4. Virtues of wisdom, 9:13–11:8

5. The joys and challenges of youth, 11:9–12:8

6. Editorial additions, 12:9–14[8]

After introducing the reader to the problems to be examined (1:1–11), the author investigates things that might bring satisfaction: wisdom (1:13–18), pleasure and fame (2:1–11), and folly (2:12–16). The author's search prompts him to make observations about life: legal justice (3:16–27), envy and oppression (4:1–3),

---

8. James M. Efird, *Biblical Books of Wisdom* (Valley Forge, Pa.: Judson Press, 1983), 52–53.

covetousness (4:7–8), companionship (4:9–12), kingship (4:13–16), worship (5:1–7), wealth and poverty (5:8–6:6), and righteousness and wickedness (7:15; 8:14–15).[9]

Koheleth continues to extol the virtue of wisdom (9:13–11:8). He focuses on keeping on trying, persevering in hope. There seems to be a sense of satisfaction in this struggle. Koheleth concludes that young people should enjoy their youth (11:9–12:8). Finally in 12:9–14 he concludes that only God gives meaning to life. Even a cursory study of Ecclesiastes reveals many topics that relate to today's audiences. Persevering life and learning the wisdom gained by Koheleth's faith can help produce sermons that relate to people's needs.

The Prophetic Books

Most books of the Old Testament come under a category of literature known as the Prophets. Scholars differ on just which Old Testament books belong in the prophetic category. Many Old Testament scholars put Isaiah, Jeremiah, Ezekiel, and Daniel in a group known as the Major Prophets. Some scholars do not put Daniel in the prophetic category but in a group of apocalyptic writings. Twelve books of the Old Testament have been called the Minor Prophets because they are relatively short, even as the Major Prophets are so called because of their greater length. Depending on the literary classification of Daniel, fifteen or sixteen books were written between 760 B.C. and 460 B.C., and they contain a vast array of messages from God.

The Nature and Character of Old Testament Prophets

To preach effectively from the prophetic books, a preacher needs to learn about the nature and character of Old Testament prophets. Some view the prophets as social reformers and preachers of ethics. Others think they were political observers who read the signs of the times and declared the consequences of individual and corporate actions. In the minds of some, a prophet was a person who foretold the future. To correct some erroneous ideas about the prophets, a preacher needs to read and study carefully the prophetic books. Robert L. Cate said, "The prophets were essentially people whose minds were able to comprehend both God and man at the same

---

9. Achtemeier, 180.

time."[10] The Holy Spirit, according to the record of the prophetic books, sensitized the hearts and minds of the prophets. They proclaimed God's Word to specific historical situations. The prophets seemed to illumine where God was at work in the world, whether in the realm of nature or history.[11]

The ordinary Hebrew word for prophet was *nabhi*, meaning "spokesperson." The Old Testament prophets were primarily God's mouthpiece to the people of that time, denouncing their sins, pleading for a return to God, and encouraging people to follow God's will in all phases of life. The prophets taught the *Torah* or law. On the basis of divine insight and in light of Israel's sacred traditions, the prophets were agents showing how to live godly lives. The faithful Hebrew prophet felt as if he had been deputized to speak on God's behalf.

In addition to being a spokesperson for God, the Hebrew prophet was also an *intercessor*. Amos interceded twice with the Lord on behalf of Israel. In a vision, Amos saw a plague of locusts, and he pleaded with God not to destroy the nation with this plague (see Amos 7:2). The Lord honored Amos' intercession and stopped the plague. In another vision, Amos saw a great fire which was about to consume the land. Again he interceded, and for a second time the Lord withheld destruction. Many intercessions occurred. Some succeeded, others failed. Jeremiah was told, "As for you, do not pray for this people, and do not lift up cry or prayer for them, and do not intercede with Me" (Jer. 7:16).

In addition to being spokespersons and intercessors, the prophets were also *suffering servants*. The prophets identified with the people so much that they felt deeply to the point of suffering. The prophets agonized over the rebellion of the people. They announced with great hurt that their society was on the road to destruction. The prophets became so identified with the sinful people that they suffered physically and emotionally. Hosea felt the grief of God with his wife's infidelity. Jeremiah suffered from God's prohibitions for him to marry, to go to a party, and to attend a funeral. Ezekiel was commanded to experience the horrors of the Babylonian siege. Isaiah's picture of a prophet was one of a vicari-

---

10. Robert L. Cate, *An Introduction to the Old Testament and Its Study* (Nashville: Broadman Press, 1987), 282.

11. Achtemeier, 110.

ous sufferer for both Israel and the nations (see Isa. 52:13–53:12). The prophets internally bore the calling of people to repentance and the announcement of judgment.

The nature and character of the Hebrew prophets demonstrated that they had the mind to comprehend both God and people at the same time. Understanding the prophet as spokesperson, intercessor, and sufferer helps with preaching from prophetic books. The prophets were not people who castigated society and individuals for their sins, functioned as mere social reformers, or looked into a crystal ball to foretell the future. The prophets maintained a relationship with God and an identification with society, and these relationships kept them in constant tension. The prophets heard God's word and sensed his will, and then they spoke God's word to the people. They did not speak God's word without deep feelings because they interceded with God on behalf of the people and interceded with people on behalf of God. The prophets so identified with people that they suffered over the people's rebellions and the consequences of the rebellions. By understanding the prophets as spokespersons, intercessors, and sufferers, expositors are more equipped to comprehend the messages of the prophetic books and to preach intelligently from these books.

Literary Forms in the Prophetic Books

The prophet's messages were spoken first and written later. The prophet's voice is silenced but the prophetic message continues in written form. Expositors must study the prophetic books as literature. A close examination of these books reveals both prose and poetry.

Prose. The prose in the prophetic books falls into two classifications: autobiographical and biographical forms.[12] The autobiographical forms are in the first person and share information only the prophet would know. The call reports—the form in which the prophets related how they became prophets—furnish a primary example of the autobiographical form. Usually this form contains a divine confrontation, a commission, a response from the prophet, and frequently a sign confirming the reality of the experience. In addition to call narratives, the prophets gave autobiographical vision reports. In these reports, the prophets told something they

---

12. Cate, 286.

saw with their eyes or conceived in their minds. Through these visions God gave the prophets special revelations. The prophets also gave autobiographical reports of their symbolic acts. These reports included God's commands to perform symbolic actions, a report of the actions, and an interpretation of the meaning of these actions.

The biographical reports found in the prose material of the prophetic books are always in the third person. These reports were told about the prophet by someone else. Prophetic biography usually describes events that happened to the prophet. Oftentimes, these biographical events were inserted as an introduction or a conclusion to a prophet's address or a collection of addresses.

Poetry. Most literary material in the prophetic books appears not as prose but as Hebrew poetry. The prophets used synonymous, antithetical, and synthetic parallelism. The prophetic speeches, which were in poetry, were called oracles. Just as students of New Testament letters think paragraphs, students of the prophetic books need to think oracles. The prophets used four common oracle forms.

- *Woe oracles* usually began with the word *woe*. Scholars believe that the background of the woe oracle was a lament offered by mourners at a funeral. Woe oracles generally consisted of an announcement of distress, the reason for the distress, and a prediction of doom. Generally, when doom was the theme of the woe oracle, it began with "therefore" or "because" (see Zeph. 1:2–2:3). Employing the woe oracles was common among many of the prophets (see Isa. 5:8–30; Hab. 2:6–8; Mic. 2:1–5).

- *Lawsuit oracles* represent God as a prosecuting attorney standing against his people. His people are arraigned in the oracle and called to offer a defense. The full lawsuit oracle contains a summons, a charge, evidence, and a verdict. In Isaiah 3:13–26 the elements of the oracles include: a lawsuit is brought against Israel (13–14a); the indictment is spoken (14b–16); the evidence shows Israel to be guilty, and a sentence is announced (17–26). This special oracle form helps get the message to the people.[13]

---

13. Fee and Stuart, 160.

- *Disputation oracles* present the prophet as God's defender who engages in a dispute with the audience. The Book of Malachi contains six disputation dialogues. These disputation oracles consist of a statement of a basic truth, a consideration of objections to the truth, and a response to the objections.

- *Promise oracles* (or salvation oracles) resemble woe oracles but end with a prediction of deliverance instead of an announcement of disaster. The typical introduction to the promise oracle is "hear this word" (Amos 5:1). The typical promise oracle contains the following elements: reference to the future, mention of change, and the disclosure of blessings. Amos 9:11–15 contains these three elements: the future, "in that day" (v.11); a radical change, described with the restoration of "the fallen booth of David" (v. 11); the exaltation of Israel over Edom (v. 12); and the return from the exile (vv. 14–15). Blessings are enumerated throughout the oracle. (See also Hos. 2:16–22; Isa. 45:1–7; and Jer. 31:1–9.)

The literary form of the prophetic books probably grew out of devoted disciples of the prophets—they collected or remembered oracles of the prophets and committed them to writing. Many Old Testament scholars suggest that every prophetic figure had a disciple or group of disciples who collected and kept the utterances of the prophets. These disciples could have helped the prophets write down their oracles. Isaiah entrusted his oracles to a disciple (see Isa. 8:16), and Jeremiah committed his prophecies to Baruch the scribe (see Jer. 36). Knowing the literary characteristics of prophetic books helps expositors preach effective individual sermons and plan a series of sermons from these books.

Historical Contexts of Prophetic Books

Preaching from the prophetic books requires a knowledge of the nature of the Old Testament prophets and the distinctive literary nature of the books bearing their names. Also, to preach effectively, expositors need to consider the prophet in light of when and where the message was delivered. Prophets uttered their oracles in the context of specific historical situations. To preach effectively from the prophetic books, expository preachers need to examine the overall historical context of the prophets. To get this historical perspective, the prophets will be studied in three eras: the eighth, seventh, and sixth centuries.

Eighth-century prophets. Israel divided in about the year 930 B.C. Ten tribes (often called Israel or Ephraim) separated from the tribe of Judah. As soon as the northern tribes left, their leader, Jeroboam II, took advantage of territorial expansion. "He restored the border of Israel from the entrance of Hamath as far as the Sea of the Arabah . . . and how he recovered for Israel, Damascus and Hamath" (2 Kings 14:25–28). With this territorial expansion came prosperity. The wealthy exploited the middle and lower classes.

In addition to the political and economic successes during the reign of Jeroboam II, the religious shrines were thronged with people. But the worship consisted of an assimilation of Baal worship and the worship of Jehovah. The fertility cult of Canaan, with the sacred prostitutes and utter sensuality, led the people away from the Lord.

After Jeroboam II, Israel was ruled by a series of kings whose leadership was not godly and whose reigns were short-lived. A typical expression about a northern king was, "And he did evil in the sight of the Lord, as his fathers had done" (2 Kings 15:9a). Amos and Hosea prophesied to the Northern Kingdom, and they spoke God's Word to the historical situations. These prophets saw the facades, the oppressions, and the injustices. To understand the messages of these two prophets, an expositor would need to know the history, geography, social conditions, and religious practices of the eighth century.

Amos appeared first on the scene of the eighth-century prophets. He lived in the Southern Kingdom of Judah and prophesied in the Northern Kingdom of Israel. He prophesied to a group of people who outwardly appeared to be happy, prosperous, and religious. His prophecy was written as follows:

1. The historical superscription, 1:1

2. The messages of Amos, 1:2–6:14

3. The visions of Amos with a biographical interlude, 7:1–9:15

Amos proclaimed that a true relationship with God produced practical righteousness. For Amos a false religion was the source of sure distinction. Yet Amos proclaimed that God's judgment was redemptive. According to Amos' prophecy to eighth-century Israel, both the present and the future rest in God's hands.

Hosea was the second prophet to appear in the Northern Kingdom. Unlike Amos, Hosea was from the North and had no problems with being considered an outsider. Hosea seemed to have received his messages from a personal tragedy with an unfaithful wife. He understood what Israel's rebellion or infidelity did to God and how much God continued to love Israel. The primary theme of Hosea seems to be God's relentless attempt to win the faithfulness of his unfaithful people. Hosea's oral messages may be outlined as follows:

1. The superscription, 1:1

2. The prophet's lesson from an unfaithful wife, 1:2–3:5

3. The prophet's various messages to the people, 4:1–14:9

From Hosea's personal tragedy came one of Israel's greatest revelations about the nature of God. The love of God can reform infidelity into an arena of blessing.

As events transpired in the Northern Kingdom of Israel, events also took place in the Southern Kingdom of Judah. Historical circumstances differed from the north. Judah did not prosper as much as Israel. Also, the rise of Baalism was not as pronounced in Judah, where the worship of Jehovah remained relatively pure in the Temple of Jerusalem. Assyria's defeat of the Northern Kingdom in 722 B.C. posed some threat to Judah's security. Sennacherib, an Assyrian ruler, invaded Judah in 701 B.C. but did not capture it.

Isaiah and Micah prophesied to the Southern Kingdom amidst chaotic internal political transactions and external threats from the Assyrians. To understand the messages of these prophets, an expositor should become familiar with Judah's political history. An expositor who wishes to preach from Isaiah or Micah needs to read the reigns of the four southern kings—Uzziah, Jotham, Ahaz, and Hezekiah—from the Kings material (see Isa. 1:1; Mic. 1:1). Isaiah's word to Judah was written and collected as follows:

1. The superscription, 1:1

2. Messages addressed to Judah and Israel, 1:1–12:6

3. Messages addressed to surrounding nations, 13:1–23:18

4. Messages about God's sovereignty, God's wisdom, and God's vengeance and blessing, 24:1–35:10

5. Messages about God's redemption of his people, 40:1–55:13

6. Messages about God's new people, 56:1–66:24

Micah prophesied shortly after Isaiah began his ministry. Micah's messages were written and arranged in the following manner:

1. The superscription, 1:1

2. The judgment on Israel and Judah, 1:2–3:12

3. The prophecy about a future Messianic Kingdom, 4:1–5:15

4. The courtroom oracle, 6:1–7:20

Seventh-century prophets. Following the ministries of Micah and Isaiah was a period of almost three-quarters of a century of silence of prophetic voices. With the fall of Israel in 722 B.C. the national identity was centered in Jerusalem. During the era of silence the people passed through the latter part of Hezekiah's reign, the brief reign of Amon, and the beginning of Josiah's reign. In about 626 B.C. the prophetic silence was broken with the words of Jeremiah and Zephaniah. They were soon joined by Habakkuk, Nahum, and Obadiah. The messages of these prophets can be understood only in light of historical happenings of the seventh century B.C.

The seventh century arrived in the final years of the reign of good king Hezekiah. He was followed by a son named Manasseh (649–642 B.C.) who was known primarily for his evil. Manasseh restored the worship of the Assyrian gods and some of the Canaanite gods. He brought idols into the temple at Jerusalem. When people rebelled against Manasseh's evil practices, he suppressed the rebellion with bloodshed. Manasseh's son Amon (642–640 B.C.) followed in his father's evil ways. Amon was killed, and his eight-year-old son Josiah (640–609 B.C.) became king. Josiah grew up and sought the ways of the Lord. He cast out Assyrian influences. He led the nation in many religious reforms, including the restoration of the temple worship and covenant commitment to the Lord. Soon after Josiah came to power Assyria declined as a world power, and Babylon began its slow rise to power. Babylon would be a significant historical factor in the proclamation of the seventh-century prophets.

Jeremiah and Zephaniah began their ministries during Josiah's reign. Jeremiah's call is dated precisely in the thirteenth year of Josiah's reign (626 B.C.). Jeremiah prophesied during the reigns of Josiah, Jehoahaz, Jehoichin, and Gedeliah. Preaching consecutively from Jeremiah's prophecy is difficult because the materials are not arranged in historical sequence. Fred Wood suggests a chronological approach to Jeremiah, even though the chapters and verses do not follow consecutively:

1. The superscription, 1:1–3

2. Messages and events during Josiah's reign (626–609 B.C.), 1:4–19; 2:1–6:30; 8:4–13; 11:1–8; 11:18–12:6; 17:19–27

3. Messages and events during Jehoahaz's reign (609 B.C.), 8:14–9:1; 22:10–12

4. Messages and events from the reign of Jehoiakim (609–598 B.C.), 6:16–21; 7:1–8:3; 9:2–26; 10:1–6, 17–25; 11:9–19; 12:7–17; 13:1–7; 14:1–15:21; 16:1–17:18; 18:1–23; 19:1–20:18; 22:1–9, 13–23; 25:1–38; 35:1–19; 36:1–36; 45:15

5. Messages and events from the reign of Jehoiachin (598–597 B.C.), 13:18–27; 22:24–30

6. Messages and events from the reign of Zedekiah (597–586 B.C.), 21:1–14; 23:1–40; 24:1–10; 27:1–28:17; 29:1–32; 32:1–33:26; 34:1–22; 37:1–21; 38:1–28; 39:1–18

7. Messages and events from the time of Gedeliah and afterward (587–586 B.C.), 30:1–31:40; 41:18; 42:1–44:30

8. Undated messages about other people, 46:1–51:64

9. Historical appendix, 52:1–34[14]

Zephaniah also began his ministry during the reign of Josiah. He preached against idolatrous practices. He spoke primarily about judgment with a redemptive purpose. The written record of Zephaniah's prophecy follows:

1. The superscription, 1:1

2. The punishment of God's people, 1:2–23

3. The punishment of the nations, 2:4–15

4. The ultimate grace of God, 3:1–20

Nahum also prophesied in the seventh century. As with the other prophets, expositors must understand the world of the Near East and Judah to preach from Nahum. Nahum preached before the fall of Nineveh in 612 B.C. He predicted the fall of Assyria and Nineveh its capital. Nahum's written prophecy is as follows:

1. The superscription, 1:1

---

14. Fred M. Wood, *Fire in My Bones* (Nashville: Broadman Press, 1959), 168–70.

2. The revelation of the nature of God, 1:2–15

3. The destruction of Nineveh, 2:1–13

4. Three reason for Assyria's fall, 3:1–19

Nahum's word to Assyria was that a kingdom built on violence ends with destruction.

Habakkuk prophesied near the end of the seventh century. Like Jeremiah, Habakkuk referred to the imminent Babylonian invasion, so he probably prophesied just before Nebuchadnezzar's first invasion of 597 B.C. Habakkuk seemed to question God about the suffering of his people rather than assault the people for their sins. Habakkuk may be divided in three sections:

1. The superscription, 1:1

2. The serious questions of the prophet, 1:2–2:20

3. The confidence of the prophet, 3:1–19

Obadiah also prophesied during the seventh century B.C. Obadiah is the shortest book in the Old Testament; it contains only twenty-one verses. The prophet Obadiah addressed a historical situation. When a major calamity had befallen Judah, the Edomites, instead of coming to the aid of their brothers, gloated over the problem, looted, captured fugitives, and turned them over to the enemy. Obadiah proclaimed God's justice would come to the Edomites.

1. The title verse, 1:1

2. The severe message to Edom, 1:2–14

3. The vindication of God's justice, 1:15–21

At least three great sermon themes can be proclaimed from this short book: the ineptness of self-exaltation, the absolute certainty of divine justice, and the promise of hope.

Sixth-century prophets. Four Hebrew prophets ministered during the sixth century: Ezekiel, Haggai, Zechariah, and Daniel. The Book of Daniel falls in the category of the Writings, but it will be considered in the prophetic books. These sixth-century prophets spoke during turbulent internal and external circumstances. The Babylonians invaded Judah in 597 B.C. Jehoiachim, king of Judah, died probably by assassination, and Jehoiachin became king. He surrendered to Nebuchadnezzar, and he and other leaders from Jerusalem were carried as captives to Babylon. Zedekiah became king of Judah and led a rebellion against Babylon. Nebuchadnezzar besieged Jerusalem and the city fell in 586 B.C. Zedekiah and others from Jerusalem were transported to Babylon.

Gedeliah became governor over Judah after Zedekiah, but Gedeliah was soon assassinated. Many Hebrews fled to Egypt. The Babylonian armies carried more captives to Babylon. The Hebrews lived in Babylon, Palestine, Egypt, and other places throughout the Near East.

In 539 B.C., Cyrus defeated Babylon. He allowed the Hebrew captives to return to Judah and to rebuild their sanctuaries and cities. Two prophets, Haggai and Zechariah, ministered to the people, urging them to return and to rebuild the temple and other significant places. The period of the captivity and the restoration furnish the historical setting of Ezekiel, Haggai, Zechariah, and Daniel.

Ezekiel began his ministry in "the fifth year of King Jehoiachin's exile" (Ezek. 1:2). These words mean that Ezekiel began his ministry in 593 B.C. His last recorded oracle was in 571 B.C. Ezekiel was then taken into Babylon as a captive by Nebuchadnezzar in 598 B.C. He strengthened the faith and hopes of the captives. The Book of Ezekiel falls into three major sections:

1. Judgment on Judah and Jerusalem, 1:1–24:27

2. Judgment against the nations, 25:1–32:32

3. Oracles of hope, 33:1–48:35

Haggai delivered five prophecies in 520 B.C. These messages were dated in the second year of Darius, king of Persia. Haggai's prophecy had one objective, to encourage the rebuilding of the temple in Jerusalem. His messages seem to have been written during or soon after their delivery, because they do not mention the completion of the temple in 516 B.C. The division of Haggai's five messages follows:

1. The command to build, 1:1–11

2. The promise of God's presence, 1:12–15

3. The encouragement for the discouraged, 2:1–9

4. The call for patience, 2:10–19

5. The promise of God's approval, 2:20–23

Zechariah also encouraged the rebuilding of the temple. The book which bears Zechariah's name has two noticeably different parts, 1–8 and 9–14. In the first part, the whole world is pictured with peace, but in the second part the nations were restless and a siege of Jerusalem seemed imminent. Some Old Testament scholars suggest that Zechariah wrote the book late in his life as an apocalyptic drama. The book falls into two parts:

1. The messages of hope for difficult days, 1:1–8:23

2. Messages of glory about the Messianic Age, 9:1–14:21

Daniel lived in turbulent and dangerous times. Many Old Testament scholars chart Daniel's life and ministry as beginning in 612 B.C. with the fall of the Assyrians and ending about 539 B.C. with the decree of Cyrus. Scholars disagree about who wrote the book and when it was written, though the events it records occurred in the sixth century B.C. Its message is relevant for the twentieth century and in every age when people need to hear about the triumph of good over evil. The book is divided into two parts:

1. Narrative about Daniel and his friends, 1:1–6:28

2. Visions of Daniel, 7:1–12:13

Other books. Jonah, Joel, and Malachi have unique circumstances with regard to historical background. Jonah probably did not write the book which bears his name. He prophesied during the reign of Jeroboam II (2 Kings 14:25), but the book was written after the destruction of Nineveh in 612 B.C. The main message of the Book of Jonah is that God loved all peoples of the world just as much as he loved Israel. The book has four sections:

1. The prophet's rebellion and the Lord's response, 1:1–16

2. The prophet's prayer and the Lord's response, 1:17–2:10

3. The prophet's obedience and the Lord's response, 3:1–10

4. The prophet's resentment and the Lord's response, 4:1–11[15]

Joel ranks as one of the hardest prophets to assign a specific period, either with the date of the prophet's ministry or the book's writing. Two prominent views about the date of the book prevail: it was composed during the reign of Joash in Judah (837 B.C.), or it was written after the exile (400 B.C.). The date of the book does not affect its message. The prophet witnessed a locust attack on Judah and interpreted it as God's judgment. The prophet called for repentance. Joel may be divided as follows:

---

15. Billy K. Smith, "Jonah," in *Layman's Bible Book Commentary*, vol. 13 (Nashville: Broadman Press, 1982), 137–53.

1. The superscription, 1:1

2. The locust plague and drought, 1:2–20

3. The coming day of the Lord, 2:1–17

4. God's blessings on the people's repentance, 2:18–3:21

Malachi bears either a particular person's name or a title. The word literally means "my messenger." Malachi was probably the name of a prophet who ministered during the times of Ezra and Nehemiah. The temple had been rebuilt, and worship in it had been taking place for some time. Malachi sought to call for repentance amid decadent and indifferent religious people. The content of Malachi's message can be divided as follows:

1. The superscription, 1:1

2. God's love for Israel, 1:2–5

3. The failure of the priests, 1:6–2:9

4. The failure of the people, 2:10–4:3

5. The call for repentance, 4:4–6

No book and no author can fully treat the preaching possibilities inherent in the Old Testament. The books of the Old Testament are a golden lode with inexhaustible riches and surprising treasures.[16]

Through the discussion of the five literary characteristics of Old Testament books and through a brief mention of most of the books in these genres, expositors have been introduced to the immense possibilities of preaching series of sermons from Old Testament books. A simple preaching plan for preaching from Old Testament books could include preaching from various psalms each year and choosing one book each year from the pentateuchal books, the historical books, the wisdom books, or the prophetic books. In the lifetime of a dedicated expositor, Old Testament books need to be the source for many series of sermons.

---

16. Achtemeier, 26.

CHAPTER 10

Preaching from New Testament Books

Abundant opportunities for timely sermons and diverse sermon series await expositors who select and study New Testament books. A conscientious preacher seeks to proclaim the entire Bible. The Old Testament closes with an uncompleted story—God's people failed to fulfill his purpose. With the opening of the New Testament account, the story resumes about the people of God and the witness about one saving message for all human beings—a message

245

that proclaims Jesus Christ. In about A.D. 320, Augustine said that "the Old Testament is implicit in the New, the New Testament becomes explicit in the Old. "[1] Jesus Christ's coming into the world fulfilled the history of Israel and closed the Old Testament. In the Gospels, the Acts, the Letters, and the Apocalypse, the New Testament history of God's people centers on Jesus Christ.

The challenge of New Testament preaching is different from the challenge of Old Testament preaching. The Old Testament contains an account of the story of God's people over a historical period embracing almost two thousand years, but the New Testament contains a record of a period of time less than one hundred years. The Old Testament writers enlarged on God's dealing with people throughout the two centuries by including many areas of national and individual life. But the New Testament writers concentrated primarily on one subject—that Jesus Christ is the one and only Savior who must be proclaimed to the entire world. New Testament writers spoke of fulfillment or completion in Jesus Christ. In Jesus Christ, God's promises about the Messiah to the people in the Old Testament era were fulfilled, and God's reign was inaugurated through his Son, the Messiah. The New Testament books contain the recording of Jesus' beginning God's reign, establishing the new Israel or the church, and promising the ultimate completion of God's reign beyond history. The New Testament writers related how the church became empowered by the Holy Spirit for its mission to the world, which involved taking the good news of God's salvation in Christ to all people. The Old Testament writers related the beginning of God's story, and the New Testament writers told the completion of the story. No expositor needs to neglect any part of the story of God's people, but expositors need to be aware of differences in the Old and New Testament stories.

Just as the gist of the Old Testament story needs to be kept uppermost in an expositor's mind, so do the salient points of the New Testament story need to be kept in mind. The New Testament story starts in the four Gospels with John the Baptist's announcement of the coming Messiah. The main character of the story is Jesus, the long-awaited Messiah, the Son of God. The primary part of the New Testament story line contains what Jesus said

---

1. Quoted in Neil Richardson, *Preaching from Scripture* (London: Epworth Press, 1983), 80.

and did from the day he was baptized until he was crucified and raised from the dead. The primary theme of the story is the inauguration of God's reign. The four Gospels contain many details of Jesus' story—his baptism by John; the temptation in the wilderness; the ministry of teaching, preaching, and healing throughout Palestine; the transfiguration; the confession of Peter at Caesarea Philippi; the journey to Jerusalem to die; the crucifixion; and the resurrection. Associated with these events and other episodes, the Gospels record Jesus' words about the reign of God. So, the Gospel writers related the words and works of Jesus Christ.

The Book of Acts follows the Gospels and continues the New Testament story. This book is a bridge between the Gospels and the rest of the New Testament. Acts relates how Christ's special messengers, led by the risen Lord and filled with the Holy Spirit, carried the good news of salvation to Jews in Jerusalem, to places across the Middle East, and to Rome, the capital of the first-century world. Acts tells of the founding of churches in Corinth, Philippi, Ephesus, Thessalonica, and many other places. In the twenty-one Epistles, various inspired writers explain and interpret Christ's words and deeds in light of their pagan environment and in light of problems in Christian living found in corporate relationships and in individual lives. John, in the last book of the New Testament, Revelation, relates how the story would end with God's purposes actualized ultimately in Jesus Christ. To preach effectively from any New Testament book, a preacher needs to see what part of Jesus' story any New Testament book contains.

The expositor also needs to recognize the kind of literature used to relate the story. Four Gospels, one theological-historical book, twenty-one Epistles, and one apocalyptic book tell about the earlier life and ministry of Jesus Christ and his continued work through his people after his resurrection. The New Testament contains four unique dominant genres: gospels, history, epistles, and apocalypse. The qualities that make these New Testament books unique have more to do with their content and theological claims than with their literary forms. Nonetheless, expositors can profit by noting some distinctive literary features that characterize New Testament books.

Leland Ryken, while stressing the superiority of content and theological claims over literary form, gave some distinctive literary features of New Testament books. The first feature of the New

Testament is that it is *religious literature*. The literature has a strong, persuasive, theological purpose. The Gospels concentrate on the purpose and work of Christ. The Book of Acts and the Epistles focus on the world-changing impact of the indwelling Christ in the life of the church.

The second feature of the New Testament is that it is *simple and realistic literature*. New Testament writers included everyday details. Their readers lived in an ordinary world of farming and nature, buying, selling, and journeying. A natural symbolism was at work; sowing seed and baking bread and putting on armor became more than normal activities. The New Testament writers opened the concrete sensory world into a spiritual world.[2]

A third feature of the New Testament is that it is *oral literature*. Addresses, sayings, and dialogues dominate the narrative parts of the New Testament (the Gospels and Acts). Individual units probably circulated orally before being collected in written documents.

The fourth feature of the New Testament is that it is *popular literature*. The New Testament is a book of the people. Its language is for the most part the language of everyday speech.[3]

The New Testament is literary at the levels of both content and form. At the level of content, the writers demonstrated more interest in presenting the person of Christ and in re-creating experiences with the risen Christ than in sharing abstract ideas. At the level of form, the New Testament books fall into general genres and possess a high degree of artistry, special resources of language, and master images. Expositors need to know the story about which the New Testament books report; expositors also need to know the style of writing which the authors used. To help with preaching from New Testament books, we will examine the four general genres of gospels, history (Acts), epistles, and apocalypse.

Gospels

Four books in the New Testament come under the category of biblical literature known as gospels. The term *gospel*, when used to designate a kind of literature, probably originated when the first line of Mark was abbreviated as if it had been intended for the title

2. Leland Ryken, *Words of Life: A Literary Introduction to the New Testament* (Grand Rapids: Baker Book House, 1987), 24–25.
3. Ibid., 25–26.

of that book: "The beginning of the gospel of Jesus Christ." If any of the literary forms in the New Testament is original with the Christian community, it is the gospel.[4] When comparing the New Testament Gospels with other types of biographical accounts in the world at that time, it becomes clear that Mark and others created a new literary form to convey understandings and interpretations of Jesus.

A large portion of the minister's preaching should come from the four Gospels. Some preachers follow a lectionary that includes readings from the Synoptic Gospels on a three-year cycle with interspersed selections from the Fourth Gospel. Any year which is divisible by three begins the B cycle with the Gospel of Mark. Matthew, or the A cycle, can be placed in the year before Mark; Luke, or the C cycle, can be placed in the year after Mark. Preachers who do not follow a lectionary can select texts frequently or preach series periodically from the Gospels.

The Origin of the Gospels

Anyone who prepares sermons from a gospel needs to know that the gospel circulated orally before it was written. Three historical contexts figure into an understanding of the origin of any written gospel: (1) the context of the time in which Jesus lived; (2) the context of the time when the gospel circulated orally; and (3) the context of the times when the four Gospels were written. Understanding a written gospel begins with studying the times when Jesus lived on earth, namely the first three decades of the first century. According to the Gospel of Mark, the gospel began with the good news of Jesus' birth, life, teachings, death, and resurrection. Jesus was born into historical circumstances. Expositors of the Gospels should immerse themselves in the political Greco-Roman situations and the religious situations among the Jews. The gospel stories, sayings, events, and other materials originated in the historical events of Jesus' earthly life and ministry.[5] To preach from any one of the four Gospels, an expositor needs to know as much as possible about the times of Jesus. Good reading offers this kind of

---

4. Fred B. Craddock, *The Gospels in Interpreting Biblical Texts* (Nashville: Abingdon Press, 1981), 24.

5. William M. Ramsey, *The Layman's Guide to the New Testament* (Atlanta: John Knox Press, 1981), 23.

information. The following two books would be useful in knowing the background of the first three decades of the first century:

Joachim Jeremias, *Jerusalem in the Time of Jesus* (Philadelphia: Fortress Press, 1969).

Eduard Lohse, *The New Testament Environment* (New York: Seabury, 1973).

To preach effectively from the four Gospels, an expositor also needs to know about the thirty or more years from the time of Jesus' resurrection to the writing of the first Gospel (perhaps about A.D. 65). During this time, few if any written records of Jesus' life and ministry circulated other than some theological insights from Paul's letters. Those were three decades of "the oral tradition." During those years, Jesus' words and deeds were communicated orally, though whole gospel accounts did not yet exist.

Students of the Gospels need to know something about this time of oral tradition. Luke related how he wrote in part from reports of those who were "eyewitnesses and servants of the word" (Luke 1:2). Those first preachers told the story of Jesus' life, relating stories and sayings from his ministry. Later, the Gospel writers selected and arranged the material from these oral expressions to write their gospel accounts. Luke, in his opening insight about eyewitnesses and servants of the word, helps us understand that much material existed orally about Jesus during the time of the oral tradition.

Fifty or more years after Jesus' resurrection, Luke provided even more insights about the time of the oral tradition. In Acts, Luke gave an account of what the messengers said. The content of the first preaching can be reconstructed by examining the summaries of sermons in Acts and by comparing these summaries with passages in Paul's letters. In a highly influential book, *The Apostolic Preaching and Its Developments*, C. H. Dodd pointed to the common characteristics of the messengers in the early church. Dodd used the Greek word *kerygma* to refer to the content of the earliest Christian preaching. The addresses in Acts and some passages in Paul, which represented the content of the Gospels during the time of the oral tradition, may be summarized as follows:

> The prophecies are fulfilled, and the new Age is inaugurated
> by the coming of Christ.
> He was born of the seed of David.
> He died according to the Scriptures,
> to deliver us out of the present evil age.

He was buried.
He rose on the third day according to the Scriptures.
He is exalted at the right hand of God,
as Son of God and Lord of quick and dead.
He will come again as Judge and Savior of man.[6]

Most of what an expositor could know about the time of the oral tradition comes from the records of the four written Gospels, the speeches in Acts, and the letters of Paul. Many New Testament scholars think that some kind of document consisting of a collection of Jesus' teachings existed in about A.D. 50. Scholars call such a supposed collection Q from the German word *Quelle*, which means "source." They think Matthew and Luke used it when they composed their written documents. The existence of Q cannot be proved absolutely. Even though such a collection of Jesus' teachings could have existed, the important factor an expositor needs to know is that the gospel circulated orally before it was written in documents known as Gospels. Early preachers related many reports, narratives, teachings, and other information from Jesus' life. Those materials, delivered for about thirty years, became part of the substance used for the written Gospels.

In the providence of God, writers were inspired to write accounts of Jesus' life and ministry. Just as expositors need to know more than the first three decades when Jesus lived on earth and the next three decades when messengers told Jesus' story, the expositor also needs to know the times when the four Gospels were written. From the vast amount of material that existed about Jesus, the Gospel writers selected and arranged this material for their special purposes. Luke helped readers understand that he selected and arranged materials from many sources and for a specific purpose: "Inasmuch as many have undertaken to compile an account of the things accomplished among us . . . so that you may know the exact truth about the things you have been taught" (Luke 1:1, 4). Evidently Luke examined many stories about Jesus that circulated during the time of the oral tradition. He then selected by God's guideline material that was appropriate to the situation of his original readers and to his purpose.

6. C. H. Dodd, *The Apostolic Preaching and Its Developments* (New York: Harper and Brothers, 1962), 17.

John also seems to have selected and arranged materials about Jesus for his purpose and for the situation of his original readers (see John 20:30–31). Matthew and Mark also picked materials about Jesus and arranged their written accounts according to historical situations and according to their purposes. Expositors can easily observe that the shape and substance of the written Gospels were affected by the life and times of both the original authors and readers.

Fred Craddock observes that the written Gospels were not addressed "to whom it may concern" but to particular Christian communities.[7] One would expect this material about Jesus Christ to address the needs of those communities. They faced legalism, persecution, zealotism, false prophets, abused grace, excessive emphasis on Christ's return, and even a collapse of expectation for his return.

Knowing the times and the circumstances of the years when the Gospels were written helps the modern reader understand the Gospels. The Gospel writers tried to preserve the exact truth of the gospel and to interpret it to the issues vital to the life and faith of Christian churches. The four authors wrote similar books, but each is different because each writer addressed the different issues facing the particular churches.[8]

Particular Christian communities had needs that had to be addressed. Four writers possessed sources about the sayings and events of Jesus' life and ministry. Bringing the needs of the community together with the Jesus material resulted in the written Gospels. Expositors who preach today can take these Gospels and expose truth, understanding the needs of the people then and exposing these truths which can still relate to people in new circumstances, yet in a way that is not discontinuous with the life and teaching of Jesus of Nazareth.

Differences become apparent as readers study the four Gospels. The Gospels are different for several reasons. Each writer selected from the material available from what Jesus said and did. Then each writer arranged this material to convey a desired meaning. Each author expanded or abbreviated the existing material and, by

---

7. Craddock, 26.
8. Ibid.

comments, introduced or concluded the account of an act or a teaching of Jesus.[9]

In the beginning was the Christ event. It has been called "the gospel." Jesus lived and taught during the first three decades of the first century. About thirty-three years after his birth, he died and arose three days later. He spent forty more days on earth after his resurrection. During the Jewish feast of Pentecost, the Holy Spirit came upon all believers, and messengers went to all the ancient world heralding the gospel. Eyewitnesses reported stories, sayings, events, and teachings from Jesus' life and ministry. According to the consensus of most scholars, no written record existed for more than thirty or more years after his ascension. Because of the need to preserve the truth of the gospel and the need to interpret the gospel to Christian communities, literary documents known as gospels came into being. Learning how the gospel was communicated through written gospels can help anyone who wishes to preach from any of the Gospels. Having observed how the gospel message came to be produced in written gospels, the student of Scripture needs to look at some of the distinctive characteristics of these written works.

Literary Characteristics of the Gospels

The New Testament begins with a collection of four works that relate the life and ministry of Jesus Christ. Each presentation of Jesus has its own peculiar emphases and presentation. These four written accounts about Jesus are called Gospels from the Greek word *euangelion*, which means "good news." Comparing these four written works with other types of biographical accounts in the ancient world leads to the conclusion that the writers developed a new literary form to convey the church's understanding and presentation of Jesus. The Gospel writers used history, biography, teachings, and other materials to present the story of Jesus. Each of the Gospel writers was concerned with the life and ministry of Jesus Christ.[10]

Four divinely inspired writers produced a written account of Jesus. Most New Testament scholars think that Mark was the first

---

9. Ibid.

10. James M. Efird, *How to Interpret the Bible* (Atlanta: John Knox Press, 1984), 90–91.

Gospel written (ca. A.D. 65). The next two Gospels written were Matthew and Luke; scholars think both of these writers used Mark as a source. Of the eighty-eight paragraphs found in Mark, only three are not in either Matthew or Luke. Obviously, both Matthew and Luke used the same material found in Mark, but they adjusted it to fit their style and purpose. Some scholars think that Matthew and Luke also used a source known as Q for much of the teachings of Jesus.

The first three Gospels are similar in content, origin, and structure. They may be easily compared by placing them in parallel columns. They are called the "Synoptics," which means "to see together." The Gospel of John differs from the Synoptics, though it tells the same story of Jesus as the other Gospels. The Synoptics focus on the events of Jesus' life that happened in Galilee, but John concentrated on Jerusalem. John also differs in form; the Synoptics have parables, but John reported no parable stories. He wrote in long monologues, figures of speech, and engaging interviews. Perhaps the greatest contrast of John to the Synoptics is that John reported Jesus' propensity to proclaim openly that he was the Christ, the Son of God. But the writers of the Synoptics presented that Jesus kept his messiahship a secret. Through the years scholars have been trying to reconcile the differences of John with the Synoptics. No easy answers exist to the challenge, but one axiom is clear: All four Gospels present the life and ministry of Jesus Christ. All four have the same hero. Everything in the Gospels focuses on Jesus Christ, his personhood, acts, and sayings. The consistent concentration on Jesus Christ becomes the chief characteristic of the Gospels.

The Gospel writers told the story of Jesus in writing, but they did not narrate strictly by chronology. Instead, they related the story of Jesus from his birth to his resurrection by a collection of materials. Certain scholars identify some of these collections as *pericopes*, which means material in self-contained units. Expositors need to think more of collections of different materials rather than a sequential, chronological account of Jesus' life and ministry. To understand the characteristics of these collections, expositors need to observe and understand some of the obvious units of collection and writing.

First, expositors need to observe the *annunciation and nativity stories*. Matthew and Luke begin with a series of stories surrounding the birth of Jesus. In the annunciation announcements, angels appear to people with news about Jesus' birth and other related incidents. The nativity stories relate what happened when Jesus was born. Only Luke includes a boyhood story of Jesus in the temple at age twelve. Neither Mark nor John contains collections of annunciations and nativity stories.

All four Gospels contain collections of *calling and encounter stories.* Calling stories relate Jesus' calling persons to follow him. These incidents include both the calling of the apostles and other followers. Closely akin to calling stories are the encounter stories. The Gospel writers included Jesus' encounter with a person or a group. The story of Zaccheus (see Luke 19:1–10) and the Samaritan woman (see John 4:1–41) represent examples of encounters. The encounter stories involve dramatic dialogue between Jesus and the person or group.

Also included in the collection for the Gospels are *conflict stories.* These stories could be grouped with encounter stories, but the essential difference seems to be Jesus' conflict with a person or group. These stories reflect a back-and-forth rhythm coupled with Jesus' strategies of defense and offense. A prominent example of a conflict collection appears in Mark 2:1–3:6, which records a series of stories about Jesus in conflict with religious authorities.

Pronouncement stories are another distinctive type of collection used by the Gospel writers. Such a story linked an event in Jesus' life with a memorable saying or proverb by Jesus. Usually the event led to the saying, and the saying or pronouncement culminated the event. The saying was so embedded in the narrative that both the event and the saying could be remembered easily. The saying either interpreted or illustrated the event. An example of a pronouncement story may be found in Mark 2:23–28. As Jesus walked through a grain field on the Sabbath, he plucked and ate some of the wheat. Some Pharisees observed the action and accused Jesus of violating the Sabbath by threshing grain. Jesus replied, "The Sabbath was made for man, and not man for the Sabbath (Mark 2:27). The saying concluded the event.

Gospel writers also included *miracle stories* in their collections about Jesus. A typical miracle story includes: (1) notation of a need, (2) seeking Jesus' help, (3) an expression of faith from the person in need or from acquaintances of the person in need, (4) the miracle performed by Jesus, and (5) people's response to the miracle.[11] The Gospel writers included a wide range of the kinds of miracles Jesus performed. They depicted Jesus' power over the natural world, disease and handicap, the unseen world, and death. The writer of the Fourth Gospel selected seven signs or miracles to present the life and ministry of Jesus (see John 2–11).

The Synoptic Gospel writers included *parables* spoken during Jesus' earthly ministry. On some occasions, parables existed alone, and on other occasions the writers selected and grouped parables in larger blocks. The parable of the good Samaritan (see Luke 10:30–37) appears in Luke just after the seventy disciples had been sent out and had returned with their reports. The parable of the good Samaritan arose out of a discussion of a lawyer with Jesus. When the lawyer asked, "And who is my neighbor?" Jesus responded with the parable of the good Samaritan. The parable is not followed immediately with other parables.

In another kind of use of the parable, the writers of Matthew, Mark, and Luke selected and grouped parables together. Matthew recorded seven parables in succession (see Matt. 13:1–52). Mark included three parables together that described the Kingdom (see Mark 4:1–34). Luke grouped the parables of the sheep, coin, and father to illustrate that God includes everyone as a prospect for the Kingdom (see Luke 15).

The Gospels include various kinds of parables. Some parables are stories: the good Samaritan, the prodigal son, and many others. Other parables are parabolic sayings that include metaphors and similes. One such parabolic saying was, "You are the salt of the earth" (Matt. 5:13). Another form of parable is the similitudes. Jesus used illustrations of leaves, the sower, mustard seed, and other everyday likenesses to make a point about the Kingdom. Much of the material in the Synoptic Gospels includes parable materials of stories, parabolic sayings, and similitudes.

The Gospel writers also included collections of Jesus' *teachings*. Many of Jesus' teachings appeared within other collections such as parables, miracles, and pronouncement stories. However, some unique teaching sections may be noted in the Gospels. For example, Matthew has five distinguishable units of Jesus' teachings: the Sermon on the Mount (see Matt. 5–7), Jesus' instructions to the twelve (see Matt. 10), seven parables about the Kingdom (see Matt.

---

11. Ramsey, 27.

13), Jesus' teachings on the way to Jerusalem (see Matt. 18–20), and Jesus' eschatological discourses (see Matt. 24–25). Matthew ended each one of these teaching sections with the phrase: "The result was that when Jesus had finished these words" (Matt. 7:28; 11:1; 13:53; 19:1; 26:1).

The writer of the Fourth Gospel also included sections of Jesus' teachings. Immediately after Jesus' performing a sign or miracle, the Gospel writer included a teaching discourse related directly to the sign. For example, after the feeding of the five thousand, the writer gave Jesus' teaching discourse on the bread of life (see John 6:22–71). The writer of the Fourth Gospel also included a large unit of Jesus' teachings in John 13–17. This material represents Jesus' instructions to his disciples in the upper room on the night before he was crucified.

All four Gospel writers included the *passion stories* in their account of Jesus' life and ministry. The events surrounding the trial, death, and resurrection of Jesus form a large part of the climax of all four Gospels. Leland Ryken lists the following percentages of passion material in the Gospels: Matthew, 29 percent; Mark, 38 percent; Luke, 25 percent; and John, 38 percent.[12] Obviously the Gospel writers considered the passion stories highly important. The Gospel writers generally included Jesus' travel to Jerusalem for the Passover, his time of teachings with the apostles in the upper room, his arrest and trial, his crucifixion and burial, his resurrection, and his postresurrection appearances. Each of the Gospel writers narrated the passion account from tragic circumstances to a triumphal ending.

None of the collections of materials used by the Gospel writers fit in one exclusive category. Often the units of material converge in other units of collections. For example, miracle stories often become pronouncement stories, and parables can be viewed as teaching materials. Despite the combination of elements, the way the writer handled the material makes the collection type the dominant element. Expositors need to be able to recognize the different kinds of collections in the Gospels and the way the writers arranged the material to narrate the life and ministry of Jesus Christ.

---

12. Ryken, 40.

Sermon Methods with the Gospels

A significant number of texts need to be preached from the Gospels each year. Using the lectionary ensures extensive use of Gospel texts. The text selections are based on a three-year cycle—A, B, and C. In the A cycle text selections come from Matthew, in the B cycle text selections come from Mark, and in the C cycle text selections come from Luke. Over a three-year period the preacher will have weekly text selections from one of the Synoptic Gospels with text from the Fourth Gospel interspersed throughout the three years. If expositors use the lectionary, they will preach many sermons from a Gospel during the course of a year.

If an expositor chooses not to follow a lectionary, a definite decision needs to be made to preach extensively from the Gospels. Earlier in this work, the suggestion was made that a preacher should preach from one Old Testament and one New Testament book each year. A Gospel may or may not be a part of the New Testament selection. A preacher might include a Gospel each year in addition to another New Testament book. For example, an expositor may devise a personalized lectionary using a Gospel each year for selected texts and topics. The first year might begin with Matthew, and the next three years would use Mark, Luke, and John for an annual emphasis. Choosing texts from a selected Gospel means that during the year the preacher reads, studies, and selects texts for preaching on the life and ministry of Jesus Christ.

Matthew. The Gospel of Matthew probably emerged from somewhere in Palestine late in the first century, perhaps A.D. 80–100.[13] The work appears to have been written by a Christian who had formerly been a Jew and who wrote to similar persons in the midst of a larger Jewish culture and community. Perhaps the perspective of authorship and readers explains the strong emphasis in Matthew on the fulfillment of "true Judaism."[14]

Matthew portrayed Jesus as a king and a magnificent teacher. In preaching from Matthew these ideas of king and teacher should be considered. William M. Ramsay gave an outline of Matthew which develops the theme of Jesus as king:

1. The King is born, 1–2

---

13. Efird, 103.
14. Ibid.

2. The King gets ready for rule with baptism and temptation, 3–4

3. The Kingdom is proclaimed, 5–7

4. Conflicting responses to the King, 8–15

5. The King is recognized, 16–17

6. The cost of the King's reign, 18–20

7. The King is crowned, 21–28[15]

William E. Hull, in an article entitled "Preaching on the Synoptic Gospels," offers a preaching approach from Matthew based on the teaching sections. Matthew inserts large blocks of teaching material within the narrative. Five such discourses alternate with narratives (see 5–7; 10–13; 18; 24–25); each of the teaching sections concludes with a transitional formula (see 7:28–29; 11:1; 13:53; 19:1; 26:1). William Manson even suggests that Matthew's grand design was to prepare a "New Torah," parallel to the five books of Moses.[16] Whatever an expositor thinks about a theory of a New Pentateuch, clearly a good preaching plan for Matthew must emphasize the teaching sections. Hull's sermon suggestions for the didactic units of Matthew follow:

1. The Sermon on the Mount, 5–7

2. Equipping God's People for a Hostile World, 9:35–11:1

3. Parables of the Kingdom, 13

4. The Church as Community, 18

5. Talk about the Future, 24–25[17]

Many other preaching approaches from Matthew, other than the themes of King and Teacher, could be taken. Such approaches could range from a systematic, consecutive preaching approach to a random selection of preferred texts or texts applicable to personal or community needs.

Mark. The Gospel of Mark was the first of the Gospels to be written. To understand Mark, the interpreter needs to know that Mark was writing to the Christian community in Rome which had

---

15. Ramsey, 39–61.

16. William Manson, *Jesus the Messiah* (London: Hodder and Stoughton, 1943), 51–55.

17. William E. Hull, "Preaching on the Synoptic Gospel," in *Biblical Preaching: An Expositor's Treasury* (Philadelphia: Westminster Press, 1983), 177–80.

experienced a period of extreme persecution at the hands of Nero. Mark wrote his Gospel basically to depict Jesus as the unique Son of God. Mark gave a theological interpretation of who Jesus was: Christ and Son of God (Mark 1:1). As the unique Son of God, Jesus inaugurated a new Kingdom. Jesus was interpreted as Messiah, but a different kind of Messiah than most Jewish people were expecting. Jesus was a suffering Messiah, and Mark interpreted Jesus' ministry against that axiom.

Mark's emphasis on a suffering Messiah relates closely to Mark's insistence that the disciples of Jesus were called on to suffer also. Mark stresses discipleship because that was the message the believers in Rome needed to hear. Interestingly enough, the disciples depicted in Mark's Gospel did not understand why Jesus had to suffer or why they should have to suffer. Mark emphasized Jesus' suffering in a way that the other Gospel writers did not because this aspect of his life was more important to the people to whom Mark was writing.

William E. Hull suggests three possible ways to tap the message of Mark:

- Preach a series of sermons on commitment stories to develop discipleship.

- Preach a series of messages on conflict stories. Mark gave greater prominence to controversy than any other Gospel writer. Each message must define the issues between Jesus and his opponents.

- Preach a series of messages on miracles. These miracles dramatize the intervention of the divine in life.[18]

Other selective approaches, such as a consecutive, paragraph-by-paragraph or verse-by-verse preaching approach, also await an expositor.

Luke. Unlike the other Gospels, Luke was written as the first volume of a two-volume work, Luke-Acts. In both prologues of these New Testament books, readers find the works addressed to Theophilus, a Roman official. Luke depicts Jesus, the Messiah of the Jews, as the Savior of the entire world. To portray the significance of Jesus, Luke collected and interpreted many materials available. Some scholars think that Luke wrote the first Christian

---

18. Ibid., 181–186.

apology, a defense of Christianity before Rome. Though the prologues to Luke-Acts have that flavor, most of the Gospel and much of Acts seem unconcerned about a legal defense of the Christian faith. No single hypothesis concerning Luke's purpose in writing seems to fit into themes and motifs found in the materials Luke used. One impression about Luke's purpose seems to be clear: in the Gospel of Luke, Luke told how Jesus was the Savior for the entire world, and in Acts he told how the followers of Jesus moved from a group within Judaism to a worldwide movement. Luke presented the story of Jesus (what Jesus began to do) and the story of the church (what Jesus continued to do) as one continuous narrative.[19]

The Gospel of Luke contains material found in Matthew and Mark, but it also includes new material. The expositor should consider all the material in Luke, both the repeated found in Matthew and Mark and the new materials. Some of the new materials include Luke's stories about Jesus' birth, infancy, childhood, and his resurrection narratives. Luke has some parables not present in Matthew or Luke including the prodigal, the Pharisee and the publican, the good Samaritan, the rich man and Lazarus. Readers also notice that Luke explained the ministry of Jesus with Old Testament quotations. A preaching approach from Luke could easily emphasize the universality of Christianity. The universality of Christianity was portrayed by Luke in describing Jesus' ministry to social outcasts. Luke presented Jesus as a friend of sinners in such stories as the woman who washed his feet with her tears and the extortioner, Zaccheus. Luke also wrote of the place of women in the ministry of Jesus, referring to them thirteen times; these references are not paralleled in the other Gospels.

Another proclamation emphasis from Luke could be the emphasis of Jesus on prayer. On at least ten strategic occasions, Luke recorded the prayer life of the Lord. Moreover, Luke also mentioned Jesus' entreaty to the disciples that they should pray. Luke alone gave three parables on prayer: the friend at midnight (see 11:5–8), the persistent widow (see 18:1–8), and the Pharisee and the publican (see 18:9–14). Only Luke gave the four prayers of the infancy narratives: the *Magnificat* (see 1:46–55), the *Benedictus* (see 1:68–79), the *Gloria* (see 2:14), and the *Nunc Dimittis* (see 2:29–32).

---

19. Craddock, 100.

Scattered throughout the Gospel are many teachings on prayer (see 6:28; 10:2; 21:36; 22:40–46). Such material on prayer could provide a preaching angle from Luke.

The sheer volume of material in Luke presents expositors with a challenge. The series of sermons could select themes from Luke's unique emphases and from material Luke adapted from Mark; or the series could be a consecutive approach from Luke. The following outline may help the expositor see the flow of Luke's Gospel.

1. Prologue, 1:1–4

2. Birth and childhood of John and Jesus, 1:5–2:52

3. Ministry of Jesus in Galilee, 3:1–9:50

4. Teaching on the way to Jerusalem, 9:51–19:27

5. The days in Jerusalem, 19:28–24: 5[20]

John. The Fourth Gospel differs in many respects from the first three. John states his reason for writing: "Many other signs therefore Jesus also performed in the presence of the disciples, which are not written in this book; but these have been written that you may believe that Jesus is the Christ, the Son of God; and that believing you may have life in His name" (John 20:30–31). The writer relates how he selected carefully what he told, but he selected only those materials that suited his purpose. John 2–11 is often called "The Book of Signs," because this section includes seven miracles. The signs were reported so readers might believe, which could refer to outsiders becoming believers or to those with faith to strengthen it. John's expression, "Jesus is the Christ, the Son of God" evidently discloses that the writer wanted readers to understand Jesus. Then John added that those who believe in Jesus Christ will have life— the life lived in Christ now and forever.

Though some facts can be known about John's purpose, specifics are hard to determine about the origin of and circumstances surrounding the writing of this Gospel. The author challenged the community to become a community of faith through inward relationship with Jesus.

John structured the Gospel to present Jesus as the revealer of God. Fred Craddock says that "every story, every sign, and every

---

20. Ibid.

discourse makes this point."[21] Craddock's outline of John helps make visible the permeating and controlling nature of this theme:

1. Prologue: God revealed in Jesus, 1:1–18

2. The Revealer of God ministers on earth, 1:19–12:50

3. The Revealer of God suffers and returns to glory, 13:1–20:31

4. Epilogue: That people know God in Jesus, 21:1–2 5[22]

Craddock adds that, because of John's emphasis on Jesus as the revealer of God, three kinds of materials prevail in the Gospel: revelation discourses, the signs, and the passion narratives.

John has a lot in common with the Synoptics. John included the accounts of John the Baptist, Jesus' going to Galilee, his feeding the multitudes, his walking on water, the miraculous catch of fish, Peter's confession, Jesus' entry into Jerusalem, the cleansing of the temple, and other accounts. Noticeably absent from John are acts of exorcism, the parables, the wilderness temptation, and the struggle in Gethsemane. New stories include the wedding at Cana, Nicodemas' interview, the woman at the well, the healing at the pool, and the raising of Lazarus.

Preaching from John affords many stimulating opportunities. In addition to the standard procedure of continuous exposition, expositors could also choose other approaches, such as the encounters of Jesus with people; the seven signs; the "I am" sayings (see 6:48; 8:12; 8:58; 10:7; 10:11; 11:25; 14:6; 15:5); and Jesus' teachings in the upper room (see 13–17).

Four Gospel writers presented the same historical Jesus who was and is the eternal Son of God. Yet each writer presented him in a distinctive manner dictated by historical situations of both the author and the readers and by divine selection and guidance of the materials. The richness of proclamation of the four accounts of Jesus' ministry and teaching become evident with the study of each Gospel. Tremendous opportunities await expositors who select and preach a series of sermons from a Gospel!

Acts

The author of Acts wrote a history of the growth of the early church. But it was history in the same sense as those presented in

---

21. Ibid., 127.
22. Ibid.

the Old Testament narratives of Samuel, Kings, and the Chronicles. Classifying the genre of Acts as history does not go far enough. Acts was written with a theological purpose. Materials were selected and arranged according to an overall theological intention. A more accurate genre identification of Acts could be "theological history." Acts is both history and theology. When preparing sermons from Acts, the preacher needs to consider both sides of this genre factor—Acts is a special kind of history, a history with a theological purpose.

Preaching from Acts allows an expositor to inform audiences about people, churches, places, events, and many other historical matters. But preaching from Acts challenges a preacher to interpret the historical matters in the light of their overall theological purpose. Hearers of the messages from Acts will become more informed about how the church moved from the boundaries of Judaism to the ends of the world; they also will be challenged not only to know history but also to hear what the Lord wants them to be and to do as individuals or as a Christian community.

The Origin of Acts

References as early as A.D. 175 refer to Luke as the author of one of the Gospels and the Book of Acts.[23] One argument for Luke as author of Acts is based on a comparison of Luke 1:1–4 with Acts 1:1. Acts 1:1 was addressed to the same person and referred to an earlier book, almost certainly the Gospel. These two books appear to have been written by the same person. Furthermore, the "we passages" from Acts 16:10 to the end of the book suggest that the author was a companion of Paul during much of the latter part of Paul's life. Coupled with this is the fact that in Colossians 4:14 Paul spoke of his companion, "Luke, the beloved physician," and 2 Timothy 4:11 relates the faithfulness of Luke. The tradition that Luke was the author of Luke-Acts seems valid.

Luke appears to have written Acts during or soon after the Jewish-Roman War (A.D. 66–70)—probably just after. This crisis for both Jews and Christians undoubtedly hastened the break of the Christians from the synagogue and the turning of the Jews from Christianity. Luke probably wrote Acts when the break between Judaism and Christianity appeared. Judging by these circumstances

---

23. Ramsey, 22.

Luke might have written to show how Christianity progressed from a group within Judaism to a worldwide movement. The Gospel of Luke presents Jesus as the universal Savior; Acts presents the church proclaiming Jesus as the Savior for all peoples.[24]

The discovery of Luke's reason for writing Acts affords good insight in understanding and proclaiming the book. Any biblical writing was governed by purpose. Though some have designated the purpose of Acts to be the "acts of the apostles," the book itself does not substantiate that assertion. Seemingly Luke had no interest in giving biographies of the apostles. James is the only apostle whose death is recorded. Peter dropped out of the narratives after he endorsed the Gentile mission recorded in Acts 15. Apart from John, the other apostles were not mentioned, and Luke's interest in Paul centered around the Gentile mission.

Furthermore, Luke's reason for writing Acts does not appear to be a description of church organization or polity. The seven men selected in Acts 6 were not specifically called deacons. Luke did not tell how leadership in the Jerusalem church passed from Peter to James, the brother of Jesus. Also, Acts does not describe the churches' polity or leadership, except to report the appointment of elders.

Many think Acts was written to describe the geographical expansion of Christianity. Nothing could have been further from the author's purpose than the disclosure of a geographical expansion of the church. If this was Luke's purpose, he failed to mention how Christianity moved to many places. Church history per se was simply not Luke's reason for writing.

Frank Stagg, in *The Book of Acts: The Early Struggle for an Unhindered Gospel*, proposed the theory that Luke's purpose in writing Acts came from the use of the Greek adverb *akolutos*, meaning "unhindered." The adverb appears in Acts 8:36; 10:47; 11:17; and 28:31. According to Stagg, Luke used this adverb in developing the idea that the gospel moved unhindered through religious, racial, and national barriers. At first only Jews embraced Christianity, but then Hellenistic Jews (Stephen and Philip) and proselytes accepted the gospel. Then Samaritans, or half-Jews, received the gospel, and finally, Gentiles came into Christianity.[25]

---

24. Frank Stagg, *The Book of Acts: The Early Struggle for an Unhindered Gospel* (Nashville: Broadman Press, 1955), 22.

25. Ibid., 13.

The key to understanding the origin of Acts seems to be Luke's telling of the story orchestrated by the Holy Spirit about how the gospel moved from its Jerusalem-based, Judaism-oriented beginnings to its becoming a worldwide Gentile phenomenon. Any purpose that does not consider the Gentile mission and the Holy Spirit's role in that mission will have missed the main point of Acts.

Knowing the origin of Acts helps immensely with preaching from Acts. The way God used the author to narrate history can help modern hearers of Acts to view the triumphant, joyful, fervent-moving expansion of the gospel, which was directed by the Holy Spirit. Preaching sermons with Luke's purpose in mind can cause hearers to see how the gospel, empowered by the Holy Spirit, changed lives and created the church. Sermons prepared with Luke's purpose in mind can help people see that God's purpose for the church, yesterday and today, is the gospel, hindered by neither Sanhedrin nor synagogue, dissension nor narrow-mindedness, prison nor riot. Nothing can stop the gospel. Luke told the story of how the Holy Spirit worked in the church, and the story still stands as a model of how individuals and churches can continue to progress.

The narrative of Acts ends abruptly, but the ending may fit its purpose. The story stops with Paul in Rome, and his mission was incomplete. Perhaps the open-ended conclusion could have been a version of the serial story with the premise "to be continued." The story told in Acts of the gospel's breaking through barriers and changing lives did not end. It is still continuing.

The Arrangement of Acts

Many suggestions about the arrangement of Acts have been proposed. Some divide the material on the basis of the author's interest in Peter (chapters 1–12) and in Paul (13–28). Still others divide the book according to the geographical expansion of the gospel mentioned in Acts 1:8: Jerusalem (1–7), Judea and Samaria (8–10), and the ends of the earth (11–28).

Gordon D. Fee and Douglas Stuart arrange Acts according to the summary statements in 6:7; 9:31; 12:24; 16:4; and 19:20.[26] In each case the narrative seemed to have a transition in the action

---

26. Gordon Fee and Douglas Stuart, *How to Read the Bible for All Its Worth: A Guide to Understanding the Bible* (Grand Rapids: Baker Book House, 1979), 90.

before going in another direction. Their approach divides Acts into six sections or panels. Each section presses the movement forward from its Jewish setting in Jerusalem with Peter as the predominant figure to a predominantly Gentile church with Paul as the predominant figure and with Rome, the leading city of the Gentile world, as the goal.

The outline of the Book of Acts may look like a geographical exposition, but the arrangements represent a more theological movement. The arrangement traces how the church moved from a small group of Jews to a worldwide movement.

1. The church began in Jerusalem, 1:1–6:7.

2. A church moved to the Samaritans, 6:8–9:31

3. The church moved out to the God-fearers, 9:32–12:24

4. The church moved out to the Gentiles, 12:25–16:5

5. The church moved into Europe, 16:6–19:20

6. The church arrived at Rome, 19:21–28:30. [27]

Without question, the crucial factor in all the narratives in Acts is the role of the Holy Spirit. At every juncture in the movement and in every key person the Holy Spirit directs and empowers, playing the leading role. God willed that the gospel go forth from the Jews to all the world, and by the power of the Holy Spirit individuals and local churches executed God's will.

Sermon Methods with Acts

Preaching a series of sermons from Acts could take many interesting directions. The consecutive approach of covering texts from Acts 1:1 to Acts 28:31 presents the expositor with a challenge. Such a treatment of Acts would mean over twelve months of sermons, preaching one per Sunday. G. Campbell Morgan preached from Acts consecutively, using fifty-seven expositions. [28] Lloyd John Ogilvie also preached consecutively from Acts in twenty-six sermons. [29] The number of sermons depends on the preacher's manner of treating texts. The consecutive approach gives a complete

---

27. Ibid., 90–91.

28. G. Campbell Morgan, *The Acts of the Apostles* (New York: Fleming H. Revell, 1924).

29. Lloyd John Ogilvie, *Drumbeat of Love: The Unlimited Power of the Spirit as Revealed in the Book of Acts* (Waco, Tex.: Word, 1979).

coverage to the book and offers many texts and topics for the preacher to study and to relate to people's needs.

Many expositors will prefer the selective approach. Numerous angles from this perspective could be used. One such approach would be to preach one sermon from each chapter in Acts. This technique would not mean that every verse in the chapter would be treated, but one text within the chapter would be chosen. George and Donald Sweeting preached from Acts with one sermon from each chapter of Acts.[30]

Still another good angle for preaching from Acts could be a series on "Great Texts in Acts." The following list of sermon titles and texts represent the author's series:

1. A Charter for Christians, 1:8

2. Important Instructions, 2:38

3. The Power of a Transformed Life, 4:13

4. The Power of Prayer, 4:31

5. An Example of an Encourager, 4:36–37

6. An Example in Death, 7:59–60

7. Sharing Jesus with Others, 8:35

8. Meeting the Risen Lord, 9:4–6

9. Calling Someone Brother, 9:17

10. The Defeat of Prejudice, 10:34

11. The Answer to an Anxious Question, 16:30–31

12. The Christian Influence in a City, 19:10

13. Courage for a Crisis, 23:11

14. Almost Persuaded, 26:28–29

15. Serenity in a Storm, 27:25

16. Continuous Communication about Christ, 28:30–31[31]

As expositors preach from Acts using great texts, they can solicit from the congregation and choose other texts for another series on "Great Texts in Acts."

---

30. George Sweeting and Donald Sweeting, *The Acts of God* (Chicago: Moody Press, 1986).

31. Harold T. Bryson, "Preaching from the Book of Acts," *The Theological Educator* 42 (fall 1990): 128–29.

Another selective angle for preaching from Acts would be a series on "Personalities in Acts." Paul S. Rees preached six sermons on prominent persons in Acts.[32] Numerous personalities could be considered for a series, such as Theophilus, Sapphira, Stephen, Philip, the Ethiopian eunuch, Paul, Ananias, Cornelius, the Philippian jailer, Felix, Agrippa. Six to ten personalities would make a good series.

Preaching a selective series of sermons from Acts could involve the selection of significant events recorded in the book. Many events affected church life. The following series, grouped under the theme "Great Events in Acts," could be a catalyst for sermon selections:

1. The Ascension of Jesus, 1:9–11
2. The Choice of Church Leaders, 1:12–14
3. The Pentecost Experience, 2:1–13
4. The Choice of Deacons, 6:1–7
5. The Death of Stephen, 6:8–8:3
6. The Conversion of Saul, 9:1–19
7. The Mission to the Gentiles, 10:1–11:18
8. The Jerusalem Conference, 15:1–35
9. The Riot in Ephesus, 19:23–41
10. The Journey to Rome, 21:17–28:28[33]

No expositor can exhaust all the interesting angles of preaching from Acts. The book is so rich and preachers are so diverse that no two series are ever identical.

Letters

Twenty-one New Testament books come under the literary category of epistle or letter. Adolph Deissmann divided this literary genre into two categories: letters and epistles. Other scholars do not make such a sharp distinction between letters and epistles. Deissmann believed that letters were nonliterary, that is, they were not intended for the public but for the person or persons to whom they were addressed. In contrast to the letter, Deissmann thought

---

32. Paul S. Rees, *Men of Action in the Book of Acts* (Westwood, N.J.: Fleming H. Revell, 1966).

33. Bryson, 128–29.

the epistle consisted of an artistic literary form intended for general public reading.[34]

Deissman distinguished letters from epistles primarily at the point of form. Thousands of ancient letters have been found, and most have a form like the New Testament Letters.

1. Name of the Author

2. Names of the Recipients

3. A Word of Greeting

4. Gratitude or Petition in Prayer

5. Body

6. Final Greeting and Farewell[35]

Some exceptions exist in New Testament letters. Gratitude and petition in prayer are missing in Galatians, 1 Timothy, and Titus. New Testament books that contain most of these six parts fall into the category of letters.

Epistles lack the formal elements of parts 1, 2, 3, and 6. They are more epistolary in form rather than letters. For example, 1 John has none of the formal elements of a letter. It looks much like the body of a letter with all the formal elements of a letter omitted. Maybe a case can be built about the differences between letter and epistle in the New Testament, but the variation does not deserve such a sharp distinction as Adolph Deissmann and others gave.

Despite the differences in form, all twenty-one New Testament letters are life-situation documents. Each arose out of a specific life situation, either from the reader's side or the author's situation. God inspired human authors to give his Word to the circumstances. Most New Testament letters or epistles originated from the reader's side. Romans, James, and Philemon, perhaps, represented the author's side. Usually the life situation involved some type of behavior that needed correcting, a doctrinal error which needed to be amended, or an interpersonal misunderstanding that needed to be reconciled.

According to most New Testament scholars, thirteen letters or epistles have been attributed to Paul. Since the fourth century, seven letters have been called the Catholic Epistles or General Epistles. These are James, 1 and 2 Peter, 1, 2, and 3 John, and Jude.

---

34. Fee and Stuart, 44.

35. Ibid.

They are General Epistles because they were written for the whole church. The Book of Hebrews seems to stand alone because many will not associate it with the letters of Paul and others will not put it in the General Letters. In this work, Hebrews will be discussed in the section with the General Epistles.

The Letters of Paul

According to Deissmann's classification, Paul wrote letters. His writings resemble the customary form of first-century Greco-Roman letters. Though he used first-century letter form, Paul's content was theological. His typical greetings included theological terms such as *grace* and *peace*. The body of Paul's letters consisted of theological discussions and instructions. Even Paul's final greeting and farewell included theological content.

Like all other New Testament letters or epistles, Paul's letters were written to particular life situations in the lives of persons or of congregations. Often he wrote to defend himself or the gospel he preached. He wrote on many occasions to help with problems and controversies. He wrote letters to present the gospel amid the problems and controversies. Often he wrote to share the challenges and the content of the gospel. To understand any letter of Paul, an expositor must look at that situation or occasion that caused Paul to write. Paul communicated abiding truths while writing a particular message to a particular situation.

1 and 2 Thessalonians. Paul's earliest New Testament writings were the two Thessalonian letters. He had left Thessalonica because of opposition and traveled to Athens. He sent Timothy back to Thessalonica to check on the progress of the church. Paul then probably left Athens to go to Corinth, where Timothy came from Thessalonica with good news, bad news, and a set of questions. Paul then hastened to write 1 Thessalonians because opposition prohibited him from visiting the church. In the letter, Paul congratulated the church on the good news about them. He defended himself against the charges about them. He defended himself against the charges his opponents made. He wrote to answer questions they had asked and sent by Timothy. First Thessalonians may be outlined as follows:

1. Gratitude over good news about the church, 1:1–10

2. Concern for the church in the midst of opposition, 2:1–3.13

3. Exhortations to keep Christ's work going and to live a life pleasing to him, 4:1–12

4. Answers to two pertinent questions, 4:13–5:11

5. Final exhortation and greeting, 5:12

Paul's first letter emphasized the imminence of Christ's return. His enemies exploited this emphasis by using members of the church at Thessalonica to quit work and wait for the Lord's return. Paul received a report of the situation created by the opposition, perhaps from the person who carried 1 Thessalonians. Therefore, within a short time after the first letter, he wrote a second one. Paul sought to encourage the believers and to teach them that they would have to endure trials before the Lord's return. Consequently, Paul urged the believers to return to their jobs and to live godly lives in the world. Based on this situation, the contents of 2 Thessalonians become meaningful:

1. Gratitude and encouragement in the midst of trials, 1:1–12

2. Correction of errors about Christ's return, 2:1–12

3. Prayer for the Thessalonians to stand firm and a request to pray for Paul, 2:13–3:5

4. Closing appeal to work and to wait for Christ's return, 3:6

1 and 2 Corinthians. Paul first came to Corinth in about A.D. 51. He worked as a partner in tent making with Aquila and Priscilla, and he preached in the synagogue. Paul stayed in Corinth for eighteen months. After Paul left Corinth, he kept in touch with the church in Corinth and wrote letters to them. When he was in Ephesus on his third missionary journey in A.D. 55–56, he wrote 1 Corinthians (see 1 Cor. 16:8). Again, news from Corinth prompted him to write. He received reports from Chloe's people about problems in the church, and he also received a letter from the church at Corinth with questions for him to answer. On the basis of news about problems and answers to questions, the contents of 1 Corinthians can be observed.

1. Report received from Corinth about divisions, incest, lawsuits, disdain of rules, 1:1–6:20

2. Replies to questions about marriage, eating meat sacrificed to idols, the place of women, issue on worship, importance of spiritual gifts, and the resurrection, 7:1–15:58

3. Miscellaneous concluding notes, 16:1–24

The occasion and outline of 2 Corinthians does not come so easily as 1 Corinthians. Gunther Bornkamm proposes that 2 Corinthians contains as many as six different fragments.[36] W. G. Kümmel argues just as strongly as Bornkamm that 2 Corinthians is one complete, unified letter.[37] Other scholars argue for four letters. These scholars think that the painful letters mentioned in 2 Corinthians 2:3–4 are the material in 2 Corinthians 10–13. Furthermore, these scholars think that 2 Corinthians 1–9 was written after 10–13. Thus, according to these scholars the first letter was 1 Corinthians; the second letter was 2 Corinthians 10–13; and the third letter was 2 Corinthians 1–9.

Evidently Paul's first letter did not help with the divisions in the church. Outsiders came stirring up more trouble. They attempted to undermine the authority of Paul by leveling many criticisms against him. Paul wrote 2 Corinthians 10–13 to defend his authority and to defend the gospel he preached at Corinth.

The mood of 2 Corinthians 1–9 differs from that of chapters 10–13. Paul had been crushed by criticism, but he spoke of victory. Earlier he had sent Titus to Corinth with 2 Corinthians 10–13. Titus brought back good news, and Paul responded with 2 Corinthians 1–9. In these chapters he spoke of his restored comfort for the church. He mentioned his partnership with them. He wrote to encourage them to help him with Christ's ministry, which would include an offering for the poor Jewish Christians in Jerusalem.

About forty or fifty years after Paul wrote his letters, they were collected and put together. The collectors evidently wanted to put chapters 1–9 before the severity of chapters 10–13 to make up one correspondence, namely 2 Corinthians. Seeing the contents of the letter as a unit helps give perspective.

1. The good report of Titus about Paul's reconciliation with the Corinthians and their partnership in the gospel, 1:1–9:15

2. The severe letter defending Paul's authority and various attacks on him, 10:1–13:14

---

36. Gunther Bornkamm, *Paul*, trans. D. M. G. Stalker, (New York: Harper and Row, 1971), 244–46.

37. Werner Georg Kümmel, *Introduction to the New Testament*, trans. A. J. Mattill, Jr., (Nashville: Abingdon Press, 1966), 211–15.

Galatians. In Paul's early travels and preaching of the gospel, some Jewish Christian fanatics entered into Galatia's churches. The troublemakers attacked Paul and the gospel he preached. Many believers in the Galatian church deserted the understanding of the Christian life as Paul preached it. These fanatics told believers that law and ceremony must be added to faith in Christ; they taught that a good Christian must live by Jewish laws and ceremonies. Paul responded with a highly emotional letter to these Christians.

The Galatian letter discusses how one can be a better Christian. It is about how one is to live after initial forgiveness has been received. The contents of Galatians reflects its occasion and purpose:

1. Paul defends his authority as an apostle, 1:1–2:21

2. Paul defends the gospel, 3:1–4:31

3. Paul urges believers to live by faith, the Christian life, 5:1–6:18

Romans. Paul wrote his longest letter to a church in Rome he had not visited. After Paul went to Jerusalem with the offering for the poor Jewish Christians, he wanted to go to Rome. He probably wrote Romans from Corinth in A.D. 57 during a three-month stay on his last missionary journey. He wanted to prepare the church in Rome for his visit and to relate to them the Gentile mission. Paul described the gospel thoroughly which he had been preaching to both Jews and Gentiles alike.

1. An introduction, 1:1–17

2. The sinfulness of all human beings, 1:18–3:20

3. The justification for those with faith in Christ, 3:21–5:21

4. The sanctification for those with faith in Christ, 6:1–8:39

5. The righteousness of God in his dealings with the Jews, 9:1–11:36

6. The believers' response to God's righteousness, 12:1–15:13

7. The conclusion, 15:14–16:27

Philippians. Paul wrote four letters from prison—Philippians, Ephesians, Colossians, and Philemon. Ideas differ about where Paul was in prison—Caesarea, Ephesus, or Rome. Most New Testament scholars consider Rome as the place of writing these four letters.

The Letter of Philippians resembles a thank-you note. The church at Philippi had sent a gift by Epaphroditus to Paul in prison. While Ephaphroditus was with him in Rome, Paul became ill and almost died. Paul wrote a letter and sent it by Epaphroditus, rejoicing over his recovery. The letter contained notes of gratitude, information about Paul's circumstances, concern over false teachers, and a plea for unity between two persons in dissension. The flow of the Philippian letter discloses its diverse personal content.

1. Information about Paul's situation, 1:1–26

2. Exhortation for Christlike humility and cooperation, 1:27–2:18

3. Good news about Timothy and Epaphroditus, 2:19–30

4. Warning against false teachers, 3:1–21

5. Concluding remarks, 4:1–23

Philemon. While Paul was in prison, he also wrote Philemon. Onesimus, a slave of Philemon in Ephesus, had stolen from his master and escaped to where Paul was in prison. In some way, Onesimus came in contact with Paul. Philemon had become a Christian through Paul's ministry, and Onesimus became one also through Paul's ministry. Paul wrote to plead with Philemon to take Onesimus back as a brother. No one knows how the story ended.

Colossians. While Paul was in prison, another visitor named Epaphras visited Paul. This visit prompted the letter of Colossians. Probably Epaphras founded the church in Colossae. Epaphras brought good news about the Colossians' faith and love, but he also brought bad news about the spreading of heresy which resembled second-century Gnosticism. It threatened the supremacy of Christ's personhood and the sufficiency of his atoning work. Paul wrote to share with the Colossians the supremacy of Jesus Christ and the sufficiency of his atoning work. The report of Epaphrus and the thoughts of Paul may be seen in the content of the letter.

1. The prayers of Paul, 1:1–14

2. The supremacy of Christ, 1:15–2:15

3. The rejection of the ethics of the false teachers, 2:16–3:11

4. The plea for the morality of believers, 3:12–4:6

5. Concluding personal notes and greetings, 4:7–18

Ephesians. Specific circumstances can be cited about Philippians, Philemon, and Colossians. But no commentator has related the Letter of Ephesians to any particular conflict or situation. Ephesians has a timeless quality about it. Perhaps it was general because Paul sent it as a circular letter to several churches in Asia Minor. It is a celebration letter. Paul celebrated that, in Christ, God is accomplishing his purpose in history, the uniting of all peoples in Christ's church. Notice its contents.

1. The celebration of God's plan to unite all people in Christ, 1:1–23

2. The actualization of God's plan with the Jews and the Gentiles, 2:1–22

3. The prayer that people catch the vision of God's plan, 3:1–21

4. The challenges to Gentile converts, 4:1–6:20

5. Concluding personal note and benediction, 6:21–24

1 and 2 Timothy. Three books in the New Testament—1 and 2 Timothy and Titus—have been called "the Pastoral Epistles." Traditionally these epistles have been attributed to Paul because the letters list Paul as the author. They are filled with numerous personal references; they have ideas typical of Paul; and they are attributed to Paul by the Muratorian Canon and other early documents. Others do not think these epistles were written by Paul because the style and vocabulary are not like Paul's, the church organization is more advanced than Paul's day, and other reasons. Linking Paul as the author of these three books does not destroy their essential messages.

Timothy was a young pastor at work in Ephesus. Heresy was spreading in the area, and Paul wrote 1 Timothy to advise Timothy and to fight errors. Paul wrote to remind Timothy of the sound doctrine that had been given him and to exhort Timothy to teach the true faith and to help him in leading the church. Paul wanted Timothy to let only godly persons guide the church. He gave specific instructions about church officers, women, widows, and even slaves.

1. The charge to teach the truth, 1:1–20

2. The instruction about proper worship, 2:1–15

3. The requirement for church officers, 3:1–13

4. The disclosure of sound doctrine, 3:14–4:16

5. The conduct pertaining to particular groups, 5:1–6:2a

6. The spiritual life and the secular life, 6:2b–19

7. A closing charge, 6:20–21

Paul continued to write to Timothy in an epistle known as 2 Timothy. Integrity of doctrines in a church led by men of integrity was the theme of 1 Timothy. This theme was repeated in 2 Timothy, but a new emphasis was added: the idea of being faithful to the gospel. In a time when many were deserting Paul and the gospel he preached, Paul urged Timothy to carry on the legacy of a faithful witness. Paul's example of his life and teaching may be observed in the contents of the letter.

1. Timothy's heritage of faith, 1:1–18

2. Timothy's charge from Paul to be true to his heritage, 2:1–26

3. Timothy's defenses against heresies, 3:1–17

4. Timothy's charge to be faithful, 4:1–5

5. Personal appeals by Paul, 4:6–22

Titus. In the Epistle of Titus, Paul addressed Titus, whom he had left to be the pastor in Crete. Titus' situation in Crete resembled Timothy's circumstances in Ephesus. Paul gave Titus some advice on his words as a pastor. The emphases centered around sound doctrine and good deeds. The letter, or epistle, bears the marks of its occasion and purpose.

1. A reminder to select good leaders, 1:1–16

2. A series of exhortations to teach every group proper behavior, 2:1–15

3. A reminder to have appropriate lives, 3:1–15

The General Letters

Since early in the fourth century the church has given the name *Catholic Epistles* or *General Epistles* to seven letters: James; 1 and 2 Peter; 1, 2, and 3 John; and Jude. For the discussion in this work, Hebrews will be added to the group. The exact reason for the title of the category is uncertain. More than likely, the title came because of the general character of the readers to whom the epistles were addressed, even though 2 and 3 John seem to be addressed to individuals. In *Handbook of the New Testament*, Claus Westermann labels these eight books as "The Remaining Epistles." Balanced preaching from New Testament books most include these "remaining epistles."

Hebrews. The Epistle of Hebrews is a mystery. It bears no author's name. Paul, Barnabas, Luke, Apollos, and Priscilla have been suggested as its author. Its recipients are also uncertain. The traditional view is that the epistle was written to a group of Jews who had become Christians and were tempted to drift back into Judaism. The author presented Christ as superior to all that Judaism offered. Judging from its contents, Hebrews had a twofold purpose: to present the superiority of Christ and to encourage believers to move forward in their faith.

1. Christ is better than the angels, 1:1–2:18

2. Christ is better than Moses, 3:1–4:13

3. Christ is better than the old priesthood, 4:14–7:28

4. Christ's new covenant is better than the old, 8:1–10:39

5. Old Testament people went forward in their faith, 11:1–40

6. Encouragement for present believers to move forward, 12:1–13:25

James. Some person named James wrote a general letter to Christians scattered over the world. Nothing concrete or specific is mentioned about the life situations of the readers. The epistle seems to be a collection of moral instructions to believers. It is a book of what New Testament scholars call a paraenesis, meaning a collection of exhortations or instructions. The moral instructions come out of a Christian's faith in Christ.

1. The proof of faith during trials and temptations, 1:1–18

2. The practice of the Word of God in deeds, 1:19–27

3. The showing of partiality, 2:1–13

4. The relationship of faith and works, 2:14–26

5. The power of the tongue, 3:1–12

6. The marks of godly wisdom, 3:13–18

7. The problem of selfishness, 4:1–10

8. The warning against judging others, 4:11–12

9. The warning against false security, 4:13–17

10. The prosperity of the selfish and their judgment, 5:1–11

11. Various admonitions, 5:12–20

1 and 2 Peter. Suffering of Christians during the persecutions of the Roman emperor Nero seems to have occasioned the writing of 1 Peter. Christians in Rome and throughout the Roman empire experienced persecution. The letter was written to help believers face trouble with courage and hope. It was written as an exhortation to witness to their pagan neighbors with their Christlike conduct.

1. The call to hope and happiness, 1:1–2:10

2. The instructions on how to live holy lives in a pagan world, 2:11–3:12

3. The Christian witness to the pagans in a time of persecution, 3:13–4:11

4. The duties during the times of persecution, 4:12–5:11

5. A closing postscript, 5:12–14

During the times of persecutions, false teachers arose and gave teachings which bothered believers. Precisely what they taught is not clear. Thus, 2 Peter was written. The author wanted to remind the readers of the true faith given by Christ and the apostles. The author wanted believers to judge all teachings on the basis of Christ's teachings.

1. The encouragement to seek the apostolic faith, 1:1–21

2. The warning against false teachers, 2:1–22

3. The instructions about final judgment, 3:1–18

1, 2, and 3 John. Heresy was rampant in the first century. According to tradition, John the apostle wrote 1 John to fight heresy. Something of what the false teachers taught can be inferred from quotations in the epistle. John wrote for two purposes: to help them be assured of their belief in Jesus and to inspire them to obedience to God through love for others.

1. A brief summary of the Christian message, 1:1–2:17

2. A warning against the false teachers, 3:1–24

3. The tests between the true and the false, 4:1–5:12

4. Postscript repeating some themes, 5:13–21

John wrote two more letters, 2 and 3 John. The second letter appears to be a brief summary of the first. The letter offers encouragement for true belief and a warning against false teachers. The second letter claims to have been written by the elder to the church. The letter closes with a mention of hospitality for itinerant evangelists and teachers. The design of 2 John gives its contents:

1. The salutation, vv. 1–3

2. The prayer of gratitude and petition, vv. 4–6

3. The warning against heretics, vv. 7–11

4. The elder's announcement of a visit, vv. 12–13

In 3 John, the elder wrote to a friend named Gaius, a respected leader in the church. He urged Gaius to provide hospitality for a traveling teacher named Demetrius. A person in the church named Diotrephes refused to receive these people. The design of 3 John also discloses its contents:

1. The salutation, vv. 1–2

2. The compliment of Gaius for his hospitality, vv. 3–8

3. The rebuke of Diotrephes for refusal of hospitality, vv. 9–10

4. The conclusion, vv. 13–15

Jude. The Letter of Jude, according to tradition, came from Jude, the half-brother of Jesus. Whether or not this fact is true does not change the author's purpose of writing a summary of the gospel. News of false teachers prompted the writing. The letter denounced the false teachers by means of presenting the apostolic orthodoxy.

1. The salutation, vv. 1–2

2. The exhortation to contend for the traditional faith, v. 3

3. The false teachers, vv. 4–19

4. The admonition to build up the faith, vv. 20–23

5. The doxology, vv. 24–25

The body of the Epistles or Letters represents a lot of diversity. Planning a series of sermons from these books could ensure a variety of sermon topics and emphases. Preaching from Paul's letters allows for an assortment of timely topics. Not all of Paul's letters are alike. Furthermore, the General Epistles provide diverse opportunities for stimulating series of sermons. No preacher's repertoire of sermon series selection would be complete without selections from the Letters or Epistles.

Apocalypse

Of all the literary types found in the Bible books, none differs so drastically as the Book of Revelation. Instead of narratives and letters containing plain statements of fact, the Book of Revelation is filled with angels, seals, trumpets, earthquakes, dragons, beasts, and bottomless pits. Because the Book of Revelation is unusual, most preachers do not attempt to preach a series of sermons from Revelation. John Calvin, the sixteenth-century Reformation preacher, wrote commentaries on many books of the Bible, but not Revelation because he admitted that he did not understand it.

Other preachers attempt to relate the Revelation to current events. Many profess to discover symbolic predictions of events in their own times that show the "signs of the times," indicating that the end of the world is at hand. Various and unusual identifications have been given to symbols such as Armageddon, the mark of the beast, and the great prostitute seated on many waters. Sermons on Revelation abounded in Europe as the year A.D. 1000 approached, declaring history to be at an end with the millennium. During World War II, many preachers declared that the numerical reference of 666 in Revelation 13:18 was a cryptogram for the name of Mussolini and others; these same preachers interpreted Russia and Germany as Gog and Magog to show that Armageddon was at hand.

In his best-seller *The Late Great Planet Earth*, Hal Lindsey related many symbols in Revelation to the headlines of the late 1970s. The ten horns of the beast (Rev. 13:1) were the ten nations of the European Common Market. The Great Harlot was the World Council of Churches. Preachers in the tradition of Hal Lindsay relate Revelation directly to current events.

How should the expositor preach from the Book of Revelation? It neither needs to be neglected nor to be interpreted as if it were written just for the twentieth century. Two primary principles should guide the expositor:

- *Interpret Revelation in light of its historical content.* Like any other Bible book, Revelation was written in a specific historical situation, and knowing that will help with understanding the book. Whatever the lessons for subsequent ages, the expositor must first see what Revelation meant to the first readers.

- *Interpret Revelation in light of other apocalyptic literature.* Many such books have come down to us from both Christian and Jewish sources. These books were written in times of persecution, and almost all picture cosmic conflict and almost all indicate that victory and judgment by God are at hand. Studying the life situation and the kind of literature to which it belongs can help produce truthful and useful sermons from Revelation.

The Occasion of Revelation

The expositor must first reconstruct the situation in which the Revelation was written. The writer was in exile because of his faith, and the original readers were suffering for the gospel, too. Reliable tradition dates Revelation as being written during the persecution of the church under the emperor Domitian about A.D. 90–96. The historical situation is clear: The Christians and the Roman government were in conflict.

Many believers suffered martyrdom during the reign of Domitian. The Roman government demanded lordship to the Roman emperor. The Christians confessed the lordship of Christ and would not worship the emperor. As a result they either lost their lives or they were persecuted severely. The cult of emperor worship prevailed throughout the Roman empire during the reign of Domitian.

John wrote Revelation as a tract for troubled times. He helped the readers view the persecution they faced from the perspective of heaven. He wrote to help believers see history from the perspective of followers of the One who was himself martyred, but who had risen to glory.

The figurative language of apocalyptic seems strange to many today, but it was the genre needed for the time. Apocalyptic language concealed the message from the secular Romans and revealed the message to the persecuted believers. For example, to predict forthrightly, the downfall of Rome would have meant destruction of the document. But to write of a beast or of Babylon would have appeared harmless to the Romans. The book was written as a secret, coded word of encouragement to Christians who may die for their faith rather than worship the emperor.

Revelation and Other Apocalyptic Literature

The Book of Revelation belongs to the genre of apocalyptic literature. This kind of literature has six common characteristics:

- *Apocalyptic used symbols that only insiders could understand.* The contents of Revelation contain visions and dreams, and its language is cryptic (having hidden meanings) and symbolic.

- *Apocalyptic professed to give secret messages about the future.* By the unusual pictures, the author of Revelation depicted the fall of Rome and the supremacy of God's reign.

- *Apocalyptic presented this world from the perspective of heaven.* The author watched events on earth from the point of view of some heavenly being.

- *Apocalyptic predicted the imminent climax of history.* The blackest moments would come in the period just before the climax of the story.

- *Apocalyptic depicted the victory of God's legions in the cosmic battle between the forces of good and evil.*

- *Apocalyptic depicted a great judgment day when the righteous would be vindicated and the evil would be punished.*

From the opening of Revelation, the author informed readers to interpret his words symbolically. The book opens with a vision of the risen Christ presented in symbolical language. This then follows later to seven churches, the original readers of Revelation. In Revelation 4 the author summoned the readers to look at human history from the perspective of heaven. In Revelation 5 the author focuses on the Lamb, who is of course Jesus Christ and who controls the destiny of the world.

From the perspective of heaven, the writer looked at the course of human history by the drama of the opening of the seals. The seven seals turn into seven trumpets. The last trumpet introduces seven bowls. The seals, trumpets, and bowls depict the troublesome course of history with the end in God's control.

The writer interprets the opening of the seals, the blowing of the trumpets, and the pouring of the bowls to introduce a dragon, a beast out of the sea, and a beast from the earth. These represent the enemies of the church—Satan, world powers, and local implementation of emperor worship. The writer of Revelation used symbols of cosmic conflict to depict the defeat of evil world power—Satan.

The writer closes Revelation with an artistic picture of the eternal reign of God's people and the tragic punishment of evil. An outline will help observe the contents of Revelation.

1. A symbolic opening vision of Christ, 1:1–20

2. Seven churches: the recipients of Revelation, 2:1–3:22

3. A vision of heaven and the opening of the book, 4:1–5:14

4. The seven seals, 6:1–8:1

5. The seven trumpets, 8:2–11:19

6. The enemies of God's people, 12:1–14:20

7. The seven bowls, 15:1–16:21

8. The destruction of God's enemies, 17:1–20:15

9. The end of history and final destruction, 21:1–22:21

Preaching from New Testament books helps hearers listen to the greatest story ever told. The Old Testament records the beginning of God's story, and the New Testament records the rest of God's story. The New Testament contains the record of how Jesus came to earth to redeem the human race. After his death, resurrection, and ascension, Jesus' followers, empowered by the Holy Spirit, took the gospel to many parts of the first-century world. The Gospels tell Jesus' story; Acts and the Letters continue the story of Jesus' work through his followers. The Book of Revelation tells how the human race will end with the triumphant, eternal reign of God.

Preaching from New Testament books happens in random selection of texts and in systemic preaching plans. The plan proposed in this book suggests preaching a series of sermons from one Old Testament book and one New Testament book each year. Some texts from the Gospels may be used annually in addition to selecting one of the other twenty-three books. Preachers who use lectionaries have a selection of texts from the Synoptic Gospels in a three-year cycle. Preachers could also choose to adopt a Gospel each year on a four-year cycle, making their own personal lectionary. Along with the Gospel, the expositor would then choose to preach a series from Acts, the Letters, or Revelation. Many possible preaching plans await the creative expositor who wishes to preach from New Testament books.

The Homiletical Plotting of a Bible Book

Selecting an Old Testament or a New Testament book for a series of sermons and studying that book is not the end of the process. Preparing sermons from a Bible book continues with planning the direction for the series. After selecting and studying the book for a sermon series, an expository preacher needs to do some preliminary planning. Some preachers select a Bible book and plunge immediately into the series without planning their direction or knowing how many sermons they will preach. The most effective expositors take time to plan a scheme for the series. This planning procedure is called "homiletical plotting."

Homiletical plotting of a Bible book may be compared to marking out housing plots from a undeveloped area of land. Suppose a developer bought a thousand acres of land to create a luxurious housing development. Before the first house could be built, many hours of planning would have to be devoted to the plot of land. More than likely, the topography of the land would have to be studied to determine the best location for lots, lakes, and streets. Plans would have to be prepared for the number and direction of the streets. Projecting the place of lots would influence the location of water, sewer, and utility services. Developers do not just purchase property and start building houses haphazardly. Instead they plan and diagram the design of the development before the project begins.

Preaching a series of sermons from a Bible book resembles the procedures for developing a plot of land into a housing development. After a Bible book has been selected, the preacher's personal plan for proclaiming the book must be developed. Some plotting begins to take shape during the background study, the analysis, the exegesis, and the interpretation processes. Perhaps the best material to help with homiletical plotting is the analysis because it helps reveal the flow of the Bible book and its separate themes. Usually some plan of the scheme for a series of sermons will begin to emerge while an expositor is analyzing a Bible book. The analysis becomes the primary catalyst for charting the direction of the series.

The homiletical plotting of a Bible book enhances the effectiveness of the series and of individual sermons in the series. Plotting each selected book requires special consideration. One primary consideration includes determining the direction for the series. Will the series of sermons be a consecutive treatment of the Bible book? Or will the series of sermons be a selective treatment of the Bible book? Choosing to treat every verse in a book affects the number of texts and sermons in the series. Plotting a book with a consecutive approach simply involves marking out where texts start and stop. Obviously, lengthy Bible books will have many texts, and shorter books will have fewer texts. Consecutive exposition is more popular than selective exposition, but some Bible books do not lend themselves to consecutive treatment.

Adopting a selective approach for preaching from a Bible book requires more personal creativity. Various directions could be chosen for plotting a series from the selective approach. The personality and proclivities of the preacher, the nature of the biblical material, and the features of the audience affect the plotting process. Plotting from a selective scheme involves choosing several texts for a series from among many texts. No book on expository preaching could exhaust the possibilities of choosing a selective treatment of a Bible book. Observing several of the published sermons series from a selective style and hearing the ways different preachers preach from the same Bible book could convince a preacher to utilize the selective method of homiletical plotting.

Expository preachers need to see three values of homiletical plotting. First, homiletical plotting prevents fragmentation. Dividing the Bible into verses has both a positive and negative effect. The versification of Scripture lets us find and identify passages quickly, but it has created the impression that each verse is a separate unit of revelation to be used apart from other verses. Texts are often torn from their setting and pressed in a new, often forced, strand of thought. To prevent fragmentation and to present the book within its setting, a preacher might preach a book sermon as an introduction to the series of sermons. This book sermon gives a general perspective of the Bible book and of the sermons from that book. It divides the general biblical plot of material into smaller segments.

The second value of homiletical plotting is that it helps the preacher establish a style for the series. Just as individual sermons have a unique style, each series of sermons needs a distinctive style.

The third value of homiletical plotting is that it helps the preacher project the number of sermons in the series, which determines the length of the series. Failing to plan ahead could lead to an excessive number of sermons from the earlier part of the Bible book and a lesser treatment of other texts. Preliminary plotting of the Bible book seems to be much better than haphazardly plunging into starting a series.

Finding disadvantages for homiletical plotting is difficult. The values overshadow any problems that may be present. Plotting is not homiletical busywork but a valuable homiletical procedure that devises a scheme for a series of sermons from a Bible book.

Plotting with Entire Books

Several writers on preaching have suggested using the entire Bible book as a basis for one sermon. This is called the "book sermon." Book sermons have been used in two ways:

- Some preachers open an expository series with a book sermon. Chalmer E. Faw calls this the "introductory book sermon."[1] This first sermon helps the audience get acquainted with the book and with subsequent sermons from the book.

- Other preachers preach a series with each sermon based on a book in the Bible. Andrew W. Blackwood suggested selecting from shorter and simpler books such as Ruth, Jonah, or 1 John.[2]

Dwight E. Stevenson, a homiletics teacher, suggested preaching consecutively on each book as they are arranged in the English Bible. This latter procedure falls outside the confines of our definition of expository preaching, but the practice of sixty-six sermons from the Bible book would be a profitable venture. Discussion of selecting an entire book will fall under the introductory book sermon and under the series of sermons from the book of the Bible.

The Practice of Doing Book Sermons

Choosing to preach one sermon on an entire Bible book has been a practice for many years. Perhaps one of the most prominent preachers to practice such an act was G. Campbell Morgan, pastor for many years at the Westminster Chapel in London, England. In his work *Living Messages of the Books of the Bible*, he left the record of his book sermons to the Westminster Chapel. He preached consecutively from the heart and contents of each Bible book. Each sermon in the series is divided into two major parts: (1) The Essential Message and (2) The Application.

Stevenson wrote two books to help preachers prepare sermons from an entire Bible book. In both books he looked into all sixty-six books of the Bible with two main headings in each discussion: (1) Working Your Way into the Book and (2) Preparing Your Own Book Sermon. The first section contained basic information about

---

1. Chalmer E. Faw, *A Guide to Biblical Preaching* (Nashville: Broadman Press, 1962), 42.

2. Andrew W. Blackwood, *Preaching from the Bible* (Nashville: Abingdon Press, 1941), 170–81.

the Bible book, and the second contained homiletical suggestions about preparing a book sermon on that particular book.[3]

Eric W. Hayden, pastor of the Spurgeon Metropolitan Tabernacle in London from 1952 to 1962, preached each Sunday from one Bible book until he had covered the entire Bible. The record of his series is in *Preaching Through the Bible, Volume One*. Later, in that same pastorate, Hayden preached from famous chapters in each book until he had covered all the Bible again. These sermons have been published under the title *Preaching Through the Bible, Volume Two*.

Effective expositors still preach single sermons from an entire book. Charles R. Swindoll, while serving the First Evangelical Free Church of Fullerton, California, preached through the Bible using one sermon for each book. He called the series "The Bible Book by Book." Each sermon contained mentions of background material, an outline of a book, and an emphasis on the main theme of the book. More than one-third of these messages were devoted to the relevancy of the book's theme to today's world.[4]

With our definition of expository preaching as preaching a series of sermons from a Bible book, only one sermon would be plotted from the entire book to introduce the series. This type of sermon would be the first in the series to launch the series of sermons. People need assistance in background material and with the analysis of content; a sermon from the entire book would help in these two areas.

Prerequisites for Preaching Book Sermons

As you prepare a book sermon, you might apply the following fourfold test of prerequisites:

Prerequisite #1: The effective book sermon, like any other sermon, combines divine truth with human need. Dwight E. Stevenson said, "A book sermon needs to be something more than a Bible

---

3. Dwight E. Stevenson, *Preaching on the Books of the Old Testament* (New York: Harper and Brothers, 1961) and *Preaching on the Books of the New Testament* (New York: Harper and Row, 1956).

4. Charles R. Swindoll, "Genesis: Where It All Begins," sermon delivered November 5, 1978, First Evangelical Free Church of Fullerton, California.

lecture."[5] Every sermon needs to have God as its sender and people as its receiver.

Prerequisite #2: The effective book sermon is selective. Every Bible book has lots of material that could not be presented in one sermon. Stevenson called for a sermon of an entire book "to be an experience of the book itself and not merely an introduction to it."[6] No book sermon can be exhaustive. Selectivity is best achieved by citing the crucial ideas within the book, narrating the story of the book, and locating a few key verses that express the main theme and a few words that support the theme. Notice the selective process in a book sermon on Romans:

Key Verse:	Romans 1:17
Theme:	Righteousness
Introduction:	Paul talked about righteousness, 1:1–17
Body:	1 Human beings are not right, 1:18–3:20
	2. Human beings are made righteous in Christ, 3:21–5:21
	3. Human beings made right live right, 6:1–8:39
	4. God does what is right, 9:1–11:36
	5. God shows us how to do right, 12:1–16:27

Deciding to focus on righteousness and using basic ideas within Romans to support that theme make the sermon have a single idea and stay within a reasonable time limit. Being selective requires knowing the book thoroughly, choosing a prominent theme, and using the contents of the book to support that theme.

Prerequisite #3: The effective book sermon is relevant. If a preacher is not careful, the book sermon will become nothing more than a Bible lesson about people who lived long ago. Today's mind wants to see a relevance of ancient truth. Exegesis and interpretation need to be intertwined at many points within a book sermon.

5. Stevenson, *Preaching on the Books of the New Testament,* 10.
6. Ibid., 13.

Charles R. Swindoll, in a book sermon entitled "Ruth: Interlude of Love," narrated the ancient story of Ruth. Throughout the narration, he related the truths to today's world. After narrating the story and intertwining the application, he gave about one-third of the sermon length to application.[7] From beginning to end, Swindoll wove Scripture and applications into one fabric.

Prerequisite #4: The effective book sermon is a true sermon, not simply a Bible lesson. It must possess homiletical qualities. These sermonic qualities include the prevalence of one main point throughout the sermon, use of some type of structure, and use of emotional persuasion and cognitive knowledge.

Procedures for Preparing a Book Sermon

Little attention has been given in homiletical literature to instructing preachers how to prepare a book sermon. Most of these works do not even mention the practice, though a few devote a single chapter to the book sermon. The procedures for preparing a book sermon may be somewhat different from proceedings on a smaller text. The following three steps will help the expositor prepare a sermon on an entire book of the Bible:

Step #1: Concentrate on the book's contents. Nothing substitutes for reading the book many times, allowing the whole book to begin to make an imprint on the expositor's mind. A preacher should check several translations but use one primary translation. The analysis which has been prepared on the book will be a valuable aid in concentrating on the contents. Commentaries and other helps need to be consulted to master the contents of the book. With repeated readings and consulting of commentaries and other helps, a main or dominant theme of the book should emerge.

Step #2: Build on the book's background. Each Bible book exists for a reason. The story of its origin and purpose helps the preacher get all of the concentration on content in the proper perspective. Studying the book's life situation provides an invaluable aid in preparing a sermon on the book's background.

Step #3: Shape the book's material into a sermon. Reading for content and studying for background produce material, but it is formless and void. The Spirit of God and the preacher's creative

---

7. Charles R. Swindoll, "Ruth: Interlude of Love," sermon delivered February 11, 1979, First Evangelical Free Church of Fullerton, California.

skills must work together to shape the material into a sermon. Homiletics for a book sermon involves projecting one point for the sermon. This point can come from the book's main theme or from one of the minor themes. Other materials from the Bible book can be used to support the point. A standard homiletical structure for a book sermon involves two parts: The first part narrates and explains the book, and the second part interprets or applies the book. Another structure style is to explain the contents of the book with a didactic outline, giving ample application or interpretation throughout the message.

Plotting with Paragraphs

The most frequent literary unit in a Bible book is its division into paragraphs. Paragraphs have been regarded by some people as the most natural unit of thought in the Bible.[8] The paragraph divisions may not have been the structural thought of the original writers and a part of the divine inspiration, but paragraphs represent transitions in thought and emphases, turns in a narrative, or shifts in the development of thought. A paragraph consists of two or more sentences with a coherent, unified thought.

According to Andrew W. Blackwood, the paragraph is the basic unit of composition in the Bible; it furnishes a valuable literacy unit for the preacher and for the construction of the sermon.[9] Most paragraphs offer enough material for preaching. The paragraphs in a Bible book offer an excellent procedure for plotting a series of sermons. Each Bible book generally contains numerous paragraph divisions; thus, an expositor could plot a series of sermons using paragraphs.

The Identification of Paragraphs

Paragraph designations have not always been a part of the Bible. The original languages of the Bible probably had no designation of paragraph divisions. The indentations and designations of units of thought, which are usually called paragraphs, are the work of editors—both ancient and modern—who have attempted to designate the rhythm of thought of the original authors. Early Hebrew and Greek editions included signs dividing Bible books into paragraphs.

---

8. Faw, 196.
9. Blackwood, 94.

As various English translations began to appear, paragraphs became part of the translations. These paragraph divisions varied from edition to edition, whether in Hebrew, Greek, or the modern languages.

Translation of the *King James Version* caused people to read and to think of the Bible in separate, individual verses instead of paragraphs. The *American Standard Version* of 1901 made tremendous strides in helping English readers think in paragraph divisions rather than separate, individual verses. Many subsequent English translations divide the Bible into paragraphs. The *American Standard Version* of 1901 divided Bible books into longer paragraphs, but subsequent versions such as the *Revised Standard Version* and the *New International Version* have many more paragraphs. For example, in 2 Corinthians: 8–9 of the 1901 *American Standard Version*, four large paragraphs appear in thirty-nine verses. In the *New International Version* nine paragraphs appear in those two chapters. In most cases, the *New International Version* and the *Revised Standard Version* have more paragraphs than the 1901 *American Standard Version*. Perhaps the best procedures for studying the Bible and plotting sermons by paragraphs would be to consult various translations and to consult the personal analysis of a Bible book.

Identifying Paragraphs. An expositor who chooses to plot a Bible book by paragraphs for a series of sermons needs to learn to identify and delineate the paragraph. No expositor can depend altogether on what others have done in translations and commentaries for paragraph designations. These resources help greatly, but expositors also need to learn to identify paragraphs and to learn their makeup. Generally speaking, a paragraph contains several sentences on a common thought and normally possesses a single topic or a sequence of events. A paragraph consists of an assertion or thematic proposition with supporting propositions; or it may narrate a primary story with reporting of supporting incidents. It contains the framework for expressing and developing a single idea.

Expositors who desire skill in plotting a series of sermons with paragraphs need to develop expertise in identifying a paragraph unit. Walter C. Kaiser, Jr., lists five characteristics of a unit of thought:

1. A paragraph has a unifying theme. Generally, the several sentences will relate to a common topic.

2. A rhetorical question often introduces a paragraph. The question or questions aid transition in thought.

3. The vocative form of address introduces a new thought, and subsequent sentences develop the thought.

4. Sudden changes in the text introduce new paragraphs. This is one of the best ways to detect the beginning of a paragraph. These may be an abrupt shift in the chief actor or participant; the mood, tense, or voice of the verb; the location of the action; or the topic. The use of a striking introductory connective, whether it is a conjunction, preposition, or relative pronoun, can also be an indicator for a paragraph designation.

5. What appears at or near the end of one paragraph is often taken up and developed more fully in the next paragraph. Biblical writers often mentioned a thought in a block of material and took the discussion to a fuller treatment.[10]

Types of Paragraphs. In addition to identifying a single paragraph, the expositor also needs to recognize the various kinds of paragraphs. The pure *narrative paragraph* is a complete story and the designation of turns in a story. For example, in Jesus' story of the loving father, the common theme is a father's love, but in the *New International Version* the story has nine paragraphs. These paragraphs help with the moves in the story; each paragraph needs to be kept in the context of the overall theme of the narrative. Another example of narrative paragraphs is David's confrontation with the Philistine giant Goliath (see 1 Sam. 17). The story has one common story, but the *New International Version* has thirty paragraphs in the narratives to designate story turns or movements. In the narrative type of paragraphs, smaller narratives need to be set in the context of the larger narrative.

The *discourse paragraph* presents a fairly complete unit of thought that revolves around one basic idea or theme. The discourse paragraph also needs to be related carefully to the development of thought in the larger unit or section of which the paragraphs are a part. Discourse paragraphs appear in the Epistles, in the collection of teachings from the Gospels, and in books of the Prophets. Paragraphs in the Letter to the Romans can be designated as follows:

---

10. Walter C. Kaiser, Jr., *Toward an Exegetical Theology: Biblical Exegesis for Preaching and Teaching* (Grand Rapids, Mich.: Baker Book House, 1981), 96.

1. The introduction to the letter, 1:1–17
2. The sinfulness of the pagan world, 1:18–32
3. The sinfulness of the Jewish world, 2:1–3:6

These three designations mark the larger discourses, but smaller paragraph units may be found in these larger discussions. The *New International Version* has seven paragraphs in 1:1–17, five paragraphs in 1:18–32, and eight paragraphs in 2:1–3:6. Another example may be seen in Matthew 5 of the Sermon on the Mount.

1. The introduction to the sermon, 5:1–2
2. The characteristics of the Kingdom persons, 5:3–12
3. The influence of the Kingdom persons, 5:13–16
4. The righteousness of the Kingdom persons, 5:17–48

Just as in the illustration from Romans 1:1–36, the *New International Version* divides 5:1–2 into just one paragraph, 5:3–12 into two paragraphs, 5:13–16 into two paragraphs, and 5:17–48 into nine paragraphs.

The *stanza*, or strophe, is the poetic equivalent of the paragraph. Stanzas are found in the Book of Psalms, in poetic sections of Job, and in large sections of the Prophets. Modern translations including the *Revised Standard Version* and the *New International Version* designate stanzas. Particular study of the stanzas, or strophes, should be given to the form and place of such a stanza in the total poetical structure and to its thought contribution to the whole. Notice the stanza arrangement of Psalm 46 from the *New International Version*:

1. Psalm 46:1–3
2. Psalm 46:4–6
3. Psalm 46:7
4. Psalm 46:8–10
5. Psalm 46:11

Each stanza expresses a separate thought that is related to the overall theme of Psalm 46, which seems to be God's presence during a crisis. Expositors need to be careful not to take a stanza out of the context of its poem. A knowledge of the nature of Hebrew poetry, its parallelism, and the repetitious character of its stanzas and refrains can save expositors from many errors and vagaries of interpretation.

The expositor who learns to identify an individual paragraph and to distinguish the different kinds of paragraphs discovers a valuable resource for plotting a series of sermons from a Bible book. By using various translations which break books into paragraphs and by using the analysis, parameters of texts in a book can be designated for sermons in the series.

The Popularity of Paragraph Plotting

Using paragraphs in a Bible book for texts has been a practice of expositors over the years, and this practice increased after the *American Standard Version* appeared in 1901. G. Campbell Morgan, Alexander Maclaren, and F. B. Meyer used the paragraph discourse extensively. In preaching a series of sermons from Hosea, G. Campbell Morgan used the following selection:

1. The Prophet's Story, 1:1–2:1
2. The Door of Hope, 2:2–3:5
3. Joined to Idols, 4:1–19
4. The Departure of God, 5:1–6:3
5. The Difficulty of God, 6:4–11
6. Unconscious Decadence, 7:1–11
7. God Mislaid, 8:1–14
8. Distorted Vision, 9:1–17
9. A Degenerate Vine, 10:1–15
10. The Compassion of God, 11:1–12:1
11. Israel Becomes Canaan, 12:2–13:1
12. Idols and God, 13:2–14:8[11]

Alexander Maclaren divided each Bible book into paragraphs, and he usually chose a key verse from the paragraph for the main theme of his sermon.

Popular expositors still use paragraph plotting. James T. Draper, Jr., a popular Southern Baptist preacher, has preached consecutively from the Book of Amos with the following themes and texts:

1. The Conscience of a Nation, 1:1
2. The Response of a Nation, 1:2–2:3

---

11. G. Campbell Morgan, *Hosea: The Heart and Holiness of God* (London: Marshall, Morgan, and Scott, Limited, 1948).

3. The Peril of Privilege, 2:4–8

4. Rejecting God's Provision, 2:9–16

5. The Voice of the Lord, 3:1–8

6. The Results of God's Judgment, 3:9–15

7. Corruption and Ecclesiasticism, 4:1–5

8. Divine Warnings in Nature, 4:6–13

9. Repentance or Disaster, 5:1–11

10. The Fruit of Repentance, 5:12–15

11. The Dark "Day of the Lord," 5:16–20

12. Vain Worship, 5:21–27

13. The Lap of Luxury, 6:1–6

14. Impending Judgment, 6:7–14

15. Trying God's Patience, 7:1–9

16. Religious Opposition to the Truth, 7:10–17

17. A Basket of Summer Fruit, 8:1–3

18. Imminent Judgment, 8:4–14

19. Inescapable Judgment, 9:1–10

20. God's Restoration, 9:11–15[12]

Draper plotted twenty paragraphs. Only one text (The Conscience of a Nation, 1:1) came from a single verse and that verse presented a book sermon, a general introduction to the Book of Amos.

Warren Wiersbe, former pastor of Moody Church in Chicago, preached frequently from Bible books. His predominant system of selecting texts and topics from a book involved the paragraph approach. In preaching from 1 Thessalonians, he used the following selections:

1. A Church Is Born, 1:1

2. What Every Church Should Be, 1:1–10

3. Helping the Baby Grow Up, 2:1–12

4. Growing Pains, 2:13–20

5. Take a Stand, 3:1–13

---

12. James T. Draper, Jr., *The Conscience of a Nation* (Nashville: Broadman Press, 1983).

6. How to Please Your Father, 4:1–12

7. The Comfort of His Coming, 4:13–18

8. Don't Walk in Your Sleep, 5:1–11

9. It's All in the Family, 5:12–28[13]

Wiersbe used the first sermon from 1 Thessalonians 1:1 as an overview of the book's themes and structure. All the other text selections were paragraphs.

Lloyd John Ogilvie, minister of First Presbyterian Church of Hollywood, California, demonstrates a propensity for paragraphs when he preaches from Bible books. Ogilvie preached from 1 Thessalonians, using the following arrangement:

1. The Authentic Life, 1:1

2. U-Turns Absolutely Required, 1:2–10

3. Love As It Was Meant to Be, 2:1–20

4. Don't Check Out, 3:1–18

5. Distinctively Different, 4:1–12

6. Hope in a World Like This, 4:13–5:11

7. Seven Steps to Spontaneity, 5:16–22

8. Wholeness for the Fragmatic, 5:23–24[14]

The first sermon in the series repeated an introduction to Ogilvie's theme of the series from 1 Thessalonians. The subsequent sermons were based on paragraphs with two sermons coming from entire chapters in 1 Thessalonians.

John R. W. Stott, a popular expositor who served as rector of All Souls Church in London, preached frequently from Bible books. He most often used paragraphs for text selection. His texts from Galatians follow:

1. The Apostle Paul's Authority and Gospel, 1:1–5

2. False Teachers and Faithless Galatians, 1:6–10

3. The Origin of Paul's Gospel, 1:11–24

4. Only One Gospel, 2:1–10

5. Paul Clashes with Peter in Antioch, 2:11–16

---

13. Warren W. Wiersbe, *Be Ready* (Wheaton, Ill.: Victor Books, 1979).

14. Lloyd John Ogilvie, *Life as It Was Meant to Be* (Ventura, Calif.: Regal Books, 1980).

6. Justification by Faith Alone, 2:15–21

7. The Folly of the Galatians, 3:1–9

8. The Alternative of Faith and Works, 3:10–14

9. Abraham, Moses, and Christ, 3:15–22

10. Under the Law and in Christ, 3:23–29

11. Once Slaves, but Now Sons, 4:1–11

12. The Relation Between Paul and the Galatians, 4:12–20

13. Isaac and Ishmael, 4:21–31

14. False and True Religion, 5:1–12

15. The Nature of Christian Freedom, 5:13–15

16. The Flesh and the Spirit, 5:16–25

17. Reciprocal Christian Relationships, 5:26–6:5

18. Sowing and Reaping, 6:6–10

19. The Essence of the Christian Religion, 6:11–18[15]

Stott preached consecutively through the Galatian letter with paragraphs. Each sermon was based on more than five verses of a paragraph.

Charles R. Swindoll, an expositor in the Evangelical Free Church tradition, preaches frequently from Bible books. He uses the paragraph approach in selecting and using texts. His treatment of Philippians illustrates his paragraph plotting.

1. A Letter That Makes You Smile (Philippians)

2. Confident Enough to Be Joyful, 1:1–11

3. What a Way to Live, 1:12–21

4. Between a Rock and a Hard Place, 1:21–30

5. The Most Christlike Attitude on Earth, 2:1–11

6. How to Keep Your Balance, 2:12–18

7. Two Men Worth Knowing, 2:19–30

8. Human Rubbish Is Divine Righteousness, 3:1–11

9. Hang Tough ... Regardless, 3:12–16

10. Bad World, Big Job, Bigger God, 3:17–4:1

---

15. John R. W. Stott, "The Message of Galatians," in *The Bible Speaks Today* (Downers Grove, Ill.: InterVarsity Press, 1968).

11. Counsel to Christians Who Clash, 4:1–3

12. Escape Route for Anxiety Addicts, 4:4–9

13. Maturity on Display, 4:10–19

14. Glory, Greeting, Grace, and God, 4:20–23[16]

Like most of his preaching from Bible books, Swindoll introduced his Philippians series with a book sermon. Then he followed on subsequent Sundays with messages from paragraph, of at least six verses.

Judging by these examples and by observing other preachers who preach from Bible books, the paragraph plotting is the most popular method of plotting sermons in a series from a Bible book. Expositors plot by paragraphs because they are the most obvious units of thought in a Bible book. Surveying the paragraph sections of a book also helps mark the parameters of a text. Seeing paragraph divisions in contemporary translations contributes to paragraph plotting being a widely used system.

The Procedure for Plotting with Paragraphs

Preaching a series of sermons from a Bible book by using paragraphs does not just happen. An expositor must have disciplined use of resources. The most valuable resource for plotting with paragraphs consists of a personal analysis of the book and the various translations which divide the book into paragraphs or stanzas. Both of these resources help expositors observe the various units or sections of a Bible book. A personal analysis designates themes for the paragraphs, and even many translations label main sections of material for the reader.

When an expositor uses these two resources of analysis and translations, some procedures for plotting sermon series with paragraphs may be used.

Procedure #1: Mark the paragraphs in the Bible book and decide which ones to use in the series. The designation of paragraphs would have been done with the analysis and with the translations, but an expositor needs to review the book carefully for the specific intention of marking paragraphs which become parameters for texts. Comparing the number of paragraphs observed by the expos-

---

16. Tape Catalogue of *The Shepherd's Voice: First Evangelical Free Church of Fullerton*—1990–91 Addendum.

itor with the number designated by the translators would be helpful in plotting the series. One can easily see that differences exist in the translator's markings of paragraphs.

For example, suppose an expositor has chosen to preach from Colossians. In reviewing the *New International Version*, the expositor observes twenty-eight paragraphs, nineteen paragraphs in the *Revised Standard Version*, and sixteen paragraphs in the *New American Standard Version*. With the expositor's own analysis and a review of the translation's paragraphs, the expositor might choose to have fourteen consecutive paragraphs from Colossians for the series. One sentence in most literary opinions is not considered a paragraph, but one-sentence statements and situations could be stretched to be labeled paragraphs. The expositor's markings of paragraphs depends greatly upon the propensity of the preacher. Personal choices decide on units of material and on the number of units plotted for the series.

Procedure #2: Label the theme of each paragraph. The common theme is what makes a group of sentences a paragraph. Labels for paragraphs can be taken from the analysis, translations, or during the time of plotting. Not everyone will label a paragraph with the same theme; in the *New International Version* Colossians 1:15–23 has the theme "The Supremacy of Christ." But in the *New American Standard Version*, Colossians 1:13–23 has the title "The Incomparable Christ." The words may differ, but the thought in both themes remains the same and generally will be the same in most paragraph designations. In many cases the theme of the paragraph will help determine the theme of the sermon. Determining the parameters of paragraphs and deciding on themes for the paragraphs will be an invaluable process in plotting a Bible book with paragraphs.

Procedure #3: Decide how many paragraphs to use and whether to use them consecutively or selectively. These decisions will determine the length of the series or the number of sermons in the series. Books like Colossians lend themselves to consecutive plotting. Books like Jeremiah lend themselves to selective plotting. The expositor's personal preference and the literary nature of a Bible book affect the choice of the number of paragraphs.

Without a doubt, the paragraph system is one of the best and more popular ways to plot a series of sermons from a Bible book. Plotting with paragraphs helps fix the parameters of texts in the book; it helps the preacher know where one text begins and ends. Plotting with paragraphs also helps lay the Bible books in sections, which enables the expositor to choose which paragraphs to use for the series and whether the paragraphs will be consecutive or selective. Using paragraphs also helps with selecting paragraphs preceding each other and paragraphs immediately following each other.

Plotting with Diversified Techniques

No one system, such as the paragraph method, exists as the sole means of plotting a series of sermons from a Bible book. Each book is dynamic and each expositor is unique. The expositor has many options. Reading and studying a Bible book leads to diversified techniques in plotting a series from that book. This section presents only a few of the available techniques.

Conceiving a Course with Chapters

Since most books in the Bible have been divided into chapters, this unit could be conceived as a means of plotting a series of sermons. Not all chapter divisions contain just one single idea. For that reason no one needs to be rigid in thinking that every verse in every chapter of a Bible book has to be used. Maybe with the exception of most of the Book of Psalms, most chapters have more than one theme. First Corinthians 13, Luke 15, and Isaiah 53 could be proclaimed with a single theme. But the makeup of most Bible books does not have a majority of the chapters with a single thought. Most books have chapter designations which contain several ideas. Nonetheless, plotting a series with chapter divisions can still be a useful technique.

Suppose an expositor chooses to preach a series of sermons from the Gospel of John. Each chapter in John, or any other Gospel for that matter, contains numerous ideas or topics. To preach from all or many of these ideas would lead to an extremely lengthy series of sermons. Just three sermons from each chapter preached one per Sunday would lead to more than a year of sermons. To preach the entire chapter would inevitably lead to a lack of a single theme for a sermon and a proliferation of ideas.

An expositor can conceive of another way to plot a series of sermons using chapters from John. The preacher can plan to preach one chapter each week from the Gospel. The Gospel has twenty-one chapters, so the preacher could spend about five months preaching from John. But does the expositor use the entire chapter? No, the expositor starts reading and studying from John 1. Many ideas exist in that chapter; but the one text and topic that emerges from the study of John 1 will become the text and the sermon. Numerous other ideas can be found in chapter 1, but the following week the expositor should move to reading and studying John chapter 2. The text and topic which emerges from chapter 2 becomes the next Sunday's sermon. The expositor would then proceed to chapter 3 for the next week.

When this process of using chapters from the Gospel of John is finished, the expositor will have preached twenty-one sermons from John. But the expositor will have a reservoir of sermon texts and topics encountered while studying John; this reservoir can be used at a later time.

Preaching one sermon from one chapter of a Bible book and moving the next week to the next chapter make an easy system for plotting a series of sermons. Some chapters in Bible books could be omitted. No rules would be broken if two or more ideas came from one chapter, but a good guideline for plotting seems to be one sermon from one chapter. Homiletical rules are not arrogant masters but helpful friends, so rigid adherence to one sermon from one chapter does not have to be followed. Seemingly, any book in the Bible could be plotted using a sermon from each chapter. Short books such as Philippians could be plotted with just four sermons selected from one of its four chapters. Longer books such as 1 Samuel could be planned with thirty sermons, one from each chapter. Probably next to the plotting of a Bible book with paragraphs, the choice of one sermon from one chapter of the book is the next most popular method of plotting.

The Selection of Sentences from a Book

Some expositors might not choose to plot one sermon from a chapter or to use paragraphs. They might decide to plot a Bible book by selecting significant sentences from the book. The division of the King James Version into verses helps with the choice of sentences. Using one verse or a sentence has been popular with expositors as they preached from Bible books. F. B. Meyer often used what he called the pivot-text method. Meyer wrote: "The expositor needs to discover the pivot sentence in each group of verses being considered. The phrase *pivot sentence* is important. Each paragraph has one sentence on which it revolves or a point on which it impinges. "[17] In most of his *Expositions of Holy Scripture,* Alexander Maclaren, like Meyer, used a pivot sentence as the theme for the sermon.

Plotting a series of sermons with sentences involves reading and studying the book, then selecting many sentences that could become texts and topics for sermons. The following texts and topics could be a series from Philippians plotted with sentences:

1. Bringing a Good Work to Completion, 1:6

2. Abounding in Love, 1:9

3. Preaching Christ Is All that Matters, 1:8

4. A Philosophy of Life and Death, 1:21

5. Getting a New Mind, 2:5

6. Working Out What Is on the Inside, 2:12

7. Risking Life for Christ's Service, 2:30

8. Being in Christ, 3:9

9. Growing in Christ, 3:9

10. Living with Stress, 4:6

11. Thinking Good Thoughts, 4:8

12. Learning to Be Content, 4:11

13. Power to Master Life, 4:13

14. Getting Needs Supplied, 4:19

Fourteen sentences have been selected from Philippians to use as the bases of sermons. Other sentences claimed attention, but these represent the ones selected for this series.

Plotting a book with sentences is not especially complicated. The expositor must become familiar with the contents of the book and choose the desired number of texts. Selection of sentences is left to the expositor's discretion. The series can be long or short, depending on the number of sentences the expositor chooses to select.

One word of warning: the sentence that contains a hint of truth needs careful study in many contexts. The danger exists that the text could be wrestled from its setting and made to say something

---

17. F. B. Meyer, *Expository Preaching Plans and Methods* (London: Hodder and Stoughton, 1912), 32.

foreign to its true meaning. The only safeguard is to approach it through its larger contexts and its general background. Chalmer E. Faw tells of a busy pastor called to preach a funeral service. The pastor did not take time to search the context of a particular text. The pastor preached that "the Lord had need of him." Later, the pastor was shocked to discover that the context of the passage was that the Lord had need of a donkey![18] Examples such as this one signal the need that each sentence selected for a text in a series needs to be examined in context. Its meaning must not be distorted, misappropriated, or misunderstood.

The Preference for Personalities in the Book

Many Bible books contain the stories of various people, and much of the literary method has a narrative nature about it. When an expositor has chosen a book with many personalities, the expositor could have a preference for choosing various personalities in the book. It could be preaching from a Bible book using narrative sermons or biographical material. The Book of Genesis lends itself to plotting with personalities. Consider a few of the personalities: God, Satan, Adam, Eve, Cain, Abel, Seth, Enoch, Noah, Abraham, Sarah, Lot, Isaac, Esau, Jacob, and Joseph. These sixteen personality studies could be the course of the series.

The Gospel of John and the other Gospels also lend themselves to plotting by the use of personalities. Some have chosen to preach a series on John by using the various women and men who encountered Jesus. Just a casual preaching of John will disclose that Jesus had meetings with many people. Each sermon in the series could focus on the meeting.

The preference for plotting with personalities usually stems from an expositor's desire to preach sermons with concrete imagery: biographical sermons, narrative sermons, or inductive sermons. Experiences, feelings, attitudes, and actions of Bible characters can be related to people's needs in today's world. Preaching from a Bible book with the use of personalities could represent a different approach than the series based on chapters, paragraphs, or sentences. Not all of the books of the Bible can be plotted for a series with personalities. The literary nature of some books is narrative, and they lend themselves to a series based on persons in the

---

18. Faw, 137–38.

book. The literary nature of some books is didactic, and plotting would best be done with paragraphs, chapters, or sentences. For example, an expositor would have difficulty in plotting the Book of Romans with personalities because the first fifteen chapters of Romans have few references to persons while the sixteenth chapter mentions over thirty persons.

A series of biographical sermons should be more than a narration of facts and events from the ancient past. The expositor needs to exegete the Bible character; the expositor also needs to interpret how that character can relate to people living in today's world.

The Use of Smaller Units in a Bible Book

Every Bible book has chapters, paragraphs, and verses. Within these larger units exist even smaller particles, such as clauses, phrases, single words, and themes. In plotting sermons and texts for a series, these smaller units may become the basis for selection.

Clauses. One such smaller unit is the clause—a group of words with a subject and predicate but does not complete a thought. Principal clauses function in the sentence structure as parts of speech— nouns, adjectives, and adverbs. The interpreter needs to pay special attention to a clause to see if it is a coordinate, causal, or purpose clause. Its exact function within a sentence will enable the interpreter to understand the meaning intended by the writer. Like a sentence, clauses need to be interpreted in light of immediate and general contexts.

Generally, clauses are not consistent occurrences throughout a Bible book; thus, expositors might have difficulty plotting a series with all clauses. Perhaps no literature of the Bible has more clauses than the Letters or Epistles. Though clauses can be frequently found in the Epistles, plotting an entire series with clauses might be extremely difficult.

Phrases. Because they are more abundant than clauses, phrases are more frequently used in series plotting. A phrase is a group of two or more words that form a sensible unit, either expressing a thought fragmentarily or as a sentence element not containing a predicate serving as a single part of speech. Phrases often suggest a candid shot. Jesus characterized the Pharisee and the publican in superb phrases. "The Pharisee stood and was thus praying *to himself*" (Luke 18:11a; *italics mine*). This phrase depicts how much the Pharisee centered his praying to himself. Notice also other phrases: "But the tax-gatherer, *standing some distance away*" (Luke 18:13a; *italics mine*). The tax collector did not wish to be conspicuous, for he knew his unworthiness. Just a verbal phrase gave a candid picture of the tax collector.

Phrases also color events. Often a single phrase will add a wealth of meaning to an event. Examine the story of the conversion of Saul (see Acts 9:1–19). Within the story is the ministry of Ananias, a disciple the Lord commissioned to help Saul. After some reluctance, Ananias went to minister to Paul. His account of ministry has many colorful phrases: *laying his hands on him* and *Brother Saul* (see Acts 9:17). Just the mention of a touch of Ananias on Saul depicts love and help for Saul, the persecutor. The phrase, *Brother Saul*, gives the color of one who accepted and forgave a convicted persecutor of the church.

Truth often flashes in the form of a phrase. The Epistles have many expressive phrases. Three prepositional phrases in 1 Thessalonians 1:2–3 express the truth of the Thessalonians' experiences of Christ. "For our gospel did not come to you in word only, but also in power and in the Holy Spirit and with full conviction" (1 Thess. 1:5a). Each of the three prepositional phrases flashes some insight about how the Thessalonians experienced the gospel when Paul preached to them.

Reading and studying a Bible book will yield the discovery of. many candid, colorful, sparks of truth. On some occasion, the expositor could plot an entire series of sermons from a Bible book just by the use of catchy, communicative phrases. Yet plotting a book with phrases should be more occasional than routine.

Words. The smallest unit in all of the biblical record is the individual word. By inherent content, frequent use, or strategic portion, a word can become the basis for a sermon, and words within a Bible book can become the basis for a series of sermons. Words contain internal power and await the expositor's knowledge and skill to unleash their possibilities.

Almost any book in the Bible could be plotted with a series of words serving as the basis of sermons. Writers used words to express their dominant thoughts. John often used the words *commandment, light, righteousness,* and *love.* An expositor could preach from 1 John just using four words and give the main thoughts of the writer. Some of the richest words in the New Testament appear in the Epistle to the Romans: *grace, gospel, faith, sin, righteousness, justified, sanctified, glorified.* These and other words from Romans could become the basis of a series.

Themes. A series could be projected on the themes and doctrines found in a book. For example, one could preach from Romans using the following doctrinal ideas:

1. The Doctrine of Revelation, 1:18–23
2. The Doctrine of Sin, 1:18–32
3. The Doctrine of Justification, 3:21–31
4. The Doctrine of Faith, 4:1–25
5. The Doctrine of the Grace of God, 5:1–21
6. The Doctrine of Sanctification, 6:1–23
7. The Doctrine of the Holy Spirit on a Believer's Life, 8:1–39
8. The Doctrine of the Sovereignty of God, 9–11
9. The Doctrine of the Christian's Life, 12:1–21
10. The Doctrine of the Governmental Responsibilities, 13:1–14

Not every book can be plotted with themes, but those that can, at times, need to be used with the doctrinal themes.

Smaller units such as clauses, phrases, words, and themes arise as possibilities for plotting. But most series of sermons will be based on chapters, paragraphs, and sentences. The smaller units can be scattered in the series, but fewer series of sermons from Bible books will use the smaller units exclusively. No homiletical rule prohibits a variety of plotting techniques. An expositor could plot a series from a book with one sermon from the entire book, several sermons plotted from sentences, several plotted from words or phrases, several plotted from character studies, a few plotted from doctrinal themes, and a lot of selections plotted from paragraphs. Most expositors will plot one sermon on the entire book and choose the rest of the sermons consecutively or selectively from paragraphs.

CHAPTER 12

Structuring Sermon Ideas from a Bible Book

Summarizing a Text
    The Study of the Text
    Stating the Summary of the Text
Determining the Sermon Idea
    One Idea of the Sermon
    Stating the Essence of the Sermon
The Sermon Objective
    Domains of a Sermon Objective
    Stating the Objective
Developing the Sermon Idea
    Using the Text in the Developmental Method
    The Mechanics of Development
Expanding the Major Divisions
    Expansion by Textual Analysis
    Expansion by Explanation/Application
    Expansion by Multiple Combinations
    Expansion by Facet Observation
The Introduction, Transitions, and Conclusion
    The Introduction of a Sermon
    The Transitions in a Sermon
    The Conclusion of a Sermon

To this point, most of the chapters in this work contain some general rules for preaching a series of sermons from a Bible book. Most of the discussion in the previous chapters involved skills for securing substance or content from passages in a Bible book. Expositors know that the process of preparing to preach does not stop with discovering substance.

Content needs to be communicated with some type of organization. The structure of substance serves as a means of getting relevant biblical truth from one person to other persons. Substance needs to be shaped so an audience can comprehend and follow the movement and thought patterns of the expositor. The expositor inevitably has to move from exegesis and interpretation of a biblical text to shaping or structuring an idea inherent in the text. Homiletics, which is the science of structuring sermons, goes along naturally with hermeneutics, which is the science of understanding and interpreting a text.

Homiletics at times has suffered both from an excessive stress on structure and a lack of emphasis on substance in the structure. Since Augustine, the classical and traditional mode of sermon structure has been to project a series of main ideas and subpoints to carry an argument. Augustine insisted that both *sequentia* and *eloquentia* are needed in effective discourse. He took these terms from classical rhetoric; they relate to the invention of ideas and the arrangement, ordering, or disposition of ideas.[1]

Soon after Augustine's deductive emphasis on the arrangement of ideas in a sermon, other homilists began to overemphasize the parts or the structure of a sermon. The *points* in the sermon seemed to be stressed more than the *point* of the sermon. Writers on homiletics from the fourth to the twentieth century overemphasized the parts, or points, making analysis become an end in itself. V. L. Stanfield, who revised John A. Broadus' nineteenth-century work on homiletics, wrote about "the excessive multiplication of formal divisions and equally formal sub-divisions."[2] The syllogistic model, which is the typical three points more or less, has prevailed through the years.[3] Clyde Fant labeled the homiletical overemphasis on

---

1. David L. Larsen, *The Anatomy of Preaching: Identifying the Issues in Preaching Today* (Grand Rapids: Baker Book House, 1989), 61.

2. John A. Broadus, *On the Preparation and Delivery of Sermons*, 4th ed., rev. Vernon L. Stanfield (San Francisco: Harper and Row, 1979), 89.

3. Larsen.

structure as "neoscholastic preaching."[4] Fant defined preaching as the points overemphasized with the main point getting lost in the proliferation of the points. Such an excessive stress on structure generally produces sermons with many points, subpoints, sub-subpoints, and sub-sub-subpoints which leads to the query, What is the point?

Overemphasis on sermon structure has led to a de-emphasis on sermon structure or organization. The general reaction against structure and analytical excess came about a century ago when Matthew Arnold argued that a sermon should be more of an informal address without any observable parts or divisions.[5] The trend today in some sermonic emphases has been a reaction against traditional homiletics where ideas are all sliced and diced. Paul E. Johnson in his work, *Modern Times*, asserted that in 1919 the world of Newtonian physics, with its eminently comprehensible straight lines and right angles, yielded to Albert Einstein's relativistic or nonstructural universe.[6] Such an emphasis in today's mind-set on nonstructuralism has led preachers to develop what might be called "oral essays."[7] David L. Larsen complains that such essays become pools of literary protoplasm flowing in all directions simultaneously.[8] Søren Kierkegaard and other existentialists, as well as pragmatists and logical positivists, have de-emphasized structure.[9]

Somewhere between the preoccupation with points and the disdain for structure exists functional, usable homiletics. God created the substance of heaven and earth, and then he shaped the substance in divine designs. Sermons, likewise, need to have shape, not for the purpose of shape but as a means of sharing the content with others. Points should exist to get the point across. Clyde E. Fant calls this "gestaltic preaching" because the whole is greater than the sum of its parts.[10] David L. Larsen also advocated a gestalt pattern with a strong emphasis on the point and a lesser emphasis on the

---

4. Clyde E. Fant, *Preaching for Today*, rev. ed. (San Francisco: Harper and Row, 1987), 182.

5. Larsen, 62.

6. Paul E. Johnson, *Modern Times: The World from the Twenties to the Eighties* (New York: Harper and Row, 1983), 1.

7. Larsen, 62.

8. Ibid.

9. Ibid., 60.

10. Fant, 182.

points and subpoints.[11] On some occasions, gestalt preaching comes with a deductive design; the preacher begins with an idea and then elaborates on that idea. At other times, gestalt preaching begins with an inductive design in which narrative seems to dominate the content.

Perhaps one of the greatest needs in the shape of sermons is variety. Preachers and hearers grow weary with the same type of structure in sermons each week. Variety in structure is especially needed when preaching a series of sermons from a Bible book. Every sermon does not have to derive all of the points and subpoints from the text. Instead, the point can be derived from the text, and then different designs can be used to communicate the point. Deductive expositors can diversify their predominant design with other deductive alternatives, and they could include some inductive designs in their homiletical repertoire. Expositors who use inductive designs can diversify with other inductive patterns and can add some deductive designs in their selections of sermon structures.

Preaching a number of sermons from a Bible book calls for a variety of sermon structures. This chapter examines a system of structuring a sermon known as "the developmental design."[12] Generally speaking, such a structural pattern begins from a deductive perspective where a single point is secured from a Bible passage, and that single point is developed into points so each point relates directly to the point. The basic technique of the developmental design has the potential for diversification from either the deductive or inductive perspective and from personal preference in designing a sermon. Chapter 13 will provide help with variety in both the deductive and inductive designs. Sermons in a series from a Bible book do not have to be the same in structure or design. Studying other designs can help expositors diversify the packaging of the product of biblical truth.

Summarizing a Text

In most cases, the developmental method of sermon preparation begins with the text. But it can start with a human need and then move to a biblical text. Whether a sermon originates with the exe-

---

11. Larsen, 62

12. A more extensive explanation of the developmental design is given in Harold T. Bryson and James C. Taylor, *Building Sermons to Meet People's Needs* (Nashville: Broadman Press, 1980).

gesis of a human need or the exegesis of a text, expositors need to consider seriously both a biblical revelation and a contemporary situation. These two poles influence the shape of a sermon.

Most preachers who preach a series of sermons from a Bible book begin preparation of the individual sermon with the text, the biblical revelation. When the text has been determined, sermon preparation with the text is a natural process. Expositors who begin sermon preparation with the text need to proceed to contemporary situations which relate to the text. At times, an expositor can emphasize the text without considering contemporary needs. For example, Karl Barth insisted that a preacher must be faithful both to the text and life, but he added that "it is always better to keep too close to the text."[13]

In the developmental design, as with numerous other designs, the preacher may discover an idea from a contemporary situation in life and then proceed back to a text. Some preachers are attracted to contemporary situations and their sermon beginnings have a propensity for person-centered, life-situation, inductive preaching forms. Their sermon ideas may come from illustrations, literature, and involvement with a human soul. Afterward their ideas are matched with the teaching of a text, and the idea is structured with the contemporary situation and the biblical revelation in mind.

The inclusion of the biblical revelation and the contemporary situation is never an either-or effort. It is a both-and process. No homiletician should announce that sermon preparation in a series from a Bible book must begin either with the biblical revelation or the contemporary situation. A good homiletical principle to adopt is that some sermon preparation will begin with the biblical revelation, and other sermon preparation will begin with the contemporary situation. Perhaps variety in preparation could be enhanced with those who have a predominant tendency toward either one of these places of beginnings to change from one to the other as occasions arise.

The Study of the Text

The word *text* comes from the Latin word *texere* which means to weave. This image of weaving conveys the idea that the truth and

---

13. Karl Barth, *The Preaching of the Gospel*, trans. B. E. Hooks (Philadelphia: Westminster, 1963), 77.

thoughts of the text are woven into the substance and shape of the sermon. To use the image of weaving, expositors need to think of the text as being extremely obvious in the content and design of the sermon like a black thread evident in a white garment. Yet another garment might be multicolored and include black threads. At first glance, the black thread might not be obvious in the multicolored garment. But closer observation causes an observer to see the presence of the black thread. Sermons may be seen in the same way. Some sermons may show an obvious, direct connection with the text. Other sermons will have the text woven into the content, and the relation to the text may not be quite so obvious at first, but close attention will confirm that the text, though not directly, relates to the sermon.

Whether an expositor chooses to use a text in a sermon directly or indirectly, the necessity of studying the text carefully needs to be attempted. Chapters 4, 5, and 6 of this work discuss the study of background, exegesis, and interpretation of Bible passages. These disciplines need to be applied to the study of a text for a sermon. Academic study of a text should lead to the practical statement of a summary of the text in a simple sentence of fifteen words or less. To understand the summary statement of the text, some procedures need to be studied.

Step One in moving toward a summary of the text is determining the parameters of a text. This exercise includes designating where the text starts and where it ends, with the contents containing a unit of thought. In the morphological definition of expository preaching, which stresses the length of the text, the parameters of each text in the Bible book would have to exceed two or three verses. But fortunately in the eclectic emphases on expository preaching, the parameters of a text may vary from part of a verse to many verses. Freedom exists for establishing the length of texts.

Ordinarily, locating the beginning and ending of a text is not difficult. The preacher will do this work by personal involvement with the text, observing the analysis of the book, and checking later with the exegesis. The clues for beginnings and endings of a text are usually of two kinds: thematic and literary. A single theme makes Ruth 1:6–18; Matthew 5:3–12; and Colossians 1:15–23 single units. Literary clues provided by the writers may be brief introductions to the material (see Isaiah 1:1) or notations about the time (see Mark 1:32), place (see Matt. 5:28), or occasion (see John 5:1). Sometimes units are completed with summary statements (see Acts 16:5). In most cases, careful reading of a Bible book and close observation will yield beginnings and endings of units.

Observing the parameters of a text allows for a summary of the entire unit in the larger unit without violating the meaning of the text. Consider James 1:2–12 as a large unit of thought on the theme of the trials of a Christian. The preacher could write a summary of this large unit. But closer consideration yields the observation of several smaller units in the larger unit of James 1:2–12. Such themes as the results of trials, 1:2–4; securing divine wisdom, 1:5–8; the trials of possessions, 1:9–11; and the blessedness of enduring trials, 1:12, exist within the larger unit. The preacher could write a summary of the larger unit, or the preacher could write summaries of the smaller units, depending on the text selected. In the eclectic perspective of expository preaching, nothing prohibits sermons on the larger unit or on all four of the smaller units.

Step Two in moving toward a summary of the text is historical background study. Each text needs to be studied in the light of its historical origin. An extensive discussion about historical background appears in chapter 4. Every text in a Bible book was written against its background, and the text's meaning will relate directly to what God inspired the original author to communicate to the original readers. Knowing factors in the life situation of a text helps to move closer to summarizing a text.

Step Three is analysis. While the analysis discussed in chapter 5 examines a Bible book generally, the specific study of a text for a sermon involves looking more specifically into analytical matters. It does not mean another analysis but a more expanded diagnostic breakdown of a specific text with thoughts moving toward summarizing the text.

Step Four is exegesis. Chapter 6 on exegesis and chapter 7 on interpretation can help greatly. Studying the literary type, the context of the text, word meanings and usages, and syntactical matters helps the expositor make a precise summary of the text. With the parameter of a text prescribed and the exercises related, the preacher is ready to think of writing a simple summary sentence of a truth in the text.

Stating the Summary of the Text

No person can predict when a summary statement of a text will emerge. It may come with just a casual reading of a text, during serious study of the text, or even when the preacher is not reading or studying that particular text. Ordinarily though, a summary of a text comes during or after careful study. For a preacher who is beginning sermon structure, putting the essence of a text in a sentence is the catalyst for beginning. Organizing the sermon begins with a point in the text, not with many points. Even if a preacher starts the sermon structure with a human need, moving to a text and a summary sentence of a text is a natural process.

Ordinarily in the developmental method, the expositor starts with the text. After studying the text carefully, the expositor should write a summary sentence. Such a sentence is called the essence of the text in a sentence (ETS). The sentence needs to be a simple one which does not exceed approximately fifteen words. It should always be stated in the past tense because it seeks to summarize what the text meant. The essence of the text can be stated from all of the text or part of the text. Look again at James 1:2–12 for some examples of summary sentences of the text.

	Text ETS
James 1:2–12	James prepared the first-century Christians for the trials of life.
James 1:2–4	James helped believers to see some positive results of trials.
James 1:5–8	James urged Christians to seek wisdom from God during life's hardships.
James 1:9–11	James sought to get believers to adjust their attitudes toward possessions.

Expositors need to remember that numerous sermon summary possibilities can be discovered in texts. Texts do not have just one specific meaning. Texts have a general meaning based on their original life situation, but multiple meanings can be derived from the general meaning. Different expositors usually put a different slant on the summary of the text, resulting from their private interpretation and their personal manner of summarizing the text. If ten preachers wrote an essence of the text in a sentence from the same text, variety would be observed but kinship to the general meaning of the text on all cases would probably be noticed. Each text may have numerous truths, but only one truth will be selected for a sermon and for the structuring of a sermon.

The ETS may emerge from a text in at least two general ways:

- The essence of the text may emerge directly from the text. The expositor might even use the words of the text. For example, an ETS of Genesis 5:24 could be: Enoch walked with God. This text is not too hard to summarize because the words come directly from the text.

- The essence of the text may be suggested by the text. Such a summary statement suggested by the text does not mean that the essence of the text will be less biblical. It means that study of the text leads, at times, to a summary statement suggested or inferred by the text. The idea of self-image is suggested by the text of Luke 15:11–24. An ETS could be: The younger son struggled with his self-image. The story of the younger man in that text suggests a struggle for an adequate self-image.

Stating a summary sentence from a text is a good way to begin structuring a sermon. The essence of the text has numerous homiletical usages. It helps start the sermon idea with a biblical concept. It also serves as a catalyst for moving to a sermon in a sentence that will be the main idea of the sermon. The essence of the text works as a guide throughout the sermon preparation for the introduction, outline, and conclusion. Getting that one sentence—the summary of the text—is a valuable process for initiating the developmental method.

To learn the mechanics of the essence of the text, some examples need to be observed. Each of these summary statements represents hours of study and meditation. Four examples of an ETS will be furnished. These examples will be observed again in the discussion about the other mechanical elements of the developmental method.

	Text ETS
Philippians 1:3–8	Paul shared Christ's ministry with the church at Philippi.
Philippians 2:5–10	Paul described the mind of Christ.

	Text ETS
Philippians 3:20–21	Paul described the church at Philippi as a colony of heaven.
Philippians 4:10–13	Paul learned some of his most valuable lessons out of life's experiences.

Determining the Sermon Idea

Getting an idea from a text and summarizing the text fulfill the necessity for having biblical context, or the *then*, of the text. But sermons from a Bible book cannot be structured in the past tense, for no book in Scripture originated or exists for mere historical posterity. Every Bible book was inspired by God and written to address human needs from the moment of its writing until history's consummation. Structuring an idea from the text needs to move to the contemporary situation, the *now* of the text. Preparing and preaching a sermon from a text in a Bible book involves making a trip from the historical biblical revelation to the contemporary human situation or from the current human need to the ancient text. Such involvement could be called the hermeneutical arch.

Hermeneutical Arch

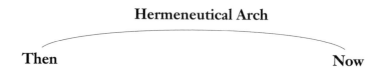

Then   **Now**

The homiletical process on the *then* side of the hermeneutical arch involves the statement of the essence of the text. This sentence ties an idea from the text to the sermon idea. The homiletical process on the other side of the *now* involves two procedures—a statement of the essence of the sermon in a sentence and a statement of the objective of the sermon in a sentence. After settling on a suitable summary of the text, an expositor should proceed to the mechanics of stating the sermon idea in a sentence and stating the objective for the sermon. This discussion will focus on the essence of the sermon, and a subsequent section will give insights about the objective of the sermon.

One Idea of the Sermon

Most writers on homiletics teach that the sermon should have one prominent idea supported or illuminated by other ideas subservient to the main idea. If the sermon preparation is conducted from a deductive direction, the sermon should have one general point supported, proved, or developed by means of several points. If the sermon preparation is conducted from an inductive perspective, the point or the plot needs to be investigated with experiences. The inductive investigation may have moves or turns instead of points, but the inductive procedure still seeks to help get the main idea across to people.

Homileticians in the deductive tradition have many different names for the one idea. These terms seem to be synonyms for a single idea in a sermon. In 1870, John A. Broadus in his work, *A Treatise on the Preparation and Delivery of Sermons*, labeled the one idea the subject of a sermon. Austin Phelps in his book, *The Theory of Preaching*, also published in 1870, proposed the one idea of a sermon as the proposition. Charles W. Koller in his work, *Expository Preaching Without Notes*, described the main idea for a sermon as the thesis or proposition. Many other writers on homiletics such as J. H. Jowett in *The Preacher: His Life and Work*, Andrew W. Blackwood in *The Preparation of Sermons*, J. Daniel Baumann in *An Introduction to Contemporary Preaching*, and V. L. Stanfield in the revision of John A. Broadus' 1870 work, *On the Preparation and Delivery of Sermons* (4th ed.), called for a sermon to have a proposition or the sermon to be stated in one main sentence. Henry Grady Davis labeled the one point of the sermon as the idea of a sermon.[14] Brown, Clinard, and Northcutt called the one idea of the sermon the central idea.[15]

All these homileticians are describing a one-idea sermon, or "the essence of the sermon in a sentence."[16] Such an expression means a simple sentence stated in either the present or future tense of fifteen words or less which states the main point of the sermon.

---

14. Henry Grady Davis, *Design for Preaching* (Philadelphia: Fortress Press, 1958), 20.

15. H.C. Brown, Jr., H. Gordon Clinard, and Jesse J. Northcutt, *Steps to the Sermon: A Plan for Sermon Preparation* (Nashville: Broadman, 1963), 46.

16. Bryson and Taylor, 63–68.

The essence of the sermon in a sentence (ESS) ordinarily comes from the essence of the text. Getting the main sermon idea from the text helps make sermon and text congruent with each other. In many cases, writing the essence of the sermon in a sentence involves little more than putting the essence of the text in either the present or future tense. These two sentences have an inseparable relationship. One serves as a homiletical device for getting an idea from biblical revelation, and the other serves as a device for putting biblical truth in sermonic or contemporary language.

Every essence of a sermon in a sentence needs to have singleness of expression. For this reason, the essence of the sermon needs to be a simple sentence, not a compound or complex one. Simple sentences contain a single idea, but compound or complex sentences comprise several ideas. From the start of structuring the sermon in the developmental method, only one idea needs to prevail. That one idea has been derived from a biblical text and then directed to a single sermon idea.

In developing a sermon sentence, an expositor needs to be sure the sentence can be developed further. The main point prevails while points emerge from the point. The process involves a series of declarations which amplify the point, a series of statements to support the main point, or a series of points which embellish the point. If, after careful study and constant practice, an expositor cannot derive points from the point, another essence of the sermon should be written.

The essence of a sermon does not need to be complicated; it should be a simple sentence that states one clear, unambiguous sermon idea. If the sentence is a simple one of about fifteen words or less, it will not be loaded with exaggerations or unnecessary embellishments.

Stating the Essence of the Sermon

A sermon needs to have a point before it has points. The points need to relate to the point. When an expositor has studied a text carefully and stated a summary of the text, the next step is to move to the summary of the sermon in a sentence. The essence of the sermon in a sentence may be stated in a variety of ways. Six of these statements of the essence of the sermon are illustrated from James 1:2–12.

1. A *possibility statement* expresses an optimistic outlook: "Christians can master the truths of life."

2. A *predictive statement* declares what can happen in a person's life: "The Christian's life can be enriched by the mastery of trials."

3. A *persuasive statement* induces the hearer to believe something or to do something: "God wants you to believe that he can help you with your trials."

4. A *comparative statement* spells out differences or similarities: "Trusting God during trials differs drastically from doubting God during testing times."

5. An *evaluative statement* ascertains the value or benefit of an action: "Mastering trials leads to the best kind of life."

6. A *declarative statement* merely states a fact: "Mastering life's trials involves listening to God's instructions."

These are only a few of the many ways to state a sermon sentence. Looking at the truths in a biblical passage and observing human needs can reveal the potential for many sermon sentences. Not all texts have the potential for discovering numerous sermon summary sentences as James 1:2–12. More than likely, the particular types of sermon sentences will be determined by the context of the audience, the needs of the hearers, the expositor's personality, and the Holy Spirit's illumination. Each essence of the sermon sentence type will suggest a slightly different direction for the message.

Learning happens when people see theories actualized. Notice in the following examples that the essence of the sermon relates closely to the essence of the text.

	Text ESS
Philippians 1:3–8	Believers share a partnership in God's work.
Philippians 2:5–10	Believers need the mind of Christ.
Philippians 3:20–21	God's people live as residents of heaven on earth.
Philippians 4:10–13	Christians can learn some valuable lessons from life's experiences.

The Sermon Objective

Each sermon in a series of messages from a Bible book needs to have a reason for existence. Sermons do not need to be prepared and proclaimed just because they are next in the series. Wise expositors seek to determine what people need to do as a result of hearing a sermon. Perhaps some sermons from Bible books err because they represent almost pure didactic presentations.

Each expository sermon must have a clear, specific objective. Each text was first written to comfort, correct, challenge, persuade, or censure. The sermon and the text continue to act. The text did something *then*, and it is to do something *now*. Arriving at a sermon objective involves considering what the text was intended to do for the original hearers and moving that historical purpose to a contemporary action.

Domains of a Sermon Objective

Each sermon should address the three domains of learning:

- The cognitive domain (intellect)
- The affective domain (feelings)
- The psychomotor domain (action)

These domains can relate to preparing a sermon objective. All three domains need to be in a sermon. Information and feelings need to be in each message, but the specific sermon objective needs to be a sentence which calls for action.

Imparting information comprises a large part of delivering a sermon. Expositors decline Greek nouns, parse Greek verbs, explain Hebrew words, give insights about syntactical constructions, and impart other informational matters. But these facts do not represent the ultimate objective of a sermon. Preaching is not just imparting information but also persuading people to action. The ultimate goal for a sermon is not transmitting information, as important as that is; rather, the goal is to transform human beings. Perhaps one of the greatest criticisms of traditional expository preaching has been the overload of technical, exegetical, and historical information. The best way to remedy the problem is to use cognitive content in persuading people to act.

Help comes at the point of an example. Suppose an objective was written on James 1:2–12. After exegetical information has been investigated, an objective in the cognitive domain would be: "I want people to know about the trials of life." Such an objective would be achieved by giving facts. After the sermon has been delivered, a hearer might ask, "So what?" Obviously the sermon objective needs to be moved from the cognitive domain to the psychomotor domain—the domain of skill and performance.

Arousing feelings is also part of sermon delivery. The content in Bible books naturally causes both the preacher and the audience to have feelings. Charles Silvester Horne said, "Nobody ought ever to go into a pulpit who can think and talk about sin and salvation and its Cross of Christ . . . without profound emotion and passion."[17] Yet the cognitive and affective domains should dominate the sermon. Feelings aroused without appeal to action can be just as bad as information imparted without persuasion to performance.

Assistance again comes at the point of example. An objective written on James 1:2–12 could be this: "I want people to feel good about the trials of life." Such an objective lies solely in the realm of human emotions. People do not need to feel good or bad about something. They need to do something. Again the sermon objective needs to be moved from the affective domain to the psychomotor domain.

Calling for action should be the dominant domain for a sermon objective. Actually, preachers impart information and include favorable feelings toward the content so that hearers can apply the facts. The preeminent objective of a sermon is to persuade people to be and to do something. A better objective from James 1:2–12 would be: "I want people to master the trials of life with God's help."

Stating the Objective

Up to this point, we have developed two statements in structuring a sermon: the essence of the text and the essence of the sermon. The third sentence states the objective of the sermon. This sentence needs to come under the psychomotor domain, which means a stated desire from the preacher for action of the hearers. The sermon objective needs to be a simple sentence of fifteen words or less in either the present or future tense. The sermon objective needs to possess at least three distinguishable traits.

---

17. Charles Silvester Horne, *The Romance of Preaching* (New York: Fleming H. Revell, 1914), 256.

Trait #1: The sentence objective should be specific. Vagueness about the sermon's purpose hampers the effort to achieve action. Working on a specific objective takes time, but it helps the sermon's preparation and delivery to be focused. "I want people to pray more" is too general. A more specific objective would be, "I want people to vary their emphases in prayer."

Trait #2: The sermon objective should be attainable. It should prescribe an action that people can reach with God's help. A certain idealism is in order, but a sermon's ideals need to be presented so that hearers recognize the possibility of achieving the ideal. "I want people to get rid of all their anxieties" is an unrealistic objective. A more attainable objective would be: "I want people to begin trusting God today with their worries." Hearers are more inclined to apply the latter objective.

Trait #3: The sermon objective should be measurable. If, indeed, a sermon objective is attainable, it should be measurable. Hearers and observers of the hearers should be able to see altered actions as a result of sermons. Objectives need to be prepared so they can be measured. For example, with the objective on prayer, hearers should be able to determine if they vary their emphases on prayer after the sermon. With the objective about anxiety, hearers could measure daily whether they worry more or whether they trust the Lord with their anxieties. Obviously, if hearers heed and practice sermons, people associated with the hearers will observe the results. Actually, God measures the action of each sermon heard.

Writing an objective for each sermon requires discipline. First attempts will be difficult because moving from the cognitive and affective domains to the psychomotor domain is not easy. The most persuasive expositors state in a sentence what they want hearers to do.

Having practical theories helps the credibility of the homiletical ideas presented. Examples of essence of the text and essence of the sermon have been presented. Now examples of the sermon objective in a sentence need to be observed in connection with the relationship of the two other sentences.

	Text OSS
Philippians 1:3–8	I want people to work together as partners in Christ.
Philippians 2:5–10	I want people to live out the mind of Christ.
Philippians 3:20–21	I want believers in Christ to give their allegiance to the Kingdom agenda.
Philippians 4:10–13	I want people to apply the Lord's will to the hard trials of life.

Developing the Sermon Idea

This entire chapter focuses on a system of structuring a sermon known as the developmental method. This method, simply defined, means getting points from the point. The word *development* is a homiletical synonym for main divisions, major points, outline, predicate, or just the word *points*. In most cases in this chapter and in the developmental method, the word *points* is preferred. The verbal form of development describes the process of enlarging an idea by means of some simple homiletical devices. The developmental method is a means of getting points from the point, ideas from the idea, an outline from a proposition, and a predicate from a subject.

Sermon structures are criticized for two defects: for being pointless and for being a proliferation of points. Correctly using the developmental method results in a sermon with just one point and prevents multiplying unrelated points. The process of developing points from the point does not produce separate ideas from the main idea. Instead, it helps expositors relate every main division to the main idea. The point holds preeminence over the points, and these points become a means of communicating the point. The developmental method represents *a* system, not *the* system, of structuring a sermon. It exists as one means among many means. The developmental method deserves careful study because it can be used extensively in preaching a series of sermons from a Bible book and because of its possibility of variation.

Using the Text in the Developmental Method

Every system of structuring a sermon needs to use the text in some manner. Most definitions of expository preaching emphasize either the length of the text or securing points directly from the text. The definition of expository preaching as the art of preaching a series of sermons from a Bible book does not hold strict regulations about the length of the text or the points proceeding directly from the text. Infinite variety for structuring each sermon in the series needs to be available to expositors. No kind of structure makes a sermon more or less biblical. If the main idea of the sermon relates to the text in a way which has kinship to the original life situation, the structure of the sermon will be biblical. The text may be used in at least two ways in the developmental method.

1. The expositor can derive the point and the points from the text. This type of development occurs when the text has the potential for such a structure. Some texts, such as narratives, parables, and short texts, would not fit in the category of getting both the point and points from the text. Even with this method of using the text for an outline, the point of the sermon needs to be the essence of the sermon, or the point not the points. Perhaps the best way to learn about how the text may be used for the point and the points is to observe an example.

Text   1 Corinthians 13:1–13

Topic   The greatest gift of a Christian

ETS   Paul described God's kind of love as the greatest gift of a Christian.

ESS   Believers need to practice Christian love.

OSS   My objective is for Christians to put God's love in action.

Points   1. Christians need to practice love because it possesses superior value, 13:1–3.

            2. Christians need to practice Christian love because it possesses outstanding actions, 13:4–7.

            3. Christians need to practice Christian love because it possesses eternal permanence, 13:8–13.

In this sermon, the point came from the entire chapter of 1 Corinthians 13. The point prevailed throughout the points. Each point came from the text, and each related directly to the main point. The text becomes the source for both the point and the points. When the shape of the text allows this possibility, it represents a good method of developing the point and the outline from the text.

2. The expositor can derive the point from the text and derive the points from the point. Just because the major divisions do not come from the text does not make a sermon less biblical. Getting the point from the text makes the sermon biblical. The points emerge from the one point, which is the summary of the text. Seeing how to get a point from the text and points from the point might help.

Text   Matthew 9:9

ETS   Jesus invited Matthew to become a disciple.

ESS   Jesus invites people to become his disciples.

OSS   I want people to decide to follow Jesus.

Points   1. Following Jesus means making an initial decision.

           2. Following Jesus means growing in the relationship.

           3. Following Jesus means sharing a companionship.

           4. Following Jesus means going in his direction.

           5. Following Jesus means arriving at his destination.

The point of the sermon came from Jesus' words in Matthew 9:9, "Follow Me." The point develops an implication or enlarges on Jesus' idea of following him. None of the points came explicitly from the text, but careful examination yields the conclusion that each point relates to the point, which relates directly to the text.

The Mechanics of Development

The concept of the developmental method should be clear by now. The major divisions proceed from the one-point sentence, the essence of the sermon. Usually outlines in the developmental method contain one to seven points. Homiletical procedures used to get those points from the point include the following: asking a probing question, answering the question with sentences, and uniting the points with a unifying word.

Step #1: Asking a probing question. Getting an outline from one main point starts by asking a probing question to the essence of the sermon. Only one probing question will be used per sermon. Several possible interrogatives exist: who or whom, what, why, how, which, when, and where. After three or four probing questions have been used, the preferred question will be chosen for developing the sermon outline. Going through the probing process of three or four questions can help select the most appropriate question for the sermon development.

Step #2: Answering the question with sentences. After a probing question has been addressed to the essence of the sermon, answers begin to emerge. These answers ultimately become the major divisions, or the outline. Preliminary processes of asking the probing question and answering the question yields many responses. As many as a dozen answers could come from the probing question in the preliminary process. However, not all these answers will be used in the completed outline. When as many answers as possible have been written to the probing question, the finishing procedure should begin. This process involves examining all the answers with the purpose of eliminating, adding, revising, or combining answers so the answers represent from two to seven points related to the point.

The processed answers become the outline, or the development, of the essence of the sermon. These answers need to have several distinguishable characteristics.

- Each point should be written in a sentence in the present or future tense. No past tense sentences should be present in outlines.

- Each point should relate directly to the essence of the sermon. In some way the points need to enlarge, unfold, or develop the main point.

- Each point should have parallel construction. If the first point is a declarative sentence, subsequent points should be declarative sentences. If the first point begins with a verbal construction, subsequent points should have a verbal construction.

- Each point should be mutually exclusive. Each point will be distinct from the other points, yet be interrelated.

- Each point should be balanced. No point needs to be excessively longer or shorter than the other points.

Step #3: Uniting the points with a unifying word. When several answers have been processed into a finished outline, the mechanics of development continue with harmonizing the points with a unifying word. Such a word is either a plural noun or the plural form of a verb. In plural form, the unifying word covers all the points, and in its singular form, the unifying word characterizes each major division. For example, in a sermon from Matthew 9:9 the probing question might be: What does it mean to follow Jesus? Each point answers that question. The unifying word is meanings, which covers all five of the points, and each division represents a meaning of following Jesus. Numerous selections for unifying words exist. It always needs to be a plural word. It can be used in the statement of the major divisions, or it can be implied though not stated.

The following examples can provide additional understanding of the developmental method. Note how the outline or points come from the point.

Text   Philippians 1:3–8

ESS   Believers share a partnership in God's work.

PQ   What do believers share in common?

UW   Experiences

Development

    I. Believers share a common experience of Christ as Savior.

    II. Believers share a common experience of friendship with Jesus.

    III. Believers share a common experience of working for Christ's mission.

Text   Philippians 2:5–10

ESS   Believers need the mind of Christ.

PQ   How can believers have the mind of Christ?

UW   Ways

Development

    I. One way a believer can have Christ's mind is to be selfless.

    II. Another way a believer can have Christ's mind is to be a servant.

III. A final way a believer can have Christ's mind is to be submissive.

Text   Philippians 3:20–21

ESS   God's people live as residents of heaven on earth.

PQ   What are the distinctions of God's colony on earth?

UW   Distinctives

Development

    I. God's colony has a distinctive of a unique leader.

    II. God's colony has a distinctive of a different lifestyle.

    III. God's colony has a distinctive of a glorious future.

Text   Philippians 4:10–13

ESS   Christians can learn some valuable lessons from life's experiences.

PQ   What lessons can Christians learn from life's experiences?

UW   Lessons

Development

    I. Christians learn the lesson of adjusting their attitudes.

    II. Christians learn the lesson of keeping priorities in perspective.

    III. Christians learn the lesson of depending on inner resources.

Expanding the Major Divisions

The developmental method involves more than a point and some related points. Each major division in the outline needs to be developed further. Such amplification is called *expansion*. Many books on homiletics label the expansion as subpoints. Either expansion or subpoints could be an acceptable label, but seemingly the word *expansion* best describes what is taking place. Expansion involves enlarging or developing in greater detail the idea indicated by each major division. Actually, expansion puts content with the major division statements.

Materials used to expand major divisions may come from many sources. This material may also be arranged in many different ways, depending on the preference of the preacher, the shape of the text, and the function of the sermon. John A. Broadus gave three main methods of expanding major divisions: explanation, argumentation, and application. He called these processes the "functional elements of a sermon." Broadus also declared that illustration was largely auxiliary to these elements.[18] To enlarge or expand major divisions, skill needs to be acquired in using and arranging these functional elements. Ordinarily the same expansion type needs to be used throughout all the major points of a sermon.

Expansion by Textual Analysis

A basic way to expand major divisions comes by continued analysis of a text. The point and the points come from the text, and the expansion blocks, or subpoints, also come directly from the text. Expansion by textual analysis happens only when the text has the shape of possible expansion. Shorter texts, narratives, and various other types of text do not have the possibility of using the textual analysis method of expansion.

Expansion by textual analysis represents a traditional morphological concept of expository preaching which advocates that its major point and the subpoints must proceed directly from the text.[19] Having to shape every sermon in this manner would be a rigid assignment because not every text selected would contain the possibility of textual analysis. Nonetheless, in preaching a series of sermons from a Bible book, there will be opportunities to get both points and subpoints from texts. Such a system of expansion does not need to be viewed as *the* way but *a* way of expanding major divisions.

Getting points and subpoints from the text depends on the shape of the text. How could points and subpoints be derived from narratives or short texts? Points and subpoints come more readily when the material is longer and of a didactic nature. Points that amplify major divisions should be selected from the text. An example of the textual analysis method based on Philippians 2:5–10 follows:

I. One way a believer can have Christ's mind is to be selfless, 2:5–6.

   A. The life of Jesus Christ represents a selfless life, 2:5.

---

18. Broadus, 128–29.
19. Davis, 188.

    B. The life of Jesus Christ represents a life which does not hold on to personal privileges, 2:6.

II. Another way a believer can have Christ's mind is to be a servant, 2:7.

    A. Jesus assumed the role of a servant, 2:7a.

    B. Jesus identified with the human race so that he might serve them, 2:7b.

III. A final way a believer can have Christ's mind is to be submissive, 2:8.

    A. Jesus humbled himself to do the Father's will, 2:8a.

    B. Jesus submitted himself to the point of death, 2:8b.

Each point and subpoint in the sermon came from the text because the text had that capability.

Expansion by Explanation/Application

The functional elements provide many possibilities for getting substance for the major point, and this content may be arranged in many ways. Therefore, a prominent way of setting subpoints or expansion blocks in order is by the explanation/application arrangement. Such organization includes two large blocks of information associated with each major point. The first block of material deals with the explanation of the text as it is relates to the major division. It treats the *then* of the text and the major point. The second block of material deals with the application of the text as it relates to people's needs. It treats the *now* of the text and the major point. Almost every sermon development could be treated with the explanation/application arrangement.

Arranging expansion by explanation/application happens easier by observing an example. The points from the sermon based on Philippians 4:1–13 are expressed first by explanation and second by application.

I. Christians learn the lesson of adjusting the attitude.

    A. Paul kept a good attitude in many kinds of circumstances.

    B. Christians need to adopt a Christian attitude to the changing circumstances of life.

II. Christians learn the lesson of keeping priorities in perspective.

A. Paul kept the Gentile mission uppermost in mind.

B. Christians need to keep God's will for their lives uppermost in their minds.

III. Christians learn the lesson of depending on inner resources.

A. Paul sought God's strength to cope with life's circumstances.

B. Christians need to seek God's help for developing inner strength.

Expansion by Multiple Combinations

Two other functional elements exist in addition to explanation and application. These elements are argumentation and narration. Combining three or four of these elements would constitute another means of expanding major divisions. The arrangement could be in any order of the three or four elements. A multiple combination could be illustrated as follows:

I. Believers share a common experience of Christ as Savior.

A. In order to be a Christian, a person has to trust Christ. (Explanation)

B. Though every Christian trusts Christ, the kinds of experience vary. (Argumentation)

C. The people in Philippi became Christians in different ways. (Narration)

D. Sharing Christ means that believers have someone in common. (Application)

Expansion by Facet Observation

At times enlarging a major point occurs only by making observations about the point. With this method an expositor attempts to look at every possible angle of the major division. Every possible idea associated with the major point should be observed. Content comes as a result of facets of the major division. The facet observation method may be observed in the development of Philippians 3:20–21.

I. God's colony has the distinctive of a unique leader.

A. No other leader compares with Christ.

B. Christ possesses impressive qualifications.

C. Christ's term of office never expires.

All of the subpoints relate directly to the major divisions. The three expansions give some facets of the idea stated in the division.

The Introduction, Transitions, and Conclusion

In structuring a sermon, the parts exist for functional rather than aesthetical reasons. Instead of focusing on the beauty of sight or sound, the parts exist to communicate an idea to the audience. The prevailing purpose of the developmental method is to be noticeably holistic. The point comes from the text. The point is directed to the needs of the people. The points come from the point, and the expansion emerges from the major divisions. Each part in these structural elements plays a part in creating a one-idea sermon.

In addition to the parts already mentioned in the developmental method are three more parts: the introduction, transitions, and the conclusion. These parts have a function in the holistic concept of the sermon. The introduction brings people to the idea; transitions lead people through the idea; and the conclusion leads people from idea to action.

The Introduction of a Sermon

Ordinarily the introduction comes after the outline in sermon preparation. By coming after the outline, the preacher has an idea to introduce. Various methods and techniques may be employed to lead people to the idea.

Functions of the Introduction. The expositor needs to understand and recognize three functions of the introduction.

- The introduction *catches the interest of the hearers.* The beginning of a sermon needs to have stimulating and interesting material that would motivate listeners to hear what follows. In many cases, attention is won or lost in the introduction.

- The introduction *makes contact with the hearers.* H. Grady Davis said that the introduction "furnishes a significant encounter with the idea, the beginning of an experience shared by preacher and people."[20]

- The introduction *presents the basic idea of the sermon.* Davis wrote: "The introduction should introduce the central idea,

---

20. Davis, 188.

whether subject, proposition, message, question, or narrative. It should do this as quickly as possible, with as strict economy of means as it can. It should avoid every word that does not point toward the central idea, for any extraneous thought is liable to be a false lead."[21] The point of the sermon needs to be mentioned as skillfully and as quickly as possible. It can be either direct or subtle. Beginning a sermon without the clear function of leading people to the main idea can be a bad start.

Segments of the Introduction. Not only do expositors need to know the functions of an introduction, but they also need to know some techniques for accomplishing these purposes. In many cases the purpose of an introduction can be accomplished by preparing three interrelated segments to precede the outline: attention-getting, textual, and relational segments.

- The *attention-getting segment* leads the audience to the sermon idea. The preacher must choose from a wide range of materials which would interest the audience. A case study, an episode from literature, a personal experience, a news item, a quote, a statistic, a line of poetry, a hymn, a reference to a book, an excerpt from a conversation, a question, a humorous incident, and other sources could be used to gain attention of the audience and relate it to the sermon idea.

- The *textual segment* relates the attention-getting material and the point of the sermon to the text. The expositor states the essence of the text as skillfully as possible in this segment. Pertinent biblical information about the text could be introduced. So far, the expositor has started where people are and has taken them to the text.

- The *relational segment* relates what the text meant to what the text means to today's hearers. In this segment the essence of the sermon needs to be used as skillfully as possible. The expositor starts where the people are, takes them to the text, and finally relates the main point of the sermon to their needs.

The Transitions in a Sermon

Effective sermons move from beginning to end with clarity and smoothness. The transitions carry listeners from one aspect of the

---

21. Ibid., 187.

main idea to another without departing from the main thought. Generally there are three main areas in the developmental method where transitions need to be present:

- from introduction to development,
- from point to point within the development,
- and from development to the conclusion.

Expositors make transitions in several ways. One popular method is the *relational sentence*. It is a compound sentence in which one part of an idea is stated in the first part of the compound, and another part of an idea is stated in the second part of the compound. The relational sentence may have several stylistic formulations. One facet of an idea may be stated indirectly on one side of the compound and stated directly on the other side. It does not matter which side of the compound sentence is direct or indirect. For example, in the development of Philippians 2:5–10, the transition from point I to point II may be: We have examined one way to have Christ's mind, and now let us examine that another way to have Christ's mind is to be a servant.

Another formulation of the compound sentence is to be directly stated on both sides of the compound. Notice the example: We can have Christ's mind by being selfless, but we can also have Christ's mind by being a servant. Still another way to make a move in a sermon by the relational sentence is to be indirect on both sides of the compound. For example: We have noticed one way to have Christ's mind, and now we are ready to look at another way.

Yet another prominent means of making transitions is to use *connecting words and phrases*. Various hinge words help move from one thought to another. The most traditional type of word transitions are: *first, second, third, likewise, besides, moreover, furthermore, additionally, thus, whereas,* and *next*. In addition to words, phrases may be used to create movement. Such expressions as *in the next place, on the contrary, added to that, after that,* and *moving on to* can help build bridges for hearers from one idea to another.

Another means of making transitions is to use *questions*. The same questions used to probe the essence of the sermon could be used throughout the sermon on Philippians 2:5–10. At almost every point of movement in the sermon, the question, How can a person have Christ's mind? can be used. Asking a question leads naturally to an interactive answer with the audience.

The Conclusion of a Sermon

The ending should be an appropriate conclusion in which the expositor leads people from idea to action. Conclusions exist in sermons not just for stopping but for accomplishing a worthwhile purpose.

Functions of the conclusion. Knowing three functions of a conclusion helps with the preparation:

- The conclusion brings the sermon to an appropriate stopping place. Preparing a conclusion based on the point of the sermon can prevent the expositor from meandering to other material. It concludes, it doesn't just stop; it finishes, it doesn't just trail off.

- The conclusion applies the main idea of the sermon. The conclusion is the speaker's last chance—the final opportunity to drive home some eternal truth, to exalt a worthy ideal, or to persuade wills in performance of duty.[22] H. Grady Davis wrote: "The conclusion is the moment in which listeners can come nearest to seeing the idea whole and all at one time. It is the moment in which the issue can be seen at its clearest, felt at its sharpest, and carried back into life where, if anywhere, it must be resolved."[23]

- The conclusion drives home the objective. No sermon is complete until the challenge has been made to act on a truth. Conclusions also help move the message to an invitation to private decision and to public commitment.

Segments of the conclusion. Knowing the purpose of a conclusion would be pointless without being able to actualize the purpose. Ordinarily the intents of a conclusion can be accomplished by preparing three interrelated segments—the reproduction, application, and invitation segments.

- The *reproduction segment* gives the final view of the central thought of the sermon. The essence of the sermon needs to be rephrased in a single, brief comprehensive statement that reproduces the main truth of the entire discussion.

---

22. John Killinger, *Fundamentals of Preaching* (Philadelphia: Fortress Press, 1985), 92.

23. Davis, 192.

- The *application segment* points out the relevancy of the sermon specifically to the hearers. In this segment, the objective of the sermon needs to be used in a creative manner along with other material.
- The *invitation segment* calls hearers to act on the idea. H. H. Farmer said that "a sermon has failed, indeed it has not been a sermon, unless it carries to the serious hearer something of a claim upon, or summons to, his will."[24] On the basis of the point of the sermon and the discussion of the point, hearers will be invited to act on the idea.

The developmental method does not represent the only way to structure sermons from a Bible book, but it does represent *one* method. By using the developmental method, an expositor starts with the text, gets a main point, develops that point with points, expands those points with content, leads people to the idea with an introduction, leads them through the sermon with transitions, and leads hearers from idea to action in the conclusion. The developmental method is a basic system of structuring a sermon that has possibilities of many variations. No expositor has to choose the developmental method for every sermon because other possible structural choices may be chosen.

---

24. H. H. Farmer, *The Servant of the Word* (Philadelphia: Fortress Press, 1942), 65.

CHAPTER 13

Variations of Sermon Structures in a Bible Book

Didactic Designs
    Exegetical Paragraph Design
    Dualistic Design
    Interrogative Design
    Commentary Design
    Syllogistic Design
    Multitext Design
    Classification Design
    Sentence-Slicing Design
    Subject Design
Explorative Designs
    Unfolding Exploration
    Hegelian Exploration
    Problem-Solving Exploration
    Inductive Investigation
    Experience-Exposure Exploration
Narrative Designs
    Narration-Implication Design
    Story-Line Design
    Shared-Story Design
    Dominant-Metaphor Design
    Explained-Narration Design
    Multiple-Story Design

Structuring a sermon may be compared to packaging a product for sale. The contents have more importance than the packaging, but the container helps purchasers buy and transport the product. Coca-Cola uses many containers to market their popular soft drink. They sell their drink in six- and eight-ounce glass bottles, six- and eight-ounce plastic bottles, sixteen- and twenty-ounce bottles, two and three liter plastic bottles, and a liquid formula to be mixed in a fountain. The Coca-Cola Company affirms that the formula for their drink is the same in all manners of distribution. Consumers of Coca-Cola make personal choices of containers for the drink because they have personal preferences for Coca-Cola from their choice of container. Coke's market research shows that the public prefers diversity. Though the content is the same in all the containers, the marketing differs because of public preference.[1]

The product or content of expository preaching has been, is, and will remain the same—the truth of God's Word recorded in the Scriptures. Through the hundreds of years of preparing and proclaiming sermons, numerous wrappings or structures have been used to communicate the substance of Scripture. People living in different ages, different cultures, different mentalities, and diverse circumstances have used many different forms to package or communicate truth from the Bible. Expositors could benefit from a study of the art of preaching throughout its twenty centuries of existence.[2] In all of the years of Christian proclamation, sermon structure has never had a fixed form. The forms have varied with individuals, generations, and cultures. H. Grady Davis said: "There is no ideal or standard form which every sermon should take. The sermon is not a species with fixed and invariable characteristics, as the form of the violet, the lily, the leaf of the red oak, the twig of the weeping willow is fixed. There is no preexistent mold into which the substance of thought must be poured in order to make a sermon."[3] Through the years and in preaching today, sermon form varies from a simple commentary on a text to a complicated, multipoint presentation of a biblical truth.

1. Harold T. Bryson, "Shape Up Your Sermons," *Proclaim* (October-November-December 1991), 45.
2. E. C. Dargan, *The Art of Preaching in the Light of Its History* (Nashville: Sunday School Board of the Southern Baptist Convention, 1922).
3. H. Grady Davis, *Design for Preaching* (Philadelphia: Fortress Press, 1958), 9.

During different eras in Christian history, various sermon structures have taken center stage. For two or three hundred years after the preaching of the apostles, sermons had little or no structure. Preachers merely explained and applied texts from the Old Testament and the New Testament. Because of the influence of Augustine and his use of secular rhetoric form on sermons, another design began to occupy the stylistic, structural spotlight. Sermons began to be packaged in the secular rhetoric wrappings of introduction, body, and conclusion. For over a century, the wraps of rhetoric dominated the form of the sermon. Then the sixteenth-century Reformers turned away from the rhetorical form to a commentary style. They packaged the truth of Scriptures in the form of a verse-by-verse preaching style.

With the publication of John A. Broadus' work entitled *A Treatise on the Preparation and Delivery of Sermons* in 1870, the rhetorical method of introduction, body, and conclusion became prominent again. Since the first appearance of Broadus' work, other authors have revised his work, and still others with homiletical books have sought to keep the rhetorical method prominent. Other variations of sermon structures have appeared on the stage of sermon preparation and delivery. Preachers now have numerous choices in packaging the substance of sermons. Options now exist from the numerous variations of the traditional rhetorical form to inductive and narrative designs. Studying homiletical trends over the past fifty years yields an immense array of structural choices for a sermon.

Expositors have the benefit of studying different designs of sermons through the centuries. They also have the benefit of current writers who propose new trends for packaging sermons. Over the years, homileticians have focused primarily on the way a preacher should prepare a sermon. This perspective comes from the designer and deliverer. One of the new emphases in homiletics in the latter part of the twentieth century involves the way people listen to sermons, thus affecting the way sermons need to be designed and delivered.

In preaching a series of sermons from a Bible book, expositors must choose how to structure truth. The typical form of sermons preached from Bible books in recent decades involves the traditional three- to five-point outline taken directly from the text. In many cases, this sermon form characterizes all of the sermons in a series from a Bible book. Expositors do not have to use the same homiletical cookie cutter for every sermon in a series where a mash-down occurs on the dough of the text and out pops another three- to five-point outline similar to the previous ones.[4] Fred Craddock challenged preachers to seek variation in sermon structure: "It will not take a lengthy exposure to such studies of the lively modes of discourse used by Jesus and the early evangelists to cause the average preacher to look upon his own standardized sermon outlines with a new lack of appreciation."[5] Preachers should ask themselves, "Why should the gospel always be impaled upon the frame of Aristotelian logic?"

Challenging the standard three to five-point sermon does not mean that it is ineffective or incorrect to use it. No form for a sermon seems to be improper when the truth of the text gets across to the hearers. Any form, whether from the perspective of narrative or Aristotelian logic, used excessively might get hearers accustomed to form, and the lack of suspense might cause hearers to miss the substance. Expositors not only need to master the content of Bible books, but they also need to seek various ways to design these truths.

Discussion about sermon structure currently centers around the words *deductive* and *inductive*. These terms describe the pattern of sermon structure. The inductive approach moves from the particular to the general, while the deductive pattern involves movement from the general to the particular. Sidney Greidanus summarized the major options an expositor might choose from the inductive, deductive, or a combination of the two:

1. Deductive: The general point is stated, then the point is particularized with deductive statements. The pattern is theme—particulars (I, II, III, etc.).

2. Inductive: The particulars are presented, and the point comes near the end from the particulars. The pattern is particulars—theme.

3. Deductive/Inductive: The theme is stated, the particulars are presented, and then the theme is restated at the end. The pattern is theme—particulars—theme.

---

4. Clyde E. Fant, *Preaching for Today* (New York: Harper and Row, 1975), 110.

5. Fred B. Craddock, *As One Without Authority* (Nashville: Abingdon, 1971), 45.

4. Inductive/Deductive: The particulars are presented first, the theme is then stated, and then implications are worked out. The pattern is particulars—theme—particulars.[6]

The most traditional form for sermon structure is the didactic design. This design usually follows the deductive direction. It is a structuring system where the point is stated and various aspects about the point are developed one after the other, usually by way of points or outline. The most prominent attraction of the deductive or didactic structure is that the point of the sermon is clear from the beginning and can be reinforced throughout the sermon. Hearers generally know from the outset where the preacher is going, and they can follow the road that leads to the destination.[7]

The least traditional form for sermon structure involves an explorative design. This pattern usually follows the inductive line of reasoning. It is a systematic search of particulars or specifics to arrive at a discovery of a truth. In most cases of the explorative design or inductive reasoning, a point or a theme comes from the search. Fred Craddock, in his case for the inductive design, said that "a preaching event is a sharing in the Word, a trip not a destination, an arriving at a point for drawing conclusions and not handing over the conclusion."[8] Craddock shared how preachers make explorations in their study in the pursuit of a sermon subject. He advocated that the preacher should not hand over conclusions to hearers but give them an opportunity to make explorations for discovery of truth on their own.[9]

According to George M. Bass, the form of preaching turned a "narrative corner" in the beginning of the 1970s.[10] A sermon idea may be shaped in the form of a narrative of a story involving events, persons, actions, and words. The idea or the point of the sermon is generally embodied in a structure of events and persons rather than in a structure of verbal generalization. Like the didactic and the explorative designs, the narrative design allows for a number of

---

6. Sidney Greidanus, *The Modern Preacher and the Ancient Text: Interpreting and Preaching Biblical Literature* (Grand Rapids: William B. Eerdmans, 1988), 142–44.

7. Ibid., 143.

8. Craddock, 146.

9. Ibid., 57.

10. George M. Bass, *The Song and the Story* (Lima, Ohio: C. S. S. Publishing, 1984), 83.

varieties in sermon construction. Expositors may choose from many narrative designs.

In preaching a series of sermons from a Bible book, an expositor does not have to structure sermons from just one category. Sermons from the didactic, explorative, or narrative perspectives could be used in a series. Choice of structural designs most often depends on the nature of the audience, the personality of the preacher, and the shape of the text. Generally speaking, most expositors use the same structural design for almost every sermon. Many of the texts in Bible books have the possibility of being structured in several different ways. Hearers generally adapt to different designs, and they probably would welcome structural variety. Examining and using new kinds of structural packaging for biblical truth will help the expositor have structural variety. A structural style does not make a sermon more or less biblical. If the theme or main idea is biblical, the structure exists to expand the one main truth. Sermon structures may be grouped in three design categories: didactic, explorative, and narrative. Within these general categories are several specific designs. The substance or content of sermons remains constant, but packaging may vary.

Didactic Designs

The didactic manner of designing sermons ordinarily follows the deductive line of reasoning. The theme usually comes at the beginning of the sermon and is subsequently divided into logical points and subpoints. The theme comes from the text, and the points that develop the theme come directly from the text. Didactic design has been the most prominent style for structuring sermons for over fifteen hundred years. It is a manner of designing sermons which has existed since Augustine married secular rhetoric to the art of preaching in the fourth century. Through the years, the didactic design has had many variations.

Exegetical Paragraph Design

Ordinarily the exegetical paragraph design goes under the label of an expository sermon because of the length of the text and the source for major divisions. The exegetical design structure usually requires several verses for a text, and the theme and main division come from the unit of verses. Andrew W. Blackwood and others advocated that an expository sermon was one based on a text longer than two or three consecutive verses.[11] Brown, Clinard, and North-cutt, along with other writers on preaching, stressed that an expository sermon was not only based on a biblical passage, but the major points and the first subpoints came directly from the text.[12] Though the exegetical paragraph design represents just one form possible in a series of sermons from a Bible book, it is most often called an expository sermon.

The length of a text or the source of major points and subpoints does not determine whether a sermon is expository. All sermons, no matter the structural form they take, are expository because of the exposure of a biblical truth and a human need.

Preaching a series of sermons from a Bible book does not mean that every sermon in the series will fit the exegetical design. Such a venture would be impossible because of the nature and length of texts in a Bible book. Furthermore, using the exegetical paragraph design exclusively in a series would create a sameness of structure. Perhaps more structural variety needs to be employed. But the exegetical paragraph design is an excellent way for structuring sermons. It represents a sermon shape which takes a paragraph of Scripture, gives the paragraph a theme, and then secures points directly from the text to elaborate or develop the theme.

The exegetical paragraph design appears to be the most popular structural form used by expositors who preach a series from a Bible book. It has been used by popular expositors such as G. Campbell Morgan, Alexander Maclaren, and F. B. Meyer. It continues to be a popular style in the latter half of the twentieth century. John R. W. Stott, former rector of All Souls Church in London, England, structured most of his sermons according to the exegetical paragraph design. In a series of nineteen messages from Galatians, he structured all of the sermons along the exegetical paragraph design. In a sermon from Galatians 1:11–24 centered on the apostle Paul, he used the following structure:

    I.   What happened before his conversion, 1:13–14

    II. What happened at his conversion, 1:15–16a

---

11. A. W. Blackwood, *Preaching from the Bible* (Nashville: Abingdon Press, 1951), 38.

12. H. C. Brown, Jr., H. Gordon Clinard, and Jesse J. Northcutt, *Steps to the Sermon: A Plan for Sermon Preparation* (Nashville: Broadman Press, 1963), 134–35.

III.   What happened after his conversion, 1:16b–24[13]

In all of Stott's sermons from Galatians, he had a paragraph for the length of the text, a theme for the paragraph, and points taken directly from the text to develop the theme.

R. Kent Hughes, pastor of College Church in Wheaton, Illinois, preached twenty-one sermons from Colossians. He used the exegetical paragraph design in all of the messages. In a sermon entitled "The Supreme Reconciliation," based on Colossians 1:19–23, he outlined the sermon with points from the text.

I.   The Father's reconciling pleasure, 1:19–20a

II.   The Father's reconciling method, 1:20b,22a

III.   The Father's reconciling purpose, 1:21–22

IV.   The Father's reconciling condition, 1:23[14]

In other series of sermons from James, Ephesians, and Mark, Hughes used the exegetical paragraph predominantly.

Warren Wiersbe, a popular preacher of sermons from a Bible book, also used the exegetical paragraph design predominantly. In Wiersbe's series of sermons from Galatians, he used twelve texts. He structured each sermon according to the exegetical paragraph design. His sermon "Bad News About the Good News," based on Galatians 1:1–10, had the following outline:

I.   He explains his authority, 1:1–5

II.   He expresses his anxiety, 1:6–7

III.   He exposes his adversaries, 1:8–10[15]

Brian L. Harbour, a Southern Baptist expositor, frequently preaches series of sermons from Bible books. In a series of messages from Ephesians, Harbour used a similar structural style of Stott, Hughes, and Wiersbe. In a sermon based on Ephesians 4:1–16 entitled "Growing Up in Christ," he used the following exegetical paragraph design:

I.   Developing the character of the Christian life, 4:1–3

II.   Discovering the commonalities of the Christian life, 4:4–6

III.   Demonstrating the calling of the Christian life, 4:7–13

---

13. John R. W. Stott, "The Message of Galatians," in *The Bible Speaks Today* (Downers Grove, Ill.: InterVarsity Press, 1968), 29–37.

14. R. Kent Hughes, *Colossians and Philemon: The Supremacy of Christ in Preaching the Word* (Westchester, Ill.: Crossway Books, 1989), 35–41.

15. Warren W. Wiersbe, *Be Free: An Expository Study of Galatians* (Wheaton, Ill.: Victor Books, 1978), 10–22.

IV. Displaying the culmination of the Christian life, 4:14–16[16]
Harbour used the same exegetical paragraph design for all thirteen
sermons from Ephesians.

Expositors need to make an objective evaluation of the exegetical
paragraph design. This structural system has much to commend it.
The points come directly from the text, and the hearers can follow
the flow of the sermon in a didactic manner. A unit or paragraph of
Scripture comes under the heading of one theme, and the theme
receives support from points directly from the text. The exegetical
paragraph design carries with it an apparent authoritative source
for sermon content. All of these factors seem to make a clear,
coherent structure that provides the hearers with a solid, logical
framework for understanding a sermon.

Yet the exegetical paragraph is often overused. Hearers get
accustomed to the same structural style. Some expositors at times
force a text into the exegetical paragraph design. When preaching
from a Bible book, an expositor can look for appropriate opportunities to use the exegetical paragraph design, but it does not have to
be used for every sermon in the series. Other didactic options exist.

Dualistic Design

A prominent method of structuring sermons from a didactic perspective is the dualistic design. It is a sermon structure with two
major points and has several variations. The dualistic design
involves a problem and a solution. The first major point involves a
thorough discussion of a prominent problem, and the second major
point follows with consideration of a probable solution to the problem. As an expositor prepares sermons from a Bible book, opportunities may arise to use the problem-solution formation. For
example, in 1 Kings 19:1–18 the subject of depression could be
treated with the following structure:

I. People have a problem with depression.

II. People can get help for depression.[17]

The dualistic design may also take a contrasting direction. In
such an outline the second major division differs with the first
major division. Often the shape of many texts involve contrast, and

---

16. Brian L. Harbour, "Living Abundantly," in *Living the Christian Faith*
(Nashville: Broadman Press, 1992), 60–71.

17. Bryson, 43.

the contrasting dualistic design makes a natural way for structuring a sermon. Notice the contrasting structure from Psalm 1.

    I. The picture of the godly life is presented, 1:1–3.

    II. There is the picture of the ungodly life, 1:4–6.

Closely related to the problem-solution structure is the question-answer dualistic design. The first major division poses a question, and the second division seeks to answer the question. In designing a sermon from Matthew 16:23–28, a possible arrangement could be:

    I. Who do people think Jesus is?

    II. What I think of Jesus.[18]

The English preacher F. W. Robertson (1816–1853) was a master craftsman of the dualistic design. E. C. Dargan described Robertson's two-point sermons: "He made a careful expository study of the Scriptures, usually taking full notes. The division is nearly always twofold. He was fond of thinking in pairs and antithesis."[19] James R. Blackwood also said: "In choosing his text and in outlining the message, Robertson laid stress on the paragraph of balance. Partly for this reason, he excelled in writing a sermon with only two main points."[20] Two of F. W. Robertson's sermon outlines demonstrate the use of the dualistic design:

The Irreparable Past

Mark 14:41–42

I. The irreparable past

II. The available future[21]

Joseph's Forgiveness of His Brothers

Genesis 50:15–21

    I. The petition of his brothers

    II. Joseph's forgiveness[22]

The dualistic design does not need to be forced on a text. When the shape of the text permits and the subject allows, the dualistic

---

18. Ibid.

19. E. C. Dargan, *A History of Preaching*, vol. 2 (New York: George H. Doran, 1912), 523.

20. James R. Blackwood, *The Soul of Frederick W. Robertson* (New York: Harper and Brothers, 1947), 105.

21. Frederick W. Robertson, *Sermons Preached at Brighton* (New York: Harper and Brothers, 1871), 426–36.

22. Ibid., 745–51.

design will be appropriate. Like every other type of sermon structure, the dualistic design could be forced, and it could be overworked in the course of one series of sermons from a Bible book.

Interrogative Design

Another popular design is the art of structuring an outline with every major division stated in the form of a question. This interrogative design can help explore a subject in an interesting and indirect manner. Like most other structural types, it is built around one main idea taken from a text. Questions relating to the main idea arise, and selected questions become the major divisions.

The interrogative design seems more occasional than frequent. Only a few preachers select this design for most of their sermons. Guy H. King, a competent expositor, used the interrogative design in a sermon entitled "In," meaning "In the faith" based on 2 Corinthians 13:5.

    I. Are you in?

    II. Are you far in?

    III. Are you getting others in?[23]

King regularly used the exegetical paragraph design, but occasionally used the interrogative design.

The interrogative design offers a good option for structure when preparing a series of sermons from a Bible book. Usually when a biblical theme needs to be structured, the interrogative design is an excellent choice. For example, notice the structural treatment of "The New Birth" based on John 3:1–15:

    I. Who needs the new birth?

    II. What does it mean to be born again?

    III. How can one be born again?

    IV. What happens when one is born again?[24]

Interrogative outlines create a dialogical interaction with the preacher and the audience. If the questions asked in each major division assume what hearers want to know about a subject, mental dialogue occurs. Using interrogatives as major divisions also helps facilitate movement and transition within a sermon. Audiences expect answers to follow questions. Perhaps the greatest problem

---

23. Guy H. King, *Brought In: Talks on the Positive Side of Christian Experience* (London: Marshall, Morgan, and Scott, 1949), 1–6.

24. Bryson, 43.

with an interrogative design is that it can lead to idea explosions where each point or question becomes a subject within itself. Separate questions, if not shaped carefully toward one point, deprive a sermon of unity.

Commentary Design

With the commentary design, an expositor reads a portion of a text and makes comments on the words, phrases, and grammatical constructions. The name for such a plan comes from the format design of a Bible commentary, which has explanations of words and phrases in the verses. After making remarks on one verse or a portion of the text, the expositor moves to the next verse and makes comments. Such a scheme resembles the exegetical paragraph without the points or outline of the section of Scripture. The commentary design usually has explanation, application, exhortation, argumentation, and illustration. Faris D. Whitesell called the commentary design "the running commentary" method.[25]

The commentary design existed before the influence of secular rhetoric on the structure of the sermon. During worship in the synagogue, the Jews practiced the systematic reading of existing Old Testament Scriptures; they also initiated the practice of making comments on the selected readings of the day. The comments came to be known as "the homily." Most books on preaching refer to the homily as a structural form, but actually the homily existed before secular rhetoric made its impact on the form of sermons. More than likely, the word *homily* came from the comments on the Scripture reading. The Greek word *homologomen* could be the word of origin for the term *homily*. A literal translation of *homologomen* could be "to say the same thing." The term *homily* could have referred to the function of the comments rather than to the form of the comments. If so, the function of the homily was to say the same thing in the comments that was said in the Scriptures. Actually, every sermon should be a homily in whatever form the comments take because the meaning of the text also needs to be conveyed in the sermon.

Effective preachers through the centuries have used the commentary design. John Chrysostom (347–407) usually followed the

---

25. Faris D. Whitesell, *Power in Expository Preaching* (Westwood, N.J.: Fleming H. Revell, 1967), 21.

order of the text in something like a verse-by-verse design. At times he digressed from the commentary on the text to insert comparisons, but in most cases he returned to commenting on the text. Martin Luther (1483–1546) preached by simply explaining and applying the text as he went. John Calvin (1509–1564) used the running commentary method in preaching through many books of the Bible. The commentaries of Luther and Calvin are composed of sermons following the commentary design. Faris D. Whitesell evaluated the commentary design when he said: "Regardless of the defects in structure and unity, it has a noble history."[26]

The commentary design represents one of several variations of the didactic structure. Like all of the other designs, the commentary design has its positive and negative qualities. Positively, the system focuses on exposing or teaching the truths of the Bible. Abundant information of biblical truth usually comes with this method. Many people gravitate to the didactic presentation of Scripture. Negatively, the commentary design leads to a proliferation of ideas without a strong concentration on one idea. Other people in an audience may not relate to a didactic presentation but hear sermons best when there is a focus on a single truth from Scripture. Like any system of structuring a sermon, the commentary design is one way among many of communicating biblical truth. The commentary design does not make sermons more biblical. Expositors who choose to use this design will need to study thoroughly the techniques of explanation, application, argumentation, and illustration.

Syllogistic Design

The syllogism can be traced to Aristotle's work *Organon*. The syllogistic design moves from a general truth to a specific truth. A simple syllogism consists of three statements: the major premise, the minor premise, and the conclusion. In a syllogistic sermon design, the first two major points will be the two premises, and the third point will be the conclusion; thus the syllogistic design will always be three main points. Donald L. Hamilton in his work *Homiletical Handbook* gave a good discussion of the syllogistic method and formulated two good examples.

---

26. Ibid., 27.

The Claim of Jesus

Mark 2:1–12

I. Forgiveness of sin comes from God only, 2:7. (Major premise)

II. Jesus claimed to forgive sin, 2:10–12. (Minor premise)

III. Therefore, Jesus claimed to be God. (Conclusion)

Being Led by the Spirit

Galatians 5:16–26

I. Christians have the choice of walking in the flesh or walking in the Spirit, 5:16. (Major premise)

II. Christians must not walk in the flesh, 5:24. (Minor premise)

III. Therefore, Christians must choose to be led by the Spirit. (Conclusion)[27]

If stated correctly, the conclusion will always be true if the two premises are true and are properly related.

Multitext Design

The multitext design chooses a subject and then develops the subject by points from several Scripture selections. James S. Stewart shaped many of his sermons with a multitext design. He used the following structure based on the theme "He Is Able."

I. He is able to succor those who are tempted (Heb. 2:18).

II. He is able to save to the uttermost (Heb. 7:25).

III. He is able to keep you from falling (Jude 24).

IV. He is able to subdue all things to Himself (Phil. 3:21).

V. He is able to keep that which I have committed (2 Tim. 1:12).

VI. He is able to do more than we can ever think (Eph. 3:20).[28]

While preaching from a Bible book, an expositor could select a subject from the book and then use selections from other books to develop the subject.

Classification Design

The classification design divides people, structures, or needs into different classes, or types. A typical pattern points out different

---

27. Donald L. Hamilton, *Homiletical Handbook* (Nashville: Broadman Press, 1992), 92. [Wording has been altered by the author.]

28. James S. Stewart, *The Wind of the Spirit* (Nashville: Abingdon Press, 1968), 158–69.

ways an issue can be met. For example, an expositor may preach "How to Meet Trouble" based on 2 Corinthians 4:8–9 and classify how people handle trouble: Some get better. Others give up. Still others keep going, upheld by their faith.[29]

Expositors throughout history have designed sermons by classification. Many of Jesus' parables involve some type of classification: the talents, the sower, and the good Samaritan. Some of the best-loved fairy tales have divided things and people into classes. "Goldilocks and the Three Bears" has the recurring classification with the first porridge being too hot, the second too cold, and the third just right; the first bed too hard, the second too soft, and the third just right.[30]

One popular sermon comes from 1 Corinthians 2:14–3:10 where Paul described three kinds of persons. The outline for a sermon may follow Paul's classification of people.

I. The natural or unregenerate person

II. The carnal Christian

III. The spiritual Christian

Halford Luccock cited John Hayes Holmes' sermon on the three kinds of people among the Israelites journey through the desert.

I. One group wanted to go back to Egypt.

II. The second group was satisfied with where they were.

III. The smallest group wanted to go forward.[31]

The classification design creates interest in helping the audience think through types, identify with people's actions, and choose among several options.

Sentence-Slicing Design

The sentence-slicing design selects one sentence for a text and slices that sentence into parts that relate to a common theme. The parts divided from the text become major divisions of the sermon. Generally the shape of the text determines whether this design may be used. It resembles the exegetical paragraph except that the text is shorter. It also resembles the commentary design with the addition of labels for words or phrases within the text. Notice the sentence-

---

29. Halford E. Luccock, *In the Minister's Workshop* (Nashville: Abingdon-Cokesbury Press, 1954), 138.

30. Ibid., 138–39.

31. Ibid., 139.

slicing design from Matthew 16:24 on what it means to follow Jesus.

I. Contemplation—"If any man will come after me."

II. Renunciation—"Let him deny himself."

III. Dedication—"And take up his cross."

IV. Invitation—"And follow me."

Homileticians have called the sentence-slicing design the textual sermon. According to David L. Larsen "the textual sermon consists of a verse or two in which the development of the main points fall right out of the word order in the text."[32]

Subject Design

Perhaps the most prominent method for designing a sermon from the deductive, didactic perspective is the subject design. An expositor determines a subject from a selected text or texts and then offers a sequence of statements that enlarge or support the subject. H. Grady Davis called such a design "a subject discussed." Davis contended that the main or central idea is the subject, and the main points constitute a "distributed predicate." The points are necessary to enlarge and to make the subject complete.[33]

John A. Broadus proposed a subject design for sermons. Broadus suggested that an expositor should get a plan or a focal idea for a sermon. Broadus called this process the subject. Then Broadus proposed that the preacher devise some divisions about the subject. In Broadus' concept, the body or the outline of a sermon was called the discussion of a subject.[34]

In most cases throughout Christian history, homileticians have labeled the subject design the topical outline. Ordinarily in this system, a subject suggested by a text will be chosen. The subject becomes the focal point of a sermon, and ideas related to that subject become the points. Note the following example:

Let's Get Serious About Sin

Romans 3:23

I. The reality of sin

II. The regrets over sin

---

32. David L. Larsen, *The Authority of Preaching: Identifying the Issues in Preaching Today* (Grand Rapids: Baker Book House, 1989) 32.

33. Davis, 141–45.

34. John A. Broadus, *A Treatise on the Preparation and Delivery of Sermons* (New York: A. C. Armstrong and Son, 1889), 257–77.

III.   The results of sin

IV.   The remedy for sin

In the example, the subject of sin originated in Romans 3:23. The four divisions or points come from a discussion of the subject of sin. The topic was derived from the text, but the points came from the subject. The subject was divided and treated according to its own nature. Donald Grey Barnhouse and D. Martyn Lloyd-Jones frequently took a small biblical text and brought various facets together to discuss a subject.

Using different didactic structures in preaching from a Bible book has its positive qualities. It opens options for didactic diversity and prohibits having to structure every sermon in a series the exact same way. Didactic designs are biblical because the main point, subject, theme, or proposition comes from the text either directly or indirectly. The expositor can choose to have the points of discussion come directly from the text, or the expositor can choose to focus on a subject taken from the text and get an outline from the subject. In both cases, getting the main point from the text makes the sermon biblical. These didactic structures allow for a logical, understandable packaging of the content for preaching. Sidney Greidanus commended the didactic approach when he said, "It makes for a clear, coherent structure that provides the hearers with a solid, logical framework for understanding the sermon."[35] Different expositors gravitate primarily to one or two of the nine didactic choices. No series of sermons of a Bible book has to have every structure in the same didactic manner.

The didactic structure is not without its critics. Don Wardlaw equated the didactic form with Greek rhetoric. Wardlaw contended that the earliest Christian preaching was narrative, and when Christianity spread into the Greco-Roman world, it took the form of secular rhetoric, which means to marshal an argument in logical sequence.[36] Fred B. Craddock critiqued the didactic structural design because it lacks democracy; the preacher hands over conclusions to hearers rather than allowing them to check out particulars and arrive at a conclusion for themselves.[37] David Buttrick in his work *Homiletic: Moves and Structures*, objected to the deductive, or

---

35. Greidanus, 146.

36. Don Wardlaw, "Introduction: The Need for New Shapes," in *Preaching Biblically* (Philadelphia: Westminster Press, 1983), 11–25.

37. Craddock, 57.

didactic, form because he thought along a story line rather than an argument in logical sequence.[38] These critics and other evaluators of sermon structures prefer an inductive or narrative perspective for the sermon. No ideal or fixed structure exists for packaging biblical content. Expositors need to look into many possible options for pouring the substance of a sermon. With nine didactic options in mind, the expositor can proceed to examine five explorative designs and six narrative designs.

Explorative Designs

The explorative manner of designing sermons ordinarily follows the inductive line of reasoning. With this design, the thoughts move from the particulars of experiences that have a familiar ring in the listener's ear to a general truth or conclusion. Sermons designed inductively usually sustain interest and engage the audience in exploration. The inductive or explorative design does not have points any more than a narrative or story does, but it does have a point or a main idea. Preaching using the explorative design gets the point across by allowing listeners to explore particulars and come to conclusions by their own reasoning.[39] Explorative designs begin with the particulars of life experience and point toward principles, concepts, and conclusions. The expositor explores with the people before telling what is found. It involves a quest for discovery. It can disarm, interest, and involve the people in exploration and capitalize on the process of learning by experience.[40] Rarely does a pure inductive sermon exist, but the explorative design is an approach which is primarily inductive. Several explorative options seem to be available for the expositor who wishes to vary from didactic designs.

Unfolding Exploration

The unfolding exploration design affords opportunity for inductive reasoning. The system begins like the blooming of a flower where a bud appears and, step by step through a series of openings,

38. David Buttrick, *Homiletic: Moves and Structures* (Philadelphia: Fortress Press, 1987), 403–4.

39. Haddon Robinson, *Biblical Preaching: The Development and Delivery of Expository Messages* (Grand Rapids: Baker Book House, 1980), 125.

40. Ralph L. Lewis with Gregg Lewis, *Inductive Preaching: Helping People Listen* (Westchester, Ill.: Crossway Books, 1983), 32.

comes to a full-blown conclusion. Halford Luccock called the unfolding design the "ladder sermon." It takes an audience from point to point like the rungs of a ladder. It is a design suited to argument, persuasion, and appeal to reason.[41] Actually the discussion of the unfolding design could fit in the didactic designs or in the explorative designs because it represents an inductive-deductive approach to reasoning. Merrill Abbey likened the unfolding design to a telescope where each point picks up the previous term and adds some further thought.[42] Whether the metaphor is a flower, a ladder, or a telescope, the important aspect is that the points progress from the previous point on the way to a final point which is the conclusion.

The unfolding design seems to be used sparingly by expositors. That neglect is unfortunate because it allows a reasonable, explorative way to present biblical truth. This structural system creates suspense until the end because the conclusion does not come until the final point. Perhaps the following example will be helpful.

Handling Life's Problems

Matthew 17:14–20

I. All of us have problems.

II. All of us make mistakes with our problems.

III. All of us can have help with our problems.

The structure unfolds from a basic premise that every person has problems. No sermon needs to stop with this proposition, so the structure proceeds to share how people make mistakes with their problems. Neither point 1 nor point 2 represents a conclusion. Therefore, the final point came to a conclusion that everyone can have help with their problems. The point progressed from a previous point on the way to a final conclusion.

Hegelian Exploration

Hegelian design follows the dialectic progression through thesis, antithesis, and synthesis. The first point presents a truth from one view, then forms its opposite in the second point; the third and final point presents an angle that gathers strength from both points. The explorative process begins with the expositor presenting a thesis

---

41. Luccock, 134–35.

42. Merrill R. Abbey, *Communication in Pulpit and Parish* (Philadelphia: Westminster Press, 1972), 166.

generally acceptable to the congregation; then the probing process adds an antithesis about which some in the audience may disagree. Finally the expositor arrives in an explorative process with a synthesis generally accepted by most of the congregation. An example of a Hegelian outline has been cited by V. L. Stanfield:

The Nature of the Gospel

Romans 1:16

    I. The gospel is personal.

   II. The gospel is social.

  III. The gospel is both personal and social.[43]

The Hegelian method is especially useful in presenting biblical truth because the structural system starts where the people are and then proceeds to explore a subject on the way to a conclusion.

Problem-Solving Exploration

H. A. Overstreet in his book, *Influencing Human Behavior*, listed "the chase technique" as a valuable means of communicating with an audience.[44] Such a system, in essence, involves getting an audience to explore a problem and to pursue a solution rather than merely announcing the result to them. Hearing a conclusion and then proceeding to pursue a subject leaves an audience with little to do at the outset of the sermon but accept or reject the conclusion. When a speaker is telling an audience, instead of inviting them to think with the expositor, the sermon is static. An explorative design would be to imply, "Let's think together and try to find a solution to this problem." Such an attitude possesses the power to win careful and continuous attention because it has a mutual explorative quality.[45] Probably a better name for this technique would be a problem-solving exploration rather than Overstreet's term "the chase technique."

Critics of the explorative designs often think that such techniques as the problem-solving method detract from the authority of biblical revelation. Instead, exploration represents a method of persuading people to accept for themselves the authority of biblical revelation. Exploration techniques have authority in proclamation, but they come across as an expositor without authority. The form

---

43. John A. Broadus, *On the Preparation and Delivery of Sermons*, rev. V. L. Stanfield (San Francisco: Harper and Row, 1979), 71.

44. Quoted in Luccock, *In the Minister's Workshop*, 143.

45. Ibid., 143–44.

of a problem-solving design could be: Is it this? No. Is it this? No. Is it another thing? Yes.[46]

Clarence Edward Macartney, pastor of First Presbyterian Church in Pittsburgh, Pennsylvania, in the early 1900s, used the problem-solving exploration frequently. In a collection of sermons entitled *The Greatest Words in the Bible and Human Speech*, most of the sermons had the problem-solving structure. In one sermon, "The Most Beautiful Word," Macartney began with a question, "What is the most beautiful word, in the Bible or out of it, spoken in heaven, or upon earth?"[47] He continued the development of the sermon, exploring many answers until he arrived at his conclusion: The most beautiful word is *forgiveness*.

Oddly enough, Bruce Thieleman, pastor of First Presbyterian Church in Pittsburgh, more recently, affirmed that his favorite technique for planning a sermon was the problem-solving method.[48] Thieleman designed many sermons based on moves within the problem-solving technique. In the first move, the problem which needed to be addressed would be stated. Then the next move in the sermon involved exploring some possible solutions to the problem. The last move in the sermon was the presentation of a solution, which seemed more biblical to the problem.[49]

Inductive Investigation

Ralph Lewis writing with his son, Gregg, proposed a system of preaching that may be called inductive investigation. Lewis began sermon design with some particular life experiences and moved toward a conclusion. He advocated exploring first before declaring conclusions. Lewis contended that such a preaching style is a "quest for discovery."[50] It involves an expositor's attempt to lead rather than push. Inductive investigation has the capacity of interesting the audience and involving the hearers from the beginning to the end of a sermon, capitalizing on the psychological process of learning from experience.

---

46. Ibid., 144.

47. Clarence Edward Macartney, *The Greatest Words in the Bible and Human Speech* (Nashville: Cokesbury Press, 1938), 21.

48. Bruce Thieleman, "The Planning of Preaching," *Message for the Moment,* sermon delivered at First Presbyterian Church, Pittsburgh, Pennsylvania.

49. Ibid.

50. Lewis, 32.

The inductive investigation sermon differs from the didactic, deductive designs. Inductive sermons start with specifics such as facts, statistics, illustrations, experiences, and examples. Deductive sermons begin with propositions, assertions, conclusions, or principles. Induction goes beyond the specifics with which it starts. Deductive designs define, dissect, defend, or delimit the major premise proposed. Inductive examples precede and lead to conclusions, and deductive examples follow and support conclusions already made. In an inductive preaching format, proposition, assertions, or declaration flow out of concrete or illustrative material. Simply stated, the deductive expositor begins with a truth and then seeks to develop that truth. The inductive expositor uses particulars to help listeners come to a conclusion.[51]

Generally speaking, most expositors have been trained in the deductive design for structuring sermons. Few books on homiletics have helped with the practical matter of designing an inductive sermon. Lewis gave a basic rule of arranging an inductive sermon when he urged to begin with specific instances that serve as evidence leading to a conclusion. This is in contrast to a deductive outline that starts with points and these points are followed by examples and evidence.[52] Fred Craddock gave a visual picture of the traditional deductive design.

Introduction
Body
   I.
      A.
         1.
         2.
   II.
Conclusion[53]
He also sought to give a visual picture of the inductive design.
         1.
         2.
      A.
         1.
         2.
     B.
  I.[54]

---

51. Ibid., 81.
52. Ibid.
53. Craddock, 152.
54. Ibid.

The intended impression for the inductive sermon designer is movement up to, rather than down from, a point.

Lewis helped readers understand how to design an inductive investigation sermon. He suggested the starting point as "Common Ground," which could be a life-related experience, a problem, a question, a need, or a conflict of some other tension point. From the point of common ground Lewis suggested inductive sermon designers should use numerous inductive ingredients and explore them before coming to a conclusion. Some of the inductive ingredients that could be used are life experiences, biographical cases, narrative, analogy, case studies, Bible incidents, dialogue, questions, comparisons, and numerous other inductive ingredients. From these specifics, the expositor moves from evidence to a conclusion. Using inductive exploration, Lewis designed a sermon entitled "Deliver Us" based on Matthew 6:13. His movements were as follows:

Move 1   Facts, anecdotes, and reminders of needs of deliverance.

Move 2   Numerous anecdotes of contemporary deliverance.

Move 3   Examples of people delivered from the Bible and history.

Move 4   Conclusion that people can be delivered.[55]

The key to Lewis' concept of inductive investigation centers on moving from specifics to general by using inductive ingredients and by involving the listeners in the process of moving through the sermon.

Experience-Exposure Exploration

Closely akin to all four previous explorative designs is an arrangement used by Fred Craddock, which may be called an experience-exposure exploration. The key to understanding Craddock's method of planning a sermon centers primarily in the word *experience*. These particular life experiences, unlike the traditional deductive method of illustrating a truth, furnish the point of the sermon. While listening to several concrete experiences in a sermon, Craddock thought listeners could identify with truth, given new perspective, and make conclusions for themselves. These experiences are not to be regarded as illustrative of something, but they consist of the "stuff of the sermon." Like a play, the plot is in the narrative.

---

55. Ibid., 167–82.

Likewise, Craddock contends that particular experiences relating to a single biblical contemporary idea will yield a point to an audience.[56]

Close study of Fred Craddock's theory of preaching in *As One Without Authority* and *Preaching*, as well as his published and recorded sermons, will disclose many experience-exposure arrangements of sermons. Usually Craddock shared about a half dozen or more experiences that related to a single theme based on a Bible text. He started the sermon by sharing a life experience and related it to the text. He then proceeded to give exposure to experiences that most of the time related to a truth in the Bible text. After sharing these experiences, listeners generally had the main theme of the sermon in mind without having been told, "The theme of the sermon is."

Nothing helps an expositor learn the experience-exposure exploration any better than a good example of such a sermon design. Craddock preached a sermon entitled "When the Roll Is Called Down Here" based on Romans 16:1–16. His experience exposures were as follows:

Experience 1: The call of the roll of 240 prospective jurors in Dekalb County, Georgia

Experience 2: The sociological profile of the names in Romans 16:1–16

Experience 3: The quilt with the names of all the church members which Craddock's church made for him

Experience 4: The ministry element of some people mentioned in Romans 16:1–16

Experience 5: The list of the names on the Viet Nam War Memorial

Experience 6: The invitation to write a list of names of people for whom listeners are thankful

Experience 7: The experiences of the baptism candidates in Craddock's church

Experience 8: The showing of the list made by the listeners to Peter in Heaven[57]

---

56. Ibid., 62.

Early in the sermon, listeners could enjoy Craddock's interesting and humorous manner of telling about lists of names. As the sermon move, most listeners could see that Craddock was emphasizing the importance of God's people in the lives of God's people. Though he never made such a conclusion, almost everyone could get the point. The message came from the stories rather than the stories being used to support the message. Craddock exposed one experience after another with the main point becoming more evident with each disclosed experience.

Using explorative designs in preaching a series from a Bible book has positive qualities. It allows a structural choice different from the deductive perspective. Explorative designs are concrete. Expositors seek to communicate with the people whose experiences are concrete. People live inductively, not deductively. Instead of general talk about the reality of death, the explorative designs have particulars, such as "Mr. Jones' son is dying," and the listeners give attention. Explorative designs also allow hearers to participate in the movement of the sermon and arrive at a conclusion on their own. Explorative designs allow for a fresh way to hear biblical truth, removing the listeners' predictability of what point is coming next. Explorative designs seem to have the element of unpredictable surprise. The explorative design comes across as Craddock intended, "as one without authority." This type of sermon arrangement is not so direct. God's Word comes across, but it comes in a more indirect manner to the listeners.

The explorative methodology comes under heavy criticism, especially from those expositors deeply entrenched in the deductive perspective. One noticeable pitfall is that preachers can become so enchanted with the explorative design that they disdain or eliminate the use of didactic designs. They make the same mistake of those who are married to the deductive forms—using one to the exclusion of the others. Some criticize inductive forms saying that they do not have biblical authority. The critics raise the question whether the inductive method makes too much dependent on the listeners. Objectors think that too much subjectivity resides in the inductive form where they say there can be as many truths as listeners in the room. Closely akin to all the objections is the criticism of

---

57. Fred B. Craddock, "When the Roll Is Called Down Here," *Preaching Today*, sound cassette, no. 50.

too much indirectness and not enough directness in the inductive forms. Actually no structural form can guarantee a decision.

The explorative designs are only one way, among others, to arrange sermons. The explorative design options allow expositors to choose another way to communicate biblical truth. God's Word never changes, but the way of presenting truth can change. With many didactic and explorative designs in mind, an expositor has still another set of options for structuring sermons with choices from the narrative designs.

Narrative Designs

Narrative designs for sermons do not represent a new creation for communicating God's Word. Ancient Israel told stories around campfires of God's involvement in history. Prophets gained the interest of audiences by telling stories. Jesus preached and taught often with stories called parables. The apostles and early disciples preached by reciting stories of the deeds of God and the words and works of Christ. As time passed, other forms began to emerge for communicating God's Word. Augustine in the fourth century used the techniques of Greek rhetoric to preach God's Word. Such a craft emphasized an introduction, points and subpoints, and a conclusion with a few illustrations placed to illuminate the points and to interest the audience.

Narrative designs have had times of resurgence throughout the twenty centuries of Christian proclamation. George Bass said "preaching began to turn 'the narrative corner' at the beginning of the 1970s."[58] Clyde E. Fant thought the narrative turn in sermon designs was due to laypersons' discontent with redundant means of communicating God's Word.[59] The emergence of story or narrative as a technique for preaching has found an enthusiastic reception, evidenced by the publication of books on the subject. Writing in 1958 as a homiletician ahead of his time, H. Grady Davis said that a sermon may take the forms of "a story told."[60] Davis wrote: "But we preachers forget that the gospel is for the most part a simple narrative of persons, places, happenings, and conversation. Nine-tenths of our preaching is verbal exposition and argument, but not one-

---

58. Bass, 83.

59. Clyde E. Fant, *Preaching for Today*, rev. ed (New York: Harper and Row, 1987), 193.

60. Davis, 157.

tenth of the gospel is exposition. Its ideas are mainly in the form of a story told."[61] Edmund A. Steimle, Morris J. Niedenthal, and Charles L. Rice took up H. Grady Davis' concept of story and wrote *Preaching the Story* in 1980. Richard Jensen followed in 1981 with his work *Telling the Story* in which he stressed narrative preaching. Other homileticians such as Eugene Lowry in *The Homiletical Plot* and *Doing Time in the Pulpit* sought to help narrative designs have a place in structuring sermons. Other articles and books on narrative style continue to appear, reflecting the popularity of the narrative sermon.

Homileticians vary in theory about the use of a subject or theme in the narrative sermon. Some contend that a subject or a theme needs to prevail in the narrative design. Eugene Lowry did not call the main idea in a narrative sermon the theme or subject. Instead he called the main idea the plot. Richard Jensen and others dispensed with the use of a theme because they left the interpretation of the main point with the listeners. Sidney Greidanus and others thought a theme did not need to prevail because the word in Scripture had a point or theme or main idea and that point should be transferred openly to today's hearers. While the language may differ, sermons need to have a point or a plot because it will keep the sermon on track, ensure the unity, promote movement, and focus the application.[62]

Writers on preaching often question whether a narrative sermon comes from a deductive or inductive perspective. Like other structural forms, the narrative designs can come from the arrangement either from an inductive direction or a deductive direction. Few forms can be purely inductive. Withholding the conclusion of a narrative to the end seems to be more inductive while making the theme known at the beginning and then developing the sermon seems to be more deductive in the narration. Thus, narrative designs can be deductive or inductive. No one work could exhaust all narrative designs, but a few examples could help expositors begin to arrange sermons from a narrative direction.

---

61. Ibid.
62. Greidanus, 149–50.

Narration-Implication Design

One of the most popular narrative designs is the narration-implication format, which consists of two main parts. The first part, which is the larger part, involves relating the Bible story. The second part, which is the smaller part, involves applying the story with an implication. In the narration segment a theme needs to prevail in the storytelling. It can be obvious, or subtle hints to the theme can be made throughout the telling of the story. The narration-implication design represents one of the simple ways of arranging a narrative design. For example, suppose an expositor was preaching from Genesis and came to the narrative about Jacob. Just giving the chronological aspects of Jacob's life would not represent stimulating and relevant material for the listeners. Many ideas could be observed about the life of Jacob. Suppose an expositor chose the theme about the importance of worshiping God. While telling Jacob's story, discernable and subtle mentions could be made about the importance of worship in Jacob's life. Following the twelve to twenty minutes of narrative, some ten to fifteen minutes could be used to give several lessons drawn from the narrative about the importance of worship.

Paul Powell has shaped some of his sermons in the narration-implication fashion. He preached a sermon entitled "Joseph: Dealing with Bitterness" based generally on Genesis 37–50 and specifically on Genesis 50:19–20. Powell began the sermon with a story from the life of Winston Churchill that illustrated the providence of God. After this illustration, he narrated the life of Joseph from his beginning as a youth to his death in Egypt. Powell related bad experiences Joseph had with his brothers, with Potiphar's wife, with the butler, and with other hardships. With care, Powell gave short, subtle references about how Joseph could have become bitter over these situations. The narrative closed with a disclosure of Joseph's amazing attitude about his misfortune. Then Powell gave three truths, which he felt hearers needed to learn from Joseph's experiences: (1) The working of God is often imperceptible. (2) The working of God is always redemptive. (3) The working of God is progressive.[63]

The narration-implication design represents one of the better ways to shape a sermon. It requires discipline in studying the narra-

---

63. Paul Powell, "Joseph: Dealing with Bitterness," *Preaching* 3, no. 6 (May-June 1988): 26–31.

tive for a major theme, skill in telling the story with the theme explicit or implicit, and perception about the implications arising out of the narrative. Expositors who have not tried narrative design might begin with this technique.

Story-Line Design

Narrative preaching means more than creating pleasure and conveying cognitive biographical information. Storytelling involves conveying truth. Frederick Buechner wrote: "The storyteller's claim, I believe, is that life has meaning. The power of stories is that they are telling us that life adds up somehow, that life itself is like a story. And this grips us and fascinates us because of the feeling it gives us and that if there is meaning in any life—in Hamlet's, in Mary's, in Christ's—then there is meaning also in our lives."[64] Novelists follow a direction known in the world of literature as "the story line." It is what Eugene Lowry labeled as "the homiletical plot." It means to tell the story with a purpose. Preparing and designing sermons along the story line involves engaging in thoughtful plotting. Characters need to be selected, events sequenced, descriptions visualized, and purposes proposed. The process of story development is a homiletical art form within itself just as in the didactic design of getting a subject, points, an introduction, a conclusion, and several illustrations.

Some of the basic skills in storytelling are needed for an effective story-line story to be created. A basic beginning starts the story with time, place, and circumstances. After the setting has been established, action needs to begin with a device known in storytelling as "a turn." After the action begins, something suspenseful needs to happen. Good storytellers introduce tension. It is the beginning of the unfolding of the main plot of the story. Good storytelling demands continuity and singleness of purpose. The story does not need to be diluted with ambiguous characters or subjects. Thematic cohesiveness will not tolerate extra stories or interruptions. Action follows action in a purposeful manner to arrive at another turn. After the climax of the story, the action falls and brings the story to a conclusion. The story line fits naturally into

---

64. Frederick Buechner, *The Magnificent Defeat* (New York: Seabury Press, 1966), 60.

shaping a narrative sermon. The turns in a sermon may be shaped as follows:

- The setting of the story
- The main turn of the story and the beginning of action
- The resolution of the plot of the story
- The climax of the story
- The brief implication of the story (implicit by the story or explicit with didactic material)

Eugene L. Lowry in *The Homiletical Plot: The Sermon as Narrative Art Form* gave the same general format of the traditional story line, but he gave the design new homiletical names. Lowry gave five stages needed to design a narrative sermon.

1. Upsetting the equilibrium. The plot begins by eliciting interest and engaging the audience.
2. Analyzing the discrepancy. The plot moves to an analogy or a diagnosis of a problem.
3. Disclosing the clue to resolution. The plot arrives at some explanation which accounts for the problematic issue.
4. Experiencing the gospel. The plot prescribes a solution to the problem.
5. Anticipating the consequences. The sermon comes to the point of creating closure.[65]

Shared-Story Design

H. Stephen Shoemaker in *Retelling the Biblical Story: The Theology and Practice of Narrative Preaching* built on the prevalent concept of narrative theology and devised a homiletic for narrative preaching. Shoemaker's concept of preaching carried a narrative quality to it when he wrote: "Preaching is the telling of the Biblical Story, the gospel of God's redeeming activity from creation to consummation."[66] Shoemaker's narrative theology may be summarized in four helpful axioms:

---

65. Eugene L. Lowry, *The Homiletical Plot: The Sermon as Narrative Art Form* (Atlanta: John Knox Press, 1980), 27–73.

66. H. Stephen Shoemaker, *Retelling the Biblical Story: The Theology and Practice of Narrative Preaching* (Nashville: Broadman Press, 1985), 148.

1. God is a story-making God. The actions and words of God create stories.

2. Human beings find meaning in becoming part of the story. Abundant life in the kingdom of God is to be involved in God's work, thus stories occur.

3. The Bible contains the narration of God's ways with human-kind. Through the Scripture, God invites humans to enter the drama of his redemptive purpose in the world.

4. Preaching, then, means to tell God's story. It involves more than arguing a line of logic or elucidating a set of points. Sermons do not just present propositions or teach points. Instead, they take hearers on a journey where they meet God.[67]

Using these narrative theology axioms, Shoemaker built a narrative on the word *retelling* where he sought in a narrative sermon to re-create the preacher's world, the hearer's world, and the biblical world. The preacher seeks to combine all of these re-creations in what Rice and Niedenthal called a "shared sermon."

Perhaps the best way to understand the idea of retelling the story would be to observe a sermon fashioned with this design. Shoemaker designed a narrative sermon on Job with the retelling technique. He began the sermon with the human world which is filled with suffering and the inadequacy of human reasoning to explain the idea of suffering. Then Shoemaker moved to relating factual data about Job's life and misfortunes. He retold the conversations of Job with his friends. He then proceeded to conclude the message with God's conversation with Job. Interspersed within all these moves were the insights about the biblical world, the people's world, and the preacher's world.[68] It was not a sermon with these insights following in a sequential fashion as points coming after each other. Shoemaker's primary point of reference was the biblical world of God, and from that basic foundation he mixed personal confession and life situations. For an expositor to design the shared story model, the biblical story needs to be mastered and then it needs to be interspersed with both personal and people experiences.

---

67. Ibid., 148–54.
68. Ibid., 108–16.

Dominant-Metaphor Design

The two previous narrative designs focused primarily on the biblical story and then proceeded with the people's story. Another narrative design which may be called the dominant metaphor starts with a secular story and then a biblical narrative is linked to it. Something in the secular story becomes a presiding metaphor. It becomes a controlling image which ties the entire sermon together and moves the sermon to a conclusion. Secular stories process power "to provide images which endure, even after the details of the story are forgotten."[69]

The homiletics of a dominant metaphor sermon involves combining two stories, one secular and another biblical. Bruce Salmon gave a dominant-metaphor sermon entitled "Lies, Flies, and Alibis," based on Acts 5:1–11. He started the sermon with a story about a cheater at a hospital parking garage tollgate. Salmon compared the cheater's actions with that of Ananias and Sapphira. He used the dominant metaphor of the cheater at the tollgate and the cheating of Ananias and Sapphira to apply to people's behavior in today's world. The contemporary story blended with the biblical story provided the dominant metaphor for the sermon.[70]

Explained-Narration Design

Narrative incidents in the Bible have lessons in the stories, but in preaching, these narrative incidents can be used with explicit lessons. One excellent way to prepare and to preach a narrative sermon is to relate the story of the Bible incident and to interject in the story labels that serve as application. Like all sermons, a theme needs to prevail throughout the sermon, and the expositor could take listeners through the sequence of events in the biblical incident, making sure to relate the theme to the events.

John C. Holbert in *Preaching Old Testament: Proclamation and Narrative in the Hebrew Bible* sought to give instructions for a sermon that may classify as an explained-narrative design. In his sermon "The Best Laugh of All" he narrated Genesis 22. As a storyteller, Holbert focused on Abraham. He told about Abraham's taking wood, fire, and knife. He introduced the idea of God's call

---

69. Bruce Salmon, *Storytelling in Preaching: A Guide to the Theory and Practice* (Nashville: Broadman Press, 1988), 93.

70. Ibid., 83–93.

recorded in Genesis 22:1, and he reviewed several times how God had called Abraham. At the outset, Holbert stressed the obedience of Abraham, and that theme prevailed throughout the sermon. In a rather sequential fashion, Holbert developed the various moves within Genesis 22, giving emphasis to obedience in all the moves.[71]

In encountering texts of a narrative nature, a preacher may simply shape the sermon by relating the incident with a dominant idea in mind. At major turns in the story, application could be made. It involves explaining truths in the story as the story is told and moving toward a climax.

Multiple-Story Design

In the narrative design variety, one story is followed by another story. Instead of points being followed by points, stories are followed by stories. If a story is a good one, listeners can usually get the point of a story. If a storyteller relates a tale or someone tells a joke and then has to explain the story, something is wrong either with the story or with the telling of the story. Jesus often used several stories to get his point across. He told the story of a lost sheep, a lost coin, and a lost boy to get across the point that God loves sinners. Few people read these stories of Jesus and miss the point.

Sermon designs do not fit rigidly into neat categories. Fred Craddock's experience-exposure explorative could just as easily be called a multiple-story design. In a sermon entitled "Who Cares?" based on Acts 4:32–35, Craddock told seven stories, one after the other. With the telling of each story, hearers could grasp the idea of the church's care for human beings.[72] Multiple-story does not mean that a sermon consists of a string of stories. It does contain several stories, but each story makes a point that relates to the point of the sermon.

Expositors have numerous choices for preaching a series of sermons from a Bible book. Being true to the biblical text and relating that truth to the needs of people are two dogmatic principles. Relativity comes in the way a sermon needs to be structured. Biblical truth does not have to be shaped in sermons in only one form.

71. John C. Holbert, *Preaching Old Testament: Proclamation and Narrative in the Hebrew Bible* (Nashville: Abingdon Press, 1991), 79–92.

72. Fred B. Craddock, "Who Cares?" *Preaching Today*, sound cassette, no. 17.

Choices abound for shaping sermons. In preaching a series of sermons from a Bible book, an expositor can choose to use one, two, or a dozen or more designs. Because of the varied shapes of texts, the proclivity of people who listen, and the varied personality types of expositors, choices may need to be exercised in shaping the sermons from a Bible book. No particular design makes a sermon "more biblical," but different designs offer options for hearing God's Word.

The Content for Sermons in a Bible Book

Sermons need biblical and contemporary substance. Structural designs in sermons should help communicate that substance. Focusing primarily on structure in sermons makes messages appear pedantic, or stilted—mere homiletical skeletons. Interesting novels contain plots, and effective speeches possess outlines. Novelists arrange content around the plot, and speech makers include various kinds of material in the general sketch of a speech.

Effective expositors concentrate on putting content into structured designs. Outlines or plots alone do not make a sermon. They only delineate the abridgement, or sketch, of a sermon idea. Just as a ceramics crafter pours plaster into many kinds of molds to make ceramic art, an expositor pours sermonic content into didactic, explorative, and narrative molds. Various kinds of sermon substance can be poured into these designs. Effective sermons use structure to communicate content. In a book concerned with sermon content, H. C. Brown, Jr., wrote, "A sermon outline never stands alone as a complete sermon. The outline must be filled out and developed before a sermon exists. The preacher cannot produce an adequate sermon by outlining the major thoughts and then dividing and redividing those thoughts. At some point the preacher must stop dividing and must begin to develop, to expand, and to fill out his structure."[1]

Cookbooks list ingredients and explain how to combine them. Like cookbooks, homiletical books explain how to combine the various substances to make a sermon. Homiletics is worthless without knowledge of substance. Expositors need to know what goes into a sermon and how to arrange content to make the sermon effective.

John A. Broadus distinguished between four "functional elements" of the sermon.[2] These functional elements are explanation, argumentation, application, and illustration.[3] Broadus separated the element of illustration from the other three elements. He described the function of illustration as "solely auxiliary, coming to the support now of one and now of another of the principal elements."[4] H. C. Brown, Jr., followed Broadus, "One effective procedure for placing authentic biblical content in sermons is through the functional

---

1. H. C. Brown, Jr., *A Quest for Reformation in Preaching* (Waco, Tex.: Word Books, 1968), 55.

2. John A. Broadus, *On the Preparation and Delivery of Sermons*, 3d ed., rev. Jesse Burton Weatherspoon (San Francisco: Harper and Row, 1943), 155.

3. Ibid., 155–21.

4. Ibid., 196

elements of preaching—explanation, application, and argumentation."[5]

Broadus' functional elements fit the didactic or deductive designs, but other kinds of content need to be used in the explorative and narrative designs. Different sermon structures call for different kinds of content. The four functional elements presented by Broadus and Brown fit didactic structure, but other kinds of content need to be studied for other structured styles. Together with explanation, argumentation, application, and illustration, we will study the elements of imagination and narration. While these six elements do not represent all content choices, they do represent the primary ones.

Within each sermon, the content elements are not completely separate and distinct from each other. Instead, the content elements overlap and complement each other. They often appear to be one element and then another.

Explanation

One basic function of preaching is the explanation of God's Word. Expositors seek to discover the meaning of Scripture and relate that meaning to people's needs. The Bible is a foreign book to most people. It originated long ago in foreign lands among people with unique customs, events, and ideas. Expositors need to give information about the Bible's words, phrases, sentences, names, places, customs, persons, and ideas.

The element of explanation should be the content for many sermons. Explanation means "to make clear," "to explain," or "to make understandable." As expositors study both biblical and non-biblical data, they need to clarify what hearers do not understand.

The Need for Explanation

God differs from his creation. He is infinite, and his creatures are finite. God has chosen to make himself known by means of natural and special revelation. With his acts of creation and redemption, God sought to explain his ways and his character to humans. His greatest explanation of himself came with the incarnation. "No man has seen God at any time; the only begotten God, who is in the bosom of the Father, He has explained Him" (John 1:18). Jesus

---

5. Brown.

explained, made clear, and made understandable the nature and character of God. God always wants his character and his ways to be known to humans. The Lord has given the Bible as a means for people to know him. The Lord wants his Word to be understood; thus, he uses servants of the Word to explain the truths of Scripture.

Relevant sermons need the element of explanation. Preachers have the task of recognizing and explaining anything that might be unclear. Faris D. Whitesell said: "The average hearer will esteem no part of the sermon more than good explanation. People revere the Bible and wish to increase their understanding of it."[6]

The problem of distance necessitates explanation in sermons. Every text a preacher uses bears the mark of distance in time and culture. Preaching builds a bridge from the ancient past to the present. Expositors study a text which originated in ancient times and seek to understand its original meaning. Then, with that understanding in mind, expositors attempt to clarify ancient truths to an audience. The background of a text will often need clarification. Sometimes matters of Bible history need to be shared so hearers may understand. At other times geographical, cultural, archaeological, or sociological matters need to be clarified.

Expositors need to explain not only background, which affects the understanding of a text, but also exegetical data within a text. Many words, phrases, sentences, names, places, persons, and ideas need clarification.[7] The exegesis of texts, or the process by which a preacher comes to understand them, was discussed in chapter 6 of this work. Explanation differs from the preacher's personal and private exegesis. A preacher presents in explanation the results, not the processes of exegesis. The intention of explanation is to take the results of exegesis, select from appropriate areas, and explain information in the text in a clear, brief, and understandable manner.

Hearers often need insight into Bible doctrines or themes. Some of the most important biblical concepts remain imperfectly understood. Expositors need to study many biblical themes for understanding and then seek some means of explaining these biblical

---

6. Farris D. Whitesell, *Power in Expository Preaching* (Westwood, N.J.: Fleming H. Revell, 1967), 31–32.

7. Broadus, 156.

ideas to hearers. Many matters of Bible truth are unclear and, without help, will remain unintelligible to people today.

People have many questions for which expositors must seek explanations. How can I become a Christian? What is God like? Why do good people have to suffer? How can I become a better Christian?

Effective expositors listen to the hearer's questions and then seek to offer some explanation or answer from the truth of Scripture. John A. Broadus said, "A thousand questions as to what is true and what is right in the practical conduct of life perplex devout minds and call for explanation."[8]

Some sermons will include a large amount of explanation. Others will have less explanation and more of another element or elements. Generally speaking, both the text and the structured type will dictate the type of content. Some texts need more explanation than others. Also, didactic designs naturally contain more explanation than explorative or narrative designs. Explanation will be present to a degree in every sermon from a Bible book because preaching is not merely persuasive and convincing, but eminently instructive.

Means of Explanation

When an expositor preaches on a biblical text or deals with an idea, the facts have to be laid out first. After stating the facts, the expositor explains them. To explain the facts, definitions, examples, and comparisons, other factors will be used so hearers not only know the facts but know what they mean. Such a means of explanation is called *exposition:* the exposure of facts and the explanation of the meaning of facts. John A. Broadus said, "However congregations may shrink from elaborate exegesis or bungling and tedious attempts to explain, they will always welcome the felicitous introduction and quick, vivid elucidation of passages from God's Word."[9] In exposition a preacher uses techniques much like those used by writers of Bible commentaries. Many contemporary Bible commentaries reflect a concern for exegesis and interpretation.

Structure. H. C. Brown, Jr., in *A Quest for Reformation in Preaching*, listed the sermon structure as a primary means of explanation.

---

8. Ibid., 158.
9. Ibid.

He wrote: "Division is properly a way to explain. A minister by pointing out, in sequence, the two or three or four normal parts of an idea, assists the audience to understand that idea."[10] John A. Broadus also included the dividing of a subject into parts as a major means of explanation. Using structural data forces a preacher to determine the main thought of a text. Once the main thought is expressed, it is explained through the major and minor points related to that thought. The art of choosing a subject and stating divisions of that subject is a major method of explanation.[11]

Definition. A main task in preaching is helping some people understand the terms used. Definition is often necessary to explain. Definition involves telling what a term meant. Words and phrases often need clarification. Defining a word in its etymology and its usage helps to clarify.

Comparison. The expository may use comparison through contrast and analogy. Jesus explained the nature of the Kingdom with comparison, "the Kingdom of heaven is like." Jesus compared spiritual truth with earthly matters. Jesus' use of comparison reminds expositors of how desirable it is to derive comparison from matter familiar to the hearers.

Question and answer. Rhetorical questions and answers provide another effective means of explanation. Anticipating questions which an audience might ask about a Scripture passage or subject and asking those questions begins the explanation process. Answering the question helps clarify the issue. Paul often used this method. It was called diatribe. In his letter to the Romans, he wrote of the grace of God. Paul anticipated that some readers would say, "If saved by grace, why not sin more so grace could abound?" Paul asked the anticipated question and dealt with the answer in Romans 6.

Cross-referencing. Expositors use Scripture for the support of truth in another text. Care should be exercised in using cross-references to "proof-text" a human speculation rather than explain divine revelation. The cross-reference Scripture passage must mean essentially the same thing as the text compared. The Scriptures are brought in to amplify and to undergird the truth in the text of a sermon.

---

10. Brown, 57.
11. Broadus, 166.

Example. Many people do not readily comprehend abstract ideas. An idea becomes more vivid and interesting when some example is used. It is difficult to explain pride to an audience, but giving an example of a prideful person could communicate a picture of pride. Giving an actual, concrete instance of a word or idea helps explain it.

Narration, argumentation, application, illustration, description, and imagination offer excellent means of explanation by example. As previously stated, all the content elements overlap, aid, and assist each other and often appear to be one element and then another. The expositor needs to learn the art of using explanation to put content in the sermon.

Argumentation

A choice for content of sermons also includes argumentation. Books written over twenty-five years ago by John A. Broadus, T. H. Pattison, and David R. Breed dealt extensively with argumentation. But more recent writers, such as H. Grady Davis, Fred Craddock, Thomas Long, James W. Cox, and Haddon Robinson, hardly mention argumentation. In recent years, argumentation has been associated almost exclusively with detailed, logical reasoning, especially when the purpose is to refute or to defend. A broader concept of argumentation might motivate more expositors to include that element in sermons. Argument does involve reasoned discourse and defensive efforts, but it also involves persuasion and affirmation of truths. In preaching sermons from a Bible book, argumentation should be included in some messages. To be effective, an expositor should know the meaning and methods of argument.

The Meaning of Argumentation

Argumentation has a much broader meaning than the defense of truth and the refutation of error. From the earliest beginnings of Christian proclamation, preachers included the apologetic substance in their sermons. These preachers affirmed the certainties of the Christian faith, and they also defended the Christian faith against error. Therefore, the apologetic or argumentation notion of preaching in the first three or four centuries involved both defense and affirmation. Preaching in every century needs to possess some element of argumentation because error always appears and the Christian faith always needs presenting in a reasonable manner.

The larger view of argument involves persuading, proving, convincing, or refuting. Argument includes reason and discussion as well as controversy and dispute.[12]

Persuade. Argumentation attempts to persuade people to act. Persuasion is a term used by most homileticians to describe the art of changing people. J. Daniel Baumann said, "Persuasion is a conscious attempt by one person to change the behavior of another person or persons toward some predetermined end through the transmission of some message."[13] An expositor presents the facts and explains what is essential, presenting the basis for decision in a credible manner. The expositor then moves the hearers to make a decision about what they have learned and believed. Persuasion presents learners with options. The hearer's freedom is inherent in authentic persuasion because persuasive preaching is not compliance behavior. Genuine persuasion is giving a message to others who can receive it and respond in freedom. Persuasion uses opportunities within a sermon to confront people, through the Holy Spirit, with biblical truth and to urge them to act on truth. Emory A. Griffin wrote, "Any persuasive effort which restricts another's freedom to choose for or against Jesus Christ is wrong."[14] Persuasive argument asks people to quit something or to start doing something on the basis of a relationship with Jesus Christ.

Prove. Argumentation uses the art of reasoning in a logical presentation of some element of the Christian faith. Argumentation also involves establishing a truth so application can be justified. Too many sermons contain authoritative assertions and impassioned appeals without an approach in the line of reasoning. Centuries ago, the secular rhetorician Aristotle complained that previous writers on rhetoric had concerned themselves only with efforts at persuasion by appeals to feeling and prejudice.[15]

Refute. In addition to the positive meanings of persuasion and reason, argumentation includes the negative meanings of defense and refutation. Doctrinal errors and improper human behavior often must be refuted. At times in preaching from a Bible book,

---

12. Brown, 64.

13. J. David Baumann, *An Introduction to Contemporary Preaching* (Grand Rapids: Bible Book House, 1972), 223.

14. Emory A. Griffin, *The Mind Changers: The Art of Christian Persuasion* (Wheaton, Ill.: Tyndale, 1976), 28.

15. Quoted in Broadus, *On the Preparation and Delivery of Sermons*, 167.

there will be opportunities to defend the Christian faith against heresy. In a homiletical argument, a preacher knows or assumes that some kind of differences in opinion between the preacher and various persons in the audience exist. Refutation becomes the means of argumentation used to speak to those who hold opinions in need of change. Broadus gave wise advice about the negative elements of argumentation: "Let a man be honest in his choice of arguments, frank in his recognition of serious difficulties, and wise to arrange his reasoning so as to effect clear understanding and stable conviction, remembering always that his interest should not be triumph and praise but truth and life."[16]

Understanding the broader view of argumentation can help expositors include it in the content of sermons. The facet of argumentation to be used depends primarily on the needs of an audience and on the teaching of the text. When people in an audience need to make changes, the element of persuasion should be used. When truths need to be presented so that people can understand and act on them, logical reasoning should be used. Whenever errors prevail, an expositor would choose to defend, to refute, or to confront.

Methods of Argumentation

One basic method of argumentation is argument from experience. The experience can come from the personal experience of the preacher or the experience of others. Thomas G. Long emphasized that in many ways the preacher becomes a witness of experience to others.[17] In regard to personal experiences, the expositor needs to be careful about whether the data involves fact, opinion, hypothesis, supposition, or illustration.[18] The speaker's credibility is the key issue. Audiences tend to believe information from a person with a reliable character.

Argument through experience also involves using the experiences and judgments of others. Presenting the reliable, trustworthy experiences of others helps convince or refute error. Like the personal experiences of the preacher, distinction should be made between the use of fact and opinion. Credible witnesses make argu-

---

16. Ibid., 190.
17. Thomas G. Long, *The Witness of Preaching* (Louisville, Ky.: Westminster/John Knox Press, 1989), 19–59.
18. Brown, 65.

ments stronger, and the reliability of the witnesses makes an assertion or a denial stronger.

Another basic method is deductive reasoning. Deductive reasoning begins with a general principle—the major premise. It continues with related subfacets of that general principle—the minor premises. From the major premise and the minor premises come a conclusion. This method of deductive reasoning may be traced to Aristotle. Many sermons contain three syllogistic reasonings, which start with a major premise and move to a minor premise followed by a conclusion.[19]

Logical reasoning can also proceed from an inductive direction. In using induction for sermon content, preachers need to move from particular cases or incidents to a general answer or conclusion. People, in most cases, do not start thinking from general truth as much as they start with particular experiences to arrive at a general truth. To include inductive reasoning in sermon content would involve selecting and using credible examples or experiences that could lead to establishing a general truth.

John Dewey identified five processes of inductive reasoning:

1. A felt difficulty, an awareness that something needs to be changed;

2. An analysis of the cause of the difficulty and a definition of the need;

3. Identification of possible solutions that would satisfy the need;

4. Evaluation of various solutions and selection of the best;

5. Proposal of the preferred solution.[20]

Still another method of argumentation is the use of logic. H. C. Brown, Jr., gave six special techniques or forms of logic:

1. Argument *a priori* which reasons from cause to effect.

2. Argument *a posteriori* which reasons from effect or result back to cause.

3. Argument *a fortiori* which reasons from weaker examples to strong ones.

---

19. Ibid., 65.
20. See John Dewey, *How We Thank* (Boston: Heath, 1910).

4. Argument *ex concesso* which argues from that which has been granted or conceded.

5. Argument *reductio ad absurdum* which reasons by reducing an issue to the absurd.

6. Argument *ad hominem* which reasons by appealing to the personal feelings and interests of the hearer.[21]

At first glance these reasoning techniques may seem difficult to use. Yet H. C. Brown, Jr., said, "They are often used by men who have had absolutely no formal training in argumentation and debate."[22] Many ministers use these forms without being conscious of their use. Study of these special forms of logic could enhance any expositor's ability to prove, to affirm, or to refute.

Various preachers prefer one or another method of argument. Generally speaking, a preacher will be more skilled in managing the methods of personal preference. But personal preference should not exclude other methods of argumentation. Choosing the methods of argument should not depend on the preacher's choice alone, but also on the constitution, intelligence, and emotions of the audience. The expositor needs to use arguments from many sources and arrange them into various forms. The use of argumentation is a process of putting content in sermons to communicate God's truth.

Application

Sermons rise or fall in application. It is a waste to provide extensive exegesis and appropriate argument and then to slight the matter of application. Preachers do more than provide information; they use that information to bring hearers under the truths of Scripture. Application includes relating, involving, and moving people to action. John A. Broadus said, "If there is no summons, there is no sermon."[23] Preachers work between two worlds, and a genuine biblical sermon builds a bridge between the biblical and contemporary worlds with a thorough acquaintance of both worlds.

Rudolph Bohren said that the act of applying truth in a sermon is "the crisis of preaching."[24] It is the challenge of fusing together

---

21. Brown, 65–66.

22. Ibid., 66.

23. Broadus, 210.

24. Rudolph Bohren, *Preaching and Community*, trans. David E. Green (Richmond, Va.: John Knox Press, 1965), 79.

responsibly the prior biblical revelation and the present actual situation. Often a gulf exists between the text from the past and the sermon for today. Bohren called the gulf "the dilemma between text and sermon."[25] Some solve the dilemma by isolating the text from application. Such an expositor studies with detail the grammar and syntax of the text and reconstructs the historical situation. But such an expositor fails to share any relevance of the text to an audience. Harry Emerson Fosdick said that most people do not "come to church desperately anxious to discover what happened to the Jebusites."[26]

Others solve the dilemma of bridging the gulf between text and sermon by interpreting the text in light of today and disregarding its past. Bohren said that such a preacher interprets the text essentially without any regard to the historical and exegetical study of the text.[27] In an article on "The Use of Application in the Sermon," Freeman wrote, "The challenge is to negotiate the passage between the prior biblical revelation and the hearer's present situation, thus escaping the dilemma."[28] Application then involves negotiating the gap between the Bible and life.

Approaches of Application

How should a preacher approach the matter of application? J. Daniel Baumann described three basic ways of handling application: making direct application to the listener, making application in an indirect or suggestive manner, and leaving the application entirely to the hearers.[29] Adopting the last approach can cause serious questions whether the address would be a sermon. Such a method could be strong biblically, theologically, and exegetically; but practically it is deficient. Expositors who leave application to the hearers argue that application is the task solely of the Holy Spirit.

Direct application. Some writers call for a direct approach in application. Faris D. Whitesell said, "It is better to make definite,

---

25. Ibid., 83.

26. Harry Emerson Fosdick, "What Is the Matter with Preaching?" *Pulpit Digest* 63 (September–October 1983), 8.

27. Bohren, 94.

28. Harold Freeman, "Making the Sermon Matter: The Use of Application in the Sermon." *Southwestern Journal of Theology* 27, no. 2 (spring 1985): 34.

29. Baumann, 247.

searching application than to imply or hint at it."[30] Examples of direct application follow: You are a sinner who needs salvation. You are a Christian, and you need to forgive. You are a Christian, and your agenda is to love your neighbor. Harvey Cox said: "Our preaching today is powerless because it does not confront people with the new reality which has occurred and because the summons is issued in general rather than in specific terms."[31]

One textbook in communication indicated that an audience generally is more affected by an explicit conclusion. An explicit statement of purpose does not necessarily alienate those audience members opposed to that purpose, and an explicit method should prove more valuable to the less intelligent members of an audience.[32] Experiments with college juniors and seniors revealed a preference for direct application. A report on the experiment said, "The speech with the explicit conclusion elicited significantly more attitude change than the speech with the implicit conclusion."[33] So a book on communication theory and a laboratory experiment indicated that direct communication was more effective than indirect communication in eliciting a desired conclusion.

Direct application involves using clearly defined directories. Explicit exhortation clarifies the issues and leaves listeners with a minimum amount of ambiguity regarding the expected response. Some expositors prefer using a more direct approach to application.

Indirect approach. Some homileticians suggest a severe abbreviation or entire elimination of explicit application, opting for a more suggestive approach. Indirect application gives stimulation in a particular direction, then allows hearers to assess and to decide. Rather than being direct, it is subtle. The trend toward indirect rather than direct approaches in secular communication theory has attracted homileticians. J. Daniel Baumann asserted that "good preaching need not make explicit application, but may often serve its purpose—and more effectively so—through implicit, subtle, and suggestive application."[34] Fred B. Craddock advised preachers to

---

30. Whitesell, 92.

31. Harvey Cox, *The Secular City* (New York: Macmillian, 1966), 122–23.

32. Burt E. Bradley, *Fundamentals of Speech Communication: The Creditability of Ideas* (Dubuque, Iowa: William C. Brown, 1974), 92–93.

33. Stewart L. Tubbs, "Explicit Versus Implicit Conclusion and Audience Commitment," *Speech Monographs 35* (March 1968): 14.

34. Baumann, 250.

deliver sermons in such a way that they would be "overhearing the gospel."[35] Craddock and others called for preachers to build application implicitly into the sermon, allowing hearers to infer truths for themselves. The preacher becomes a prompter rather than a dispenser of all wisdom. Indirect application has gained use in recent years because individuals are becoming more reluctant to accept explicit application. Individual application implies that one person leads other persons to discovery, and the preaching event does not become one person telling others what they should do. Frank Dance said: "The most persuasive thing in the world is participation. If I want to change behavior, I must engage the other person whose behavior I want to change in the decision to change his own behavior. I will not change his behavior by telling him to."[36] Carl Rogers argued that "self-discovered and self-motivated behavior are, in the long run, the only ones which produce significant changes."[37]

Effective preaching does not have to have explicit application. Often application can be achieved through an implicit, subtle, and suggestive manner. J. Daniel Baumann said this is indirect application: "The preacher becomes a midwife who assists in the encounter between God and man."[38] Hearers do the deciding; the preacher merely assists in the discovery.

Choosing which approach in application to use is not, in most cases, an either/or choice; it is a both/and decision. No one method is the right one. Three theorists in communication gave three factors in deciding which application approach to use: the nature of the communicator, the nature of the audience, and the nature of the subject.[39] While keeping all three of these factors in mind, an expositor needs to arrive at a personal conclusion about the best approach to use in applying biblical truth. Using both approaches according to the subject discussed and the audience addressed seems to be an effective technique.

---

35. Fred B. Craddock, *Overhearing the Gospel* (Nashville: Abingdon, 1978).

36. Frank Dance, "Communication Theory and Contemporary Preaching," *Preaching*, 3 (September-October, 1968): 31.

37. Donovan J. Ochs, "Videotapes in Teaching Advanced Public Speaking," *The Speech Teacher*, 17 (March 1968): 111.

38. Baumann, 250.

39. Carl I. Houland, Irving L. Janis, and Harold H. Kelley, *Communication and Persuasion* (New Haven: Yale University Press, 1953), 100.

The Placement of Application

Where in the sermon to relate or to apply biblical truth to people's lives is a point of dispute. Application may be used at any point in a sermon. The approach an expositor uses in application determines where in the sermon application appears. Direct application can appear throughout the sermon. In most cases indirect application moves toward an impact or a change, so application appears near the end of the sermon.

In the direct approach, application can begin at the beginning of a sermon. It can even start with a sermon title. Some titles suggest in their wording how the message will relate to a person's life. Furthermore in the didactic sermon structure, application can be made in each major division. A typical pattern of placement in a didactic sermon could be as follows:

I. Major Point

    A. Explanation

    B. Application

II. Major Point

    A. Explanation

    B. Application

Application can appear in the introduction, throughout the body of the sermon, and in the conclusion. Some deductive preachers spend much of their time in explanation or argumentation and wait for application until the end. Others choose to apply all along the way and to relate the truth in a poignant manner at the end.

Generally speaking, the indirect method of application does not begin to relate truth at the beginning of a sermon. It has more subtle application; thus, relevancy is woven into the material. In the explorative and narrative designs, applications appear late or at the end of the sermon. Saving the application until later helps with the movement of the sermon. If the sermon has a narrative design, the relevancy of the story will move toward a climax. Nathan did not spoil the story he told to David by telling him, "You are the man," before it was time (see 2 Sam. 12: 7).

No rigid rule can be established about where to place application in a sermon. It can come anywhere in a sermon, but the expositor should be aware that the structural design chosen will affect the placement of application in the sermon.

Methods of Application

Preachers who want to relate biblical truth to people's needs should learn about various methods of application. Many ways to apply truth are available. The techniques of application differ in the direct and indirect approaches.

Direct methods of application. At least eight methods may be chosen in the direct approach.

- Declaration. The expositor affirms in an explicit manner that the sermon data does relate to the hearers. When Isaiah spoke to Judah in the eighth century B.C. he told them with several assertions what to do: "Wash yourselves, make yourselves clean; remove the evil of your deeds from my sight. Cease to do evil, learn to do good; Seek justice, reprove the ruthless; defend the orphan, plead for the widow" (Isa. 1:16–17). The prophet told the people what to do. Sometimes the contemporary communicator needs to apply with assertions.

- Demonstration. The preacher may present a course of possible action along with possible steps to take. Practical procedures may be outlined in applying a truth. The preacher may use various means to demonstrate with practical procedures how a truth is relevant.

- Justification. The preacher tells hearers the relevancy of an issue. Because of the expositor's conviction about an idea, the method in the sermon will be presented so hearers know the speaker wants them to respond.

- Interrogation. Questions that the preacher poses to an audience become another form of direct application. Questions tend to force hearers to interact with the speaker about a truth presented. Asking questions changes the preaching process from a monologue to a dialogue. The questioning method of application becomes an effective means of relating and involving people with a biblical truth so they can see how the truth is suitable, fitting, or appropriate to them.

- Visualization. In using visualization the preacher describes results produced by following actions suggested. By giving in concrete terms the specific advantages to be gained by a decision, the expositor applies the message, allowing the audience to see the results of a decision before it happens. The main problem with visualization as application is exaggeration. In almost all cases, exaggeration is not deliberate deceit but eagerness pressed too far.[40]

- Exhortation. By using exhortation, the preacher gives sincere and earnest pleading for an audience to act or respond. Exhortation gives practical advice or earnest warning. Pressure tactics and exhortations are not synonymous. Exhortation is a plea for people to take action that is best for their lives. It is a warning against attitudes and actions that could harm their lives.

- Exaggeration. Hyperbole arouses the listener by overstatement. Jesus often used hyperbole as application. He said, "And if your right hand makes you stumble, cut it off" (Matt. 5:30). Jesus was not encouraging the mutilation of the body; instead he spoke of the radical nature of discipleship by using exaggeration. Exaggeration may be used to arouse people from lethargy and inactivity.

- Invitation. The expositor invites and urges people to make a public or a private decision. The call for decision represents the actualization of biblical truth. The invitation is a practical disclosure of how to put biblical truth in action.

Direct application represents explicit, direct, and overt speaking to people. Indirect application represents suggestion, implicit and indirect speaking to people. Indirect application encourages the hearer to move in a particular direction but trusts listeners to make their own conclusion or decision.[41] Rather than being overt, it is subtle.[42] Not all sermons need to have explicit application. Some sermons can be served best with implicit, subtle, and suggestive application.[43]

Indirect methods of application. Four methods are commonly used with indirect application.

- Illustration. A concrete example drawn out of contemporary life helps bridge the chasm from the biblical world to today's world. Illustrations do not need explanation; therefore, they

---

40. Brown, 62–63.

41. Baumann, 249.

42. Donovan J. Ochs, "Videotape in Teaching Advanced Public Speaking," *The Speech Teacher*, 17 (March 1968): 111.

43. Baumann, 250.

are suggestive and implicit. J. Daniel Baumann gave some qualification for illustrations as application: "Typical, not unique; believable, not stronger than fiction; current, not dated; possible, not unlikely; life-situational, not theoretic."[44] An illustration simply told becomes its own method of application.

- Option. The speaker can enumerate possible options. Jesus spoke of two entrances, two ways, and two foundations (see Matt. 7:13–27). He gave a choice to the hearers in an indirect manner. Joshua gave the Israelites three choices: serving the gods of their forefathers, serving the gods of the Amorites, or serving the Lord (Josh. 24:14–15). Contemporary preachers can apply by option. They can suggest the opportunities or choices open to the hearer. Listeners are allowed to make a decision.

- Narration. Retelling biblical stories often brings home a lesson or lessons to listeners. The biblical narrative originated for a theological purpose; thus, relating the story can carry a message within itself. While hearers listen to the flow of a story, lessons begin to emerge subtly. For example, a preacher might preach about the Old Testament character Joseph and relate God's providence in his life. If the narration sermon is presented wisely, it should have implicit application throughout. Insulting the listener by adding explicit applications is unnecessary.

- Personal attestation. A speaker may make subtle application by using personal experience. On several occasions, Paul related his personal experience of conversion. Joshua told Israel of his personal decision (see Josh. 24:15). Hearing what the speaker has decided or experienced helps hearers relate the truth to their lives.

Which method of application is best, the direct or the indirect? Probably the best criterion for choosing a technique of application is the nature of the hearers. Independent people might need an indirect approach, and dependent people might need a direct approach. Using a variety is good. The Holy Spirit plays a role in application, whether direct or indirect.

---

44. Ibid.

Illustration

Many theories exist about using illustrations for sermon content. Some preachers fear that illustrations may dilute biblical content. To these expositors, exegetical content should be prominent in sermons. Other preachers think that sermons with primary exegetical content may be too abstract for congregational understanding. The first group of preachers is concerned that biblical truth may not be heard because of the illustrations. The other group is concerned that biblical truth may not be heard without illustrations. Expository preaching should be concerned with exposing biblical truth and meeting human needs. As long as illustrations illumine truth, they should be present as content material. But when illustration becomes the end rather than the means, they should be eliminated.

In recent years, homileticians have changed their views about using illustrations. Older homiletic books assigned an auxiliary service to illustrations. John A. Broadus represented this use of illustration: "Strictly speaking, one would not call illustration a distinct element of the sermon coordinate with explanation and argument, or with persuasion. . . . Its function is solely auxiliary, coming to the support now of one and now of another of the principal elements."[45] Such a use of illustration involves giving an idea and then illustrating that idea.

Recent books on homiletics, for the most part, still retain the auxiliary role of illustration, but they also add that illustrations make the point. Homileticians who write about inductive, narrative, and life-situation preaching use illustrations as the main way to communicate truth. The formula is not truth and illustration, but the technique involves life experience and truth gleaned from the stories. Using illustrations helps rescue truth from the ethereal world of abstract dogma. Scripture becomes real, applicable, and meaningful because its messages become rooted in real life. The primary criticism of this approach is that it is weak on exposition. But most homileticians who include illustrations intend to integrate life situations with the exegesis of the Scripture.[46]

Whatever approach an expositor chooses to use with illustration, content material in sermons should make the foreign familiar, and

---

45. Broadus, 196.

46. Bryan Chapell, *Using Illustrations to Preach with Power* (Grand Rapids: Zondervan, 1992), 25–31.

the abstract real. Content material also should observe biblical truths in the context of life situations. Putting illustrations in sermons is necessary today because most hearers in today's world are not accustomed to lengthy, rational discourses. A multimedia world has caused hearers to think visually. Ours is a picture-thinking world. Using illustrations as a means of understanding biblical truth represents a legitimate way of putting content in sermons.

Purposes of Illustration

Illustrations exist for legitimate reasons. Here are nine purposes, or functions, of illustration:

- *Illustration helps explain a point.* As expositors discover biblical truth, they need to think about what is analogous to that truth in everyday life. If an expositor cannot produce an analogy, the hearer may not understand the point. Illustrations furnish listeners with examples of abstract truth. R. E. C. Browne said, "Most people, even educated people, do not listen analytically, but are affected by the pattern of imagery in an utterance."[47]

- *Illustration helps prove a point.* John A. Broadus pointed out how Paul gave three illustrations in Romans 6–7 to prove that justification by faith does not encourage sinning. Broadus cautioned against using illustrations that imply more than they prove.[48]

- *Illustration persuades people to act.* People need to understand truth, but they also need to take action with regard to biblical truth. Appropriate illustrations can do more than clarify an issue; they can compel people to act.

- *Illustration creates interest.* Sermons consisting primarily of argumentation and explanation make a tedious listening experience. Listeners long for diversity and interesting matters. Humor, a life experience, or some other type of illustration has the power to sustain or to reclaim an audience's interest. Preaching to many secular mind-sets in today's world requires preachers to include interesting content.

---

47. Quoted in Ian MacPherson, *The Art of Illustrating Sermons* (Nashville: Abingdon Press, 1964), 14.
48. Broadus, 197.

- *Illustration gives the audience a break.* Today's communication theorists claim that hearers of discourses need points of relaxation in the process. The amount of time an average congregation can listen to the same kind of content is limited. Using illustrative content at five-or-six-minute intervals could help hold listeners' attention.[49] As illustrations enlighten biblical truth, they tend to reduce the tension of sustained, consecutive thinking.

- *Illustration helps hearers remember.* Illustrative material is remembered more easily than lines of abstract reasoning. Truth seems to make a deeper and more lasting impression in the form of stories.

- *Illustration helps hearers drop their guard.* Making a direct attack against what an expositor exposes and opposes might make hearers defensive. But an appropriate illustration can penetrate human defense as did Nathan's story to David. Nathan told a disarming story, and David saw his sin before he had a chance to defend himself. Illustrations often hide truth until it is too late for hearers to guard against it.

- *Illustration touches the heart.* Hearers of sermons are more than people who just think. Hearers also are people who feel. Humanizing concepts through proper emotions is an imperative to preaching. Many effective preachers have learned to include illustrative content that touches the emotion of listeners in a wholesome manner.

- *Illustration visualizes abstract truth.* A story paints a picture. W. E. Sangster said that one purpose of illustration is to help people "see the point" of a sermon.[50] Picturing a message can keep expositors from developing pure philosophical thinking about Christianity. Keeping an interest in people and the world helps anchor doctrine to common things.

Faced with nine purposes of illustration, how can an expositor question the wisdom of making wide but discriminating use of illustration in sermons? Knowing the many kinds of illustrative possibilities will help expositors use diverse content in sermons.

49. Baumann, 172.

50. W. E. Sangster, *The Craft of Sermon Illustration* (Philadelphia: Westminster Press, 1950), 20–21.

Types of Illustration

What is an illustration? Some limit an illustration to a story or life experience. Others enlarge the concept of an illustration to include anything that throws light on an idea. Preachers have many choices of types of illustration to use in their sermons. Three major types of illustrations exist: skillful use of language, wide use of stories, and use of poetry and quotations. Though using language skillfully may not seem like an illustration, it can be used as illustrative material. *Reader's Digest* has a section entitled "Toward More Picturesque Speech." Language has the power to create pictures. Even a single word can create an image for hearers. Every letter of the alphabet was originally a picture or symbol of some object or idea. Ideas conceived in the human mind use words to communicate to others. Learning about word usage can help a preacher prepare more picturesque sermons. For example, active verbs create more action than passive verbs. Adjectives add description to nouns.[51] Calvin Miller called preachers "wordsmiths," or persons who work with words; thus the constant study of language helps preachers put picturesque content in sermons.[52]

Phrases. Phraseological forms, such as a common idiom or a simple extended metaphor or simile, can help illuminate reality. Idioms represent an expression peculiar to a language. Usually idioms are characterized by homely expressions, such as "the falling night" or "a 30 land." Metaphors and similes are condensed parables. They picture truth in tabloid form. These phrases express likenesses or dissimilarities to the things they are designed to illustrate. A simile is a comparison that uses the words like or as. A metaphor is an implied comparison. Phrases in many forms can create images for sermons, bringing life to discoveries.

Sentences. With a skillfully constructed sentence, a preacher can make a memorable picture in the mind of the hearers. Charles Haddon Spurgeon said in a sermon: "God gets his best soldiers from the highlands of affliction." Cynddylon Jones said: "You might as well try to cross the Atlantic in a paper boat as to get to

---

51. Sue Nichols, *Words on Target: For Better Communication* (Richmond, Va.: John Knox Press), 47–61.

52. Calvin Miller, *Spirit, Word, and Story: A Philosophy of Preaching* (Dallas: Word Publishing, 1989), 109.

heaven by your own good works."[53] Preachers should include at least a half dozen pictorial sentences in each sermon.

Stories. Allegories, fables, parables, life experiences, anecdotes, and historical happenings are various forms of stories. Allegory is one use of illustrative material, but it is not as popular as it once was. Perhaps one of the best uses of allegory is in John Bunyan's work *Pilgrim's Progress*. An allegory is a fictitious story which conveys an abstract truth in symbolic language. A contemporary allegory is George Lucas' *Star Wars*.

Fables. Aesop, the Brothers Grimm, Hans Christian Anderson, and Lewis Carroll created or recorded fables. These are imaginary stories, often about animals. Only the extremely gifted expositor could create fables, but any expositor can use existing fables.

Parables. Parables, both ancient and contemporary, represent a variation of a story. In the Bible, a parable was a true-to-life story that communicated a moral or spiritual truth. Jesus used parables extensively. Søren Kierkegaard, the Danish philosopher and theologian, created parables to communicate biblical truth. Strange as it may seem, contemporary preachers rarely present truth with created parables. With the help of God's Spirit, today's expositors could create contemporary parables in the sermons.

True-life experiences. Perhaps the most popular variation of a story in today's world comes from life experiences. These kinds of stories are real happenings of a biographical, autobiographical, historical, or literary nature. Such stories also include current happenings. Reuel Howe commended the life-experience type of illustration when he said, "The sermons which get my attention are the ones in which they relate a story of everyday living and use it to tell us about Christian living."[54] Recounting experiences from people's lives is an appropriate method of relating life experiences. People relate to the biographical experiences of others. Relating autobiographical experiences is also a legitimate method of using life experiences. Autobiographical disclosure involves sharing the light a preacher has found or the darkness a preacher has experienced. It is not self-exposure for the sake of pity or praise. It is shared personal experience for the purpose of illumining a biblical

---

53. Quoted in MacPherson, *The Art of Illustrating Sermons*, 51.
54. Reuel L. Howe, *Partners in Preaching* (New York: Seaburg Press, 1967), 31.

truth. Excessive self-exposure that deflects biblical truth should be avoided.

Historical incidents. Historical happenings furnish abundant illustration potential. Just because an event occurred years ago does not make it irrelevant to a congregation today. All the events of history, both secular and religious, are available for illustrative material. Retelling a historical happening in an appropriate and relevant manner can help audiences understand and apply truth to life in their contemporary world.

Current events. Preachers can also derive illustrations from the news of the day. Events that could be used to illustrate truths in sermons occur daily. These experiences are as numerous and as diverse as the news of a cat in a tree or a military clash. These happenings are full of human interest, of joy and despair, and can be effectively used in sermons.

Dramas. In most cases, illustrations from literature and films represent life experiences. Ancient and contemporary literature provide an immense field and offer a vast resource for illustrations. Novels, plays, and movies furnish realistic slices of human existence. Sermons may come alive through the wise use of drama as illustrative material.

Poems. Poetry expresses the realities of life in different language forms. Though poetry is not widely read, there seems to be a universal liking for the rhythm and beauty expressed in verse. Often a poem brings into focus an idea more beautifully and powerfully expressed than could any combination of work in prose. A few lines from a poem or hymn can add interest and effect to the sermon.

Quotations. Sayings, maxims, and proverbs provide a valuable means of stating the truth impressively and forcibly. Axioms spoken by people throughout the ages of civilization provide abundant resources for illustrative material. Axioms evaluate people and events of life; thus, they help substantiate a point or state a point in a fresh way. Jesus repeatedly used expressions which appear to have been proverbial. The Book of Proverbs, with its numerous wise sayings, can furnish preachers with abundant resources. Quotes or proverbs are especially forceful means of adding illustrative material.

Humor. Skillful use of language, stories, poetry, and quotations often invokes humor. If humor can help illumine and impact people, it can be valuable. But if humor is used to entertain or to display cleverness, it is entirely out of place. If used wisely, humor can be a means of getting a point across, establishing rapport with an audience, and applying a truth. In the latter part of the twentieth century, using humor wisely has played a large part in helping illustrate sermons.

Imagination

Content for sermons comes from the traditional, logical reasoning elements of explanation, argumentation, application, and illustration. But substance for sermons also should include the element of imagination. Urban T. Holmes III defined imagination as the capacity "to make the material an image of the immaterial or spiritual."[55]

People have the ability to create images and to use narrative logic. Imagination incarnates facts with living scenes and situations to present hidden truth. It identifies the unknown and the known and creates fresh images so hearers can understand and experience truth in a new way.

Unfortunately, erroneous ideas exist about imagination. There has been an emphasis on imagining as flight into fantasy, rather than as imaginative representation of reality. Authentic imagination uses facts which have been discovered. Imagination always comes under the control of reality; it is the power to evoke new material from that which is factually familiar. Thomas H. Troeger gave the guidelines for imagination to be "encouraged by the Spirit, disciplined by Scripture, informed by the wisdom of the homiletical city, and energized by the need of the world."[56]

Early in the 1960s, scientists presented an interesting theory about the dual nature of the human brain. This theory, if true, would definitely affect the way a preacher shaped a sermon and added content. Scientists proposed the idea that each of the brain's two hemispheres—right and left—process information in different ways. According to this theory, the left hemisphere of the brain processes information analytically and verbally, dividing information into component parts. It understands and communicates truth by analyzing. The right hemisphere of the brain deals with information

---

55. Urban T. Holmes III, *Ministry and Imagination* (New York: Seaburg Press, 1976), 97–98.

56. Thomas H. Troeger, *Imagining a Sermon* (Nashville: Abingdon Press, 1990), 28.

instinctually and visually. Scientists say the hemispheres are connected by the *corpus callosum*, allowing the two halves to interact.[57]

Over the years, preachers have been trained in traditional homiletics to process and communicate information analytically. Troeger stated that the model of homiletics is shifting toward images.[58] Such a shift would mean calling on the right hemisphere of the brain for more instinctive and imaginative sermon substance. Troeger indicated that many of the homiletical systems provide a step-by-step plan for producing sermon content analytically even when the preacher is not inspired. In speaking of the process, Troeger said, "A preacher could construct something to say no matter how cold and dry the wells of inspiration are."[59] Just as preachers develop the left brain of analysis, they also need to develop the right brain of images.

Preaching from a Bible book calls for the use of the whole brain in putting substance into sermons. Content from analytical reasoning and visual imagining could be used. Explanation, argumentation, and application come more from left brain reasoning. Illustration uses vision and imagination—both right-brain functions. To develop skills in imagination, two topics will be examined: the functions of imagination and the procedures for imagination.

Functions of Imagination

Using imagination in sermons can increase the possibility of receiving and comprehending biblical truth. Sermons sprinkled with imagination can create interest and communicate the Word of God in a fresh way. Before learning how to put imagination into sermons, expositors should know the numerous functions of the imagination.

Imagination organizes content in fresh forms. Imagination can help in shaping sermon substance. Imagination functions as a means of giving familiar materials fresh insights and interest—these familiar materials must be brought into new combinations. Just as the individual ingredients of flour, eggs, milk, salt, and yeast are not bread, piling up thoughts does not constitute a sermon. The cook creatively combines the ingredients to make bread; so too, the creative

---

57. Ralph L. Lewis with Gregg Lewis, *Learning to Preach Like Jesus* (Westchester, Ill.: Crossway Books, 1989), 37.

58. Troeger, *Imagining a Sermon*, 28–30.

59. Ibid., 13.

expositor shapes a sermon. Imagination does not create content; it organizes content in fresh forms. Much of the preparation of a sermon involves the work of a word-picture artist. Sermons begin with a basic design that resembles building a foundation. After a basic design has been chosen, materials for the sermon have to be collected. Every step in shaping a sermon is a work of imagination. Organizing the paragraphs and constructing the sentences are works of art. Factual material should be shaped in fresh ways to give fresh interest to the familiar.

Imagination creates revealing images. Imagination helps the preacher clothe abstract ideas in concrete expressions. Pictures of reality become more interesting and convincing than arguments. Jesus, the master Preacher, used imagination in many of his messages. For example, he did not give an abstract disclosure of God's love. Instead he created a picture of a shepherd looking for a lost sheep so that hearers could "see" the truth that God loves the lost. The image of a loving shepherd in action appears to be more effective than an argument. The dilemma of every expositor is how to portray the syllables of existence so that people can recognize God's Word in their daily living.

Creating revealing images is a function of imagination built on facts. The expositor should examine truth and then seek to create fresh images for the truth. If possible, an idea or thought should associate with a resemblance or an analogy where images can be formed. Revealing images do not create truth, but they help comprehension, build conviction, and awaken emotions.

Imagination narrates the biblical revelation. Recounting the events of the Bible is one of the most powerful purposes of preaching. Actually, all of the Bible happened in history; thus, a story exists behind every verse. Much of the Bible consists of narrative, and the task of the expositor is to retell the scenes and events. Narrating the Scriptures takes imagination in reproducing the scenes, persons, and events of the past. Preachers have to think back into the story and bring it forward to today, observing carefully and participating empathetically in what has transpired. Reproducing Bible stories requires a thorough knowledge of the times and empathy with ancient attitudes and actions; otherwise, expositors will fall into error and misrepresentation.

Imagination visualizes people's experiences. Expositors need to think into the feelings of people who hear sermons. Ezekiel set an example when he said, "I sat there seven days where they were living" (Ezek. 3:15). Expositors who sit with people until they know their fortunes and failures, their happinesses and hurts, their sins and virtues, their temptations and aspirations will have abundant content for sermons. Putting themselves in the place of others gives expositors an imaginative dimension to sermons. When an expositor uses empathetic imagination, hearers will listen and homiletical artistry will become secondary. Understanding the lives of listeners helps the expositor move away from generalizing truth to specifying truth.

Procedures for Imagination

Imagination is not the gift of a chosen few. It is a possession for all persons. Some people are endowed with more imagination and cultural development than others, but anyone chosen by God to preach his Word possesses the power of imagination. Some preachers seem to be born with imaginative quality, but like the less gifted they have to cultivate their inventive geniuses. Skill in imagination depends on and responds to constant cultivation.

Procedures for incorporating imagination into sermons are as much theological as methodological. Expositors should study procedures that could produce imaginative content in sermons. Imagination does not just happen. The following list of six requirements presents some courses of action.

1. Imagination requires time. Imagination comes to expositors who take time to be still and reflect in their study. Preachers act as administrators, counsel numerous people, care for congregations, and perform other duties; thus, little time is left for reflection. Imagination finds its impetus more in scheduled study than in a busy schedule. The expositor must reflect creatively on the text and engage in prayer. Thomas Troeger wrote: "It takes discipline to see and to hear the visions and voices of God in our life, discipline every bit as strenuous as exegesis. There is a sharpening of the eye and a training of the ear that can help us avoid mistaking the hollowness of our study for the absence of Spirit."[60] The invisible world becomes more visible when the expositor keeps close to the source of the vision. Rhetoric, logic, and psychology are the instru-

---

60. Thomas H. Troeger, *Creating Fresh Images for Preaching: New Rungs for Jacob's Ladder* (Valley Forge, Pa.: Judson Press, 1982), 12.

ments of preaching, but the Holy Spirit is the creative source of power and imagination.[61]

2. Imagination requires experience. When truth becomes experience, it impacts the way sermons are prepared and preached. In a way, the act of preaching is an experience in personal exposure. Expositors do not just study biblical truth; they experience truth in the text. Having had a personal experience with the text makes a preacher and the sermon real. Preachers imagine best when they listen to God speak to them about the grace reflected in Ephesians 2:8–10 and when they experience the grace of God, not when resources have to be secured to embellish God's grace. Experiencing truth and then exposing it make for credible imagination.

3. Imagination requires concrete thinking. Imagination comes to an expositor who creates images of abstract ideas. Biblical truth can be understood and communicated in images. Amos communicated prophetic truth in images of a roaring lion, the sight of a mangled lamb, the coming of grasshoppers, the use of a plumb line, and a basket of summer fruit. Jesus took abstract truth and used it to create images. When he wanted to explain how people listened, he invited hearers to look at an image: "Behold, the sower went out to sow" (Matt. 13:3b). Jesus had the ability to see the truth and communicate it with pictures. Exegetes of biblical texts should ask, "Can the listener see the truth?" In asking such a question, expositors are doing much more than gathering and arranging sermon content. They are trying to create a fresh image so listeners of their sermons also will see the truth.

4. Imagination requires vocabulary study. Imagination helps preachers work creatively with words. David Buttrick said, "With words, we name the world."[62] Words come from everywhere to make up our vocabulary. Arranging words to write or to speak ideas to others involves choosing and using appropriate words. Shaping words into sentences is a process of imagination. Since sermons consist of words, preachers work constantly with words. They need to shape sentences with variety, search for synonyms, choose active verbs, find descriptive adjectives, forceful prepositions, and specific nouns. Well-chosen words are not an ostentatious display; instead,

---

61. Broadus, 291.

62. David Buttrick, *Homiletic: Moves and Structures* (Philadelphia: Fortress Press, 1987), 9.

they clarify understanding and communicate content. Expositors who want imaginative content should always be studying words—their combinations and their usages. Selecting and arranging words take work. Writing sermons in manuscripts can help with the preacher's use of words. It does not mean the sermon has to be read in delivery.

5. *Imagination requires lifelong learning.* Imagination comes not from a few hours each week in the study but from a life-style of learning about all of life. An engaging and interesting expositor lives among people, observes their lives, listens to their ideas, learns their language and meanings, participates in their work and play, and knows their flaws and virtues. Preachers also learn about life when they read extensively. They learn what other people have imagined and how they expressed what they saw. Poetry, drama, and even some fiction depict life in picturesque and emotional language. Sermon substance comes easier when preachers live in the wide world of reading, listening, and observing life.

6. *Imagination requires meditation on everyday experiences.* Thomas H. Troeger said: "The vividness of the world feeds our creativity day by day. We are less anxious about finding homiletical resources because we have become sensitive to the richness of common experience. We use our imaginations to draw parables from life, from plain human stories that are marked by ambiguity, resolution, and renewed ambiguity."[63]

Resources for sermons develop constantly through the experience of living. Expositors do not have to order outlines or substance for sermons when the abundant riches of life's experiences exist. Expositors can draw lessons from common, everyday experienced expositors. The discipline of using life's experiences for spiritual lessons should be developed constantly. If expositors study Jesus' teachings, they will discover that he was a master of this procedure of imagination.

Using the imagination in sermons is not just a recent focus of homiletics. Almost a century ago, Henry Ward Beecher expressed strong feelings about imagination in sermons. In his famous *Yale Lectures on Preaching*, he named imagination as the most important prerequisite for effective preaching. He used a phrase calling imagination "the God Power of the Soul" by which he meant "the

---

63. Troeger, *Imagining a Sermon*, 89.

power of conceiving as definite the things which are invisible to the senses—of giving them distinct shape."[64] Imagination is a rhapsodic, rational, prayerful, meditative, all-embracing process that replicates through the limitations of human language and actions the pulsations of the heart of reality.[65] Each expositor needs to acknowledge that he has the gift of imagination and resolve to develop imaginative skills for putting content in sermons.

Narration

Much of the substance for sermons comes from the narration of biblical material or of current circumstances. Charles W. Koller named narration as a "rhetorical process," or a means of putting flesh on the bare bones of a sermon outline. He also named interpretation, illustration, application, argumentation, and exhortation as the other rhetorical processes.[66] Putting narration in sermons differs from designing a narrative sermon. The narrative sermon, rather than containing the content of narration, is a narration from beginning to end, with the entire sermon held together with a single plot or theme. Occasionally in narrative sermons, subplots, separate illustration, or lessons appear, but the plot or theme stays in force from the "once upon a time" until its "happily ever after."[67] The narrative sermon might simply be retelling a biblical narrative in a story style, or it might be a contemporary story made analogous to some biblical truth. Narrative sermons primarily contain narrative content.

Sermons that do not have a narrative design can contain narration as part of content. Along with the other elements of explanation, argumentation, application, illustration, and imagination, the element of narration is a vital element for putting substance in sermons. Narration as an element overlaps with the other six elements and complements them. The amount of narration differs from sermon to sermon, but almost every sermon needs narrative content. Narration is needed to retell the biblical story or to put the concepts of the text in a narrative form. Expositors can successfully

---

64. Ibid, 114.

65. Ibid.

66. Charles W. Koller, *Expository Preaching Without Notes* (Grand Rapids: Baker Book House, 1962), 50–51.

67. Calvin Miller, "Narrative Preaching" in *A Handbook of Contemporary Preaching* (Nashville: Broadman Press, 1992), 103.

include narrative portions in sermons and even in designing narrative sermons by observing the possibilities of narration and by learning to narrate.

Possibilities of Narration

Using narrative content in sermons creates enormous possibilities. Narration creates interest. Ears perk up when a story appears in a sermon. A narrative almost inevitably catches the hearers' attention, involving them in the sermon.

Narration clarifies abstract truth. Sharing information by logical reasoning is part of preaching, but inserting narration helps make truth plain to the hearer. Stories implanted in the preaching process help hearers understand biblical principles. Too much abstract material can create ambiguity. Inserting a story analogous to the abstraction can help move sermon content from general truth to specific examples of the truth.

Narration facilitates indirect address. The basic concern for preaching God's Word is not the transference of information. Fred Craddock learned from Søren Kierkegaard that the indirect mode of communication is the most suitable for communicating God's Word. Craddock said, "The indirect is the mode for eliciting capability and action from within the listener, a transaction that does not occur by giving the hearer some information."[68] Storytelling in preaching does not hit hearers so directly. Narrative material seems to engage the hearers, to involve them, and to invite them into the drama.

Narration aids listener identification. All stories can touch the listener in one way or another. Stories are about us. To paraphrase Pogo, "We have met the story and it is us."[69] Joseph Campbell, writing over a quarter of a century ago, entitled his famous book *The Hero with a Thousand Faces.* Campbell believed that there is really only one story and one hero, and he or she wears many faces, including our own. Every story in God's Word is everybody's story.

Narration aides the memory. Stories help people remember their history, their glories, and their sin and shame. Israelite history was preserved through oral storytelling. They did not want their

---

68. Craddock, *Overhearing the Gospel*, 82.

69. William J. Bausch, *Storytelling: Imagination and Faith* (Mystic, Conn.: Twenty-Third Publications, 1984), 58–60.

descendants to forget God's works among them or the stupidity of their rebellion against God. Expositors of God's Word use narration to help us remember and, in remembering, to celebrate God's goodness, to confess, and in confessing to be whole. William R. White wrote: "We are a forgetful people. We need storytellers. We need someone to lay the drama of God's love before us."[70] Hearers have a tendency to remember narrative material more than logical reason. Stories have the power to elicit memory and to help hearers keep remembering.

Narration helps people relax. Telling a story creates listener relief—comic or dramatic—from rational arguments. When words are too much for people, a good story can give a break without departing from the subject. Narrative material, whether humorous or serious, offers another way to present truth. Variety in the kinds of material presented gives a minibreak to listeners.

Narration enhances behavior modification. Bruce C. Salmon wrote: "Reason alone seldom motivates people to change their actions, attitudes or ideas. Human behavior is largely determined by feelings."[71] Frank Dance wrote that persons do not change behavior simply because they are told to. Rather, they must be engaged in the decision to change their behavior.[72] Such engagement appeals to the emotions. Rational argument appeals to the mind, but narrative appeals to the heart, where there is the impetus to decide.

Techniques of Narration

Expositors need to learn the skill of narrating just as much as learning the art of logical reasoning. The techniques of narrating can be learned by reading books on the mechanics of storytelling, listening to skilled storytellers, and reading great stories. The best stories and the most skilled storytellers can be found in the Bible. Studying biblical narration can help expositors learn some of the bedrock rules of storytelling.

1. Remember the point! Some preachers make the point implicit within the story. Other preachers make the point and then tell stories to substantiate, elaborate, or illustrate the point. The biblical

---

70. William R. White, *Speaking in Stories* (Minneapolis: Augsbury Publishing, 1982), 118.

71. Bruce C. Salmon, *Storytelling in Preaching: A Guide to the Theory and Practice* (Nashville: Broadman Press), 128.

72. Dance, 31.

narration presents not only information about people, places, and events but also theological reasons for existence. Before expositors put narrative material in a sermon, the following questions need to be asked: Does the story make a point? Does the story relate to the point?

2. Gets your ducks in a row! Give careful attention to the sequence of events. Read the story of Joseph recorded in Genesis 37–50. Notice how skillfully the author gave the continuity of events. Putting events in sequence is much more than giving an order of reports. A narrator needs to build response. The introduction of response makes a story different from a report. A report merely links a series of events together. Narration introduces tension or response and releases the response at the right moment. It does not take much to arouse people's interest. Jesus said: "A certain man had two sons," and with those words the Lord took listeners on a journey. The opening line created a desire to know more about the two sons. Jesus then selected the story of one son, and each episode in the story had a response. The story turned dramatically when Jesus related how the other son related to the prodigal son.

3. Clip the shaggy dog! In narrating an event, no side issues should take away from the main events. Interesting narration can be destroyed when tangential matters are introduced. Hearers lack the patience to put up with disjointed thoughts, so preachers need to keep a singleness of thought and a continuity of events in narrative.

4. Focus on words and actions! Characters in stories have a purpose. Recognizing the function of major and minor characters is important. John C. Holbert in *Preaching Old Testament: Proclamation and Narrative in the Hebrew Bible* instructed expositors to watch what characters say and do.[73] In studying people's words and actions, expositors learn character. So, in narrating an episode with people involved, expositors need to recount actions and speech. Hearers can then learn who the characters are and what they are like.

Description in narration should use adjectives wisely, insert illustrative phrases, and use sentences that portray a place or an object. Expositors need to study about places and objects, see them in their mind, and then describe them in narration.

---

73. John C. Holbert, *Preaching Old Testament: Proclamation and Narrative in the Hebrew Bible* (Nashville: Abingdon Press, 1991), 64–68.

5. *Draw implications!* Sometimes expositors must trust the story to convey its meaning. Often when stories have to be explained, the impact of narrating the story has been destroyed. At other times expositors should interpret the narration. The purpose of the interpretation is not to rob the narration of its force, but to focus on its force. There is always a chance that listeners will not hear the real part of the story. Therefore, implications of the narration should be interpreted in some way to the hearers. Such explanation need not be an elaborate discussion but a brief application.

Sermon content can be improved with the skillful use of narrative materials. Expositors through the years have been adept in using logical argument for sermon content. Now with the publication of so many books on the mechanics of storytelling and the presence of so many secular storytelling and narrative preachers, sermons can be enhanced with narrative content.

Putting content in sermons is a multidimensional pursuit. No one, two, or three elements should dominate the choice of content for sermons. All of the elements, whether explanation, argumentation, application, illustration, imagination, or narration, help expositors preach the Word. All elements of content exist to help bring the truth of God's Word to people in such a way that they can hear clearly what God is saying.

Bibliography

Preaching

Achtemeier, Elizabeth. *Creative Preaching: Finding the Words.* Nashville: Abingdon Press, 1980.

————. *Preaching as Theology and Art.* Nashville: Abingdon Press, 1984.

Allen, Ronald J. *Preaching the Topical Sermon.* Louisville: Westminster/John Knox Press, 1992.

Barth, Karl. *The Word of God and the Word of Man.* Translated by Douglas Horton. New York: Harper and Row, 1957.

Bartow, Charles L. *The Preaching Moment: A Guide to Sermon Delivery.* Nashville: Abingdon Press, 1980.

————. *The Preaching of the Gospel.* Translated by B. E. Hooke. Philadelphia: Westminster Press, 1963.

Bass, George M. *The Song and the Story.* Lima, Ohio: C. S. S., Publishing, 1984.

Baumann, J. Daniel. *An Introduction to Contemporary Preaching.* Grand Rapids: Baker Book House, 1972, 1988.

Black, James. *The Mystery of Preaching.* Reprint. Grand Rapids: Zondervan, 1978.

Bowie, Walter R. *Preaching.* New York: Abingdon Press, 1954.

Braga, James. *How to Prepare Bible Messages.* Portland, Oreg.: Multnomah Press, 1981.

Broadus, John A. *On the Preparation and Delivery of Sermons.* 4th ed. Revised by Vernon L. Stanfield. San Francisco: Harper and Row, 1986.

Brooks, Philips. *Lectures on Preaching*. Reprint of Yale lectures. Grand Rapids: Baker Book House, 1978.

Brown, David M. *Dramatic Narrative in Preaching*. Valley Forge, Pa.: Judson Press, 1981.

Brown, H. C., Jr. *A Quest for Reformation in Preaching*. Waco, Texas: Word Books, Publishers, 1968.

Brown, H. C. Jr., H. Gordon Clinard, and Jesse J. Northcutt. *Steps to the Sermon: A Plan for Sermon Preparation*. Nashville: Broadman Press, 1963.

Bugg, Charles. *Preaching from the Inside Out*. Nashville: Broadman Press, 1992.

Burghardt, Walter J. *Preaching: The Art and the Craft*. New York: Paulist Press, 1987.

Buttrick, David G. *A Captive Voice: The Liberation of Preaching*. Louisville, Ky.: Westminster/John Knox Press, 1994.

———. *Homiletic: Moves and Structures*. Philadelphia: Fortress Press, 1987.

Chapel, Bryan. *Christ-Centered Preaching: Redeeming the Expository Sermon*. Grand Rapids: Baker Book House, 1994.

———. *Using Illustrations to Preach with Power*. Grand Rapids: Zondervan Publishing House, 1992.

Cox, James W. *Biblical Preaching: An Expositor's Treasury*. Philadelphia: Westminster Press, 1983.

———. *A Guide to Biblical Preaching*. Nashville: Abingdon Press, 1976.

———. *Preaching: A Comprehensive Approach to the Design and Delivery of Sermons*. San Francisco: Harper and Row, 1985.

Craddock, Fred B. *As One Without Authority*. Nashville: Abingdon Press, 1981.

———. *Overhearing the Gospel*. Nashville: Abingdon Press, 1978.

———. *Preaching*. Nashville: Abingdon Press, 1985.

Crum, Milton, Jr. *Manual on Preaching*. Wilton, Conn.: Morehouse-Barlow, 1988.

Daane, James. *Preaching with Confidence: A Theological Essay on the Power of the Pulpit*. Grand Rapids: William B. Eerdmans, 1980.

Davis, H. Grady. *Design for Preaching*. Philadelphia: Fortress Press, 1958.

Demaray, Donald E. *Introduction to Homiletics*. 2d ed. Grand Rapids: Baker Book House, 1990.

———. *Proclaiming the Truth: Guides to Spiritual Preaching*. Grand Rapids: Baker Book House, 1979.

Diduit, Michael, ed. *Handbook of Contemporary Preaching*. Nashville: Broadman Press, 1992.

Dodd, C. H. *The Apostolic Preaching and Its Development*. New York: Harper and Row, 1964.

Eslinger, Richard L. *A New Hearing: Living Options in Homiletic Method*. Nashville: Abingdon Press, 1987.

Fant, Clyde E. *Preaching for Today*. 2d ed. New York: Harper and Row, 1987.

Fasol, Al. *Essentials for Biblical Preaching*. Grand Rapids: Baker Book House, 1989.

Faw, Chalmers E. *A Guide to Biblical Preaching*. Nashville: Broadman Press, 1962.

Flynn, Leslie B. *Come Alive with Illustrations*. Grand Rapids: Baker Book House, 1988.

Ford, D. W. Cleverly. *The Ministry of the Word*. Grand Rapids: William B. Eerdmans, 1979.

———. *Preaching Today*. London: Epworth Press, 1969.

Freeman, Harold. *Variety in Biblical Preaching: Innovative Techniques and Fresh Forms*. Waco: Word Books, 1986.

Gowan, Donald E. *Reclaiming the Old Testament for the Christian Pulpit*. Atlanta: John Knox Press, 1980.

Grant, Reg and John Reed. *The Power Sermon: Countdown to Quality Messages with Maximum Impact*. Grand Rapids: Baker Books, 1993.

Hall, E. Eugene and James L. Heflin. *Proclaim the Word: The Bases of Preaching*. Nashville: Broadman Press, 1985.

Hall, Thor. *The Future Shape of Preaching*. Philadelphia: Fortress Press, 1971.

Hamilton, Donald L. *Homiletical Handbook*. Nashville: Broadman Press, 1992.

Holbert, John C. *Preaching the Old Testament: Proclamation and Narration in the Hebrew Bible*. Nashville: Abingdon Press, 1991.

Jackson, Edgar N. *How to Preach to People's Needs*. Grand Rapids: Baker Book House, 1956.

Jensen, Richard A. *Telling the Story: Variety and Imagination in Preaching*. Minneapolis: Augsburg Publishing House, 1979.

———. *Thinking in Story: Preaching in a Post-literate Age*. Lima, Ohio: C. S. S. Publishing Company, 1993.

Jones, Ilion T. *Principles and Practice of Preaching*. New York: Abingdon Press, 1956.

Kemp, Charles F. *The Preaching Pastor*. St. Louis: Bethany Press, 1966.

Killinger, John. *Fundamentals of Preaching*. Philadelphia: Fortress Press, 1985.

Koller, Charles W. *Expository Preaching Without Notes Plus Sermons Preached Without Notes*. Grand Rapids: Baker Book House, 1962.

Larson, David L. *The Anatomy of Preaching: Identifying the Issues in Preaching Today*. Grand Rapids: Baker Book House, 1989.

Lenski, R. C. H. *The Sermon: Its Homiletical Construction*. Reprint. Grand Rapids: Baker Book House, 1968.

Lewis, Ralph L. and Gregg Lewis. *Inductive Preaching: Helping People Listen*. Westchester, Ill.: Crossway Books, 1983.

———. *Learning to Preach Like Jesus*. Wheaton, Ill.: Crossway Books, 1989.

Lischer, Richard. *Theories of Preaching: Selected Readings in the Homiletical Tradition*. Durham, N.C.: Labyrinth Press, 1987.

Lloyd-Jones, D. Martyn. *Preaching and Preachers*. Grand Rapids: Zondervan, 1971.

Long, Thomas G. *The Senses of Preaching*. Atlanta: John Knox Press, 1988.

———. *The Witness of Preaching*. Louisville: Westminster/John Knox Press, 1989.

Loscalzo, Craig A. *Preaching Sermons That Connect: Effective Communication Through Identification*. Downers Grove, Ill.: InterVarsity Press, 1992.

Lowry, Eugene L. *Doing Time in the Pulpit: The Relationship Between Narrative and Preaching*. Nashville: Abingdon Press, 1985.

———. *The Homiletical Plot: The Sermon as Narrative Art Form*. Atlanta: John Knox Press, 1980.

Luccock, Halford E. *Communicating the Gospel*. Yale Lectures. New York: Harper and Row, 1954.

———. *In the Minister's Workshop*. Nashville: Abingdon-Cokesbury Press, 1944.

Lueking, F. Dean. *Preaching: The Art of Connecting God and People*. Waco: Word Books, 1985.

MacArthur, John, Jr., and the Master's Seminary Faculty. *Rediscovering Expository Preaching*. Dallas: Word Publishing, 1992.

Macartney, Clarence E. *Preaching Without Notes*. New York: Abingdon Press, 1946.

McCraken, Robert J. *The Making of the Sermon*. New York: Harper and Row, 1956.

McDill, Wayne. *The 12 Essential Skills for Great Preaching*. Nashville: Broadman & Holman Publishers, 1994.

Markquart, Edward F. *Quest for Better Preaching: Resources for Renewal in the Pulpit*. Minneapolis: Augsburg Publishing House, 1985.

Massey, James Earl. *Designing the Sermon: Order and Movement in Preaching*. Nashville: Abingdon Press, 1980.

Meyer, F. B. *Expository Preaching: Plans and Methods*. New York: Doran, 1912.

Miller, Calvin. *The Empowered Communicator: 7 Keys to Unlocking an Audience*. Nashville: Broadman & Holman Publishers, 1994.

————.*Spirit, Word, and Story: A Philosophy of Preaching*. Dallas: Word Books, 1989.

Miller, Donald G. *Fire in Thy Mouth*. Nashville: Abingdon Press, 1954.

————. *The Way to Biblical Preaching*. New York: Abingdon Press, 1957.

Morgan, Peter M. *Story Weaving: Using Stories to Transform Congregations*. St. Louis: CBP Press, 1986.

Nichols, J. Randall. *The Restoring Word: Preaching as Pastoral Communication*. San Francisco: Harper and Row, 1987.

O'Day, Gail R. and Thomas G. Long. *Listening to the Word: Studies in Honor of Fred B. Craddock*. Nashville: Abingdon Press, 1993.

Pattison, Thomas H. *The Making of the Sermon*. Philadelphia: Judson Press, 1941.

Pearce, J. Winston. *Planning Your Preaching*. Nashville: Broadman Press, 1979.

Perry, Lloyd M. *Biblical Preaching for Today's World*. Chicago: Moody Press, 1973.

————. *Biblical Sermon Guide*. Grand Rapids: Baker Book House, 1979.

————. *A Manual for Biblical Preaching*. Grand Rapids: Baker Book House, 1981.

Piper, John. *The Supremacy of God in Preaching*. Grand Rapids: Baker Book House, 1990.

Pitt-Watson, Ian. *A Primer for Preachers*. Grand Rapids: Baker Book House, 1986.

————. *Preaching: A Kind of Folly*. Edinburgh: St. Andrew's Press, 1976.

Robinson, Haddon W. *Biblical Preaching: The Development and Delivery of Expository Messages*. Grand Rapids: Baker Book House, 1980.

————. *Biblical Sermons: How Twelve Preachers Apply the Principles of Biblical Preaching*. Grand Rapids: Baker Book House, 1989.

Salmon, Bruce C. *Storytelling in Preaching: A Guide to the Theory and*

Practice. Nashville: Broadman Press, 1988.

Sangster, William E. *The Craft of Sermon Construction*. Philadelphia: Westminster Press, 1951.

Scherer, Paul. *For We Have This Treasure*. Yale Lectures. New York: Harper and Row, 1944.

Shoemaker, H. Stephen. *Retelling the Biblical Story: The Theology and Practice of Narrative Preaching*. Nashville: Broadman Press, 1985.

Skinner, Craig. *The Teaching Ministry of the Pulpit*. Reprint. Lanham, Md.: University Press of America, 1988.

Sleeth, Ronald. *God's Word and Our Words: Basic Homiletics*. Atlanta: John Knox Press, 1986.

———. *Proclaiming the Word*. Nashville: Abingdon Press, 1964.

Spurgeon, Charles H. *Spurgeon's Lectures to His Students*. Reprint. Grand Rapids: Zondervan, 1955.

Stevenson, Dwight E. *In the Biblical Preacher's Workshop*. Nashville: Abingdon Press, 1967.

Stevenson, Dwight E. and Charles F. Diehl. *Reaching People from the Pulpit: A Guide to Effective Sermon Delivery*. Grand Rapids: Baker Book House, 1958.

Stewart, James. *A Faith to Proclaim*. Reprint of Yale Lectures. Grand Rapids: Baker Book House, 1972.

———. *Heralds of God*. London: Hodder and Stoughton, 1946.

Stibbs, Alan M. *Expounding God's Word: Some Principles and Methods*. Grand Rapids: William B. Eerdmans, 1961.

Stott, John R. W. *Between Two Worlds: The Art of Preaching in the Twentieth Century*. Grand Rapids: William B. Eerdmans, 1982.

———. *The Preacher's Portrait*. Grand Rapids: William B. Eerdmans, 1964.

Stratman, Gary D. *Pastoral Preaching: Timeless Truth for Changing Needs*. Nashville: Abingdon Press, 1983.

Sweazey, George E. *Preaching the Good News*. Englewood Cliffs, N.J.: Prentice-Hall, 1976.

Thielen, Martin. *Getting Ready for Sunday's Sermon: A Practical Guide for Sermon Preparation*. Nashville: Broadman Press, 1990.

Thompson, William D. and Gordon C. Bennett. *Dialogue Preaching: The Shared Sermon*. Valley Forge, Pa.: Judson Press, 1969.

Troeger, Thomas H. *Imagining a Sermon*. Nashville: Abingdon Press, 1990.

Unger, Merrill F. *Principles of Expository Preaching*. Grand Rapids: Zondervan, 1955.

Vines, Jerry. *A Practical Guide to Sermon Preparation*. Chicago: Moody

Press, 1985.

Whitesell, Faris D. *The Art of Biblical Preaching*. Grand Rapids: Zondervan, 1950.

Whitesell, Faris D. and Lloyd M. Perry. *Variety in Your Preaching*. Old Tappan, N.J.: Fleming H. Revell, 1954.

Wiersbe, Warren W. *Preaching and Teaching with Imagination*. Wheaton, Ill.: Victor Books, 1994.

Willimon, William H. *The Intensive Word: Preaching to the Unbaptized*. Grand Rapids: William B. Eerdmans, 1994.

———. *Peculiar Speech: Preaching to the Baptized*. Grand Rapids: William B. Eerdmans, 1992.

———. *Preaching and Leading Worship*. Philadelphia: Westminster Press, 1984.

Wingren, Gustaf. *The Living Word: A Theological Study of Preaching and the Church*. Translated by V. C. Pogue. London: SCM, 1960.

Wood, John. *The Preacher's Workshop: Preparation for Expository Preaching*. Chicago: Inter-Varsity Press, 1965.

Interpretation

Achtemeier, Elizabeth. *The Old Testament and the Proclamation of the Gospel*. Philadelphia: Westminster Press, 1973.

———. *Preaching from the Old Testament*. Louisville, Ky.: Westminster/John Knox Press, 1989.

Achtemeier, Paul J. *An Introduction to the New Hermeneutic*. Philadelphia: Westminster Press, 1969.

Allen, Ronald J. *Contemporary Biblical Interpretation for Preaching*. Valley Forge, Pa.: Judson Press, 1984.

Alter, Robert. *The Art of Biblical Narrative*. New York: Basic Books, 1981.

———. *The Art of Biblical Poetry*. New York: Basic Books, 1985.

Aune, David. *The New Testament in Its Literary Environment*. Philadelphia: Westminster Press, 1987.

Bailey, Raymond, ed. *Hermeneutics for Preaching: Approaches to Contemporary Interpretation of Scripture*. Nashville: Broadman Press, 1992.

Barr, James. *The Bible in the Modern World*. New York: Harper and Row, 1973.

Berkhof, Louis. *Principles of Biblical Interpretation*. Grand Rapids: Baker Book House, 1950.

Berkouwer, G. C. *Holy Scripture*. Translated and edited by Jack B. Rogers. Grand Rapids: Eerdmans, 1975.

Best, Ernest. *From Text to Sermon: Responsible Use of the New Testament in Preaching*. Atlanta: John Knox Press, 1978.

Blackwood, Andrew W. *Preaching from the Bible*. New York: Abingdon Press, 1941.

———. *The Preparation of Sermons*. London: Church Book Room, 1948.

Bruce, F. F. *The Message of the New Testament*. Grand Rapids: William B. Eerdmans, 1973.

Caird, G. B. *The Language and Imagery of the Bible*. Philadelphia: Westminster Press, 1980.

Carson, D. A. *Exegetical Fallacies*. Grand Rapids: Baker Book House, 1984.

Childs, Brevard S. *Biblical Theology in Crisis*. Philadelphia: Westminster Press, 1970.

Clowney, Edmund P. *Preaching and Biblical Theology*. Phillipsburg, N.J.: Presbyterian and Reformed Publishing, 1979.

Cox, James W., ed. *Biblical Preaching: An Expositor's Treasury*. Philadelphia: Westminster Press, 1983.

Craddock, Fred B. *The Gospels in Interpreting Biblical Texts*. Nashville: Abingdon Press, 1981.

Dockery, David S., Kenneth A. Matthews, Robert B. Sloan (eds). *Foundations for Biblical Interpretation: A Complete Library of Tools and Resources*. Nashville: Broadman & Holman Publishers, 1994.

Dodd, Charles H. *The Apostolic Preaching and Its Developments*. New York: Harper and Row, 1936.

Doty, William G. *Contemporary New Testament Interpretation*. Englewood Cliffs, N.J.: Prentice-Hall, 1972.

Efird, James M. *How to Interpret the Bible*. Atlanta: John Knox Press, 1984.

Fee, Gordon D. *New Testament Exegesis: A Handbook for Students and Pastors*. Philadelphia: Westminster Press, 1983.

Fee, Gordon, and Douglas Stuart. *How to Read the Bible for All Its Worth—A Guide to Understanding the Bible*. Grand Rapids: Zondervan, 1982.

Fuller, Reginald. *The Use of the Bible in Preaching*. Philadelphia: Fortress Press, 1981.

Gowan, Donald E. *Reclaiming the Old Testament for the Christian Pulpit*. Atlanta: John Knox Press, 1980.

Greidanus, Sidney. *The Modern Preacher and the Ancient Text: Interpreting and Preaching Biblical Literature*. Grand Rapids: William B. Eerdmans, 1988.

Harrison, R. K. *Biblical Criticism: Historical, Literary and Textual*.

Grand Rapids: Zondervan, 1978.

Hayes, John H., and Carl R. Holladay. *Biblical Exegesis: A Beginner's Handbook.* 2d ed. Atlanta: John Knox Press, 1987.

Johnson, Elliot E. *Expository Hermeneutics: An Introduction.* Grand Rapids: Zondervan, 1990.

Kaiser, Walter C., Jr. *The Old Testament in Contemporary Preaching.* Grand Rapids: Baker Book House, 1973.

————. *Toward an Exegetical Theology: Biblical Exegesis for Preaching and Teaching.* Grand Rapids: Baker Book House, 1981.

Keck, Leander E. *The Bible in the Pulpit: The Renewal of Biblical Preaching.* Nashville: Abingdon Press, 1978.

Keck, Leander E., and Victor Furnish. *The Pauline Letters in Interpreting Biblical Texts.* Nashville: Abingdon Press, 1984.

Klein, George L., ed. *Reclaiming the Prophetic Mantle: Preaching the Old Testament Faithfully.* Nashville: Broadman Press, 1992.

Licht, Jacob. *Storytelling in the Bible.* Jerusalem: Magnes Press, 1978.

Liefeld, Walter L. *New Testament Exposition: From Text to Sermon.* Grand Rapids: Zondervan, 1984.

Lischer, Richard. *A Theology of Preaching: The Dynamics of the Gospel.* Durham, N.C.: Labyrinth Press, 1991.

Long, Thomas G. *Preaching and the Literary Forms of the Bible.* Philadelphia: Fortress Press, 1989.

Mickelson, A. Berkeley. *Interpreting the Bible.* Grand Rapids: William B. Eerdmans, 1963.

Mounce, Robert H. *The Essential Nature of New Testament Preaching.* Grand Rapids: William B. Eerdmans, 1960.

Mumaw, John R. *Preach the Word: Expository Preaching from the Book of Ephesians.* Scottsdale, Pa.: Herald Press, 1987.

Osborne, Grant R. *The Hermeneutical Spiral.* Downers Grove, Ill.: InterVarsity Press, 1991.

Pinnock, Clark H. *Biblical Revelation.* Chicago: Moody Press, 1971.

Piper, John. *The Supremacy of God in Preaching.* Grand Rapids: Baker Book House, 1990.

Rad, Gerhard von. *Biblical Interpretations in Preaching.* Translated by John E. Steely. Nashville: Abingdon Press, 1977.

Ramm, Bernard L. *Protestant Biblical Interpretation: A Textbook of Hermeneutics.* 3d rev. ed. Grand Rapids: Baker Book House, 1970.

Rust, Eric Charles. *The Word and Words: Towards a Theology of Preaching.* Macon, Ga.: Mercer University Press, 1982.

Ryken, Leland. *How to Read the Bible as Literature.* Grand Rapids: Zondervan, 1984.

————. *The Literature of the Bible.* Grand Rapids: Zondervan, 1974.

Sanders, James. *God Has a Story Too.* Philadelphia: Fortress Press, 1979.

————. *Words of Delight: A Literary Introduction to the Bible.* Grand Rapids: Baker Book House, 1987.

————. *Words of Life: A Literary Introduction to the New Testament.* Grand Rapids: Baker Book House, 1987.

Smart, James D. *The Past, Present, and Future of Biblical Theology.* Philadelphia: Westminster Press, 1979.

————. *The Strange Silence of the Bible in the Church: A Study in Hermeneutics.* Philadelphia: Westminster Press, 1972.

Smith, Dwight Moody. *Interpreting the Gospels for Preaching.* Philadelphia: Fortress Press, 1979.

Stuart, Douglas. *Old Testament Exegesis: A Primer for Students and Pastors.* Philadelphia: Westminster Press, 1980.

Tate, W. Randolph. *Biblical Interpretation.* Peabody, Mass.: Hendrickson Publishers, 1991.

Terry, Milton S. *Biblical Hermeneutics.* 2d ed. 1883, Reprint, Grand Rapids: Zondervan, n.d.

Thompson, William D. *Preaching Biblically: Exegesis and Interpretation.* Nashville: Abingdon Press, 1981.

Toombs, Lawrence E. *The Old Testament in Christian Preaching.* Philadelphia: Westminster Press, 1961.

Virkler, Henry A. *Hermeneutics: Principles and Processes of Biblical Interpretation.* Grand Rapids: Baker Book House, 1981.

Wilder, Amos. *Early Christian Rhetoric: The Language of the Gospel.* Cambridge: Harvard University Press, 1971.

Wink, Walter. *The Bible in Human Transformation: Toward a New Paradigm for Biblical Study.* Philadelphia: Fortress Press, 1973.

Worley, Robert C. *Preaching and Teaching in the Earliest Church.* Philadelphia: Westminster Press, 1967.

Zuck, Roy B. *Basic Bible Interpretation.* Wheaton, Ill.: Victor Books, 1991.

Subject Index

Name Index

423

Scripture Index

Acts

Romans

Colossians

1 Thessalonians

2 Thessalonians